FROM THE AURORAL DARKNESS
The Life and Poetry of Robert Hayden

FROM THE AURORAL DARKNESS

The Life and Poetry of Robert Hayden

by

John Hatcher

GEORGE RONALD

OXFORD

GEORGE RONALD, Publisher
46 High Street, Kidlington, Oxford

ISBN 0-85398-188-4 (Hardcover)
ISBN 0-85398-189-2 (Softcover)

Printed and bound in Great Britain
by Billing & Sons Limited, Worcester.

Contents

Illustrations

Acknowledgments

As with any undertaking of this magnitude there are countless sources of assistance without which such a project would not be possible. Among those to whom I am most indebted are the Association for Studies on the Bahá'í Faith, which first commissioned me to begin work on a study of Hayden's poetry; Mrs Marion Hofman, who provided me with important materials and encouragement; Mr Frederick Glaysher, Hayden's secretary during the poet's last two years, who helped organize Hayden's papers and aided me greatly in starting my research; Mrs Erma Hayden, Robert's widow and my friend for more than twenty-five years, who gave me interviews and access to important papers. I am also indebted to the University of South Florida for granting me a sabbatical year during which time the bulk of this research was completed, and I am grateful to Roger Dahl and the staff of the National Bahá'í Archives for providing me with crucial materials before the Hayden papers had been processed. I am appreciative of the splended editorial assistance of my colleague Dr Robert Chisnell and of my wife Lucia Corsiglia Hatcher, to whom this work is dedicated. Finally I acknowledge the lifetime of conscientious frugality by my father whose estate assisted me in living at half my salary during my sabbatical year, as did the loving generosity of my mother – the older I get, the wiser they become.

Quotations from the poems of Robert Hayden are made with the kind permission of Mrs Erma Hayden, and of the publishers October House for the poems from *Selected Poems* and *Words in the Mourning Time*. Quotations from the two volumes published by Liveright Publishing Corporation are with their kind permission. These are *Angle of Ascent*, New and Selected Poems, copyright © 1975, 1972, 1970, 1966 by Robert Hayden; and *American Journal*, Poems by Robert Hayden copyright © 1982 by Erma Hayden. Acknowledgments for permissions to quote are also due to Faber and Faber Publishers and Alfred A. Knopf, Inc., for the extract from the poem by Wallace Stevens 'Peter Quince at the Clavier' from their respective editions of *The Collected Poems of Wallace Stevens*; and to Talonbooks for the extract from the collection of Rilke's *Sonnets to Orpheus* translated by Karl H. Siegler.

for Lucia

Foreword

'Ars Longa, Vita Brevis' – art endures, life does not – thus begins Robert Hayden's poem 'The Peacock Room'. In February of 1980 Hayden the man 'disappeared in the dead of winter', but, as with Yeats, 'The death of the poet was kept from his poems',[1] which daily acquire a vaster audience.

John Ciardi, Hayden's fellow graduate student at Michigan and a noted poet and critic in his own right, once discussed so clearly the irony of this belated recognition. In a 1958 piece entitled 'Dialogue with the Audience' he observed that the 'good poet' who dedicates himself to his art may forgo the accolades of the 'horizontal audience' (those who might praise the poet during his lifetime), but he will ultimately achieve a greater readership from the 'vertical audience' (those who in succeeding decades and centuries may read his work):

And not only for the greatest poets. Andrew Marvell is certainly a minor poet, but given time enough, more people will certainly have read 'To His Coy Mistress' than will ever have subscribed to *Time, Life,* and *Fortune.* Compared to what a good poem can do, Luce is a piker at getting circulation.[2]

Toward the end of Ciardi's fictionalized dialogue between the poet and the 'citizen', he has the poet respond to the citizen's objection that poems require too much effort, that they are too inaccessible for the average reader. 'You're going to be dead the next time anyone looks', the poet answers. 'We all are for that matter. But not the poem. Not if it's made right.'[3] Robert Hayden was read by a slim audience during the bulk of his career – only his last two books were widely available – but his poems were 'made right', and he is assured of a substantial vertical audience.

He could have had the horizontal audience too, if that had been his primary concern. The proponents of the 'Black Aesthetic' in the 1960s would have welcomed him into their ranks, to join his voice with theirs in protest and revolt – certainly publishers were eager then for these politicized voices. Probably Hayden's fellow members of the Bahá'í Faith would have honored him more had he made his poems impassioned professions of faith or explicit tributes to Bahá'í tenets or heroes.

Ironically, Hayden wrote from both of these perspectives, as a Black American in a violent society and as a Bahá'í in what he firmly believed to be a crucial period of transition for mankind. But to shape these feelings and ideas into verse, to fuse them with form and image, Hayden paid unceasing attention to what he believed to be the timeless requisites of art, because he was a 'serious artist', as he termed his calling.

If we are to appreciate his work, therefore, we must study it with the same sort of seriousness. We must approach his poems with energy and imagination, because as symbolic pieces they often reach far beyond the sometimes beguilingly accessible surfaces. Consequently, I do not presume in this study to compass his life or exhaust his art – his poems will benefit from a variety of creative examinations. What I have attempted is to hasten the gathering of that vertical audience by offering a guide for the serious reader. It is my hope that this guide benefits from my own perspective as Robert Hayden's friend, as a fellow Bahá'í, teacher and poet, and, most important, as a serious student of his work.

My reason for treating the entirety of his published volumes in chronological order, therefore, is not based on any delusion of completeness, but on my belief, as is explained in the study, that such a procedure is warranted by the continuity of his art. But since virtually none of his early works are available to the reader, I have included the tables of contents for each of his ten volumes of poetry in an appendix as an aid in following my discussion. Wherever possible I have referred the reader to the Liveright volumes *Angle of Ascent* and *American Journal*, the second of which is still in print. Indeed, the student of Hayden's poetry is most fortunate that together these two volumes not only offer a survey of the poet's best work, but also present the poems in the groups which he himself devised. A new volume, *The Collected Poems of Robert Hayden*, is due to be published by Liveright in Spring 1985.

I have begun my examination of Hayden's work with a synopsis of his life because, in an important sense, the continuity of his art is inseparable from the continuity of Hayden himself. Not that one is obliged to approach his poetry from the standpoint of historical criticism; indeed, some examinations of his poems suffer profoundly by viewing his work solely as an extension of autobiographical fact. Nevertheless, the thoroughly human and approachable persona who serves as guide throughout the poet's work is derived in no small way from the intense humanity of Robert Hayden, a man 'superb in love and logic'.[4] Ultimately, this persona's emblematic journey of search and discovery provides major clues to Hayden's symbolic purposes.

John S. Hatcher

Part I

FROM PARADISE VALLEY TO POET LAUREATE

Africa is in his soul, the world at large
in his mind and heart.

Dakar Press Release, 1966

As I listen to the resonant voice on the recording of a 1976 interview with Robert Hayden, I recall again the precise articulation of the man, the way his sentences, even in semi-formal circumstances such as these, would be masterfully formed, as if he had for some time pondered the structure of his utterances. Not too many words go by before several other common traits become apparent – the quick wit, the ironic anecdote, the off-hand quote from another poet or scholar which, from someone else, might appear pompous, but which from Robert Hayden seemed a natural part of a world he loved and knew intimately.

The slightly nervous manner he has of repeating a word or phrase several times before completing his sentences recalls his appearance – the absurdly thick lenses which distorted his kind eyes, the omnipresent bow-tie. One is reminded of Michael Harper's word portrait of his good friend as 'a man of considered reserve, with an unsuppressible elegance, his bow-ties, watch-chain and old man's comforts giving him the glow of a courtly preacher summoned to give the word, and well he did'.[1] The voice also calls to mind an anecdote told by William Meredith in a memorial piece on Hayden:

A young black man came to his office one day, not on literary business but to reproach him for his dress. 'How can you, a black man, come to your office day after day wearing a suit like that, the uniform of your white oppressor?' Hayden was elegantly dressed that morning in Providence, when he told the story. 'I've always liked to dress myself up a little,' he said then, 'and I told this boy, "I'm just coming into my style, boy. You ain't seen nothing yet."'[2]

In a Preface to a transcription of his talks with Hayden, Dennis Gendron states that while his interview yields insights into the man and his work, 'it cannot adequately reflect the intensity, candor, charm or wit of the man'.[3] Likewise the editors of *World Order* in their memorial issue to Hayden recall him as an 'irrepressible wit and humorist with a seemingly endless store of anecdotes . . .'[4]

Others have extolled his grace under pressure. Julius Lester stated in a memorial piece that Hayden was a man who 'refused to capitulate to those, who in the screaming agony of their own pain and loneliness, could do nothing but return evil for evil'.[5] In a review and assessment of Hayden's career, Robert Greenberg alludes to 'the dogged courage he displayed during his long career as a poet'.[6]

The voice on the tape is not glib. He answers each question as if it had never been posed before, complimenting the interviewer. One could not infer from that voice what the years had done. One could not guess from the gentle demeanor and manner what battles had been waged, what impediments overcome in the long trek from Paradise Valley.

1. Paradise Valley
1913–1930

... sunflowers gangled there
sometimes, tough-stalked and bold
and like the vivid children there unplanned.[1]

Robert Hayden, 'Summertime and the Living . . .'

Paradise Valley was an area in the old eastside of Detroit in the early 1900s. By the 1920s and 30s it was becoming a largely Black ghetto, though there were still some remnants of the Jewish and Italian communities which had been a part of the neighborhood. At the heart of Paradise Valley was St Antoine Street (pronounced *Anto-wine* by Detroiters). It was full of restaurants, pool halls, gambling joints. It was Detroit's own Beale Street, the crossroads of Detroit's 'colored world'. 'You stand on St Antoine,' the saying went, 'and sooner or later everybody you know or ever heard of will be passing by.' Hayden would later recall St Antoine as a kaleidoscope of 'Shootings, stabbings, blaring jazz, and a liveliness, a gaiety at once desperate and releasing, at once wicked – Satan's playground – and goodhearted'.[2]

A block away on Beacon Street lived William and Sue Hayden. He was a former coal miner and laborer who now drove a coal wagon, a staunch Baptist who ruled his household sternly. Sue Hayden had once worked on a Mississippi River steamer and had been married to Jim Barlow, a man she never forgot.[3] Both the Haydens were uneducated and Pa Hayden in particular had trouble understanding his adoptive son's obsession with books, his withdrawal into a world of reading and imagination.

The child's severe nearsightedness as a result of damage to his eyes at birth was partly to blame. Robert had playmates, but he could not participate in athletics and other such activities which would have been considered 'normal' by someone like William Hayden. But if the boy's inability to express his masculinity in ways Pa Hayden could understand was a source of tension in the family, the circumstances of the child's origin was an even more critical issue.

Robert Hayden was born on August 4, 1913, to Ruth Sheffey. Her maiden name was Gladys Finn and her home was Altoona, Pennsylvania. She was a beautiful woman who had joined a circus and run away from home in her late teens. She changed her name to Ruth, and in Detroit married a former coal miner from West Virginia, Asa Sheffey. The marriage did not last long; they divorced, and shortly after she had a son. When the child was only a few weeks old she entrusted him to the care of her friends, the Haydens, so that she could go to Buffalo, New York, to get work.

Robert knew his natural mother, saw her on numerous occasions, both at the Hayden home where she visited and even stayed for a while, and later on visits to Buffalo where his mother took him on boat rides and theater excursions. Such positive experiences deepened the love he had for his mother, an affection which never diminished. But the brief encounter with his natural father was less successful. Asa Sheffey had relocated in Gary, Indiana, and Robert went to visit him at about the age of twelve.[4] His father tried to win the boy's affection with a few gifts, or else in bouts of drinking he would demonstrate his boisterous humor or end up denouncing his former wife. Like Pa Hayden, he was unable to appreciate his son's feelings or understand the bookish boy he had fathered.

In addition to the hard life which poverty imposed there was a tension in the Hayden house resulting from the fact that Robert was not really their son, a tension that Ruth Sheffey's visits only served to heighten. The situation was almost calculated to produce ambivalence on the part of a boy who was the focal point of this struggle. His natural mother understood his needs, his sensitivity in a way the Haydens could not, and yet it was the Haydens who raised him, provided for him, who later encouraged his education. 'Get something in your head and they can't take it away from you,' Pa Hayden had told him. 'Stay in school, don't let me catch you hanging around in the streets. I don't want you to live like I've had to live. You don't have to live like this.'[5]

But that same foster father could not understand the precocious child's gifts, the way he always had his head in a book, learning to read before he entered grade school, the way he would look through an encyclopedia or dictionary, just for the fun of it. The young child was learning by five or six to escape from his environment through his imagination, radio programs, movies, or his own miniature theater for which he would compose dialogue for his make-believe characters. On one occasion, unable to understand what he thought to be unmanly behavior for a young boy, Pa Hayden ripped apart the toy theater in front of the shocked and bewildered child.

Robert Hayden never forgot the pain of scenes like that, or the periodic whippings his foster mother gave to purge her own frustrations. Later in life, through his poetry, he would try to understand better the mechanisms that formed his early feelings about the Haydens, his mother, his childhood, about Paradise Valley itself with its strange mixture of positive and negative stimuli, lively, vital, replete with an array of characters and happenings.

Aunt Roxie lived with them and worked as a waitress at a nearby Chinese restaurant which was owned by the father of Kuni, one of Robert's close friends. Some of his playmates were Jewish children, some even ex-patriate southern whites, and at night in the summertime the children would play hide and seek with the lamppost as base, wait for the crab man, the waffle wagon with its tinkling bell or watch a small crowd gather around a street-corner preacher, interested more in the Baptist hymns that two fat women with tambourines would sing than in what the preacher had to say.[6]

There might be parades for the followers of Marcus Garvey and his 'Back to Africa' movement, or on special occasions, like Halloween, grownups and kids alike would watch 'masqueraders make their surreal progress along St Antoine. Clowns, red devils with curling tails, Zulus, men in evening gowns, women in tuxedos, each sex a parody of the other.'[7] On a given day in Paradise Valley one might see real celebrities like Jack Johnson, Tiger Flowers or Kid Chocolate.

It was this vibrant aspect of ghetto life that seems to have been for Hayden a positive force, an era, a feeling, a place he would later recapture in numerous poems about these people, scenes and feelings. He never idealized the life – he spoke often of the poverty, the hard times – but it was not so important a source of his emotional turmoil and ambivalence about childhood as was the whole complex of relationships among his foster family, his natural mother and himself.

His foster parents were poor, uneducated, could not support his inherent gifts and artistic needs, whereas his natural mother encouraged him: part of Hayden's literary inspiration, he says, came from his mother, who, he explains, was lively, imaginative and beautiful. She was not well educated but encouraged his interest in books. She did this even though they lived apart.[8]

As a result, the competition for the boy's affection was fierce, especially when his natural mother came to visit. But besides this constant source of tension and confused identity on the boy's part, and Pa Hayden's inability to accept his son's visual handicap as a sufficient explanation for his inability to play sports like the other boys, there was another constant source of trouble. Sue Hayden was always haunted by her memories of Jim Barlow, and on occasion she would let Pa Hayden know that he could never give her the affection and love she had felt from this man.

In 'The Ballad of Sue Ellen Westerfield' (Sue Hayden's maiden name), the poet would later recount the details of that intense love affair, ending the ballad with the revealing lines:

> They kissed and said farewell at last.
> He wept as had her father once.
> They kissed and said farewell.

> Until her dying-bed,
> she cursed the circumstance.[9]

Now she was married to a quiet laborer who was severely religious, and the secret pain she felt from the loss of the life she had known and from the constant tension over this son who was still not legally hers she took out in anger against the boy. These wrenching moments Hayden reveals touchingly in 'The Whipping':

> And the woman leans muttering against
> a tree, exhausted, purged—
> avenged in part for lifelong hidings
> she has had to bear.[10]

On other occasions, Sue Hayden's misery manifested itself in physical pain. In one of his notebooks, Hayden sketched his recollection of going with his foster mother to visit the neighborhood conjurer-healer-medium, Old Dad.[11] She had some sort of chronic pain, and the boy hoped Old Dad would cure her so that she would be less irritable and less inclined to take out her own misery on him. The room they entered was full of cabinets, each stocked full with unguents, voodoo powders, charms and hair grease, and there was a strange pervasive smell he would always remember.

But she quit going to Old Dad after a while, and the pains continued. She would get angry at the boy, curse at him, and sure enough the pain would start. Why he had been made to feel responsible, he was never sure, but this was another childhood source of lifelong guilt and anger he would have to manage.

In part to escape these tensions and feelings, Robert found solace in books:

I learned to read before I went to public school, and I began trying to write poems and stories and plays while I was down in the grades . . . I remember that when I was in the grades the teacher gave us a list of words for spelling and told us to put the words into sentences. I made up a story out of the words instead of just putting them into sentences.[12]

He frequented the library, since there were few books in the Hayden home, and as early as the fifth grade he read books on scenario writing and would try to rewrite plays about movies he had seen. At the library he made an important friend in Marie Alice Hanson, the librarian to whom he dedicated his volume *Words in the Mourning Time* (1970):

Marie Alice would put the new books of poetry aside for me, and when I kept them out beyond the due date she would sometimes pay the fines. She encouraged my love of poetry. When I began to have a few poems published she would put copies of them on the bulletin board in the poetry room of the Detroit Public Library.[13]

He loved books in part because they took him out of his environment, partly because they fed his imagination with experiences he had never known, but mostly, perhaps, because he was beginning to love the words themselves.

Literature was not his only cultural interest; he also took violin lessons at the Detroit Institute of Musical Art with his neighborhood friend Kuni. Later he had to quit when the teacher discovered that because of his poor eyesight he was playing by ear instead of reading the music. As a result of the problem with his vision, he was placed in a special sight conservation class in high school where his reading was supervised:

We were not permitted to read small type, and we wrote on manila sheets of paper and used big, thick pencils – to this day I'm addicted to big, thick, black pencils and so on. But one of my sight-saving teachers used to read my assignments in English to me, and I remember that we were to read a book and report on it. I chose George Eliot's *Romola*. That had a tremendous influence on me . . .[14]

Before long, at the age of sixteen, he became particularly attracted to poetry, primarily to the works of Countee Cullen, 'whom I read with almost bated breath',[15] but also to the poems of Carl Sandburg, Edna St Vincent Millay, Elinor Wylie, Orrick Johns, and Langston Hughes. Soon Robert was trying his own hand at writing verse:

I read these poets and tried to write like them. And I found that I was more fascinated, more stimulated by poetry than by any other form of literature. Instead of playing baseball – I was so nearsighted I could hardly see the ball anyway the few times I played – instead of playing ball or taking part in other so-called 'normal' activities of the boys in my neighborhood, I would spend hours reading poetry and struggling to get my own words down on paper. From that summer on, I continued working at poetry, hoping some day to be known as a poet.[16]

It was during this time that Hayden accidentally discovered the volume edited by Alain Locke entitled *The New Negro*, which effectively introduced him to the poets of the Harlem Renaissance, poets whose work would greatly influence his own early work. In fact, the first two renowned poets he would meet would be Langston Hughes and Countee Cullen. Interestingly, Alain Locke, whose essay 'The New Negro' had such a significant influence on the question of aesthetics in relation to the racial point of view, was a member of the religion which Hayden himself would later join, the Bahá'í Faith.[17]

Because Hayden wanted to study Spanish, which was not offered at Miller High School in eastside Detroit, he transferred for his senior year to Northern High School, where he was one of only a few Black students. His interest in Spanish would continue later into his college studies and even in his poetry. But he was still primarily interested in becoming a poet and tried to find places to publish his work. One of these was the church paper. Hayden was very active in the Second Baptist Church, and was even urged by the church elders to consider going into the African mission field.[18]

2. The Apprenticeship
1930–1940

If poetry nags at you, if it's something you feel incomplete without,
then you'll go on because you'll have to. One cannot learn to be a
poet. One is born a poet.[1]

Robert Hayden

In 1930 Robert Hayden graduated from Northern High School with little
hope of continuing his education since neither he nor Pa Hayden could afford
the sixty-five-dollar tuition, especially now that the sudden faltering of the
American economy of the Great Depression had forced the Haydens to go on
welfare. Hayden's interest in poetry had continued as had his determination to
become a poet, but at this time the means toward that end seemed quite
concealed. Fortunately, he was able to attend some post-graduate classes at
Cass High School and thus continue his reading and writing instead of having
to get a job immediately, as most boys in the neighborhood had to do. In addition, his determination and persistence in trying to get his work published
soon paid off. He submitted a collection of his poetry entitled *Songs of the
1880s* to Harper Brothers and it was rejected, but his poem 'Africa' was
accepted by *Abbott's Monthly* and published in 1931 when Hayden was only
eighteen years old.

It was also at this time that the first in a series of important instances of luck,
destiny or divine intervention aided his progress. Of course, none of the
fateful events would have meant much had he not had talent, and later there
would seem to be just about as many forces working against him, but there
was clearly a pattern of propitious turning points in his career. This one
occurred like the plot of the Saturday morning double features he would
watch at the Arcade or Castle theaters with his neighborhood friends. As he
stood in a welfare line reading a book of poems by Cullen, the caseworker
asked what he was reading. He showed her the volume of verse and told her
brazenly that he too would publish a volume of poems some day. Several days
later, she showed up at the Hayden house to give Robert the name of a man

who she said might help him obtain a tuition scholarship at Detroit City College through the State Rehabilitation Service. 'If you're going to be a poet,' she said, 'you ought to get a good education.'[2]

It seemed a far-fetched idea – none of his family before him had ever finished grade school. But he followed the social worker's advice and went to the office of a merry little Scots-Irishman who interviewed him. Without much ado, the man said cheerfully after a few minutes, 'Of course you're going to college; that is, if I have anything to say in the matter!'[3]

Apparently the man did, and in the fall of 1932 Robert Hayden began his undergraduate studies at Detroit City College (now Wayne State University). He enrolled as a Spanish major with the intention of becoming a teacher eventually. He did not take poetry courses because they conflicted with his schedule, but he did continue his writing and reading. He also became familiar with other aspiring writers at the college, some of whom he would get to know better on the WPA project later in the 1930s.

As he stated later in an interview, during these undergraduate years he read 'all the poetry I could get hold of, and I read without discrimination'.[4] His own writing was still quite traditional, patterned largely after Cullen, Hughes, Sandburg, Crane and others:

All through my undergraduate years I was pretty imitative. As I discovered poets new to me, I studied their work and tried to write as they did. I suppose all young poets do this. It's certainly one method of learning something about poetry.[5]

He was fond of the Romantic poets and sometimes imagined himself another Keats or Shelley, answering his calling with a furious outburst of verse, then dying young. One of his classmates at the time later wrote to Hayden in 1966 about his vivid memory of the poet's romantic bent in those years:

One June night five of us took a ride to Grosse Isle in a rickety old Chevrolet I then owned. Alfred Stevenson, yourself, a lad named Woodson (we called him 'Woody' I believe), a young Italian named Delcie (I don't recall his first name) . . . When we got there it was very dark, and as we looked out over the water, each of us had a different reaction. Stevenson thought it was a good spot for a play . . . I thought it a good spot for a murder (being of the Poesque nature with a leaning towards murder mysteries) . . . and you said, 'black lacquered water'. It was the first time I had heard the expression, and I considered it a very beautiful poetic term.[6]

Not everyone could discern the poetic soul in Robert Hayden. He never forgot his experience with the one English teacher to whom he had dared show his poems. After several days, Hayden went to the teacher's office:

Without the slightest regard for my feelings he told me that my verses were quite bad, and as if that were not withering enough, he drew a scale showing the relative positions of Shakespeare, Milton, Robinson, Frost, and Millay. 'You are down here,' he said, 'at the very bottom of the scale.' He implied that that was where my paucity of talent would undoubtedly keep me.[7]

Toward the end of his undergraduate studies, Hayden began associating with other aspiring poets, like John Malcolm Brinnin, Kimon Friar, Chad Walsh, John Ciardi, and Nelson Bentley. A few of his pieces appeared in the campus paper, *The Detroit Collegian*, and in some of the Black weeklies in Detroit. Most of his poems at this time were typical of his 'socially conscious period', as he called it – anti-war poems, indictments of racial injustice, dialect pieces from the point of view of the poverty-stricken Black American.

Besides poetry, he had two other loves – his studies and the theater. He did some directing, and was always beginning plays and scenes in his notebooks, pages of dialogue, and one play on Harriet Tubman which he would finish shortly after his undergraduate work. As for his studies, he did extremely well, with the exception of physics. Mathematics gave him a little trouble, but he failed physics and could not pass no matter how many times he tried, even though it was the only remaining requirement for his degree.

In 1936 Robert Hayden finished his undergraduate work without the degree and began wondering how to make a living with a major in Spanish during the Depression. The prospects for him, especially as a Black man, were bleak; to find a job involving writing seemed even more remote. But since the Hayden family were welfare recipients, Robert qualified to apply for work with the WPA (Works Project Administration). In particular, he applied for a job as a writer on the Detroit Branch of the Federal Writers Project, and to his delight he was accepted. Not only could he support himself for the first time in his life, but he could also help support his foster family, and after helping with the food and rent he could even have a bit left over for himself.

At first the twenty-five-year-old poet felt awkward on the project among writers who had been places, who had met real poets, who had published books. He had never done any of those things, had never even lived outside Detroit:

. . . I was struggling with so many things and had so much to learn and so far to come that all of them dazzled me. I mean, I thought that all of them were better than I was and I thought that all of them would certainly, certainly do things that I could never do.[8]

It was hardly an ideal atmosphere for writing. He would go to the office in the morning at eight or nine, write all day, sometimes the same paragraph over and over as he tried to get his brain to function amid the clatter of typewriters and people coming and going. His subject was interesting – the Underground Railroad movement – and his research into the topic served to inspire some later poems, as well as his play on Harriet Tubman, *Go Down Moses*. It was not a particularly good play, but it was performed at Cass High School under the sponsorship of the Second Baptist Church. But even though he was writing, he did not feel much like doing his own creative work when he would get home at night after a day of doing nothing but writing.

Robert Hayden at age eight in Detroit

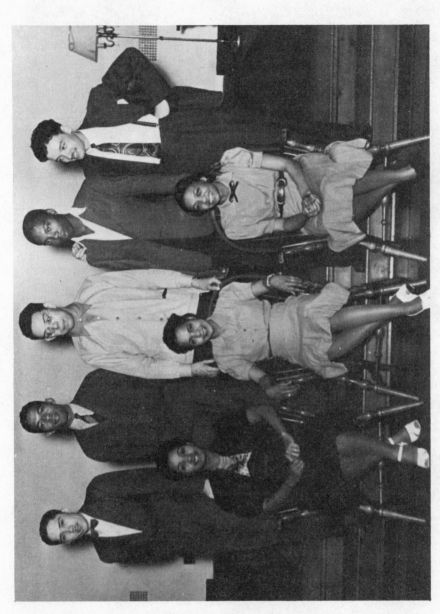

The cast of a play Robert directed for the Alpha Kappa Alpha sorority in Detroit. It was published in the Michigan Chronicle, a Black newspaper. Robert Hayden is in the middle of the back row. (Photograph Langford P. James.)

It is difficult to say exactly how much his experience on the WPA influenced his writing and thinking during this period of the late 1930s, but a few generalizations are worth noting. First, through his association with other socially-aware writers, Hayden became intimately familiar with those who advocated radical political change as an answer to the staggering economic and racial problems. Very early in these associations he also began to see very clearly, especially among those who advocated communism or ideologies akin to 'Party thinking', that he was not a group person. Whatever the source of such an inclination, he early became convinced that he could not work easily within the confines of labels, even though he was very much in sympathy with some of the ideas on the Afro-American struggle espoused by such writers as Richard Wright in *Uncle Tom's Children,* the concept of world brotherhood, and the sentiment against the impending war. Secondly, Hayden's growing awareness of writers and social and political concerns outside the more narrow province of life in Detroit heightened his growing interest in Afro-American history and his belief in the concept of Blacks and Whites joining together to bring about social change.

Hayden took part in anti-war rallies, read his poetry for the John Reed Club and at a rally of the United Auto Workers in Detroit, and he demonstrated with his fellow WPA workers for higher pay. His poems during this period, generally didactic in tone, were on these social themes, were direct pleas for the elimination of prejudice and the economic plight of the poor. As he said in a 1978 interview, he 'felt that this was the function of artists – to be spokesmen and voice for freedom, justice and so on'.[9] But his strong religious convictions would not allow him to believe that any purely economic or political cause would be a sufficient force to cure the ills of mankind:

In the first place, I didn't accept communism as the solution to everything. I still felt that . . . Well, I believe in God, for one thing, and that made a difference. I believe there is a spiritual dimension to human life. I simply did not accept their idea of economic determinism and many of them did.[10]

Certainly one of the most prominent forces in Hayden's life during this time of growth and development as a writer and thinker was Erma Inez Morris, a beautiful young pianist whom he had met at one of the theater productions he was in. In some ways she was quite different in temperament from the young poet. She was demonstrative, happy, affirmative, resilient. The granddaughter of an Episcopal priest, the daughter of parents who had met in medical school, Erma was born in Philadelphia in 1911 into a family that had infused in her expectations of college and achievement. Her family's middle-class expectations for her did not include a poor, struggling poet from Detroit's eastside who was sensitive, almost fragile in some ways and subject to despair.

But the two had a great deal in common – mutual love of theater, poetry, the arts. They were both talented artists and both shared an indomitable sense of humor. If she was the firm center, the relationship was hardly one-sided. It was not easy for her to abide his somber times, his basically negative feelings about himself and his past. But she could understand and appreciate the origin of those feelings, and she eventually came to realize, as she now says, that 'poets are in a mortal combat with life'.[11] Besides, she was a tenacious person, and having determined his talent and worth as a human being, she was not the sort to give up on him.

There were other noteworthy events in Hayden's life during the late 1930s. He directed the Paul Robeson Players, and while working with the WPA he met the first recognized poet of his career, Langston Hughes, thus beginning a relationship he was to maintain for some years to come. He was working in amateur theater at the time, and his friend Elsie Roxboro, who was performing Hughes' *Drums of Haiti,* arranged for the two to have lunch at the Lucy Thurmon YWCA. Hayden brought along a sheaf of his best poems which he shared with Hughes at what seemed the right moment.

Hughes was interested in Hayden's potential, though he was not impressed with most of these particular poems and told him so. He explained that the poems were too imitative and 'pointed out that I needed to find my own voice . . .'[12] At first the young Hayden was disheartened by the assessment of his work, but very soon he would come to agree with Hughes' observations and would always recall this meeting as an inspiring and helpful encounter: 'My meeting with Hughes is one of my pleasantest recollections, for he was the first recognized poet I'd met, the first to spend time talking to me about my own poems.'[13]

It was also during this period that Hayden established two other important relationships, one with Louis O. Martin, owner of the *Michigan Chronicle,* a Negro Weekly where Hayden got a job writing music and drama criticism, and the other with the University of Michigan at Ann Arbor, where he took graduate courses on a part-time basis during the summers. As a result of Hayden's friendship with Martin, the newspaper owner established the Falcon Press, largely as a vehicle to publish Hayden's first book of poetry in 1940, *Heart-Shape in the Dust.* This book was the culmination of Hayden's past efforts in verse and marks, in many ways, the end of Hayden's period of apprenticeship as it is reflected in his publications, though he still had ahead of him his important graduate work at the university where his style would change rapidly.

Hayden began his part-time graduate work in the summer of 1938, and in that summer also won his first poetry award, the Hopwood Minor Award, for poems that would later appear as part of the Falcon Press volume. Meanwhile, the relationship with Erma continued to flourish, though against the best wishes of Erma's parents and peers who considered this lovely, talented young woman too good for Hayden.[14] Nevertheless, in June of 1940 Robert Hayden and Erma Morris were married.

3. The Poet Comes of Age
1941–1946

He read some of my poems. There were some that he liked very much, and some he didn't like at all. The ones he liked he said were poems that were like algebra, in which you were solving for x.[1]

Hayden about Auden

Rarely is the development of a poet so clearly demarked by a shift in style as is the poetry of Robert Hayden after 1940. Simply stated, virtually all his poetry before 1940, including *Heart-Shape in the Dust*, is imitative, traditional. After 1940 his subjects and themes are much the same, but the poetry is vastly different. In his study of Afro-American writers, Arthur Davis describes this phenomenal growth:

In very few poets is the change of tone so pronounced as in the Robert Hayden of *A Ballad of Remembrance* (1962) when compared with the Robert *E*. Hayden of *Heart-Shape in the Dust* (1940). The latter shows a young novice poet following, perhaps too closely, models from the New Negro Renaissance. The Hayden of *Ballad of Remembrance* shows a mature craftsman making use of the diction, the forms, and unfortunately, some of the obscurity of contemporary verse making.[2]

While one might not agree with Davis' statement about the 'obscurity' of Hayden's later verse, the shift in style is blatant and purposeful. In fact, Hayden did not like anthologists to use poems from his first volume, even though some of them 'have an intrinsic excellence which transcends any racial or topical limitation'.[3] For the most part, the poems from *Heart-Shape in the Dust* are written in set metrical forms and rhyme schemes. Some are dialect pieces bemoaning the plight of the victims of racism and unjust economic systems. Others protest lynchings or war. Most reflect the influence of Hughes, Tolson, Wright, McKay and other Black poets who had treated these same themes.

Nevertheless, the book sold well, and despite Hayden's later threats to round up all the copies and burn them, there were positive reviews. But perhaps the most memorable reaction to the work for Hayden occurred in

1941. The Haydens were in New York while Erma was studying music at Juilliard and Robert was doing research in the Schomburg Collection at the New York City Library on materials which he would later shape into the finished poem 'Middle Passage'. Erma's uncle had known the poet Countee Cullen in college, and knowing her husband's early affection for Cullen's work, Erma called the noted poet, who still remembered Erma from her youth, and invited the couple for a visit. During the course of the evening's conversation, Cullen expressed an interest in Hayden's book *Heart-Shape in the Dust*, which he had read, and then he asked if Robert would read 'The Falcon', which was one of Cullen's favorites from the collection. Naturally the young poet was delighted to oblige.[4]

It was also during this period the Haydens decided that when they returned to Detroit, Robert should pursue his graduate studies full time at the University of Michigan at Ann Arbor where he hoped to study under W. H. Auden who was teaching a course in the analysis of poetry. Hayden had become aware of Auden's work in the late 1930s, when Hayden felt Auden was 'writing in a rather opaque manner and it was hard to get through it. But we kept on reading Auden and I think he was a real influence on poets of my generation – he and Stephen Spender.'[5] At this time in 1941, however, Hayden had come to believe that Auden was 'undoubtedly the greatest poet writing in English . . .'[6]

In the fall of 1941, at age twenty-eight, Hayden began his full-time pursuit of his MA degree in English and his association with W. H. Auden. It was a significant influence on Hayden's career, 'a strategic experience in my life',[7] as he was to describe it later. There was to be little intimate or casual fellowship between the two, but Auden showed him his 'strengths and weaknesses as a poet in ways no one else before had done',[8] and they would maintain contact for years to come.

Such a positive influence could not have come at a more crucial time. Hayden was ready to move forward with his art, having completed his apprenticeship. He would never cease changing and evolving as an artist, but he was clearly ready to strike out on his own stylistically, to find his own modes, his own voice. Auden was able to help elicit from the poet the qualities of imagery, of sound and phrasing that were distinctly Hayden's own, so that the poems that emerged from this period in the early 1940s, the historical pieces, for example, are totally different from anything Hayden had written before. No doubt such progress would have occurred without Auden's influence, but from the positive things Hayden had to say about the association, as well as from the inferences one must draw from the changed poetic technique, one can deduce that the studies with Auden at the University of Michigan served as a catalyst and accelerated the process of the poet's maturation.

Whatever lasting effects Auden contributed from 'the range of his learning, the breadth of his knowledge',[9] the one quality of poetry which in every interview and discussion about Auden, Hayden inevitably mentions is Auden's analogy between good poetry and algebra. This notion of poetry as a process of 'solving for the unknown' not only captured succinctly for Hayden the objectivist theory of the New Critical school that influenced Hayden's own poetic theory, it also conveys as clearly as anything could the vast change that occurred in his own poetry during this time. His poems in *Heart-Shape in the Dust* are arithmetic; they enunciate directly the message, and the total poetic effect is the sum of those statements. Hayden's later poetry requires something from the reader, to solve for x, to discover the meanings which the poetic images give form to.

Two other events during that same school year 1941–2 played a strategic part in the Haydens' lives and in Robert Hayden's career. In October of 1942 their daughter Maia was born, a cause for joy to be sure, but also a source of financial and emotional responsibility for the couple. In addition, Erma had during the year become acquainted on campus with a small and lively group of people belonging to the Bahá'í Faith. She quickly became enthralled with the Bahá'í teachings on universal brotherhood and the unity of religions. When she investigated the religion further and read the Bahá'í Writings, she became convinced of the veracity of the Bahá'í beliefs and determined to become a Bahá'í herself.

Robert was no less interested in the religion, but he was not yet ready to make this important commitment. He continued studying the Bahá'í Faith, what may well have been for him, with his Baptist upbringing, a radical departure from his previous religious point of view, in spite of his already acknowledged beliefs in world brotherhood, world peace and integration.

The longer he studied, the more Erma tried to convey to him the enthusiasm and excitement she felt. Finally, Robert told her outright that if she persisted in pushing him, he might never become a Bahá'í. She never said another word about it. Later in the year, however, after thoughtful study of the Bahá'í Writings and a frank and meaningful discussion with Dorothy Baker, one of the most charismatic and knowledgeable Bahá'í teachers of the time, Robert Hayden became a Bahá'í in 1943. It was not an easy decision, because he was not a group person, as he often observed. In a taped interview in 1976, Hayden stated that in the first place neither he nor Erma was at that time desperately looking for something new to direct their lives, but when they encountered this Faith and found that they believed its teachings, they had no choice but to follow the truth.[10] The intellectual and moral integrity reflected in this observation and in the decision that the Haydens made serves as a hallmark of the future decisions they would face. In all of these their beliefs would help guide them through a variety of troublesome situations.

At first Hayden was not particularly aware of the influence his decision had on his work. Later he realized that from that point on, the Bahá'í Faith shaped his themes and approaches to subjects:

I saw very little influence on my work for the first several years . . . but now I realize it has given me a base, a focus. I am not very pious, certainly not in any sense a goody-goody. Indeed, I still struggle with my faith; it harrows up my soul, as I guess it is supposed to do. And I confess that as an artist I find it extremely difficult to conform to the letter of the law. But I have learned from it that the work of the artist, the scientist, the philosopher, all sincere effort in any discipline has spiritual value and is both a form of service and a form of worship. This thought sustains me when the dark times come . . .[11]

Later, in the years at Fisk, he would encounter other problems regarding his beliefs, some as a result of trying to perceive how his art related to his religion and other problems arising from his political and social stands.

In the meantime Hayden was progressing rapidly with his poetry. He was trying to forge a series of poems on Afro-American history into a sequence for submission to the Hopwood competition at the university. His ultimate intent with the history pieces was to create a volume entitled *The Black Spear* which, in effect, would respond to the passage in Stephen Vincent Benét's *John Brown's Body* that some day a Black poet would bring forth a 'blackskinned epic, epic with the black spear',[12] to commemorate the history of the Afro-American:

I dared hope that I might be that poet. And when I met Mr Benét, several years after reading his book, I told him I also intended to write a poem of slavery and the Civil War, but this time from the black man's point of view. He was enthusiastic and encouraged me to do so.[13]

Among the poems he completed for this series were 'O Daedalus, Fly Away Home', 'The Ballad of Nat Turner' and 'Frederick Douglass'. He did not finish 'Middle Passage', so he entered the competition without it. In 1942 these poems won for him the Hopwood Major Award for Poetry. To Hayden's great delight, Auden attended the awards ceremony and afterward came up to shake his hand and congratulate him on the accomplishment.

In addition to the Hopwood award, Hayden garnered some national attention by publishing pieces in important poetry journals. In 1943 he published 'O Daedalus, Fly Away Home' in perhaps the most noteworthy of poetry journals, *Poetry*, established in 1912 by Harriet Monroe. In 1944 he published the completed 'Middle Passage' in *Phylon*, then under the editorship of the renowned W. E. B. Du Bois. A few years after that, in 1947, he published 'Frederick Douglass' in the *Atlantic Monthly*.

4. The Early Years at Fisk
1946–1960

He became my father and mother because he midwifed the writer-in-me and, after bringing it into the light, shaped and moulded the writer and me.[1]

Julius Lester

Ostensibly, Robert Hayden's career as a poet was assured. In 1944 he received both his BA degree from Wayne State and his MA degree from the University of Michigan – the administration at Wayne State (with the urging of the University of Michigan) decided it was, after all, ridiculous to withhold the degree from this brilliant young poet on the basis of one physics course. His grade point average was high enough to award him induction into Phi Kappa Phi National Honor Society, and he was also awarded a Teaching Assistantship for the 1945–6 academic year. He was accelerating in his poetry, had worked under one of the best poets alive, had won a major award, and had been published in the best literary journals. He had a loving family, aware of his talent and devoted to helping him establish himself, and he had a religious belief which supported his art and integrated the various activities of his life.

In short, by age thirty-one Robert Earl Hayden had lifted himself from the Detroit ghetto to a position far beyond anything he could have dared dream of as a child – though he had dared to dream all the same. In spite of an emotionally tumultuous childhood, maimed vision, which rendered him legally blind, had combined his talents with the determination to succeed – assisted here and there by propitious forces beyond his control. But in spite of this auspicious foothold on his career as poet, he was, ironically, not to attain any substantial success until almost twenty years later.

It was a hard decision that confronted the Haydens in 1946. Robert had received a job offer at Fisk University in Nashville, Tennessee, presumably as a teacher of creative writing in addition to other courses in English literature. They had both previously vowed that they would never live in the South, and the offer of three thousand dollars a year was not much, though it was more than the two thousand he was making as a Teaching Assistant. As they stood on the porch of the rustic cabin they rented in Brooklyn, Michigan, Robert and Erma reluctantly decided to move.

Nashville was a sprawling country town surrounded by farms, but it was also a college town, home of Vanderbilt University, Peabody College, Fisk, Tennessee A and I, Scarritt Theological Seminary and Meharry Medical School. While the Fisk campus served as an oasis from much of the racial tension, it was not sufficient to ward against the sudden changes they experienced. They could find people of good will of both races, but they were still limited in the kind of life they could lead when all public facilities were segregated – restaurants, schools, buses, even drinking fountains:

There was a time, for example, when I never went to the movies in the South, because in order to go to the movie you had to enter the theater through an alley and then go up and sit in what we used to call the buzzard's roost, a Jim Crow balcony. So I never went to the movies in Nashville.[2]

And even among those people not inhibited by racial prejudice there was a kind of provincialism which stifled the Haydens. They had become accustomed to indulging their love of modern art and modern dance, but the people in Nashville tended to socialize at home, largely unaware of the world that lay beyond their neighborhoods.

Perhaps the biggest disappointment to the Haydens, however, came not from the insult and narrow boundaries which segregation imposed, but from the exorbitant demands of his new job at Fisk, together with the almost total lack of regard by the school administration for his writing. Fisk wanted an English teacher, not a poet, and, in spite of the meager pay, they expected him to teach from fifteen to twenty hours per week.

Hayden once remarked that he taught 'in order to earn a living so that [I] can write a poem or two now and then'.[3] And yet he was a superb teacher and gave unselfishly of his time and energy:

. . . I don't resent teaching, but I don't love it. I never have loved it, and I've always been a good teacher. I'm a very conscientious teacher and also I care about my students. I try to give them a full measure. But I feel always in conflict, partly because until recently I've had to teach rather heavy loads.[4]

He had such a sense of duty to his students that he refused to short-change them, even at the expense of his own career.

It was not that Hayden needed or cherished emotional support for his aspirations as a poet; throughout his career he would wage his battles largely alone, except for the support that Erma and a few close friends could give. But what he did not need was the undermining of the most precious requisite for his work – spare time. With such heavy course loads he would exhaust himself during the day, teaching and grading papers. After dinner and some diverting moments with wife and daughter he would try to write from about twelve until three a.m.

In his *New York Times* review of *Words in the Mourning Time*, Julius Lester, a former student of Hayden's, mentions his recollection of the poet's situation at Fisk:

When I entered Fisk University in the fall of 1956, he had already been there 10 years in that miasma of black bourgeois gentility. On the campus, he was regarded as just another instructor in the English department, teaching 15 hours of classes a week, from two sections of freshman English to American literature to creative writing. No one at Fisk had the vaguest notion of what a poet's function was, not that they gave it any thought. Yet, somehow, Hayden continued to believe – in himself and poetry – though no one except his wife and a few students and friends in New York ever cared.[5]

During his second year at Fisk Hayden almost left. He had won a Julius Rosenwald Fellowship in Creative Writing in 1947 but was asked to teach two courses in the department, for which he assumed he would be paid his regular salary. Several weeks into the term he discovered he was receiving only a frac- tion of his normal pay. He immediately went to the chairman of the department to resign, and would have followed through except for the intervention of several colleagues and students who protested the resignation and the loss of Hayden to the school.

Fisk agreed to pay him his normal salary, and he stayed. But the teaching load never got much better and the pay remained low. Furthermore, it was difficult to become acclimatized to living in a segregated society, especially since Maia would soon be six and ready to enter school. So it was that in 1948 the Haydens made the difficult decision that Erma should take Maia to New York where she could enter an integrated school system, and Robert would come up in the summers until he could obtain a leave of absence.

In this same year another milestone occurred in the poet's career, though it might not have seemed so at the time. Hayden and Myron O'Higgins, another Rosenwald fellow, published the first in the Counterpoise series of poetry volumes through the funds of the Rosenwald Foundation. The volume entitled *The Lion and the Archer* contained six poems by Hayden, among them his extremely important poem 'A Ballad of Remembrance'. Nothing shows more clearly the progress of Hayden's poetry during the eight years since the publi- cation of *Heart-Shape in the Dust* than these poems which serve as a virtual credo of his liberation from traditional poetic modes. But in addition to the fine poetry the poets published a preface to the series, a manifesto by artists determined not to be casually labeled as 'Negro poets'. It was a document to which any student of Hayden's art must turn as the cornerstone of his poetics, a doctrine which he courageously maintained for the rest of his life. It reads in part:

We are unalterably opposed to the chauvinistic, the cultish, to special pleading, to all that seeks to limit and restrict creative expression. We believe experimentation to be an absolute necessity in keeping the arts vital and significant in contemporary life . . . As writers who belong to a so-called minority, we are violently opposed to having our work viewed, as the custom is, entirely in the light of sociology and politics, to having it overpraised on the one hand by those with an axe to grind or with a conscience to salve, to having it misinterpreted on the other hand by coterie editors, reviewers, anthologists who refuse us encouragement or critical guidance because we deal with realities we find it neither possible nor desirable to ignore . . . We believe in the oneness of mankind and the importance of the arts in the struggle for peace and unity.[6]

The poetry of the volume was markedly distinct from anything Hayden had done before, even from the history poems. The vocabulary was richly allusive, without dialect or propaganda. The themes, though sometimes on Afro-American concerns, were objectively presented. But beyond obvious differences of meters and sound effects, which are importantly changed, there was a heavy reliance on symbolism. Unlike Hayden's later work which was more accessible on the literal level, these poems were often difficult to penetrate and, in their lush imagery, belong to what Hayden termed his 'Baroque period'.

Published in Nashville by the Hemphill Press, the small volume was exquisitely printed, and in theme as well as form it marked Hayden's departure from what had become traditional poetic modes for the Afro-American poet. Consequently, in spite of the relatively limited distribution of the work, the collection was noted by Selden Rodman in the *New York Times* as a landmark publication: 'It is possible that this modest pamphlet, containing thirteen short poems by two young Negro poets, may come to be regarded as the entering wedge in the "emancipation" of Negro poetry in America.'[7] And, in fact, the most critically acclaimed poem in the collection, 'A Ballad of Remembrance', describes in symbolic terms the poet's own determination to speak with his own voice, as Hughes years before had bade him do. Two other pieces, 'The Invisible Circus' and 'The Lion', also deal importantly with the duty of the poet to probe courageously his innermost being, and the obligation of the reader to infer meaning through the algebraic process of working through poetic images.

The next year, 1950, Hayden was able to obtain a leave of absence from Fisk so that he could join Erma and Maia in New York. The Haydens barely managed with Erma working and Robert caring for Maia, and it was a hard routine. They rented a house in Brooklyn, and Erma had to commute to her job in Manhattan where she taught music and creative dance at the Little Red School House. The long hours of traveling left Erma constantly exhausted, and in 1951 the family moved back to Nashville. Maia was now nine years old, an extremely beautiful, bright and sensitive child. Fortunately that first year back she had an excellent, creative teacher in Pansey Williams. In the years that followed, however, Maia's teachers were of a substantially lower quality. This concern, coupled with the child's intense difficulty with allergies, was a further distraction from the poet's work, but not nearly so difficult as the continuing drain on his energies that his courses imposed. Had he been a less conscientious teacher, quite possibly he could have performed his duties mechanically and concentrated on his writing. But he cared about his students, especially those who aspired to write, and many of them went on to become successful writers – Lonne Elder, William Demby, Norman Loftis, and Julius Lester.

There would be other traumas in this his fourth decade, but before they came barreling in he had some successes. In 1954 he received a Ford Foundation grant for travel and writing in Mexico. He had longed to experience another culture, and since he had been a Spanish major in undergraduate school, he delighted in the eight months he spent there. The Mexican poems, which eventually emerged from the notes he took, formed a sequence entitled 'An Inference of Mexico'. Symbolic in nature, these poems tell on a literal level as much as anything could about his reactions to the country and the Mexican people. Generally, the pieces are studies in contrast between exquisite landscapes and a poverty-stricken populace, between a rich history and a lost identity. His imagination was stirred by the Mexican's obsession with death, as evidenced in the celebration of 'El Dia de los Muertos' (The Day of the Dead), and the *corrida*, which seemed to the poet's eye a morality play wherein man and beast act out the search for vitality in death. Within these poems are the landscapes typical of the country – the coast at Veracruz, the marketplace, the Aztec ruins:

You will see Indian vendors in regional dress selling birds in the Paseo de la Reforma, Mexico City's most elegant boulevard. Modern buildings, almost futuristic in design, will have mosaic murals – fantastic, kaleidoscopic . . . There are great pyramids of the sun and the moon built centuries ago. And the faces of the people often remind you of old Aztec masks. The Mexican past seemed remarkably viable to me, gave Mexico its special kind of ambience.[8]

Because he could speak Spanish, Hayden was able to understand the ironic contrasts beyond the stark beauty, the harsh realities of the daily rigor. He was the outsider, the *gringo*, but he also realized one of his favorite axioms: 'No place is home for me; therefore, every place is home.'[9] His firsthand experience of the universality of the Bahá'í was also very important to him:

Being a Bahá'í kept me from feeling as much a stranger as I might otherwise have. For I came to know several Mexican Bahá'ís, was invited to their homes, made trips with them. The faith we shared diminished our superficial differences, was a bond between us.[10]

Upon Hayden's return to Nashville and Fisk he was promoted to Associate Professor of English literature, something of no great note at the time, but part of a process which was to become significant later. The following year, 1955, Hayden published a second volume of verse in the Counterpoise series entitled *Figure of Time*. As yet he was still at work on the Mexican pieces and none of them were included, but the twelve poems in the volume are extremely varied in style and theme. There are a number of poems dealing with the Afro-American experience: 'Summertime and the living . . .', about his boyhood in Detroit, 'The Burly Fading One', about his Uncle Jed, 'Incense of the Lucky Virgin', about a hapless mother who ventures infanticide in the throes of despair, and 'Figure', a powerful portrait of a lynched Black man. There are also two poems explicitly about the Bahá'í Faith: 'In Light Half Nightmare and Half Vision' and 'The Prophet', both of which he revised and published in his later collections.

More than any volume he had published thus far, *Figure of Time* demonstrated the mature power of Hayden's technique. In general, the literal level of meaning is more accessible in these poems than in the pieces from *The Lion and the Archer*, but the layers of meaning resulting from his symbolism are just as evident. Above all else, the fine craftsmanship of the poet is evident, the careful selection of every word, the phrasing of lines, the organic use of structure. This polish, the honing of his verses, rapidly became Hayden's trademark and won him respect among the most severe critics. Furthermore, this constant concern for quality accounts for other noteworthy characteristics of his career. For example, because he would quite literally spend months and longer revising, reworking, reconsidering a poem, his output suffered. This obsession with quality along with his unceasing professorial duties prevented him from churning out reams of verse, but it also meant that what he did complete was finely tuned and worthy of intense examination. This care with his art also accounted for the time lag between the original impetus for a poem and the publication of the poems themselves, especially during this part of his career.

Of course, the self-imposed isolation that writing requires is difficult for any poet, and Hayden's decision to immerse himself in his art was not an easy one. He was constantly faced with the dilemma of discerning the proper balance between his art and his other loves and obligations – his family, his teaching, his religion. Interestingly, it was largely from Erma that he received the greatest encouragement to give priority to his writing. It was also Erma who most insistently reassured him that the quality of his work far outweighed the sheer quantity of his publications. Most of the struggle, the uncertainty, the twinges of guilt came from within, especially during the mid and late 1950s. During this time Hayden had to come to terms with some of the most profound emotional and philosophical dilemmas he would ever face.

Among these was the conflict Hayden felt as a result of wanting to write, cherishing his work, and yet being an intensely sensitive, sociable man. He loved people and conversation, humor, conviviality, and rejecting the comfort and delight of human companionship to pursue his calling was not easy. Gene Olson remarks in his guide to creative writing, 'Find a private place in which to write and guard it with your life; words abhor crowds.'[11] Olson further states, 'Tell your story only once . . . and tell it on paper.'[12] These dicta, simple and logical though they be, imply if taken seriously that a writer's life is necessarily one of self-imposed isolation, loneliness, and the possible sundering of healthy human relationships. Hayden, like any writer, loved his art, and cherished the time he had to work on his poems, and among his drafts of the Mexican poems in his personal papers is the following entry which portrays him exhorting himself with the same sort of axioms:

1. Refrain from criticism of others. A *poet* should be above this.

2. No longer share what is most personal with anyone – neither with wife, friend, nor child. Express it only in poetry and in an indirect or objective way.

3. No longer discuss my writing or my hopes for it with anyone. It is too special and sacred to me; no one should be expected to understand how I feel about it.

4. Seek solitude and stand alone.

5. Do not let fatigue, disappointment, professional routine and academic trivia betray finer instincts.

6. Cease complaining. And do not any longer make excuses or explanations to anyone.

7. Read and think more and talk less. Or not at all, unless in a fairly objective and impersonal way.[13]

Placed as these notes are in the midst of poetry drafts, one can imagine how some temporary frustration – an interruption, a diverting conversation which may have distracted him from his work – might have induced him to jot down such rules. But he could not long sustain such Spartan rigor among his loved ones and friends, and later, as he gained more national and international attention, he would still give most liberally of his time and thought to others.

Another source of intense introspection and emotional turmoil to Hayden during this period resulted from the concern over his identity in relation to his foster family and his natural parents, a problem which nagged and plagued him the rest of his life. His foster mother had died in 1938, his foster father in 1941, and his natural father in the early 1950s. These losses had saddened him, but they also allowed for an unhampered relationship with his natural mother, which he enjoyed immensely. But during the 1950s he began to examine his deepest feelings about his childhood. No doubt part of the stimulus for his probing was the revelation by his mother that his real name, his given name, was not Robert Earl Hayden, but Asa Bundy Sheffey. How this revelation affected him is perhaps best revealed in the poem 'Names' which he published in his 1978 volume *American Journal*:

When my fourth decade came,
I learned my name was not my name.

I felt deserted, mocked.
Why had the old ones lied?
No matter. They were dead.

And the name on the books was dead,
like the life my mother fled,
like the life I might have known.[14]

According to Hayden, however, it was hardly one event that caused this examination of his childhood. Some of the impetus derived from his sense of having reached a mid-point in his life, having turned forty in 1953, just as the century itself was at mid-point. Also, he stated, by this time he 'had enough detachment', had gained 'enough psychic or emotional distance to write these memory poems'.[15] The poems he speaks of are pieces like 'Those Winter Sundays' and 'The Whipping', the one a tribute to the work-a-day drudgery his foster father endured to provide for him, and the other an attempt to understand the deep frustration which drove his foster mother to vent her rage on her adopted child.

These lyrics, considered by many to be some of his best poems, were, according to Hayden, part of his 'need to recall my past and to rid myself of the pain of so much of it'.[16] The source of this pain is complex, and never fully explored in his poetry since it was never Hayden's purpose to use his poetry to bleed on his pages or condemn others. Indeed, his 'memory' poems attempt to explore the positive traits of his foster parents, quite in accord, in fact, with the Bahá'í principle set forth by 'Abdu'l-Bahá about concentrating on the positive qualities in others. [17] But Hayden's refusal to detail the difficulties of his childhood should not be taken as a sign that these were not, indeed, traumatic memories and emotions:

We had a terrible love-hate relationship with one another, and dreadful things happened I can never forget. They turned me in upon myself, although perhaps they wouldn't have affected me so deeply if I'd not been struggling against my own inner demons, struggling with feelings of inadequacy and self doubt. A struggle that continues to this day, I might add.[18]

It is quite possible that this tortuous ambivalence towards his foster parents was also subtly at work in his feelings towards his natural mother, who had, after all, left him in the charge of people not really able to understand his sensitive spirit, though Hayden never admitted such feelings. What is clear is that during the 1950s he was examining and sorting out these complex relationships, trying to deal with feelings of rejection and guilt, of love mixed with anger.

This period climaxed with the death of his mother in 1957, though he never fully resolved his feelings about his childhood. That Hayden emerged from such a morass of ties and emotions as a sane, sensitive and resilient individual is remarkable. That he was, beyond that, outgoing and unselfish is a tribute to his deep strength of character, his religious convictions, and the loving support of Erma and a few devoted friends.

Even the surface reminders of these problems never fled. In the mid-1970s, when he was serving as Consultant to the Library of Congress, he and Erma were invited to Bulgaria. When he applied for his passport he discovered that he was, legally, still Asa Bundy Sheffey. This revelation devastated him, especially when he had to suffer the indignity of having to change his name to Robert Hayden.

From such unsettling forces at work in the poet's life, one would well expect poems of another sort – introspective outcry, self-pity, some of the solipsistic modes so evident in much of post-modern poetry in which the self is the center of the universe around which all other realities orbit, in relation to which all other realities take their meaning. But always the focus of Hayden's work is outward, expansive, examining the larger implications of even the most personal events.

During these same years there was, beyond this problem of his identity and his childhood, another source of internal debate for Hayden – the question of the relationship between his art and his beliefs as a Bahá'í. It was not a new consideration, but it was an issue that grew in importance until he resolved his feelings. It was never a question of a conflict with the explicit teachings of the Bahá'í Faith; the problem stemmed from the sense of urgency Hayden inferred from the Bahá'í Writings concerning the obligation of Bahá'ís to teach: 'Say: Teach ye the Cause of God, O people of Bahá, for God hath prescribed unto every one the duty of proclaiming His Message, and regardeth it as the most meritorious of all deeds.'[19] This and similar statements by Bahá'u'lláh, when coupled with some of the teachings concerning the rejection of attachment to 'the dust-heap of a mortal world'[20] seemed to advocate to some Bahá'ís the abandonment of concerns for professional advancement or any activity other than the direct and specific act of conveying by word of mouth the verities of the Bahá'í Writings. Other Bahá'í Writings, however, seemed to be in contrast with this inference, commanding that the Bahá'í have a profession, and equating work done in the proper spirit with worship, and praising in particular those professions that aid mankind. Furthermore, praiseworthy professions, according to the Bahá'í Writings, are not only those which literally and directly assist people – medicine, social work and the like. The Bahá'í Writings acknowledge the possibility of a variety of methods of informing mankind of the Bahá'í teachings and a variety of ways of serving mankind: 'Not all of us are capable of serving in the same way, but the one way every Bahá'í can spread the Faith is by example. This moves the hearts of people far more deeply than words ever can.'[21]

The Bahá'í Writings also exalt the arts specifically as a praiseworthy activity:

It is enjoined upon every one of you to engage in some form of occupation, such as crafts, trades and the like. We have graciously exalted your engagement in such work to the rank of worship unto God, the True One.[22]

Great indeed is the claim of scientists and craftsmen on the peoples of the world . . . In truth, knowledge is a veritable treasure for man, and a source of glory, of bounty, of joy, of exaltation, of cheer and gladness unto him.[23]

If a man engageth with all his power in the acquisition of a science or in the perfection of an art, it is as if he has been worshipping God in churches and temples.[24]

Despite these clear affirmations, the Bahá'í artist may be surrounded in a Bahá'í community by those who define more narrowly the methods of teaching their beliefs and who exhort others to do the same. In such an atmosphere the artist's own ostensibly esoteric endeavors may appear quite irrelevant to other Bahá'ís, and to the artist himself.[25]

To someone only peripherally concerned with his beliefs as a Bahá'í, such a dilemma might never occur, but Robert Hayden had made his decision to become a Bahá'í with utmost seriousness and care, and he could not ignore this growing need for clarity in understanding the relationship between his art and his own spiritual development, as well as the relationship between his art and the Bahá'í Faith in general. Speaking about the impact of this conflict between his religious beliefs and his aspirations as a poet, Hayden later observed:

I sat in my front room one day when I was still teaching at Fisk University and was filled with a sense of cold, almost inexpressible horror, because suddenly something sort of swept over me: 'You are not really dealing with reality. Everything you are doing is false because you don't really see the connection between what you say you believe and what you are doing as a writer.' It was naturally a horrifying experience.[26]

Exactly when Hayden resolved this conflict he never clearly explained – probably there was no precise date. But what becomes evident, as I hope to demonstrate later, is that Hayden's poetry itself, quite apart from being wholly legitimized by the Bahá'í passages already cited, contains an orchestrated and coherent pursuit of major Bahá'í themes throughout, albeit largely in symbolic terms. It is sufficient here to note that Hayden's own confirmation of his coming to terms with the problem clarifies the principal insight which, in his own mind, vindicated his devotion to his art:

After that [conflict] I guess I began to try to see what the relationship was, and today I feel very comfortable in that. It lies behind everything I do. Indeed, when I was less sophisticated in my outlook, I thought that the only way that I really could serve the Cause was by writing religious poems, but later on as I pondered what Bahá'u'lláh said about the role of the artist, I began to realize that if you really had the new spiritual orientation, just about anything you did could be of service.[27]

There was another aspect of this conflict which Hayden himself could not resolve, and it troubled him, subtly and blatantly, the rest of his life. It was, in a most general way, the failure of the Bahá'í community to appreciate his work – though this sense of alienation took many forms. Sometimes it was simply his sense that the other Bahá'ís had trouble understanding his art as a service to the Faith, as opposed to the more direct kinds of teaching and committee work that Erma was always doing. As a result of this perception of his work, he felt he was regarded as less a Bahá'í. Obviously the failure on the part of his fellow believers to appreciate his art was devastating by itself and made his inherently lonely task even lonelier. But when he sensed disapproval of his endeavors as being spiritually irrelevant – and thus inconsequential – he felt an even deeper sadness.

Toward the end of his career, when he had attained national acclaim, many Bahá'ís understood profoundly how his accomplishments had served to establish the legitimacy of the Faith in the minds of the public, and yet even then he lamented how few Bahá'ís were familiar with his work. One brief anecdote illustrates well the cause for his distress. He had traveled to a community to give a reading of his poetry as part of a Bahá'í public program. At the time Hayden was much in demand to give readings, and on this occasion was not only giving freely of his services, but he was taking precious time away from his work. In preparation for introducing Hayden, a speaker was jotting down the poet's accomplishments. After noting some of the more impressive milestones in the poet's career, the troubled Bahá'í questioned Hayden, 'But what have you done in the way of *Bahá'í* service?'

As with the battles he would wage in the 1960s, when he withstood the virulent attacks by the advocates of the Black Militant Cause, Hayden contained most of these struggles within, as he had his complex emotions about his childhood. At times, in the presence of Erma or close companions, he would vent his anger and pain, try to relieve enough built-up emotion so that he could maintain stasis and pursue his work. Never in his writing or in his interviews did he betray a hint of these concerns about his fellow Bahá'ís or the depth of his suffering. But only in the light of this background can one begin to sense behind the nervous, gentle and affectionate man the strength of character which enabled him to sustain his belief in his Faith, himself and his art.

But if the decade of the 1950s was a period of coming to grips with these crucial issues, it was also a period of further advancement in his publications. In addition to *Figure of Time* (1955), Hayden's 'O Daedalus, Fly Away Home', 'A Ballad of Remembrance', 'Runagate Runagate' and 'Frederick Douglass' appeared in *The Poetry of the Negro*, an anthology edited by Langston Hughes and Arna Bontemps.[28] In 1954 'Witch Doctor', one of his most critically acclaimed poems, appeared in *Voices*, and 'Locus', 'Incense of the Lucky Virgin' and 'A Road in Kentucky' appeared in *The Midwest Journal.*

Toward the end of the 1950s he began to publish the first of his Mexican poems with 'Corrida de Toros' appearing in 1959 in S. I. Hiakawa's respected journal *ETC.*

The workload at Fisk did not abate in spite of his successes, however, and he tried on occasion to find a position elsewhere. But in the decades of the forties and fifties it was difficult for a Black professor at a Southern Afro-American school like Fisk to have much mobility, especially to a reputable university in the North where Hayden wanted to go. At one point Hayden was interviewed at the University of Chicago, but the job fell through.[29]

Thus Hayden endured at Fisk, struggling to find time to write, hoping to find a publisher for his poems. If he had thought that the situation would soon improve, he was to discover it would not. Indeed, things would get much worse before they got better.

5. The Crucial Years
1960–1969

At home, Hayden had to be content with assurances from his colleagues that he had a good underground reputation. 'I wish it would surface,' he used to say. [1]

Jo Thomas

Robert Hayden was in his late forties when the decade of the sixties began, a period which would test him utterly and yet inaugurate forcefully his ascendancy as a poet. At the decade's beginning he had not published a single volume with a commercial press, and, with regard to quantity alone, he had published relatively few single poems in literary journals, though he had been included in two important anthologies. By the end of the decade he had published three volumes of poetry, two with a commercial publisher, had been awarded the Grand Prize for poetry at the First World Festival of Negro Arts at Dakar, Senegal, and had received a full professorship at his alma mater. How such a vast change in Hayden's career came about is a story well worthy of a playwright's pen, containing as it does the intertwining of fate and the almost angelic intervention of Dr Rosey Pool.

The first of these forces to enter his life was Rosey Pool. About 1960 Hayden received a call from London where Dr Pool was doing a BBC radio show on which she read and discussed the poetry of Afro-Americans. She told Hayden that in the Nazi concentration camp where she had been a prisoner, 'she and her fellow prisoners, wishing to pray together in secret yet lacking a common faith, used lines from Negro spirituals instead, because these old songs expressed what they all felt most deeply'.[2] Now she was putting together an anthology of the work of Black poets and wanted permission to read his work on the air and use his poetry in her anthology.

Dr Pool was born in 1905 in Holland and had become interested in Afro-American poets in 1925 while a student at the University of Amsterdam. Later, when she visited the United States in the 1960s, she was surprised and disturbed to find 'that most Negro poets were unknown in their own country, or, if known, were given only a tenuous kind of recognition'.[3]

When Hitler invaded Holland, she had joined the resistance. Later she was imprisoned with her family, and her parents were executed as Jews. After the war she had attained some notoriety as the former teacher of Anne Frank, whose diary she originally translated. She settled in London, and as an acknowledged authority on Black poetry she later taught at Negro universities in the United States and lectured on radio and television. In London she acquainted a fellow countryman, Paul Breman, with Hayden's work, and a proposal was made for a series of poetry volumes to be printed in Holland and published in London. Hayden's would be the first of these limited editions.

Hayden titled this volume *A Ballad of Remembrance* and in it he included the best of everything he had done. He arranged and orchestrated the poems so that a few years later in 1966, when October House would publish his *Selected Poems*, he had to make relatively few changes to render the volume complete. The poems in *A Ballad of Remembrance* are grouped into four sections, each of which is, in a sense, a collection of remembrances, as the book's title suggests. The first section contains a miscellany of remembered places and characters, all of which have possible symbolic value. Among these are 'A Ballad of Remembrance', 'Locus' (a portrait of a southern landscape), 'Tour 5' (about the old Natchez Trace – an historic trail which Hayden uses again in a later poem 'Theory of Evil') and 'On Lookout Mountain' (a reverie at the famous Civil War battlefield). There are also recalled characters such as Bessie Smith in 'Homage to the Empress of the Blues' and Daddy Grace in 'Witch Doctor'. The second section contains a variety of childhood recollections such as 'Summertime and the living. . .', 'The Whipping', 'Those Winter Sundays', all of which deal with aspects of Detroit ghetto life, and a miscellaneous collection of some of his most weighty short lyrics – 'Lear is Gay', 'Theme and Variation', the two poems on Bahá'u'lláh and several others. The third section contains the Mexico poems, seven in all, and the fourth section contains the poems on Afro-American history: 'Middle Passage', based on the account of a slave ship rebellion, 'O Daedalus, Fly Away Home', in which a Georgia slave longs for his native Africa, 'The Ballad of Nat Turner' and 'Frederick Douglass', powerful lyrics about Black historical figures.

Thus, in 1962 the first ample collection of Hayden's work since *Heart-Shape in the Dust* appeared, as did Rosey Pool's study of new poems by American Negroes *Beyond the Blues*, which contains four of Hayden's poems – 'Full Moon', 'Belsen, Liberation Day', 'The Diver' and 'School Integration Riot'. At the time, neither publication really did much to promote Hayden's career. In his own mind (and it was an accurate appraisal) he was largely unknown and unappreciated except by a handful of admirers who discerned the quality of his work.

His own assessment of his career between 1962 and 1966, when he won the prize at Dakar, can be inferred from the following letter he received in November of 1965:

When I come down Christmas, I will beg you to make a tape recording of your poems, not only so that I'll have something worth a few bucks some day, but because I need all the samples of poets reading I can get, and speaking of it being worth a few bucks some day, I'm sure you realize you have a place in the history of American poetry assured you, if only because you are a Negro poet writing in a certain way at a certain time. I'm sure you know this and it must be damn little comfort. But it's distressing at times to talk to you or hear from you when you are bemoaning your 'pseudo career'. All careers are pseudo. You haven't had much of a career; that's true. But everyone knows, including yourself, that you are not a pseudo poet. A Poet is not a man who is published, praised and prized every so often, though blessed is the man who gets this. A Poet is a man to whom everything is symbolic, a sign, a portent.[4]

Possibly Hayden had been lamenting to his friend Clyde Watkins his inability to find an American publisher for his work. Among his correspondence, for example, one finds a letter from Macmillan and Company dated June 25, 1964, rejecting his proposed manuscript, even though the editor states that 'We believe in your work', and notes that if he could add his proposed poem on Matthew Henson (the Negro who accompanied Peary to the North Pole) 'and most of *A Ballad of Remembrance,* you would have a terrific book in hand'.[5] Certainly Hayden had to feel himself a failure at this point, in spite of the utter beauty of the Paul Breman volume, in spite of the trustworthy friends who were well aware of his talent, in spite of inner assurance that he was a good poet (an assurance which, Hayden himself admitted in a 1976 interview, never lasts very long for a writer).[6]

As Watkins succinctly pointed out in the last part of his letter, Hayden was a poet, someone who examined life, tried to discern the symbols there, the metaphors, the meaning behind the surfaces of events, of people, of nature itself. In his verse he distilled, revised and polished those perceptions, the patterns he found, until he had some notion of what meaning lay behind the largest sweeps of history or the most commonplace daily experiences.

Perhaps nothing in Hayden's papers illustrates the way he came upon these poetic ideas as tellingly and delightfully as notes he took when he entered hospital in 1961 for an operation. As soon as he hears a word, a sound, observes a hospital procedure, he is trying to correlate what he has experienced with similar occurrences, analyzing events even as they happen. This was typical of Hayden's mind – that in the midst of his own anxiety, fear and pain, he was also a sort of disembodied spirit watching himself, examining himself and his experiences, evaluating, judging, sometimes pleased, sometimes not, but always trying to find some truth, some larger implication of events. This bears out what Gene Olson describes as a common characteristic of the creative writer – the need to live life twice, to 'complete' the experience by distilling it on paper:[7]

The man a door or so down – his wife found him with his mistress and shot him. According to the doctor, his being fat (280 lb.) kept the bullets from going clear through him. I hear him moaning from time to time – next-door neighbors on a street of suffering.

I am not in pain of any sort but my morbid imagination runs wild every time I think 'operation' – which I am to have tomorrow. A sense of isolation and shelter against the outside world – death-in-life and life-in-death; the body's marvelous powers of revival; the (my) mind's fear of the body, the physical – something that goes back to the Puritan, the Calvinist in me, which I cannot free myself from. My discomfort is trivial in comparison with what my mother, what Erma and others I love have suffered, yet this is big enough for me.[8]

The notes, which later became the basis for his poem 'The Broken Dark',[9] go on to organize in an outline fashion the hospital procedures and to discuss the strengths he observes in the downtrodden, indigent patients who do not brood over their distress because they accept suffering as a natural part of life.

From such notes ideas for poems would arise, though the notes by themselves are delightful and incisive. Beginning with a line or two, sometimes this process would entail quite literally hundreds of drafts, but the end result would be a poem of acknowledged excellence which would flow with such easy grace that it would seem plucked spontaneously from the air. But always behind the deceptive ease was a mastery of sound and meter, of image and symbol, an orchestration of technique.

So it is that while one can view the series of events surrounding Hayden's winning the Dakar award in 1966 as a divine accident (since he never even entered the competition himself), it was in another sense the inevitable result of years of fine craftsmanship which, I am convinced, would have ultimately emerged successful regardless. For example, it is worth noting that Hayden considered the publication of his work *Selected Poems* by the commercial American publisher October House as a major turning point in his career, and though the book was published in September of 1966 after he had officially won the Dakar award on April 7, 1966, the book had been contracted before news of this honor. In no way does this lessen the prestige or great joy which this fortuitous episode gave to Hayden, but it does help indicate that, given his ceaseless work and determination, given the quality of his art, he probably would have succeeded.

But let me not detract from what was, at once, among the most joyful surprises and propitious events in Hayden's career, not unlike the episode with the social worker and the college scholarship. The First World Festival of Negro Arts was instigated and sponsored by Léopold Sédar Senghor (Senegal's president and a recognized contemporary French poet), Unesco and the *Société Africaine de Culture*. Painters, sculptors, composers, musicians, actors, dancers and writers of every sort responded to the call for submissions to the various categories of competition. Dr Rosey E. Pool, who herself had become a Bahá'í in 1965, was asked by the British Committee to sit as a member of the pre-selection jury for the literary prizes for poets writing in English. When she received the list of entered works, she was sad to note the absence of Hayden's work:

Two days later, Wednesday the 19th of January, Marion Hofman came to lunch with me. I told her about the pre-selection jury, showed her the list of books submitted and expressed my regret that Robert Hayden's book of poetry *A Ballad of Remembrance* was not entered. Like in a flash of lightning I realised we might still be able to do something about it. Hayden's book was published in London by Paul Breman, a young independent publisher and incidentally a Hollander, like myself. A telephone call to Paul Breman. Another call to the British Committee for the Festival. An urgent letter to the Festival Office in Paris. An airmail parcel containing twelve copies of *A Ballad of Remembrance* was hurriedly posted. Robert Hayden's book was accepted for competition.[10]

Rosey's instinct, derived from years of studying poetry by Black writers, was accurate. In February 1966, after much deliberation during which Rosey was careful not to influence the opinions of the other jurists, the pre-selection jury chose three books of poetry to contend for the award; the authors of these volumes were Derek Walcott from St Lucia, Christopher Okigbo from Nigeria and Robert Hayden of the United States.

A month later Dr Pool unexpectedly received word that she had been chosen to be among the eight judges from various nations to determine the winning volume. To accept this position of honor, however, she had to withdraw her own book *Beyond the Blues*. After some consideration she decided to withdraw her own volume, and left for Dakar, Senegal, to serve on the panel with none other than Langston Hughes, the first major poet Hayden had ever met.

Each of the judges, trained in poetry, discussed preferences at length. But in Rosey's mind Hayden's verse rang out clearly above the rest:

With me, like a prayer, even before us on the table printed in a book of poetry were Robert Hayden's thoughts singing out in pain, in joy, in recognition of love of all humanity; the voice of a true poet – background to all our discussions in the magnificent building of the Republic of Senegal's National Assembly.[11]

At length, the judges were in accord and a press release was written announcing Hayden as winner. The tribute of the judges bears repeating:

Robert Hayden, born 1913, professor of English at Fisk University, Nashville, Tennessee, ranks on every level of the critical analysis of poetry among the finest of our anglophone contemporaries. *A Ballad of Remembrance* is the work of a remarkable craftsman, an outstanding singer of words, a striking thinker, a *poète pur sang*. He gives glory and dignity to America through deep attachment to the past, present and future of his race. Africa is in his soul, the world at large in his mind and heart.[12]

A few days later on a Saturday morning, a telegram arrived at the Hayden house saying he had won the competition. He had to read the message several times before he even understood what it meant. In a letter to Rosey he said:

I was absolutely stunned! I remember walking the floor and saying the Greatest Name and feeling proud and humble and unworthy and justified all at the same time! To think that somehow my work had meaning for people beyond anything I could have imagined! Well, it made the long and sometimes bitter struggle to be a poet worthwhile. And it had – and still has – the effect on me of making me determined to dedicate myself more completely, if that is possible, to poetry.[13]

It was in this same letter written on August 12, 1966, that Hayden called Rosey 'one of the rarest and dearest souls I have been privileged to know'. In the midst of his joyful gratitude, he gave as his reason for not writing sooner 'personal problems' which had occupied his time. As usual, Hayden was not one to complain publicly, even to so dear a friend as Rosey, but the 'problems' he alluded to were no simple, passing things, but possibly the most trying experience of his career.

Ironically, the situation alluded to in the letter had begun in April of 1966, at the very time his poetry was receiving accolades in Africa. It was the First Black Writers' Conference at Fisk where Hayden was severely attacked by some participants. The background to this humiliation and to the conference itself was the progressive faltering in the civil rights movement of the non-violent strategies which had experienced such initial success in cities like Nashville. The result was an ostensibly spontaneous outburst of militancy, intolerance and violence under the leadership of some Black activists. No longer was integration perceived as attainable or even desirable, since it seemed from the militant's point of view a loss of cultural identity for Blacks and an acceptance of the White, capitalistic definition of society.

As a college professor, Hayden had already felt pressure from this philosophical change. The student population had become rebellious, intolerant of traditional studies, and curricula gave way to what were thought to be innovative and 'relevant' courses. The positive atmosphere of students involved in and caring about politics and society was quickly overshadowed, in many cases, by the narrow-minded jargon which often condemned, prejudicially, traditional literature, arts and learning.

For Hayden, on a predominantly Black campus, the situation was often intolerable. As a writer of renown, he was, the students felt, in a position to take a stand, to make public statements and receive the attention that they could not. They also felt that as a poet he was in a position of being able to put into verse their most heartfelt emotions, to give music to their battle cries. But he would not. It was not, of course, that he did not dare – his refusals required infinitely more courage and cost him more friendships and support than compliance would have. But he was determined to uphold the standards he

had carefully and conscientiously avowed almost twenty years before in the
Counterpoise preface. He would not allow his verse to become propaganda
nor would he consider himself a 'Black poet': he was a poet who happened to
be black.

From the earliest days of his tenure at Fisk, he had been admired by aspiring
student writers. His ringing lyrics about freedom, justice and slave revolts had
won him a place in the hearts of students taking pride in their identity as Afro-
Americans. Now the university had appointed John O. Killens, a resident
novelist, to organize the 1966 Writers' Conference. To the students, Hayden
seemed, in his suits, bow-ties and soft manner, an 'Uncle Tom', an 'Oreo'. To
those attending the conference Hayden was an easy target.

The June 1966 issue of the *Negro Digest* details some of the confrontation
between Hayden and other participants:

'I have said this until I almost think I'll choke and fall over backwards,' thus began a
visibly disturbed Robert Hayden, addressing himself to the argument as to whether
one is a Negro poet or, as Hayden insists, 'a poet who happens to be a Negro'.
Reading lines from Yeats, Hayden solemnly commented, 'I didn't have to be Irish to
love those lines.'
  'Let's quit saying we're black writers writing to black folks – it has been given
importance it should not have.' Hayden's anticipation of opposition gave way to a
slight stutter. 'I don't think we're consciously trying to escape.'
  His sensibility shaken to the point of anger, Hayden continued, 'Please notice this
– all you folks sitting out there waiting to jump down my neck.' He proceeded to
define poetry as 'the beauty of perception given form . . . the art of saying the impossible'.[14]

But as eloquent and sound as his words now seem, Hayden's fate was sealed
by the clear dominance of the angry and defiant mood, and his fine sentiments
were rebuked by Tolson, who denounced capitalism, by another speaker, who
denounced Hayden as having a bad influence on his students at Fisk by not
stressing their particular role as 'black poets, black teachers'.[15] Clearly what
had been intended as a writers' conference had quickly become a political/
philosophical debate, and Hayden's urging that literature not become simply
a tool for propaganda was perceived as weakness. Ironically, he was pleading
for freedom, freedom from being told how or what to write, and his statements echoed his earlier words: 'We are unalterably opposed to the chauvinistic, the cultish, to special pleading, to all that seeks to limit and restrict
expression.'[16]

Perhaps he was more of an individualist than most. The only 'group' he felt
comfortable being aligned with was the Bahá'í Faith: 'I'm not a joiner', he
once remarked in an interview. 'I don't get involved with groups. The Bahá'í
Faith is about the only organized body I can stand. I cherish my individuality
and don't want to be a conformist except (paradoxically) on my own terms.'[17]

But he felt that every man should have the right to be such an individualist, whether he be Black or White.

There were more writers' conferences, but Hayden refused to attend; he was too angry, too hurt, too discouraged. But he did not recant his stand, and when he could, he tried to address the issue. He was painfully aware that few would understand the distinction he was making – they would question how he could write such powerful lyrics about the Afro-American in an unjust society, about lynchings, growing up in the ghetto, and yet not wish his art to be judged as 'Black poetry' but simply as poetry. That same year in his introduction to *Kaleidoscope*, which he was commissioned to edit by Harcourt, Brace and World (1967), Hayden alluded powerfully to this same crucial point:

In the decades since the New Negro movement, which ended with the Twenties, protest and race consciousness have continued to find expression in the poetry of the American Negro. But other motivating forces are also in evidence. There are Negro poets who believe that any poet's most clearly defined task is to create with honesty and sincerity poems that will illuminate human experience – not exclusively 'Negro experience'. They reject the idea of poetry as racial propaganda, of poetry that functions as a kind of sociology.[18]

Obviously Hayden was referring to his own feelings, and he made this abundantly clear when later in the volume he introduced the poetry of LeRoi Jones (Imamu Amiri Baraka):

He is an advocate of art as protest and propaganda, and he favors the cultivation of a 'black' art which would reject white aesthetic values . . . As the leading 'Poet of the Negro Revolution', Jones attacks both 'Whitey' and 'Uncle Tom' with equal vehemence, but the result is more often angry abuse than it is impassioned poetry.[19]

Only someone who has been in such a peculiarly difficult situation, where relenting and being applauded for it would be so much easier than taking a stand, can fully appreciate Hayden's courage and integrity throughout this period. The abuse he received was both verbal and silent, blatant and insidious. It was the source of a pain that never fully left him and an anger he could never completely purge. According to Hugh Semple, a Bahá'í photographer who was one of those closest to Hayden during the poet's last years, Hayden would occasionally get sidetracked into a tirade against the students at Fisk who during those years had so callously abused him.[20] More than anything, Semple said, Hayden resented their hypocrisy, stereotyping him so easily with a cute word or phrase – Uncle Tom, oreo – then driving off in their Cadillacs wearing their 'Superfly' suits.

Several letters Hayden received at the time from fellow Black teachers and writers are very revealing about the magnitude and tenor of the problem. The most revealing of these is part of the correspondence between Hayden and Margaret Danner, herself a Bahá'í, a recognized Black poet, and an associate of Dudley Randall who, as a fellow Detroiter, had known Hayden over the years.[21] From the letter one can infer that Hayden had enunciated to her and other writers the danger of lending their talents to the riots. The letter also points out forcefully the relationship between Hayden's stand on these issues and his identity as Bahá'í, as well as the support which the Bahá'í beliefs afforded him in his stand on involvement in partisan politics in general:

There is so much that we should talk about, both [Hayden and Danner] being Bahá'ís and both being non-political. I think the sweetest words I have ever heard were yours when you said, 'We must stick together' when you expressed concern over Dudley Randall's seeming defection, I think is the word I want, to the Reds. Dudley knows what he is doing and he doesn't intend to become involved with those people. He will get every penny, every honor that they can bestow and then be just plain Dudley Randall . . . So don't be concerned about him. You have a kind heart and are so sensitive that it bothers you to think they have him. *They don't!*[22]

The letter goes on to describe how at a meeting of Black writers there had been an attempt to embarrass her, but Dudley Randall had come to her defense:

Dudley will be the same way about you if he thinks people are wronging you. He may be taken aback because of what you said about LeRoi, but after we have our talk, he will see what you were really saying and he will come to your defense. Not that you need him or anyone, but as you said, we must stick together, and in unity there is strength, indeed . . . If those for the peaceful way of obtaining our rights stick together, we will not be undertowed by the Reds. Oh, how glad I am that I am a Bahá'í and that you are . . . I had to tell you how grateful I am to God and to Bahá'u'lláh that you realized that we must indeed stick together.[23]

Another letter, written in 1967 by William Bernhardt, a former colleague at Fisk who had moved to Reed College, is of a lighter vein, and deals more with the pressure the students exerted than with the pressure from other writers.

Here I am in the land of lotus-eating flower children and it's some relief, I can tell you, from last year. The sense of impending social doom is perhaps sometimes just as strong as it was at Fisk, but one does not find it impinging at every moment . . . there are whole days when one can be concerned with literature and go unpunished for the indulgence. And if the students are insufferably arrogant at times, they do work during the interim. Not that Reed is without its pains, such as a colleague who berates the students in their own newspaper for their failure to have a single riot in recent years . . . I trust you had a good summer in Indiana. (For my own part, I found my own liberation from Fisk somewhat clouded by the unfolding of the long, hot summer.)[24]

Understandably, Robert Hayden was not the most emotionally secure person in the world, and like any writer, he was not always sure of his gifts or how to use them, but he was unfailingly a man of courage, principle and integrity. Poetry to him was an art and he was a consummate poet. He dedicated himself to his art, and dedicated his art to mankind. Every spare minute of his life he devoted to the cause of becoming the best poet he was capable of becoming, and this is how he saw his usefulness as an individual, whether as a Black American, as a Bahá'í, or simply as a human being. He cherished civil rights, abhorred the war in Vietnam, detested injustice and small-mindedness wherever it occurred, yet his standards for his art were inviolable.

But the sixties were not all politics and confrontation. Later in 1966 he was invited to New York for the awards ceremony for the *Grand Prix de la Poésie*. President Léopold Senghor of Senegal attended in person and presented Robert Hayden with the award. And who else should be there to congratulate Robert Hayden but Langston Hughes – it was the last time Hayden saw Hughes, who died the next year. A quarter of a century before, Hughes had told the young Hayden his verses were too conventional, and now he had come to honor the gifted voice of this innovative artist:

Langston came over to chat with my wife and me after the presentation and asked me to autograph my *Selected Poems* for him. I was deeply moved somehow, and I remember saying, as I tried to hold back the tears, 'Well, Langston, it's a new day when you ask *me* to autograph a book for *you*.' Behind my words, you know, was the memory of that afternoon years and years ago, when I was a young hopeful with a sheaf of bad poems to show him.[25]

Soon other honors began rolling in. His *Selected Poems* was reviewed in *Poetry* magazine. In 1967 he recorded his verse for the Library of Congress. His anthology of poems by American Negro poets *Kaleidoscope* was published. A record of him reading his poetry was issued by Scholastic Folkways entitled *Today's Poets*. He was appointed poetry editor of the Bahá'í quarterly *World Order* magazine. He was promoted to the rank of full professor at Fisk. In the summer of 1967 he was visiting poet-in-residence at Indiana State University. In 1968 he was a visiting professor of English at the University of Michigan. In 1969 he received the Mayor's Bronze Medal for distinguished achievement by a native Detroiter, and he served as the Bingham Professor at the University of Louisville. In the summer semester of 1969 he served as visiting poet at the University of Washington (Seattle). He topped off the decade by resigning with great relief from Fisk to accept a position as full professor at the University of Michigan.

He had entered his fifth decade in 1963 thinking himself a failure – he had been relatively unpublished, unknown, discouraged by his career, financially poor, stuck in an institution that did not seem to appreciate his talents. He had little reason to think any of this would change. Seven years later he had achieved almost every goal he had set for himself. His poems had been published by a commercial publishing house. He had received national and international recognition. He had returned, after twenty-three years of seeming exile, to his beloved Ann Arbor. He had been severely tested, and he had prevailed. But his career was hardly over – his successes or his struggles.

6. The Poet Laureate
1969–1980

> Crucial in my development has been the coming to grips with myself, my own soul, if you will, with my own realities as they have been revealed to me through my dedication to poetry and, yes, through religion.[1]
>
> Robert Hayden

It is human nature, I think, that achieving long-sought goals often deflates aspirations, blurs the identity rather than reinforcing it. Hayden had certainly achieved most of his avowed goals by the beginning of his last decade, but in no way did he accept this accomplishment as a sign that he should relax in his work. If anything, he took the position at Michigan and the growing recognition as confirmation of his greatest hopes for his work, and as a confirmation that he should proceed with even greater intensity. At last he was being taken seriously as a professional poet, not simply by a handful of followers or by the esoteric community of fellow poets, but by a prominent university which had hired him in recognition of his talent.

It is tempting, therefore, to see the last ten years of Hayden's life as a chronology of successes – four volumes of poetry, numerous awards, positions, acclaim. He was still ascending with ever-increasing velocity when his untimely death cut short what had become a truly dynamic career. But while it is valuable to note the successes so long in coming, so arduously won, it is also important to understand that his struggles were not over. As always, there was the challenge to write new poetry – that was a struggle from which he never had respite, nor wanted any.

But if he had believed that his move to Ann Arbor would provide a Utopian existence, he was soon made aware of the contrary by an undercurrent of harsher realities. One of these subtle problems occurred shortly after his arrival in 1969, when, unknown to most people, he was first offered the position of Consultant to the Library of Congress, one of the few long-cherished aspirations he still had unfulfilled. To accept the position would have meant an immediate leave of absence from his newly appointed position; therefore, Hayden went to the chairman of the English department to get approval. Incredibly, for reasons one can only guess at, the chairman told him in no uncertain terms that such a move would be ill-advised. After all, it was explained, he had just been appointed. Thus, in a move he was to regret later, Hayden decided to abide by the chairman's advice and forgo an honor he had wanted profoundly for years, an honor no Black poet had ever before received.

Another source of subtle discomfort resulted from the teaching position itself. Hayden had not earned a Ph.D., had few scholarly publications and yet he was being hired at the highest rank, full professor, above many professors who had the degree, numerous scholarly/publications and years of service at the university. Of course, Hayden was later to receive many honorary doctorates, and as a publishing writer he could not be expected to be judged by the standards with which the professors in the fields of scholarship were assessed. Nevertheless, there were some hurt feelings, and Hayden was, for a while, made to feel the culprit.

Some of his immediately forthcoming recognitions and accomplishments offset much of whatever discord his appointment had induced. He received that first year a Russell Loines Award for distinguished poetic achievement from the National Institute of Art and Letters and he became a consultant and editor for the high school division of Scott, Foresman and Company. Yet, in spite of these successes, he was urged privately by some fellow teachers to publish scholarly articles to further his career.

Hayden no doubt appreciated the irony, the almost grotesque humor of it, that here he was producing the very stuff that English teachers teach, was engaged with all his energies in becoming a celebrated writer, and some wanted him instead to write about writers. He did not let such narrow-mindedness consume much of his time or energy, but he was aware of these stirrings and he was not impervious to the pain they inflicted.

But, as usual, Hayden was not one to let such events keep him from his poetry, and in 1970 his second volume with October House was published. As the title, *Words in the Mourning Time*, implies, it is a collection centered around the succession of events of the late 1960s – the 'long hot summer' and the racial violence, the several startling assassinations of Robert Kennedy, Martin Luther King, Jr., and Malcolm X, and the ever-widening horrors of the Vietnam War.

On the surface, the collection might seem a strange blending of images from the historic and mythic past with scenes from strictly modern contexts. A closer examination reveals a carefully developed treatment of the theme of grief within the historical perspective of the Bahá'í vision of man's destiny. In this sense the title poem serves as a structural model for the development of the whole volume. It begins with the speaker in a detached mood, acknowledging his grief, but also intellectually aware that this period of mourning is temporary, that it foreshadows and precedes a period of fulfillment as described by Bahá'u'lláh:

> I grieve. Yet know the vanity
> of grief—through power of
> The Blessed Exile's
> transilluminating word
>
> aware of how these deaths, how all
> the agonies of our deathbed childbed age
> are process, major means whereby,
> oh dreadfully, our humanness must be achieved.[2]

The ten-part narrative poem then follows the speaker through rapid changes of mood as he contemplates the present bloody state of humanity and goes from anger to bitter irony, to sadness, to the haunting voice of love spoken by Martin Luther King, to a final resolution. In the end the speaker alludes to the short obligatory prayer of the Bahá'í Writings, acknowledging that without the 'transilluminating' words of Bahá'u'lláh there could be no basis for hope:

> I bear Him witness now:
> towards Him our history in its disastrous quest
> for meaning is impelled.[3]

All of the various poems relate to this theme of a future hope sensed from within a maelstrom of ever-darkening chaos. But in most of the poems the hope for solutions to identity, to racial turmoil, to international warfare are largely overshadowed by present grief.

There are several poems, however, which hint at a theme that Hayden was working on in 1970 in the poem 'The Night-Blooming Cereus', the title poem for a volume of poems he would publish in 1973. 'The Mirages', 'Monet's "Waterlilies"', 'October' and 'A Plague of Starlings' all hint at a spiritual world underlying and ultimately more real than the so-called 'real' world: the arsenals, riddles, sickness, the injustice. Ultimately, Hayden seems to imply with the last poems in the volume that there is an historical meaning to the bloodshed and a transcendence we should strive for as we confront the chaos.

The brief volume *The Night-Blooming Cereus* appeared three years later as the twentieth volume (on the tenth anniversary) of the Heritage series published by Paul Breman. It was eight pieces, all playing off the Platonic theme suggested by both the epigraph and the closing poem 'Traveling Through Fog' – that to study the images of the physical world carefully (whether in nature, in art, or in the human condition) is to perceive the essential spiritual form behind that image of reality. As in *Words in the Mourning Time*, there is no absolute and final clarity to this knowing, but the tone of the volume is, for the most part, an affirmative suggestion that, while we know this truth only hazily, it is the most significant thing that we can know in this life:

> Between obscuring cloud
> and cloud, the cloudy dark
> ensphering us seems all we can
> be certain of. Is Plato's cave.[4]

Both of these volumes were very important to Hayden. *Words in the Mourning Time* was reviewed quite favorably in the *New York Times* by one of Hayden's former students at Fisk, Julius Lester. The article praised the book, but it concentrated even more heavily on praising Hayden himself, on lamenting the neglect he had suffered as a poet and the abuse he had endured as a man. Lester ended the review with this remarkable tribute:

If we ever reach that time when man is permitted to be man, one of the reasons will be men and women like this poet, Robert Hayden, who, when pressed into the most terrifying corners of loneliness, refused to capitulate to those who, in the screaming agony of their own pain and loneliness, could do nothing but return evil for evil.[5]

The Night-Blooming Cereus, though published in the limited Heritage edition, was also extremely important to Hayden for several reasons. First, it was the product of his laboring through what he perceived to be a dry spell. Secondly, in this brief but powerful volume he took the essential theme of his previous works and advanced it, gave it a further dimension and direction – one does not simply bide his time in this life or in this period in history, Hayden seems to say; one labors to find the meaning behind the shadows. In a 1973 interview Hayden said about the work:

. . . it's my favorite book up to now. Writing it released me, also confirmed ideas and feelings I'd had before, but distrusted. I began to move in a new direction and to consolidate my gains, such as they were.[6]

In the meantime Hayden's reputation increased as did his honors and activities. In 1971 he co-edited *Afro-American Literature: An Introduction* for Harcourt, Brace, Jovanovich, and in 1972 he co-authored *How I Write* and edited the modern American poetry section of *The United States in Literature*, a text for secondary schools produced by Scott, Foresman and Company. In 1974 he served as visiting poet at Connecticut College.

In many ways the following year, 1975, was the climax of Hayden's career. Certainly his accomplishments that year established unmistakably his place in American letters. First, he published another volume of verse, a volume which in some ways surpassed all the previous volumes in importance. In a letter to the *Washington Star,* written when Hayden was in Washington as Consultant to the Library of Congress in 1977, a reader complained to the editor that Hayden's 'books are not carried by any of the city's major book stores . . .'[7]

A poetry reading at the Library of Congress before he was appointed consultant, about 1971

At Fisk University, about 1958

Several days later a letter responded saying that publishing is an industry 'which does not especially foster poets, even great ones'.[8] The reader went on to say: 'Lucky for us that Mr Hayden's *Angle of Ascent* is available from a big house; therefore we can buy it.'

The previous volumes through October House had been commercially available, but not with the wide distribution of his new volume *Angle of Ascent*, which was published with Liveright, now a division of W. W. Norton, one of the best known and most prestigious publishers of English literature texts for university use. The fact that the volume was a lengthy collection of the best of all the poems Hayden had previously published indicates the publisher's own awareness of its function in disseminating his work.

The book is not solely an anthology of his previous poems – the first section contains important new poems, among which are 'Beginnings' about his family, 'Akhenaten' on the theme of progressive Revelation, 'Stars' which contains a very powerful allusion to the Bahá'í Faith, and 'For a Young Artist', a most moving and insightful allegory examining the station of the artist in this life. In addition to these new poems there are revisions of many older pieces, all of which are arranged according to the chronology of their previous publications.

The book received a glowing tribute in the *New York Times*, reviewed by no less a poet than Michael Harper, who, like Julius Lester before him, took the opportunity to defend Hayden further against those who had previously portrayed him as too conciliatory on racial issues and against those who had been critical about the quantity of his output:

Having committed himself to the improvement of language, he has sometimes been falsely accused of timidity of commitment to the black struggle because of his refusal to 'politicize' his work for expedient and transient goals. But it is Hayden's poetry that best captures the Afro-American tradition of the black hero . . .[9]

Harper went on to extol Hayden's craftsmanship, his exquisite care in choosing just the right words and phrasing, calling him 'the poet of perfect pitch', an appellation repeated by numerous other critics. In the notes to the paperback edition of *Angle of Ascent*, Harper said, 'His poems are chiseled, honed . . . It goes without saying that Mr Hayden is in the first rank of practicing poets, of all persuasions.'[10]

Within a few months of the publication of *Angle of Ascent*, Hayden was once more offered the post of Consultant in Poetry to the Library of Congress. He was, as has been noted, the first Negro to attain this position; he was also the first Bahá'í artist to have risen to such a position. This time Hayden accepted.

Later in that same year another comparable recognition of his achievement occurred – he was elected the 1975 Fellow of the Academy of American Poets for 'distinguished poetic achievement', an award which Harper noted was 'a long time in coming',[11] an award which carried with it a welcomed stipend of ten thousand dollars.

Robert Hayden was no longer a poet with an 'underground' reputation. He had devoted himself to his art, and his persistence had finally brought some of the rewards due him. It was a mixed blessing to be sure. He was now fair game as a subject for MA theses and Ph.D. dissertations, and susceptible to the constant stream of writers wishing to write about people who write. Even more than before, he had to guard the time for his poems against the ceaseless flow of mail and other interlopers.

It is hard to say with certainty that these events, spectacular as they were to someone who had struggled so strenuously against an army of trials, were as sweet as the more subtle victories – having Langston Hughes present when he received the Dakar award, having Auden congratulate him at the Hopwood award in 1942, later reading with Auden at Columbia University in 1971. Perhaps nothing would surpass the combined surprise, delight and vindication he felt upon receiving the telegram in 1966 from Paul Breman.

Regardless, Hayden must have realized once in a while, in spite of a schedule that left little time for contemplative thought, that he had come a long, long way from Paradise Valley, that he had finally achieved his own 'angle of ascent'. And amid the pressures and demands, the barrage of honors that began to flow, there must have been some sense of accomplishment. He received honorary doctorates from Grand Valley State College in 1975, from Brown University in 1976, from Benedict College in 1977, from Wayne State in 1977, from Fisk in 1978. In 1977 he was reappointed for 1978 as Consultant to the Library of Congress, and he was also invited with other recognized poets to an Inauguration Series of Poetry Readings where he was introduced to President Carter.

Now in his mid sixties, he was beginning to notice the weight of years, and he was not particularly thrilled at the thought of reaching old age. But as he became aware of his age, he also was delighted to find that his poetic faculties were in no way diminished. In September of 1976 as he was preparing to leave for Washington, he told a reporter, 'I'm at the age people think your creative powers are gone', he said. 'My mind is working better. As I've grown older and thought about the life I've lived, I've come to understand it. One of the ways of relieving the pain of it, for me, is to write.'[12] That same year he said in another interview at the Bahá'í House of Worship:

As I get older, my mind gets clearer. When I was your age, my dear young man, I greatly feared that when I got to be in my fifties – and now, you see, I'm in my sixties – that it would be curtains, curtains, Jack. There wouldn't be anything left, you know? But I am delighted to discover that I have *more* ideas. Say *sunrise* and I can fill up pages.[13]

However furious the activity got, he did not let it deter his devotion to his work. In 1978 he published yet another volume of verse, *American Journal* with Effendi Press, and it was nominated for a National Book Award. In this work he included poems about other figures drawn from Black history – Phillis Wheatley, Paul Laurence Dunbar and Matthew Henson. There were also a multitude of personalities recalled from his childhood in Detroit in the eight parts of 'Elegies for Paradise Valley', and a moving personal lyric 'The Prisoners' based on Hayden's visits with other Bahá'ís to Jackson State Prison to read his poems to the inmates, a piece which curiously follows up the Platonic possibilities established in his previous work. There are vitally new poetic techniques in the haunting narrative 'from *The Snow Lamp*' and in the title poem '[American Journal]', a purported account by an alien visitor who tries to make sense out of the strange amalgamation of personalities and points of view that comprise the American populace. The title poem serves as an appropriate conclusion to the volume and to Hayden's work as a whole, since he, like the alien, worked among us much like a chronicler from another sphere, involved, touched, pained, while a part of him, the part that was poet, was always objective, studying, trying to find the 'real' behind the shadowy entanglements of history and emotion. Like this alien persona, Hayden's assessment of America in his poem '[American Journal]' was, despite its history of violence and injustice, basically a positive one:

> confess i am curiously drawn   unmentionable   to
> the americans   doubt i could exist among them for
> long however   psychic demands far too severe
> much violence   much that repels   i am attracted
> none the less   their variousness their ingenuity
> their elan vital   and that some thing   essence
> quiddity   i cannot penetrate or name[14]

In an important sense Hayden's poetry represents for us his own American Journal, within its collection of images from history, its assorted characters, its portraits of injustice, hopes, anger. In his poems he probed these images, handed them back to us in forms we too could examine, hoping, no doubt, that a little better understanding of ourselves would result. As Michael Harper concluded in his review of the book for the *New York Times*, 'his poems promise a blossoming evident in the continuous journal of an America he had both named and penetrated'.[15]

While he was at work on *American Journal*, Hayden's tenure as Consultant to the Library of Congress was a burdensome honor, but a burden which he, in his customary fashion, handled with a serious regard for quality. The pace was almost overwhelming, the interviews, television shows, the constant flow of correspondence. As much as he could, he added his personal touch to the position, bringing in a greater variety of poets, trying to broaden and enhance the functions of the post. There were a few battles (a senator trying to have some sweet lady, who penned lyrics now and then, recorded for posterity), and Hayden faced these with his usual tactful honesty and courage. He met with poets from other countries, arranged readings for the year, decided what poets should be recorded. He invited men and women to read together, Blacks and Whites – not then the usual procedure. He arranged for special nights for foreign poets – a night for the Chinese or the Hungarians.

In addition to this full-time agenda, he agreed to serve as poet-in-residence at Howard University where he would meet weekly with eager student poets. In his spare time he wrote. Erma tried as best she could to get him to slow the pace, but he could no more slow down than she could follow her own advice by cutting down on the massive work she too was doing, for the Bahá'í Faith and her family, tending to her piano practice in her spare time. She knew he was not feeling well, and both suspected what the cause might be, a haunting thought that kept Hayden from going to the doctor – his mother had died of cancer, and all his life he had sensed that this would also be his fate. He feared it, dreaded it, but so long as no doctor verified it, his doom was not sealed.

When they returned to Ann Arbor he felt no better, and finally, in February of 1979, a doctor confirmed what in his heart he already knew. He was not without hope – the prognosis was relatively good. He had periods of vigor, and always his sense of humor was in gear, often protecting others more than himself from the doom he felt. But early in the progress of the disease he began methodically to order his papers, to prepare for what, on some level, he sensed was inevitable. In September 1979 he hired Frederick Glaysher, a graduate student at the university, a fellow poet and Bahá'í, to be his secretary, to assemble and order the incredible volume of drafts, correspondence, notes, that had accumulated over the years.

As with every battle he had faced in his life, he exhibited a sustained determination which belied the superficial nervous manner he had – the soft voice, the quick turns of emotion, the thick-lens glasses which seemed to connote fragility. He still had fears, of death, of life, but underneath these emotions was a faith that had subsisted and strengthened through it all. It was a belief nurtured by Erma, by his close friends, but it was truly his own, a hard-won conviction and wisdom that had evolved with his verse.

On Sunday, February 24, 1980, almost exactly a year after he had received confirmation of the diagnosis, Hayden was to receive what he felt was one of the greatest honors of his life. The Center for Afro-American and African Studies at the University of Michigan scheduled 'A Tribute to Robert Hayden'. It was to include readings, drama, music, and a discussion by Michael Harper of Hayden's poetry, followed by a reading of two poems Harper had dedicated to Hayden. No doubt the thought of being honored by a department whose avowed purpose was to probe the identity of the Afro-American seemed in part to rectify some of the abuse Hayden had earlier suffered at the hands of those whose battle cry was the affirmation of that identity. If it did not erase the hurt, it at least established for him that some now understood the motives behind his stand.

That week his already worsened condition was exacerbated by a bout with flu, and Hayden himself was unable to attend. In the afternoon when the tribute was over, a few of the participants came by the house to see him. His daughter Maia helped him dress, and he went downstairs to greet his guests. Soon he had them laughing with his deft wit and loving manner.

The next day, February 25, Robert Hayden died. His work was hardly finished. A new volume, also entitled *American Journal,* was scheduled to be published by Liveright.[16] He was very much in mid-stride. He barely had the time to take stock of all he had accomplished, how far he had come, though it was not his nature to be as generous with himself as he was with others. Perhaps out of a fear of hubris, he never touted himself or systematically promoted his own career. He enjoyed the victories, he felt pain during the loneliness and struggle, but he always kept a safe emotional distance from his success.

He did not keep the same distance between himself and others. In talking with those who were dearest to him, one hears almost verbatim the same qualities extolled; he was able to see in others what was special, unique. He sincerely cared for others, whether they were Bahá'ís or not, whether they were poets or laborers, Black or White. In his presence one felt important, appreciated, loved.

Dr Niara Sudarkasa, associate director of the University of Michigan Center for Afro-American Studies, stated, 'He was the most important professor I ever had; he had the greatest impact on me.'[17] Harold P. Shapiro, president of the university said, 'His poetry helped define the landscape of human life, brightening the nooks and crannies of our existence. His life as teacher, as poet and as man enriched us all.'[18]

His passing and his impact on American letters was discussed by the *New York Times. Time Magazine* said, 'Hayden's work evoked a heroic sense of the black American past . . .'[19] William Meredith, former Consultant to the Library of Congress and a close friend, said, 'Robert Hayden lived and died ahead of a reputation that could only lag behind his accomplishments. He set himself a standard of excellence that leaves his life and work beautifully clear . . . It was his habit always to call attention to the debt he felt to his lifetime companion Erma . . .'[20] As an epigraph to Part One of the spring 1980 issue of *Empyrea,* which was dedicated to Hayden, there is a quotation from the one poem Hayden specifically asked Harper to read at the tribute, 'Frederick Douglass':

this man, superb in love and logic . . .[21]

One is struck by the way eyes light up and smiles brighten when friends recall his wit, his manner, his scoffing at pomposity, his occasional tirades, because one and all they sensed beyond the poet a gentle, caring lover of humanity. As Laurence Goldstein notes in his assessment of Hayden's career, Hayden's first love was always poetry, but through his poetry he expressed his love for mankind:

Finally the only name he would be happy with is poet. His love of poetry was boundless. He talked constantly about its intricacies, its accents and diction, its mystery . . . Nearly blind at the end, he never relaxed vigilant scrutiny of manuscripts from students, friends, and strangers. There was nothing of the *noblesse oblige* in Robert Hayden; he did not 'do his duty' to literature; rather, he acted joyfully upon his artistic instincts, making articulate the music of humanity that few of his contemporaries heard as clearly as he.[22]

Part II

THE MINOTAURS
OF EDICT

We must go on struggling to be human,
though monsters of abstraction
police and threaten us.[1]

Robert Hayden

In the poem 'A Ballad of Remembrance', which became for the poet the hall-mark of his newfound voice and elegant skills, Robert Hayden depicts three contending voices vying for the allegiance of the Afro-American. Each represents a traditional response to racial injustice acted out in the gaudy symbols of *mardi gras* costumes in New Orleans, The 'Zulu king' mutters 'Accommodate'; the 'gun-metal priestess' in her spiked bellcollar as symbol of the stark horror of slavery shrieks 'Hate!'; the 'saints and the angels and the mermaids', the choired voices of a strict Christian response of forgiveness, chime 'Love'. Caught in the 'hoodoo of that dance', in that 'schizoid city', the speaker fears the loss of his humanity, feels, perhaps, his identity ripped apart by the 'switchblades of that air'.

These three voices are not unique to the time and setting of Hayden's poem; they represent a tradition in Afro-American letters of contending points of view about how to respond to the existential dilemma of injustice, as well as to the history of grief etched in the collective unconscious of the Black race. The poem represents, more importantly, a philosophical struggle which is extremely relevant to understanding how Hayden has been received and what is likely to be the assessment of his work in the future.

To recent generations of Hayden's readers, the viability of such a struggle may seem relevant only to the violence of the 1960s when the formerly non-violent approach to civil rights following the leadership of the National Association for the Advancement of Colored People (NAACP) under Roy Wilkins and the Southern Christian Leadership Conference (SCLC) under Martin Luther King, Jr., suddenly, and seemingly mysteriously, transformed into the violent and radical response of Stokely Carmichael, Eldridge Cleaver, and the Black Power advocacy of various militant spokesmen.

To those Americans who had lived through the Depression, the vying voices might have recalled the struggle of contending philosophies during the thirties and early forties. To those even older, the contending responses may have seemed to have their foundation in the flowering of Black writers and artists in the Harlem Renaissance era of the 1920s with such spokesmen as Alain Locke in his essay 'The New Negro' (1925) or Langston Hughes in his

seminal essay 'The Negro Artist and the Racial Mountain' (1926). To those
with a cursory knowledge of the history of Afro-American letters, however,
these militant voices reflected earlier statements by Marcus Garvey and his
Universal Negro Improvement Association with his goal of acquiring economic power and building a Black-governed nation in Africa. Contending with
Garvey and his over two million followers in 1919 were A. Philip Randolph
and W. E. B. Du Bois, who had as early as 1909 established the NAACP and
advocated the ascent of Afro-Americans through higher education and the
establishment of Blacks in positions of leadership and authority, in govern-
ment and the professions. Further back, Du Bois himself had reacted against
the stand of Booker T. Washington, who in his famous speech at the Atlanta
Exposition in 1893 had advocated accommodation, as it was interpreted, by
exhorting Black Americans to 'Cast down your buckets where you are', to
acquire basic vocational skills but remain separate socially. Even that debate
took place against the backdrop of a pre-abolition dispute as to whether it
would be better to repatriate the Afro-Americans to the African continent
rather than assimilate them into the emerging American society. This 'Great
Black Controversy', as it came to be called, was the foundation for the attitudes of Garvey as well as the Black nationalists of the 1960s like Stokely
Carmichael. Even some slave diaries, which are only now being edited and
published, present various responses to the dilemma of the Afro-American, a
variety reflected in history by the violent rebellions of Gabriel Prosser in 1800
and Nat Turner in 1831, the powerful oratory and studied ideology of Frederick Douglass during the later 1800s, or the courageous leadership of Harriet
Tubman who in the 1850s led more than three hundred slaves to freedom via
the Underground Railroad.

It was in this complex historical context that the debate over the notion of a
'Black Aesthetic' was carried on during the 1960s and 70s; it was not a new
issue. It is, therefore, necessary to understand something of this background in
order to appreciate or understand Hayden's position, as well as his treatment
of Afro-American history in his poetry. For while we can see the relationship
between Hayden's position and his personal background and beliefs as a
Bahá'í, it is also necessary to understand that the dispute in the 1960s over the
concept of a 'Black Aesthetic' really had its roots deep in Afro-American
history and letters. It was not a phenomenon created solely in the cauldron of
radicalized politics of the civil rights movement.

7. The Problem of a 'Black Aesthetic'

What the colored poet in the United States needs to do is something
like what Synge did for the Irish; he needs to find a form that will
express the racial spirit by symbols from within rather than by
symbols from without, such as the mere mutilation of English spelling
and pronunciation. He needs a form that is freer and larger than
dialect, but which will still hold the racial flavor . . .[1]

James Weldon Johnson, 1921

Certainly the broad scope of Hayden's themes transcends limits of racial,
national or even religious points of view. This is not to say, however, that one
can be ignorant of the source of his images and step easily through his
volumes: one cannot. In Rosey Pool's 1962 anthology, *Beyond the Blues*,
Hayden states that his desire to be considered a poet, not a hyphenated 'black-
poet', in no way means he does not wish to concern himself with racial
problems or points of view:

On the whole, I would say that I certainly have no desire to escape the implications of
the Negro situation, but want always to deal with them as an artist rather than a
journalist or pleader of a cause. I think of Joyce and Yeats, who were both intensely
Irish and who seemingly repudiated certain aspects of the Irish struggle but nevertheless were able to use Irish materials in an artistically valid and meaningful way.[2]

In that same succinct introduction to a study of the poetry of Black writers,
Dr Pool herself states: 'Negro writers do not answer to rules other than
writers of other races. It is just that their experiences are different.'[3] That
exception has meant to many Black writers that in their work they cannot
transcend or do not wish to transcend that difference; in fact, to some it is
immoral, illegitimate and, implicitly, inartistic for the Black writer to concern
himself with aught else.

The chronicle of discussions of poetics regarding the work by Afro-Americans has its beginnings more or less with the book *The Souls of Black Folk* by
W. E. B. Du Bois in 1903. In this work Du Bois states that 'the singular spiritual
heritage of the nation and the greatest gift of the Negro people' is 'the Negro
folk-song, the rhythmic cry of the slave'.[4]

Of course, significant poetry by Afro-American writers had been produced long before 1903, but it was not until the Harlem Renaissance that the articulation of an artistic point of view relating to the racial pride of Black Americans had a prominent forum. Among the variety of discussions about the artistic expression of the Afro-American cultural heritage are the two most often cited essays by Langston Hughes and Alain Locke. Hughes, perhaps the most widely acclaimed of poets from the Harlem Renaissance, was born in 1902 and at the age of twenty-four wrote 'The Negro Artist and the Racial Mountain', which was published in *The Nation* on June 23, 1926. The article begins with Hughes' now-famous anecdote expressing the view that the Negro poet cannot separate his art from his racial identity:

One of the most promising of the young Negro poets said to me once, 'I want to be a poet – not a Negro poet', meaning, I believe, 'I want to write like a white poet'; meaning subconsciously, 'I would like to be a white poet'; meaning behind that, 'I would like to be white.' And I was sorry the young man said that, for no great poet has ever been afraid of being himself. And I doubted then that, with his desire to run away spiritually from his race, this boy would ever be a great poet. But this is the mountain standing in the way of any true Negro art in America – this urge within the race toward whiteness, the desire to pour racial individuality into the mold of American standardization, and to be as little Negro and as much American as possible.[5]

The article goes on to portray the middle and higher class Negroes as aspiring to White goals, adopting White points of view, 'Nordic manners, Nordic faces, Nordic hair, Nordic arts (if any), and an Episcopal heaven'.[6] Hughes then contrasts these middle-class aspirants to Whiteness with the majority of 'low-down folks, the so-called common element'[7] who are not afraid of their own culture, their spirituals, their shouted religion, their jazz and joy and distinctive character.

Hughes' remaining paragraphs exhort the Black artist to be unafraid of his heritage, indeed to relish the richness of it, not to strive toward the goals implicit in White culture. He affirms that most of his own works 'are racial in theme and treatment, derived from the life I know'.[8] He further disdains the complicity of affluent Blacks in perpetrating a self-hate, stating, 'An artist must be free to choose what he does, certainly, but he must also never be afraid to do what he might choose'.[9] He concludes with a phrase that could easily befit the chanted slogans of the racial movement in the 1960s:

We younger Negro artists who create now intend to express our individual dark-skinned selves without fear or shame. If white people are pleased, we are glad. If they are not, it doesn't matter. We know we are beautiful. And ugly too. The tom-tom cries and the tom-tom laughs. If colored people are pleased, we are glad. If they are not, their displeasure doesn't matter either. We build our temples for tomorrow, strong as we know how, and we stand on top of the mountain, free within ourselves.[10]

It is worth noting that in the previous week's issue of *The Nation*, an article with the opposing view appeared by George S. Schuyler, noted Black writer for the *Messenger,* in response to which Langston Hughes wrote a letter to the editor. His opening sentence states, 'For Mr Schuyler to say that "the Negro masses . . . are no different from the white masses" in America seems to me obviously absurd. Fundamentally, perhaps, all peoples are the same. But as long as the Negro remains a segregated group in this country he must reflect certain racial and environmental differences which are his own.'[11] He goes on to point out that until America has absorbed the Negro 'the true work of art from the Negro artist is bound, if it have any color and distinctiveness at all, to reflect his racial background and his racial environment'.[12]

If we are tempted now to react emotionally one way or another to this issue, certainly the urge was infinitely greater at the time of the composition of the article. It is also worth noting that this expression of racial pride, of refusing to judge Black artists by an alien standard, was being expressed by highly educated and sophisticated writers and thinkers. W. E. B. Du Bois had attended Fisk, Harvard, the University of Berlin, and had taught classical languages and history. Alain Locke, another leader of the Harlem Renaissance, was a Harvard graduate (1907), the first Black Rhodes scholar, had studied at Oxford and had received a Ph.D. in philosophy from Harvard (1918).

Locke was well-versed in African culture and urged Black artists to realize their African heritage both as a means of self-respect and as an artistic resource. His anthology in 1925 *The New Negro* contains his essay 'The New Negro', which described, and prescribed, the point of view of the rising tide of new Black artists. It was not a new insight, as Allan Spear notes in his introduction to the 1958 edition of Locke's work:

Yet long before the 1920s, some blacks had sought a cultural identity beyond weak attempts to imitate the white man or to pander to his stereotype of Negro life. Even the phrase 'New Negro' was used at least as early as 1895, and the emphasis on race pride and self-respect that lay at its core had been a continual, if often subordinate, theme in Negro history. Frequently, race pride was associated with an attempt to withdraw from American society, to abandon the struggle for integration and fall back upon the resources of the black community.[13]

In part what accounts for the New Negro movement with its consolidation of this emphasis on Black pride was the migration northward by rural Blacks to work in factories during the war years, the so-called 'Great Migration' (1915–19) which 'transformed the black people in America from a peasantry to a proletariat'.[14] The resulting fear on the part of Northern Whites led to violence – the race riots of 1917 and 1919. The returning Black war veterans, having viewed in France a society without the segregated caste system, could no longer accept passively American discrimination. The slimly populated pre-war ghettos in the North had now swelled to sizable inner cities, largely independent of White control.

The amalgamation of the Black interests, the molding of Black pride, was not always uniform and clear – some saw this breaching of White stereotyping and striving toward cultural realization as a device for pressing for acceptance and integration, while others viewed the changed tenor of Negro life as a vehicle for exalting Black nationalism and separatism. But regardless, at the core of the movement in the twenties was Harlem, vibrant, alive, the capital of Black culture and the center of artistic ferment, New York's Montmartre. Of course, the White image of Harlem as a playground of primitive gaiety belied the true worth of the artistic and intellectual climate that was also there, as had the popular White image of the antebellum South with the contented, loyal slave, and the White image of the 'docile, lazy, childlike "darky"'[15] belied the cruel reality of racism.

It was in this context that the anthology *The New Negro* was originally produced in a special issue of *The Survey* as a collection of essays, art, poetry and other creative work from the Harlem school of writers. This volume established and introduced as well as any single work could the spirit, the artists, the points of view of 'Negro Renaissance', 'The New Negro', the 'Harlem Renaissance', as it was variously called, with its lengthy list of artists (Cullen, McKay, Toomer, Johnson, Hughes, among many others). In the title essay Locke begins his description of this rapid transformation of the Black community by stating that the 'New Negro' is not so much a transformation of the Old Negro as it is the realization that the Old Negro never existed, except as a White fiction: 'The Old Negro, we must remember, was a creature of moral debate and historical controversy. His has been a stock figure perpetrated as an historical fiction partly in innocent sentimentalism, partly in deliberate reactionism.'[16]

Locke describes the effects of stereotyping of the Negro, on the Negro as well as on the White, and concludes that the new attitude of 'self-respect and self-dependence' both reflects and promulgates the 'New Negro'. He then focuses on Harlem as the prime example of the Black community 'seizing upon its first chances for group expression and self-determination'.[17]

His essay is not a polemic, but a keen analysis of the politics of the moment and the reaction against the past: 'It seems to be the outcome of the reaction to proscription and prejudice; an attempt, fairly successful on the whole, to convert a defensive into an offensive position, a handicap into an incentive.'[18] He goes on to show that as the consciousness of the Negro is made aware of the rich heritage through this black 'Zionism', so will the White become cognizant of the contributions and gifts the Black populace has subliminally infused into the culture of the South in the form of folk-art, music and humor. What now will occur, he says, is a conscious contribution by the New Negro artists, thinkers, writers who can transcend the former role of ward to become a 'collaborator and participant in American civilization'.[19]

The poetry resulting from this era, sometimes called 'The New Poetry', was characterized by Hayden himself in his introduction to *Kaleidoscope* as having the goals of 'Free verse, diction close to everyday speech, a realistic approach to life, and the use of material once considered unpoetic . . .'[20] Prompted by the literary magazines *The Crisis* and *Opportunity*, the poetry of the Harlem Renaissance was focused on themes of race, Black history and lore, Black music and the sense of nostalgia for the lost homeland. As Hayden summarized it:

Protest became more defiant, racial bitterness and racial pride more outspoken than ever before. Negro history and folklore were explored as new sources of inspiration. Spirituals, blues, and jazz suggested themes and verse patterns to young poets like Jean Toomer and Langston Hughes. Certain conventions, notably what has been called 'literary Garveyism', grew out of a fervent Negro nationalism.[21]

The protest, the pride, the newly sounded cry for identity continued in the voices of Black poets into the thirties as Hayden's poetic career began. It was never the uniformly coordinated voice one might infer from James McCall's famous poem 'The New Negro' written in the heyday of the Renaissance:

> He scans the world with calm and fearless eyes,
> conscious within of powers long since forgot;
> at every step, new man-made barriers rise
> to bar his progress——but he heeds them not.
> He stands erect, though tempests round him crash,
> though thunder bursts and billows surge and roll;
> he laughs and forges on, while lightnings flash
> along the rocky pathway to his goal.
> Impassive as a Sphinx, he stares ahead—
> foresees new empires rise and old ones fall;
> while caste-mad nations lust for blood to shed,
> he sees God's finger writing on the wall.
> With soul awakened, wise and strong he stands,
> holding his destiny within his hands.[22]

Many fine artists, in fact, saw the danger in 'art as polemic'. Not only was there danger in limiting art to a single issue and point of view, but there was, perhaps, the greater danger of being just as easily grouped with all Black writers, and chunked aside or ignored.

For example, David Lewis in his study *When Harlem Was in Vogue* describes Jean Toomer's reaction to being categorized by his publisher as 'a promising Negro writer'. To an extent, Lewis attributes the vehemence of Toomer's indignation to Waldo Frank who had cautioned Toomer in a letter: 'The day you write as a Negro, or as an American, or as anything but a human part of life, your work will lose a dimension'.[23]

Countee Cullen had a similar attitude. A Phi Beta Kappa graduate of NYU and accepted for graduate school at Harvard, Cullen balked at being typed as a Black poet, though he was well aware that his identity as an Afro-American inevitably affected his point of view:

And even though he struggled increasingly against being typed a 'Negro poet', Harlem (except for Du Bois, who reproached Cullen's parochialism) had cheered the 1923 interview in *The New York Times* quoting the Witter Bynner prizewinner as saying that race consciousness guided his muse, that 'although I struggle against it, it colors my writing, I fear, in spite of everything that I can do'.[24]

The focal issue which emerged from the ferment of this vital era, then, formed the background for the most vehement criticism wielded at Robert Hayden – the issue of whether or not a Black poet's primary identity is as a human artist among men, or as a Black artist among Blacks. And as the decade of the 1920s progressed, the sides became more clearly drawn. On the one hand were poets such as Countee Cullen and William Stanley Braithwaite, wishing to be poets, not 'Negro' poets, striving, they hoped, to avoid the 'condescension and double standard of some white critics'.[25] Opposed to this view were writers like Hughes who advocated a distinctive Black art and an emerging Black audience to receive the work:

Implicit in Hughes's essay is a call for the reeducation not only of the black artist but of the black middle class public as well; a call for the emergence of a black audience that would take the initiative in recognizing and patronizing black talent, instead of waiting for white public approval first.[26]

The basic question, then, remained vital and has affected virtually every Afro-American poet since. In the essays of Locke and Schuyler the idea of an art delineated exclusively in terms of a Black Aesthetic – apart from aesthetics of any other art – is viewed as ludicrous, or else ill-advised. Other writers and artists saw the question of aesthetics as distinct from the social and economic issues. They might aspire to racial pride and self-esteem, but they refused to acknowledge that the criteria for art would be affected by such an issue.

The Harlem era ended much as did the gaiety of all America in the 1920s, with the blight of the Depression, but it did not stop the artists themselves, not all of them. It did not stop their influence and themes of racial pride and protest. It did obliterate the phenomenon that was the Harlem Renaissance, for if the Depression hit America hard, it devastated Harlem and savaged the hopes grown so mighty during the ascendancy of the 1920s in the minds of Black Americans who had witnessed the upward mobility of Blacks in the working class and in the Talented Tenth (the ten percent of the population who are the professionals). Upwards of fifty and sixty percent of Afro-Americans had no jobs. Black financial institutions faltered and failed. Harlem rapidly deteriorated to a slum, a situation which worsened until in 1935 there was a race riot caused largely by these conditions. The Harlem Renaissance would have died out in any case, but the 'Depression accelerated a failure that was inevitable . . .'[27]

In the 1930s two new influences began to affect this issue of the Black Aesthetic, one social, the other philosophical. Both of these shaped the early work of Hayden, who was well into his apprenticeship. The first was the rising sentiment of communism among many Americans, both the working class and the humanitarian elite who saw in the philosophic concern for the masses a romanticized political hope for mankind. This sentiment was promulgated further by chapters of the John Reed Club which sprang up almost spontaneously across the land. Instead of being viewed as antithetical to the American dream, the disembodied doctrine seemed almost the fulfillment of the founding fathers' vision, which vast monopolies, the 'robber barons' and their Wall Street Empire had ostensibly destroyed. Certainly in the midst of economic chaos and deprivation, the romantic notion of the proletariat taking over from the corrupt and self-centered elite seemed a hopeful and comforting possibility.

The atmosphere later in the 1930s further contributed to the appeal of communism with the success of such socialistic reforms as the WPA programs and the vast welfare systems which accomplished what nothing else had. Consequently, Black writers and artists, such as Langston Hughes and Richard Wright, found in the ideal of communism a struggle and an implicit solution which transcended questions of race or class, which, in effect, united the disenfranchised of whatever sort in a common goal of justice:

The 1930s was a Marxist decade for Hughes as it was for some other American writers. Communism promised an alternative to the capitalist order which feeds on racism and the exploitation of the working classes. It emphasized the identity of interests of all oppressed peoples, regardless of race or nationality, and called upon them to unite and overthrow their oppressors. Unlike Richard Wright, Hughes never specifically joined the Communist Party; but he found in its ideology a fresh perspective, an effective tool of social analysis, a broader conception of the black struggle as part of a world-wide struggle against oppression.[28]

A second noteworthy contribution to an evolving Black Aesthetic was termed *négritude*, a movement begun in the 1930s, and continuing well into the 50s, which, in a French context, celebrated, as some of the Harlem writers had done, the African heritage of the Black people. Based in French-speaking Africa and the Caribbean, the term *négritude* was coined by Léopold Senghor, the leading figure in the movement, who, interestingly, was later to bestow on Robert Hayden the 1966 Dakar Award in the contest which Langston Hughes would help judge. The principal notion of *négritude* was an opposition to the ostensibly egalitarian concept of assimilation (the whole Black Controversy again) inasmuch as assimilation implied or presupposed a supremacy of White European cultural ideals over those of Africa. More to the point, the adherents of the philosophy saw integration and assimilation as the destruction of their historical and cultural heritage as Africans. Akin to much of the debate in America which had preceded it, *négritude* stressed in writing and art the richness of African society, the paucity of spiritual values in modern Western materialism, and the elevation of Black pride by the realization of how African heritage had become subverted and degraded, first through the slave trade, and subsequently by colonialism.

The effect of the movement in art and in poetry was not only to stress African themes, but also to view art as a political expression and the artist as intimately involved in the struggle for racial identity and for economic and political freedom. In her introduction to *Beyond the Blues* (1962) Rosey Pool succinctly describes the philosophical point of view *négritude* connotes:

'Négritude' is a sign, in the present generation, of men and women who prefer to be called Afro-Americans to being classified as Negroes. The latter name, invented by Portuguese or Spanish slave-importers, simply means Blacks, and is too much misery-laden for their liking. I personally think that this is a symptom of transition similar to James Baldwin's rejection of water-melon.[29]

In a more general way, the term connoted somewhat the same quality as did the 1960s slang term 'soul', a pride, a cultural identity, an awareness of heritage as something to be cherished or at least acknowledged, not to be ignored, avoided, denied or feared.

How *négritude* became expressed was totally subjective. From her own point of view as a survivor of the Nazi death camps, as well as a member of a race persecuted through the ages, Rosey Pool stated:

The stigma of slavery and persecution is one which sticks. Awareness of the injustice, the humiliation that generations of his ancestors suffered, may send one man into the desperate effort to 'erase the colour line' from his life, while another may join the Black Moslems for inverted segregation, start a Buy Black campaign, and put barbed wire between the races, from his side of the fence. These are the extremes. The third man, the one with a sound amount of *négritude*, will, I am certain, see the others lose their self-consciousness eventually. One day they will themselves acquire a healthy dose of the stuff. Or their children will.[30]

So it was that before the ideological debates of the 1960s, long before the transformation of the non-violent Civil Rights Movement into militant politics and the pens of Afro-American writers became weapons in the fight, the same issues had long been discussed. In general, the response of the Black artist to the controversy had been one of three basic attitudes – to advocate assimilation into the mainstream of Western cultural tradition, to affirm the validity of a distinct Afro-American heritage with its own critical standards but a tradition which could operate within a White culture, or to conclude that the only recourse for the Black artist was to establish his own political identity in order to promulgate his cultural heritage either by repatriation to Africa or by establishing a separate state within the White culture.Obviously not every artist fitted neatly into one of these three classifications, but this array of responses encompasses the range of possibilities and it implies something of the background to the ideological and aesthetic context which Hayden entered as an aspiring poet in the 1930s.

8. The Birth of the Hayden Stand

> He has not given up Negro subject matter, he has elevated it to a
> higher plane. He no longer writes old-fashion protest poems. On the
> contrary, he plays down the parochial and limiting elements in a given
> racial situation or incident and, by removing the racial emphasis, he
> raises the human interest involved.[1]

> Arthur Davis about Hayden, 1974.

Before the Counterpoise Manifesto, before the remarkable shift in his poetics,
Hayden reflected in his largely imitative verse three major influences. The first
of these was the Harlem Renaissance school, which in its own diversity established a variety of themes and stylistics. Still, over half the poems in
Heart-Shape in the Dust employ dialect or else treat the thematic concerns of
the Harlem poets as enumerated by one of the writers from the period,
Sterling Brown:

1. A discovery of Africa as a source for race pride.

2. A use of Negro heroes and heroic episodes from American history.

3. Propaganda of protest.

4. A treatment of the Negro masses (frequently of the folk, less often of the
workers).

5. Franker and deeper self-revelation.[2]

Since most readers are unfamiliar with these early verses, when we come upon
them with a knowledge of Hayden's later work, they appear as flat, formulaic,
forced. And yet, while the voice is imitative and consequently strained, they
accurately reflect the point of view of a poet born from the womb of the
ghetto whose identity, at least at that time, was aligned with these thematic
realities. For example, the Harlem Renaissance writer Walter Francis White
describes in his autobiography how he suddenly understood his identity as he
and his brother and father armed themselves to defend against marauding
Whites in the 1906 Atlanta race riot:

In that instant there opened within me a great awareness; I knew then who I was. I
was a Negro, a human being with an invisible pigmentation which marked me as a

person to be hunted, hanged, abused, discriminated against, kept in poverty and ignorance . . .[3]

Though in a more positive vein, Robert Hayden likewise attributed his own sense of identity at that time to his upbringing in Paradise Valley. In his auto-biographical notes he stated, 'I always knew who and what I was . . . Remember, I grew up in the ghetto, which, if mixed in those days, was predominantly Afro-American.'[4] In short, Hayden never denied his racial identity or its profound influence on his work. Later, of course, he would change his approach to many of these same themes – Afro-American heroes, the history of the Afro-American. He would find his own voice. But in these early works he relied most heavily on those techniques already established by the New Negro movement, even though its heyday had passed.

The second major influence on Hayden's early poetry was the poetic theory and practice of the English Romantics. Like Countee Cullen, Hayden had every reason to be introspective, confused, perplexed by the circumstances of his childhood and his individual identity apart from his racial heritage. Like Cullen's mother, Ruth Sheffey had left her son in the care of foster parents, but, unlike Cullen's mother, Ruth Sheffey had paid more than lip service to her son's upbringing; she visited when she could and tried to nurture the artistic gifts she sensed in her son. Nevertheless, it is clear that many of the poems in *Heart-Shape* which are imitative of the English Romantics are empowered less by a denunciation of racial injustice than by a groping for identity and understanding. There are not too many poems in this first volume disassociated from racial themes – 'Sonnet to E.', 'Monody', 'This Grief', 'Orison' and several others. Generally these are traditional love lyrics or else elegies, like 'Rosemary', and 'Obituary'. But there are enough of them that indicate even in these early poems Hayden's interests beyond the expression of racial utterance. In these pieces there is no dialect, no racial identity of the speaker, as Cullen's favorite 'The Falcon' well illustrates:

The Falcon

I saw the falcon like a scimitar
    Drop from the brittle morning skies;
The shadow of his wings was fear,
    Death was the lustre of his eyes.
His claws were cleanly-curven blades,
    Swift as arrows they sank to rest
Within the swallow's singing throat,
    Sudden and swift they clove his breast,
Sheathing themselves in song . . .
    Imperious the falcon flies
On wings emphatic as a gun;
    Death is the wisdom of his eyes.[5]

The third major influence during this period of apprenticeship was the politicized verse of social protest typical of the proletarian concerns of the late thirties, especially among the WPA writers. Various critics and biographers have attributed different degrees of interest on Hayden's part in the then rising fascination for communism. In the 1940 edition of Robert Kerlin's *Negro Poets and Their Poems*, for example (published originally in 1923 during the height of the Harlem Renaissance), Hayden's poem 'Speech' is introduced by the following brief description of the twenty-seven-year-old poet's work: 'Robert Hayden gives . . . clear proof of his proletarian point of view and of a broader outlook than that of race':

Speech

Hear me, white brothers,
Black brothers, hear me:

I have seen the hand
Holding the blowtorch
To the dark, anguish-twisted body;
I have seen the hand
Giving the high-sign
To fire on the white pickets;
And it was the same hand,
Brothers, listen to me,
It was the same hand.
Hear me, black brothers,
White brothers, hear me:

I have heard the words
They set like barbed-wire fences
To   divide you,
I have heard the words—
Dirty nigger, poor white trash——
And the same voice spoke them;
Brothers, listen well to me.
The same voice spoke them.[6]

(Heart-Shape, p. 27)

The most substantial of his poems on the proletariat theme was the eight-page 'Mass Chant' entitled 'These Are My People'. According to Pontheolla Williams' 1972 interview with Hayden, he was during these years greatly influenced by the works of Richard Wright, particularly *Uncle Tom's Children* (1938), and by the John Reed Club, for whom he read some of these early poems.[7] But, as Williams further notes, Hayden never accepted communism as a solution, partly because it denied a spiritual reality and partly because he simply was uncomfortable with the label of a group identity:

Although too religious and individualistic to join the Communist Party, as Richard Wright had, he remained on the 'periphery of the radical movement', and he gives the John Reed Club credit for his 'understanding' of what the political issues were in the United States, and the world in general, as well as the inspiration to consider cultural questions in his works.[8]

Williams concludes that this interest in Marxist ideology was the second stage in Hayden's evolving consciousness – from race, to class, and finally, after he discovered the Bahá'í Faith, to an even more expansive 'vision of world brotherhood of the Bahá'í faith'.[9]

In his essay 'The Black Aesthetic in the Thirties, Forties, and Fifties', Dudley Randall classifies this era between the decline of the Harlem Renaissance and the emergence in the 1960s of the 'Black Aesthetic' as a 'middle period'.[10] He includes as the most prominent Black poets during this period M. B. Tolson, Gwendolyn Brooks and Robert Hayden. The poetic themes during the 'middle period' Randall depicts as resulting from the dominating historical events of each decade:

In the thirties it was the Great Depression and the Spanish Civil War. In the forties it was World War II. In the fifties it was McCarthyism, the Korean War, and the beginning of the Freedom movement with the Supreme Court school-desegregation decision of 1954.[11]

The poetics of these middle-period artists, Randall observes, depart from the imitative modes which had previously characterized the work of Black poets; this was a period when 'Negro writers wanted to be accepted into the mainstream of American literature'.[12] In particular, Randall notes, as have other critics, that this new approach was strongly influenced by the techniques of 'New Criticism', the strong reliance on imagery, allusion, symbolism, the objective correlative as practiced by 'the modern experimental masters such as Hart Crane, Eliot, Pound, and Yeats . . .'[13] But clearly Hayden's poetry which reflects Randall's comments is the later verse, not the poems written before 1940.

What effected this transition in Hayden's aesthetics? Clearly no simple, concise or complete answer is possible, but between the publication of *Heart-Shape in the Dust* and the Counterpoise Manifesto in 1948 a number of influences are clearly discernible, some of which I have already mentioned. First there was Erma, a cultured, educated and supportive companion who both understood and encouraged Hayden's aspirations to become an important poet. On the one hand, some critics have attributed too much or, more correctly, the wrong kind of influence on Erma's part. Williams, for example, describes Erma as 'an ambitious woman'[14] who 'wanted him to be a success',[15] and who finally 'got her husband back into graduate school'.[16] She even goes so far as to imply that Hayden's acceptance of the Bahá'í Faith was directly attributable to Erma's influence when she says that Erma, 'assured of his intellectual opportunities as well of as a certain [sic] measure of financial security – turned her attention to his spiritual well-being'.[17] The fact is that Erma became a Bahá'í before Robert because he was adamant about not affiliating with groups in general, but particularly not one with ideological implications unless he was thoroughly convinced of its truth. Williams herself admits that Hayden did not become a Bahá'í until he had read the literature and that it was a 'serious commitment' on his part which 'had a lasting effect on the philosophical direction of his thought and thus on his poetry as well'.[18]

Hayden's acceptance of the Bahá'í Faith in 1943 was especially difficult not only because of his fundamentalist religious background, but also because he had come to distrust group thought as a result of his association with the adherents of Marxist ideology. For example, in his notes he describes his experience in reading his poetry to the John Reed Club:

Venturing to read his poems for the members of the John Reed Club, he was scathingly criticized for his lack of political awareness. And he was often accused of being too much the individualist and not willing to submit to ideology.[19]

Years later, he summed up his feelings on the subject when in a 1976 interview he stated that 'I'm not a joiner. I don't get involved with groups. The Bahá'í Faith is about the only organized body I can stand. I cherish my individuality and don't want to be a conformist except (paradoxically) on my own terms.'[20]

In short, Erma was a source of stability, understanding, affection and encouragement which was essential to Hayden's life and career, and he always acknowledged her crucial role in his work. But his desire to be a poet, his staunch individualism, his rigorous pursuit of his ambition and his decision to become a Bahá'í were clearly his own considered choices.

Another major influence in Hayden's changed attitude towards his art, then, was his acceptance of the Bahá'í Faith. As I have noted in the discussion of his life, it was not an influence he immediately perceived and understood – it confirmed his already established belief in the oneness of mankind and the essentially spiritual nature of man's existence. But, even more subtly, the Bahá'í Faith supported the direction of his art away from the subjective poetics of his Romantic verse and toward the objectivist poetics as delineated by the New Critical School; away from the didacticism of his 'social protest' poems and towards indirection. And yet in the strong statements against racism in the Bahá'í Writings, as well as in its affirmation of the arts as spiritual endeavor, Hayden found confirmation of all his major thematic interests.

Among the specific Bahá'í teachings which illustrate this influence are the beliefs in abstinence from partisan political issues, the injunctions against proselytizing and dogmatism, and the stress on world unity as a solution to contemporary problems and as the goal of human history. Perhaps the most significant of these to Hayden at this time of his poetic transformation in the early 1940s is the affirmation of independent investigation of the truth, the notion that belief must be acquired by objective study, not indoctrination; as 'Abdu'l-Bahá notes: 'If religious beliefs and opinions are found contrary to the standards of science, they are mere superstitions and imaginations; for the antithesis of knowledge is ignorance, and the child of ignorance is superstition.'[21] Likewise, in speaking of how the Bahá'í should teach others, Bahá'u'lláh states that first one must teach himself that others may see the truth in human example:

Whoso ariseth among you to teach the Cause of his Lord, let him, before all else, teach his own self, that his speech may attract the hearts of them that hear him. Unless he teacheth his own self, the words of his mouth will not influence the heart of the seeker.[22]

He further states that after one has taught himself, he must not teach others through force or coercion, so that the seeker will respond to his own investigation of that truth and not to pressure: 'Beware lest ye contend with any one, nay, strive to make him aware of the truth with kindly manner and most convincing exhortation. If your hearer respond, he will have responded to his own behoof . . .'[23]

This whole notion of teaching through example, of enabling the hearer to investigate truth for himself, is essentially the same process which the objectivist theory of poetry presented to Hayden. That is, by avoiding the 'chauvinistic and the doctrinaire', as Hayden termed more direct methods of verse, the poet forces the audience to relate to the poem, not the poet. Furthermore, Hayden recognized in the symbolic and analogical techniques of the writings of all Prophets of God, an essentially poetic process, the same algebraic quality which Auden so aptly described to his students. Hayden often noted this similarity between the technique of the poet and that of the Manifestation:

Poetry is very close to religion, and I might say tangentially that when we speak of the Prophet, and Bahá'u'lláh in particular, as being a poet, in a sense this is very true, because the Prophet uses symbols, speaks in parables, uses metaphors, and all the devices we associate with poetry.[24]

Furthermore, the Bahá'í teachings confirmed and advanced Hayden's most powerful themes of unity, racial justice, personal identity and transformation. Not only did the Bahá'í Faith confirm Hayden's belief in an essentially non-violent approach to racial problems, it further denounced racial prejudice as a key issue in the attempt to spiritualize mankind:

As to racial prejudice, the corrosion of which, for well nigh a century, has bitten into the fibre, and attacked the whole social structure of American society, it should be regarded as constituting the most vital and challenging issue confronting the Bahá'í community at the present stage of its evolution . . . White and Negro, high and low, young and old, whether newly converted to the Faith or not, all who stand identified with it must participate in, and lend their assistance, each according to his or her capacity, experience, and opportunities, to the common task of fulfilling the instructions, realizing the hopes, and following the example, of 'Abdu'l-Bahá.[25]

With such primacy given to the abolition of racial prejudice as part of the larger process of world unity and spiritual transformation, it is, perhaps, no wonder that, in addition to Hayden, the Bahá'í Faith attracted a number of other major figures in the recent history of Afro-American literature. Among the most prominent were Alain Locke, author of 'The New Negro' and a leading spokesman for the Harlem Renaissance; Margaret Danner, a poet of significant standing; and Dr Rosey Pool.[26]

The third influence on the transformation of Hayden's poetry was Auden, or, more accurately, the total effect of his renewed and intensified study of poetry at the University of Michigan. Auden's notion of poetry as a process of solving for the unknown is something that Hayden would inevitably mention as an essential key to his poetics: 'In poetry you are really solving x, looking for the unknown quantity. You are trying to say what cannot be said any other way – and, in some poems, you are trying to say what really cannot be said at all.'[27] Hayden's understanding of this essential ingredient in poetry shaped everything he did afterward. It did not direct his subjects or themes – he still wrote about his most personal insights, his analysis of racial injustice, Afro-American heroes, the need for world unity. But instead of telling the reader what to think, he employed symbols, metaphors, imagery, the persona and other devices to create an intimate relationship between the poem and the reader.

Of course, as we will see later, there is much more than this to his transformed poetics, but insofar as his racial stand was concerned, it is crucial to know that in addition to his other objections about politicized verse, he also believed it to be generally bad poetry because most often it becomes propaganda and rhetorically embellished dogma instead of art.

By the time of the publication of the Counterpoise Manifesto in 1948, then, Hayden had assimilated these external influences, as well as internal resources of change which we can only guess at. He had practiced and perfected this technique in his writing of his history poems and in the other pieces which appear in *The Lion and the Archer*. But whether or not we understand exactly the source of that change, Hayden's stand itself is quite clear – he wished to be considered and adjudged as a poet, not a Black poet, not a Bahá'í poet, simply a poet. Thus, in the Counterpoise statement, when he speaks of being opposed to 'the chauvinistic, the cultish, to special pleading, to all that seeks to limit and restrict creative expression', he is not referring exclusively to matters of racial identity. Likewise, in *Kaleidoscope* (1967) he stated his opposition to 'the chauvinistic and the doctrinaire' and to 'having his writing judged by standards different from those applied to the work of other poets'. And yet even here he was not solely referring to matters of racial identity, though in 1967, when he wrote the blurb, that was his principal concern.

Of course, twenty years later the Counterpoise statement was to be interpreted as a denial of his racial identity, which it obviously was not. Many of his most powerful poems are concerned with heroism in Afro-American history, but, as he was later to point out, his poems are not so much about race as they are about using the racial situation as a means of understanding something about mankind:

I'm not so interested in pointing out what is singularly black or Afro-American as in pointing out something about the way people live and the humanity Afro-American people share with everyone else . . .

One's particular starting point might be racial awareness or identity, but if you're a good enough artist, you can make those materials have meaning for other people . . .

Perhaps we've had to go through a phase of ethnicity, but now we must move to our common humanity. Artists need to say this . . .[28]

As he pointed out in another interview in 1976, he wrote from his perspective as a human being, not solely from his point of view as the member of a particular race:

I'm alive in my time – alive in the world. I respond to everything around me. I have my own inner personal struggles which have nothing to do with race, that are existential, you might say . . .

There is a tendency to regiment Afro-American artists and to feel that they should all say the same thing . . . But we are as complex and as various as any other people.[29]

One cannot give even a general outline of Hayden's stand, however, without noting finally how this same issue of his identity as a poet related to his beliefs as a Bahá'í. For while outwardly and most importantly the controversy he would face resulted from his refusal to be labeled a 'Black poet', he also suffered as a result of his failure to be classified a 'Bahá'í poet', though in a much more subtle way. Put succinctly, if Hayden's national reputation was largely underground until his last decade, he was even less well known among his co-religionists, because even though he was poetry editor of *World Order* magazine, a Bahá'í periodical, his own poetry was rarely a direct expression of his beliefs.

The historical background to this issue is complex, but worth alluding to in order to understand the importance of this problem to Hayden and his stand on aesthetics. The arts have always been considered to have questionable value among the adherents of institutionalized religious thought. In the medieval period the so-called Pauline Precept prevailed – the view that all art should express Christian doctrine. Art which did not was rejected as unworthy and was expunged, expurgated or destroyed. When discussing the preservation of Anglo-Saxon folk literature, the noted eighth-century monk Alcuin remarked, '*Quid Ineldus con Cristo?*' (What does Ingeld have to do with

Christ?)[30] Fortunately, some Old English works survived as our only link to that rich tribal culture, but most were destroyed.

A similarly unfortunate attitude might be possible among those adherents of the Bahá'í Faith who would question the validity or at least the priority of the arts during a period when, Bahá'ís believe, the utmost effort of the Bahá'í community should go toward assisting mankind in its transition to a new identity, a concept of world unity. To support such a contention some Bahá'ís might ignore the statements of Bahá'u'lláh and 'Abdu'l-Bahá affirming the importance of the arts, and cite only those statements which, taken out of context, might seem to imply the abandonment of all concerns other than promulgating their beliefs, statements like 'Abdu'l-Bahá's exhortation in the *Tablets of the Divine Plan,* the charter for a succession of global teaching plans: 'Now is the time that you may divest yourselves from the garment of attachment to this phenomenal realm, be wholly severed from the physical world, become angels of heaven and travel and teach through all these regions.'[31]

By no means did Hayden downplay his identity as a Bahá'í, any more than he denied his identity as an Afro-American. In fact, he often gave readings for Bahá'í groups, and ten of his hundred best poems allude explicitly to the Bahá'í Writings. And yet the reality Hayden faced was that very few Bahá'ís knew of his work, and of those who did, even fewer sensed how importantly it related to his beliefs as a Bahá'í. On one occasion Hayden was picked up at the airport in a town where he was to give a poetry reading for a Bahá'í community. A well-meaning young lady remarked as she drove him to the meeting that she used to write poetry but gave it up to do 'Bahá'í work'. No doubt the woman was totally unaware of what her statement implied – that what Hayden had devoted himself to was neither 'Bahá'í work' nor as important as more obvious sorts of teaching. Thus, within the Bahá'í community itself Robert Hayden was often known as 'Erma's husband who writes poetry'.[32]

In his essay 'Can there be a Bahá'í Poetry?' Geoffrey Nash quotes the Guardian of the Bahá'í Faith as stating that there is no such thing as 'Bahá'í art' at this time. There are at least two major implications of this statement. The first concerns the Bahá'í historical perspective – that when a new Revelation transforms civilization it inevitably calls forth expressions of this advancement in human understanding, in the arts and sciences. For example, we can see Christian art or Islamic art or Oriental art as emanating from the cultural impact of the spiritual awakening that Revelations caused. While the Bahá'í Revelation has spread throughout the world, civilization at large has not yet been affected by this new awareness, as the Bahá'í Writings assure us will be the case in the future. There is no 'Bahá'í' culture as yet. A second implication of this statement is that the inclusive nature of the Faith, affirming as it does unity in the diversity of peoples and cultures, virtually prohibits a single artistic point of view as being able to represent the 'Bahá'í' perspective.

But it is another aspect of this question that most interests Nash and which is really most importantly related to Hayden's career, and that issue is the importance of art at this crucial point of transition. Nash asks, 'Must we then turn away from the arts, as being of secondary importance at this stage of our history?'[33]

Mr Nash concludes his essay by exhorting Bahá'í poets to write 'in inhospitable circumstances among aliens or not always enlightened friends' because the very intimate examination of life which the poet provides explores the life of every man:

Through his own sorrows he must know the joy and suffering that are one. It is as though he is articulating the spiritual battles of Everyman. In these matters there can be no abstraction, no dogma . . . Bahá'ís, following the advice of 'Abdu'l-Bahá, do not merely recite verses but strive to make their lives beautiful prayers.[34]

Certainly this view of the relevancy of art and poetry in particular to the spiritual aspirations of mankind accord completely with Hayden's own statements on the subject, especially his succinct observation that for him poetry was a 'prayer for illumination'.[35] In short, the reference from both Hayden and Nash is clear – that art is a vital part of a people's spiritual life, not a superfluous trapping. What is also clear is that art by a Bahá'í can be valid and valuable even when it makes no explicit allusion to the Bahá'í Faith, its doctrine, its special jargon or historical figures.

As we will see later in this study, Hayden's poetry is in a very important sense 'Bahá'í art' because at the heart of it, organizing it, empowering its themes, are Bahá'í concepts. In fact, Hayden received criticism when he became overt in his allusion to the Bahá'í Faith. Robert Greenberg in his literary biography of Hayden states that in the poem 'Words in the Mourning Time' (which incorporates the 'Short Obligatory Prayer' of Bahá'u'lláh) Hayden is violating his own aesthetic stand by becoming doctrinaire:

Since the general audience does not share Hayden's sentiments about this prophet, his faith seems undemonstrated in the poem, an imposition on the reader. Hayden's immersion in the universalist content of Bahá'u'lláh's message may have obscured from him the fact that to Western readers it seems not so much humane and unifying as strange and sectarian. This involved Hayden in at least the appearance of a contradictory stance, since he conceived and described his poetry as 'opposed to the chauvinistic and the doctrinaire'.[36]

Hayden legitimately expected his serious readers to probe the allusions to the Bahá'í Faith and to recover those allusions, just as the interested reader might study Celtic myth to appreciate T. S. Eliot's *The Wasteland.* In short, Hayden early determined that his objective was to become the best poet he could and to write about those subjects which pursued him most forcefully.

He did not begin with a definition of what a poet should be – he rejected the easy label, referring to himself only in the most general terms as symbolist poet, but he was always aware that it was his beliefs as a Bahá'í that consolidated those symbols:

I object to strict definitions of what a poet is or should be, because they usually are thought up by people with an axe to grind – by those who care less about poetry than they do about some cause. We're living in a time when individuality is threatened by a kind of mechanizing anonymity, and by regimentation. In order to be free, you must submit to tyranny, to ideological slavery, in the name of freedom. And obviously, this is the enemy of the artist; it stultifies anything creative . . . Poetry, all art, it seems to me is ultimately religious in the broadest sense of the term. It grows out of, reflects, illuminates our inmost selves, and so on. It doesn't have to be sectarian or denominational.[37]

Hayden's stand as enunciated in his statements on poetics, then, was in no way a denial of his racial identity or a denial of his belief as a Bahá'í – it was a courageous and forceful statement of the bare requisites for good poetry and a caution against those who would dictate what the artist must say or how he should say it. It should not be confused with an advocacy of complete licence; it was the expression of Hayden's belief that we must not let 'monsters of abstraction/police and threaten us', but strive for an atmosphere where 'godliness/is possible and man/is . . ./permitted to be man'.[38]

9. The Controversy

No issue in Afro-American letters has to date generated more heat or
less light than the question of what 'black poet' means.[1]

Wilburn Williams, Jr., 1977

In 1962 Rosey Pool's *Beyond the Blues* was published in England because, as
Dudley Randall notes in his 1971 anthology *Black Poets*, 'Everyone [in the
USA] she queried said the book was too special and declined to handle it.'[2]
What had occurred in those nine years to enable Randall's collection to be
published by a popular commercial publisher when Pool's work had been the
first major anthology of Black poetry since Bontemps' and Hughes' anthology
in 1949, and the first since Johnson's *The Book of American Negro Poetry* in
1922, to give biographical insights about the authors?

The changed climate was due partly to the riots in Watts and Detroit, partly
to the resurgence of the Black pride sentiment which Hughes had described
forty years before. It was the result of the whole fervor of the Civil Rights
movement, the freedom rides, and lynchings, not of rural Blacks only, but of
White, middle-class youngsters gone South to register voters, of middle-aged
women and prominent citizenry. It was the result of collective consciousness
enlightened by such literary works as *Soul on Ice* and *The Autobiography of
Malcolm X*. It was all the things that the phrase 'the movement' signaled and
connoted, what the term *négritude* had heralded in previous decades, or
Garveyism in the 1920s, of The Great Controversy before that. It was
connoted in art by the phrase 'Black Aesthetic', in politics by 'Black Power'.

For Robert Hayden, the artistic implications of the Movement would
become a devastating and ironic attack on his poetics, on his character, an
unreasoned and unwarranted harangue from which he would never fully
recover. It began, as has been noted, with the Fisk Writers' Conference. It
centered around one simple but pivotal question, not unlike the ominous ring
of Senator McCarthy's 1950s interrogatives about one's political associations.
It asked simply: What are you first, a Negro or an artist? Implicitly, explicitly,
all Afro-American writers were similarly interrogated, and failure to reply
correctly meant instant disdain, catcalls, threats and ostracism.

In a recent conversation, Dudley Randall stated that Hayden's answer had been that he was a poet first; Randall's had been that he was first of all a Black, but he now wishes he had said that it was 'nobody's business'. 'What matters', he now affirms, 'is that you produce good poetry. You can do this from either point of view.'[3] As Hayden had put it, there is only good poetry and bad poetry.

With our present perspective, it is ironic to look back to that turning point at the writers' conference at Fisk on April 22, 1966. Most in attendance no doubt viewed Hayden as misguided, unfortunate, perhaps pitiful, his solo voice crying out against what he saw happening to discussions of literature. The portents of the event could certainly have been sensed by Hayden – any less courageous a man in his situation might have stayed away. John Oliver Killens had been appointed author-in-residence at Fisk, even though it was Hayden who had been there for twenty years, Hayden who had paid his dues there, teaching whatever they gave him: 'This meant that Mr Hayden could no longer teach creative writing. That Writer-in-Residence did much, I under-stand, to make Mr Hayden's humiliation continual by discouraging students from studying with him.'[4] The conference had been arranged by Killens, who kicked off the ensuing battle in his keynote speech with the words, 'For too long we've looked into the eyes of the white master for an image of ourselves.'[5]

This same attitude expressed at the conference was being played out politi-cally with the takeover of the civil rights movement by such figures as Stokely Carmichael, who in his 1967 book *Black Power* stated that integration, 'the goal of assimilation into middle-class America'[6] was no longer the goal of Blacks:

Our basic need is to reclaim our history and our identity from what must be called cultural terrorism, from the depredation of self-justifying white guilt. We shall have to struggle for the right to create our own terms through which to define ourselves and our relationship to the society, and to have these terms recognized.[7]

He goes on to quote from Killens in renouncing White 'structures' and the White political system as a means towards Black freedom and justice. After tracing the progress of American race relations historically, Carmichael, in his chapter 'Dynamite in the Ghetto', decries the institutionalized racism and endless cycle of disenfranchisement as the catalyst for the racial violence which was then occurring:

Herein lies the match that will continue to ignite the dynamite in the ghettos: the ineptness of decision-makers, the anachronistic institutions, the inability to think boldly and above all the unwillingness to innovate . . . They can continue to provide mobile swimming pools and hastily built play areas, but there is a point beyond which the steaming ghettos will not be cooled off. It is ludicrous for the society to believe that these temporary measures can long contain the tempers of an oppressed people.[8]

In art the so-called Black Power movement was signaled by the 'Black Aesthetic', more a political philosophy than an artistic point of view. It was foreshadowed in such comments as the review in *Poetry* in March 1964 by LeRoi Jones in which he assesses eight books by or about Black writers. Categorizing his review as possibly his 'last literal, or non-literal act', Jones examines these works in terms of their relationship to the condition of Blacks, stating that a Black poet's racial point of view is valid subject matter and that it should not be imitative of White forms. His one sentence about Hayden, interestingly, is praise – 'Robert Hayden's poems, as self-consciously bigwordy as they are, are still full of wild dream renderings in water tight rhythms that need a fuller audience.'[9]

But it was after the turning point of 1966 that the 'Black Aesthetic' really took hold. In his 1966 'State/Meant', Jones (now Amiri Baraka) gave direct vent to his fully politicized criteria for the 'Black Artist' (in 1964 it was the 'Negro Artist'):

The Black Artist's role in America is to aid in the destruction of America as he knows it. His role is to report and reflect so precisely the nature of the society, and of himself in that society, that other men will be moved by the exactness of his rendering and, if they are black men, grow strong through this moving, having seen their own strength, and weakness; and if they are white men, tremble, curse, and go mad, because they will be drenched with the filth of their evil![10]

This was hardly a lone voice, however. The emerging 'Black Aesthetic' was affirmed by a number of other poets, like Larry Neal and Don Lee. The ensuing debate between the advocates of politicized art and those opposed to it, so reminiscent of the exchange between Hughes and Schuyler, occupied a major part of the January 1968 number of *Negro Digest* (which was to become *Black World* in 1970). Then in 1971 Addison Gayle published his collection of essays entitled *The Black Aesthetic*, which compiled the most prominent discussions of the major issues.

To understand the logical extension of the Black Aesthetic viewpoint, however, one need only read the opening statement of Ron Karenga in that 1968 *Negro Digest* dialogue:

Black art, like everything else in the black community, must respond positively to the reality of revolution. It must become and remain a part of the revolutionary machinery that moves us to change quickly and creatively. We have always said, and continue to say, that the battle we are waging now is the battle for the minds of Black people, and that if we lose this battle, we cannot win the violent one. It becomes very important, then, that art play the role that it should play in Black survival and not bog itself down in the meaningless madness of the Western world wasted. In order to avoid this madness, black artists and those who wish to be artists must accept the fact that what is needed is an aesthetic, a black aesthetic, that is a criteria [sic] for judging the validity and/or the beauty of a work of art.[11]

So it was that the conference in the spring of 1966 at Fisk was spawned by this ferment. Unwittingly, most of the writers were attending a forum on the issue as orchestrated, or at least as incited, by Killens' keynote speech. But the advocates of such a view were hardly dupes or anti-art; to read the essays of Karenga, Carmichael, Baraka or Lee is to understand some weighty evidence for their hypothesis. But to Hayden it was a rehashing of the rhetoric of the thirties and early forties all over again. In his 'In Memoriam' article in 1982, Julius Lester, who at the time was an enthusiastic advocate of the 'Black Aesthetic', reflects on what this event meant to Hayden:

To Mr Hayden, who was not conceived or reborn in the womb of Black Power, such thinking was not only repugnant; it was a direct assault on the human spirit and art. By its very nature, art, Mr Hayden taught, is revolutionary, because it seeks to change the consciousness, perceptions, and very beings of those who open themselves to it. However, its revolutionary nature can be only mortally wounded if it must meet political prescriptions.[12]

Emotionally balanced on the edge of anger and sorrow, Hayden withheld nothing from the charged atmosphere of the conference:

'I have said this until I almost think I'll choke and fall over backwards,' thus began a visibly disturbed Robert Hayden, addressing himself to the argument as to whether one is a Negro poet, or, as Hayden insists, 'a poet who happens to be a Negro'. Reading lines from Yeats, Hayden solemnly commented, 'I didn't have to be Irish to love those lines.'

'Let's quit saying we're black writers writing to black folks – it has been given importance it should not have.'[13]

Hayden's plea fell on deaf ears, ears ready for the chant of slogans, and Melvin B. Tolson, who was to die later that same year, gave the audience exactly what it wanted. The 'grandfather' of the conference grinned at Hayden, and with a voice 'blazing to the rafters' of Jubilee Hall, he said, 'I'm a black poet, an African-American poet, a Negro poet. I'm no accident – and I don't give a tinker's damn what you think.'[14] After stating that 'Nobody writes in a vacuum or out of a vacuum', he went on to blame capitalism for the world's race problem, and the conference turned into a political rally with James Forman of SNCC having more sway than any artists and with John Killens arranging for a post-conference 'dialogue between the artists and the activists . . .'[15] Even a member of the audience attacked Hayden, reminding him that he had an obligation to his students at Fisk to impress upon them his special identity as a Black poet, not just as a poet.

But in spite of the politically charged tone of the discussion, the conference could not help honoring Hayden's skills as writer, as artist. The Sunday afternoon of the conference was given to poetry reading, and Hayden, as the recently heralded winner of the Dakar award, 'masterfully engaged his audience'[16] by reading 'Full Moon', an eloquent allusion to the Bahá'í Faith,

and a number of other fine lyrics which contrasted mightily with the politicized verse of Margaret Walker, the former 1942 winner of the Yale Younger
Poets award, who read her poem 'Now': '. . . time to wipe away the slime,
time to end this bloody crime.'

Fully aware of the 'personal problem' Hayden had alluded to in his letter to
her of August 12, 1966, Dr Rosey Pool in the same issue of *Negro Digest* has an
article entitled 'An Assessment: Robert Hayden – Poet Laureate'. In this
discussion of Hayden's craftsmanship and the accolades he received from the
jury who considered his work at the Dakar conference, Dr Pool indicates her
awareness of the tide of protest opinion which was already at work attacking
Robert Hayden's failure to become a participant in the voice of revolution:

Hayden is certainly not a 'protest poet' in the usual sense of the word. He would
refuse that label as he refuses to be pigeon-holed as a 'Negro poet', or as one whose
Negritude or race-identification features as a basic quality of his poetry. And still . . .
he is all that. Not primarily, not deliberately, not in propense, but naturally all that in
him is 'truly instinct, brain matter, diastole, systole, reflex action', as he himself
speaks of freedom and liberty as personified in the great Frederick Douglass.[17]

Perhaps Dr Pool sensed in the current of opinion the same subtle oppression that had previously worked to subvert the Black race as well as her own
family of European Jews. Certainly Hayden saw the parallels. He stated in his
unpublished notes how familiar it all seemed as the conference rhetoric turned
against him. Recalling the pressure to conform which the Marxists had previously exerted on him, he thought, 'This is where I came in thirty years ago.'[18]

At the time, many of Hayden's close friends and students could not
understand his inflexibility on the issue. Julius Lester later recounted:

I couldn't understand why he was so vociferous in denying that he was a black poet.
After all, he was the man who had written 'Middle Passage', 'Frederick Douglass',
'Homage to the Empress of the Blues', and 'Runagate Runagate', four of the finest
poems about the black experience in the English language. Why couldn't he admit he
was a black poet?[19]

Fellow Bahá'í Margaret Danner knew the answer to that question and shared
that understanding in her letters. Dr Pool expressed the same sentiment at the
end of that 1966 assessment of Hayden:

Robert Hayden belongs to the Bahá'í World Faith. Bahá'ís believe in the unity of all
religions, of all prophets. 'In light half nightmare and half vision' he speaks of the face
of Bahá'u'lláh, prophet of the Bahá'í faith in whose eyes Hayden sees the suffering of
the men and women who died at Dachau and Buchenwald for their specific *Négritude.*[20]

Then, virtually quoting Hayden's Counterpoise statement, Dr Pool summarized the Bahá'í belief which effectively prohibits Bahá'ís from aligning
themselves with a divisive cause or in seeing their identity as being anything
less than a 'world citizen':

Bahá'ís believe in the unity of all mankind, the universality of all God's creation. In Hayden's poem, 'The Prophet', he speaks of the 'auroral darkness which is God' and he sees 'Energies like angels dance glorias of recognition'. They too sense their group-awareness.[21]

She concludes this milestone in the assessment of Hayden's poetry, the first time any critic had noted the tremendous importance in his verse of his religious beliefs, with the resounding affirmation of his integrity as artist and as a Bahá'í:

And so, the First World Festival of Negro Arts has honored an Afro-American's artistic parity, his natural Negro-ness which is part of his natural human-ness, his American-ness along with his universal-ness: the human integrity of an artist, and the artistic integrity of a fellow-man.[22]

As Hayden himself had observed, the voices of freedom expressed by adherents to movements can themselves become enslaved by ideological boundaries, and to some extent, this is precisely what the voice of the Black Aesthetic did. To further the cause of Black pride and racial justice, individuality had to be sacrificed. In succinctly analyzing the comparison between the Movement and what Hughes avowed in his 1926 article, which according to many was the first major call for a Black Aesthetic, Dudley Randall notes this paradox:

Hughes stresses individualism ('express our individual dark-skinned selves'). In the Black Aesthetic, individualism is frowned upon. Feedback from black people, or the mandates of self-appointed literary commissars, is supposed to guide the poet. But Hughes says, 'If colored people are pleased, we are glad. If they are not, their displeasure doesn't matter either.' (Another expression of individualism.) Hughes says, 'We know we are beautiful. And ugly too.' In the Black Aesthetic, Negroes are always beautiful.[23]

But Mr Randall's observations several years after the event (1971) would not have been so easily verbalized at the Fisk conference. It did not matter that Hayden's own poems were about Afro-American history, that he had won the Dakar prize, that the very poem 'A Ballad of Remembrance', which the adherents of the Black Aesthetic had perceived as Uncle Tomish, was Hughes' favorite poem by Hayden or that at the Dakar Festival Hughes, as one of the judges, had dubbed Hayden 'poet laureate'. Even Hayden's student Julius Lester, who was then caught up in the movement and who would use his 'pen to further the revolution',[24] had to wince at Hayden's treatment:

I found myself caught between what I had learned from Mr Hayden and the new ethos. But on that day in May 1966 I felt great pain for him because, of all people, he did not deserve public humiliation at the hands of black people angered because he refused to lead them to the holy wars.[25]

But the controversy over the 'Black Aesthetic' did not end at the Fisk conference. Over the next few years, as the Black Power advocates took over the reins of the civil rights movement and the tenor of American society in general was profoundly affected by the upsurge of revolutionary rhetoric and violent anti-establishment demonstrations, Hayden's career was importantly affected by his stand, and the assessment of his poetry was inevitably related to the issue.

Hayden would not be silenced – he saw his stand as a defense not only of his own individual philosophy but of art in general. The ensuing debate was not over specific issues *per se*, though Hayden as a believer in the unity and oneness of mankind no doubt disagreed philosophically with the conclusions of the emerging leaders of the Movement. But what dominated was the question of principle, whether anyone, whatever their point of view (and here he would not have excluded his own point of view as a Bahá'í), has the right to legislate how one should write or what subjects as artist one should pursue. In one discussion he went so far as to label such 'minotaurs of edict' as 'literary nazis'.[26] He was 'purely an artist', as Margaret Danner recalls, 'but he was fearless on this issue'.[27]

And yet he was not oblivious to the courage and perspective of the activist writer, nor unsympathetic to what many of them endured to make their beliefs known. In a letter to the editor in the April issue of *Negro Digest*, Hayden publicly recanted the harshness of his tone in denouncing LeRoi Jones, who had been arrested during a demonstration:

In view of his recent imprisonment and the dubious circumstances surrounding it, I certainly have no desire to add to his pain or attack him for his 'militancy'. I am not so much a part of the 'Establishment' that I take pleasure in injuring, either by word or deed, fellow artists with whom I disagree.

It is sad to think of a sensitive and creative man like Jones behind bars. And I for one hope that justice will soon prevail and that he will be free once again to pursue his career as a writer.[28]

In 1966 David Littlejohn published *Black on White*, a study of literature by American Negroes in which he pointedly rejects the two poems 'most celebrated in Negro circles', Tolson's 'Dark Symphony' and Margaret Walker's 'For My People'.[29] Littlejohn terms these pieces weak poetically, 'at their best, eloquent declamations, at their worst valuable period pieces like the heroic WPA murals they recall'.[30] Littlejohn goes on to say that the 'two finest poems by Negroes' are Richard Wright's 'Between the World and Me' and Robert Hayden's 'Middle Passage'. While a writer of whatever background could object to such praise, the exaltation of his poetry by 'Establishment' academic critics further alienated Hayden from the increasingly anti-academic Black literati.

Littlejohn's observations were upheld, however, by the respected and increasingly militant Gwendolyn Brooks in her October review that same year of Hayden's just-published *Selected Poems*. Already at this time a recipient of an American Academy of Arts and Letters Award, as well as a Guggenheim fellow, Brooks in her review described two sorts of poets – the one who 'mixes with mud' and writes in the midst of feeling, 'his wounds like faucets above his page', and a second sort of poet who 'is amenable to a clarifying enchantment via the power of Art', who has a 'reverence for the word Art', who, in effect, is more studied, more analytical.[31] She goes on to say that while we need both sorts, Hayden is clearly the latter:

Robert Hayden, for at least thirty years, has busied himself with a very active and earnest subscription to his faith in spite of occasional light heckling from the bare-fight boys, the snarls of whom, indeed, have been at least half-affectionate because few are quicker than they to sense authentic quality in the work of 'the enemy', and to salute it.[32]

Brooks may have accurately reflected the esteem with which Hayden was then regarded, but she clearly underplays (perhaps in an attempt at conciliation) the 'switchblades of that air'. For example, underlying the lofty praise with which *Selected Poems* was reviewed in *Choice* was the growing awareness by May of 1967 that Hayden was being attacked, as the following observation implies: '*Selected Poems* reveals the surest poetic talent of any Negro poet in America, more importantly it demonstrates a major talent and poetic coming-of-age without regard to race or creed.'[33]

The tensions increased within the literary community that same year when William Styron published his controversial *The Confessions of Nat Turner*, which was severely attacked by many Black artists. Hayden, who had early written his own poetic speculation about the mystical calling of this historical figure, publicly defended Styron's artistic rights and saw the attack as another example of the undermining of the foundation of art itself, a frightening sort of fascism. In discussing the issue of Styron with Paul McClusky, Hayden stated:

Are we to be told what to write about and how to write it? Are we to be restricted in our choice of subjects? It's true that Afro-American history has been traduced. And it's true that as a people we have been stereotyped and caricatured in literature almost beyond recognition . . . But even if Styron's book were as gross a misinterpretation as some people consider it, would chauvinistic censorship be the proper remedy?[34]

The following year, twenty years since he had clearly and forcefully stated his artistic beliefs in the Counterpoise preface, Hayden restated those same principles in the introduction to *Kaleidoscope*. Here he delineated two points of view, that of the 'poets of the Negro revolution' on the one hand, and the view of those who object to the idea of 'Negro poetry' because, among other things, 'it has been used disparagingly to indicate a kind of pseudo-poetry concerned with the race problem to the exclusion of almost everything else'.[35]

At Your Heritage House in Detroit, 1979 (Photograph Hugh Grannum)

Receiving an honorary degree at Brown University in Providence, Rhode Island, 1976

At a meeting in 1967

Hayden cites Cullen as a proponent of the latter view because he 'did not want to be restricted to racial themes nor have his poetry judged solely on the basis of its relevance to the Negro struggle'.[36] Hayden's introductory essay, though clearly supporting his own accord with Cullen, does not disdain 'the Negro poet's devotion to the cause of freedom', but he does attempt to show the danger of perceiving literature by Negroes as being lumped together in a 'kind of literary ghetto', of being assessed by special or different standards, of seeing every Negro writer as a 'spokesman for his race'.[37] He further states, 'there is no denying that a great deal of "race poetry" is poor, because its content seems ready-made and art is displaced by argument'.[38] Hayden then traces the issue through a brief summary of Afro-American literature, from Phillis Wheatley through the Harlem Renaissance, and then concludes with the observation that there are Negro writers (himself obviously one) who perceive the task of the writer, regardless of race, to 'illuminate the human experience', and not to be confined to a racial point of view:

They reject the idea of poetry as racial propaganda, of poetry that functions as a kind of sociology. Their attitude is not wholly new, of course, being substantially that of Dunbar and Cullen. In counterpoise too it is the 'Beat' or 'nonacademic' view held by poets who are not only in rebellion against middle-class ideals and the older poetic traditions but who also advocate a militant racism in a definitely 'Negro' poetry.[39]

Hayden finishes by defending *Kaleidoscope* as a collection of the work of Negro poets (implicitly violating his thesis) by stating that unfortunately there is nowhere else that the student will be able to 'gather any impression of the nature and scope of the Negro's contribution to American poetry'.[40]

Nor is the heated debate reflected only in the introduction; Hayden notes in the biographical sketches of the various poets those who felt strongly one way or the other about this issue. For example, he says about Cullen, 'Although he felt the obligation to speak out against prejudice and bigotry, he avoided obvious propaganda.'[41] About Gwendolyn Brooks he states, 'Inevitably considered by some as a "spokesman" for her race, Miss Brooks has had valuable things to say, but she has said them as a poet, not as a polemicist.'[42] Whereas about LeRoi Jones he states, 'He is an advocate of art as protest and propaganda, and he favors the cultivation of a "black" art which would reject white aesthetic values.'[43] He concludes by stating that 'Jones attacks both "Whitey" and "Uncle Tom" with equal vehemence, but the result is more often angry abuse than it is impassioned poetry.'[44]

Hayden was not, in one sense, using his position as editor to strike out against those same militants who had termed him an 'Uncle Tom', to 'return evil for evil', so much as he was accurately portraying the sentiments of those writers who were also caught up in the issue. But we can infer from the tone of these remarks the importance of this issue at work in Hayden's career. Certainly, the most often quoted passsage of Hayden's in the anthology is the closing statement in his own biography, a description which was used by almost every subsequent anthologizer of Hayden's work:

Hayden is interested in Negro history and folklore and has written poems using materials from these sources. Opposed to the chauvinistic and the doctrinaire, he sees no reason why a Negro poet should be limited to 'racial utterance' or to having his writing judged by standards different from those applied to the work of other poets.[45]

Another statement which Hayden used repeatedly to encapsulate his stand Julius Lester recalls in his memorial article: 'he maintained angrily that there was "no such thing as black literature. There's good literature, and there's bad. And that's all!"'[46]

Coming in the midst of racial turmoil, *Kaleidoscope* was praised by some because Hayden had chosen the poetry according to literary quality, not social issues: as the *Saturday Review* noted, 'Although some of the verse expresses the feelings of the authors speaking as Negroes, preponderantly the selections have been made on a purely literary basis.'[47] But in *Negro Digest* there appeared a review of *Kaleidoscope* which reacted in the strongest terms to the implications of Hayden's statements in the anthology. Written by Don L. Lee, one of the most vociferous spokesmen for the Black Aesthetic, the review described Hayden's statements as an apology for being a Negro. It noted the irony of his rejecting the notion of 'Negro poetry' while concocting an anthology for Negro poets. Lee most strongly objected to Hayden's characterizing of the militant writers as perceiving poetry as an 'ideological weapon', and he proceeded to explain that all of White American society is replete with ideological weapons aimed against Blacks:

Mr Hayden, what are television, radio, movies, newspapers and weekly news magazines if not ideological weapons – white ideology? Twenty-four hours a day at every conceivable level white concepts are inforced and re-inforced [sic] upon black people. What we do not need, Mr Hayden, is people like you telling us what we need.[48]

The review then degenerates into a tirade against the 'WASP' power structure and becomes a celebration of Black Power and an apologia for the Black Aesthetic:

First, Mr Cullen and Mr Hayden continue to perpetrate a very dangerous myth in that they presuppose that poets other than black poets or black critics, are qualified to judge black or 'negro' poetry. I believe that this is an absurdity to say the least; how can one who is not a part of our culture, a part of our immediate life, a part of us, judge us?[49]

Lee states that the Black poet writes about 'racial utterance' because racial identity is the most powerful thing he experiences. Lee then terms writing according to 'white' standards and 'white' critics as prostituting one's talent by 'imitating the works of others'.[50] He goes on to decry Hayden's inclusion of Phillis Wheatley 'in all her white nothingness', and of 'ex-colored man' James Weldon Johnson.

Lee does eventually make some literary observations in his lengthy diatribe, though he resumes the ideological battle with a defense of LeRoi Jones against Hayden's accusation that some of Jones' poetry devolves into propaganda:

This is to say that some of Jones' poetry is racist, etc, etc, etc. I find *that* statement racist, and that's going some for a negro. Jones' poetry is black, which is pro-black, pro-people, pro-living, i.e., pro-tomorrow. The editor feels that Jones' poetry is favored by the 'nonacademic' poets. Does that mean that he is favored by poets who don't read and have not been 'properly' educated?[51]

This, then, was the tenor of the debate as it was emerging, and in that same issue of *Negro Digest* was a series of interviews concerned with the Black Aesthetic. Among the writers interviewed was Hayden. The editor of the piece noted that Hayden had 'received a grant from the National Endowment for the Arts to seek out promising young writers to bring to the attention of the federal agency. His recommendations helped to secure grants for several young black poets and novelists.'[52] It then noted his stand on 'militant writers', stating that he does not fall 'neatly into the reactionary category where many of his critics would facilely place him'.[53] It quotes Hayden as saying that he could 'deplore Jones' *black nazism* but recognize his power as a writer'.[54]

After repeating some of his earlier statements about the Black Aesthetic as 'racist propaganda in a new guise', Hayden affirms in the interview:

Let us direct our work toward human beings. Let us deal with the truth of life as each of us is able to comprehend it and speak to the human condition . . . I want to see black writers concern themselves with truth, justice, freedom, as writers have always done (writers worth their salt, that is).[55]

For the next several years, hardly an anthology or discussion which included Hayden did not mention the controversy regarding his stand. In *Black American Literature* (1970) the biographical blurb on Hayden states, 'An admirer of the verbal dexterities of William Butler Yeats, Hayden has provoked reaction from some recent black critics by insisting that a black poet should not be restricted to racial utterance. Despite the rhetoric of the debate, Robert Hayden, sensitively aware of his heritage, often has recreated incidents from the black man's history . . .'[56] Similarly, the anthology *Black Writers of America*, which appeared two years later, states:

His position, restated forcefully in *Kaleidoscope*, is that no poet, Black or White, should be restricted to racial themes and that any effort to evaluate him as a Black poet is both racially chauvinistic and politically doctrinaire . . . Hayden's insistence that the poet must have this freedom enriches and deepens his poetry. By striving for a broader awareness of the human condition, he can arrive at a deeper understanding of the significance of the Black Experience.[57]

In 1970 Hayden's *Words in the Mourning Time* appeared with its poems about the deaths of Malcolm X and Martin Luther King, Jr., about racial violence and the war in Vietnam. In it are also numerous allusions to the irony of using violence to achieve peace ('Killing people to save, to free them?/With napalm lighting routes to the future?'), concluding that we should strive for a world where man is 'man/permitted to be man'. The subsequent review of the book by Julius Lester in the *New York Times* was not only the first lengthy recognition of Hayden's work, it was also a substantial public vindication of Hayden's courageous stand by his former student. In the course of the touching review, Lester speaks of the trauma of the Fisk conference and then laments the fact that a Black writer is inevitably associated with a cause 'because whites only grant the right of individuality to whites':

A black is not an individual; he is the representative of a 'cause'. Unfortunately, blacks concur in this evaluation. They see each other as 'causes' and have little, if any, use for a black writer who does not concern himself with 'the cause'. Both races think the black writer is a priest, offering absolution to whites or leading blacks to the holy wars.[58]

Lester goes on to describe Hayden's stand in the turmoil of the 1960s, his demanding criteria for his art, and Lester's own painful process of coming to understand what Hayden as his teacher had meant by his stand against the Black Aesthetic:

Now, I know that his desire to be regarded as nothing more or less than a poet was not a denial of his blackness but the only way he knew of saying that blackness was not big enough to contain him. He wanted to live in the universe.[59]

Lester concludes this astounding tribute to Hayden with one of the few comments to capture the importance of Hayden's stand and the courage he exhibited:

If we ever reach that time when man is permitted to be man, one of the reasons will be men and women like this poet, Robert Hayden, who, when pressed into the most terrifying corners of loneliness, refused to capitulate to those who, in the screaming agony of their own pain and loneliness, could do nothing but return evil for evil.[60]

Other reviews of *Words in the Mourning Time* also took note of Hayden's stand. The following month (March, 1971) Jerome Cushman in *Library Journal* noted that Hayden 'knows who he is – a man who is black, but also a poet who refuses to limit his concerns to his ethnic background'.[61] The month after that in the *Saturday Review*, Daniel Jaffe remarked that Hayden was 'more than a figure suitable for a cultural occasion' and that his 'best poems merit wide distribution and not only in collections intended to celebrate the achievements of blacks'.[62]

But the war was not over, especially in *Negro Digest*, which under the guidance of Hoyt Fuller had become *Black World* in 1970. In a 1972 review of Hayden's high school literature text *Afro-American Literature: An Introduction*, Carolyn Gerald objects to Hayden's treatment of 'art-for-art's sake vs. art-for-people's sake' and 'topicality vs. universality'.[63] But while she questions the editorial presentation of the issue of whether or not there really is a 'black literature', she generally praises the book and presents her case with reason and legitimate concern.

In a 1974 study of Afro-American Writers, *From the Dark Tower*, Arthur Davis also pays careful attention to Hayden's stand. After citing Hayden's statements about the poet's goals, he notes that 'unlike Gwendolyn Brooks and others of his generation, Hayden did not adopt the militant, nationalist, anti-Western-tradition stance of contemporary Black Arts writers':

On the contrary, he has tried in every way to make even his so-called Negro poetry conform to and measure up to the best that Western civilization has produced. A superb craftsman, and a perfectionist, Hayden has consistently written for a 'fit audience, though few'.[64]

In that same year, Hayden's *The Night-Blooming Cereus* appeared, and, as with his other work, it was reviewed by *Black World*, this time by Angela Jackson. One of about three negative reviews of Hayden's poetry during his lifetime, this brief reaction to this pivotal work (containing as it does two of his most powerful pieces 'The Peacock Room' and 'The Night-Blooming Cereus') is clearly geared to the work's lack of a racial point of view: 'Most of these poems are more practiced memory of deliberate dream than memory hung in the center of life; never at the center of Black activity in this world; it dwells along the periphery, coreless.'[65] Her only positive comment regards Hayden's '"Dance the Orange"', because she can relate this piece to the Black experience – 'I keep thinking of a silhouette of a spiny and muscular African ballet or boogaloo. Maybe Hayden has some other folk dances in mind?'[66] The facetious tone of this remark provides a key to her overall conclusion that the work is 'intellectually circumscribed' and 'artificial' because it contains no apparent or easily accessible emotional content, at least not in terms of explicitly Afro-American experience.

By 1975 the issue was toning down somewhat, both in the public forum and among Black writers. But for Hayden the matter was not finished. In 1976, when Hayden was serving at his post as Consultant to the Library of Congress, Onwuchekwa Jemie published *Langston Hughes: An Introduction to the Poetry*, one of the Columbia University Press Introductions to Twentieth-Century American Poetry. The work, which traces the career and philosophy of Hughes, stressing his influence in the emergence of a Black Aesthetic, continues the rhetoric begun ten years before and lashes out against Hayden's failure to use 'black style and language' in enough of his poems.

After praising 'Middle Passage' and 'Runagate Runagate', Jemie states that Hayden's 'other poems of the black experience are written in standard academic English with no black flavor'.[67] After this implicit indictment of Hayden, Jemie goes on to say that 'the problem of language' is not so important as Hayden's 'overall problem of sensibility and viewpoint', explaining that Hayden 'repeatedly affirms the Bahá'í faith to which he belongs' but 'denigrates Afro-American religions'.[68] Jemie, who clearly had not read Hayden's poems with care, then gives as example of this 'denigration' poems such as 'Witch Doctor' (a generalized portrait of a religious charlatan), 'Idol' (which celebrates the once vital Aztec religion, not the African culture) and 'A Ballad of Remembrance' (which Jemie sees as a travesty of 'gorgeous parades and masquerades' followed by an ironic rescue by 'the Great White Father'). He concludes this caustic condemnation of Hayden's life's work with a rhetorical flourish strangely alien to a serious literary study: 'For Hayden, black tradition at its most mystical and profound is horror and chaos; white tradition is 'humanism'. What irony! Phillis Wheatley could perhaps be excused on account of her epoch and milieu but Robert Hayden . . . ?'[69]

It would not be worth while to point out the slanting of this critical estimation of Hayden's poetry – its circumvention of logic is fairly obvious (for example, Jemie indicts Hayden's allegiance to the Bahá'í Faith because it is a 'White' religion). Clearly the assessment, like Jackson's review, is motivated by visceral rage at Hayden's public stand against the Black Aesthetic. Thus, even in his last decade of triumphs, the controversy beclouded the critical estimation of his work. The furor, the pitch of it, had subsided, but the issue was still alive, still haunted and hurt him.

In 1976, after Hayden's work finally received public attention through the publication of *Angle of Ascent* and his appointment as Consultant in Poetry to the Library of Congress, Michael Harper, himself a noted Black poet and victim of similar assaults, stated in his review of Hayden's poetry in the *New York Times*:

Having committed himself to the improvement of language, he has sometimes been falsely accused of timidity of commitment to the black struggle because of his refusal to 'politicize' his work for expedient and transient goals. But it is Hayden's poetry that best captures the Afro-American tradition of the black hero . . .'[70]

Harper goes on to dub Hayden the poet with 'perfect pitch', 'a symbolist poet struggling with historical fact'. Both epithets came to be often repeated in later assessments of Hayden as artist.

To outward seeming, Hayden had attained his own angle of ascent, had escaped the claws of embittered rhetoric, the pettiness and narrow perspectives of those too engrossed in their indignation to be objective about his art. But he was never really free from the inner seething this issue created, as any of his closest friends can confirm – he had for too long stored up too much pain and anger. But the reason these emotions were suppressed is important, and if one studies the interviews with Hayden, it is apparent. Robert Hayden was a man of dignity and bearing, by nature gentle, loving, disdainful of verbal abuse. He would unhesitatingly give his frank opinion of a poem or a poetic theory, but he would usually do it rationally, calmly, responding point for point instead of vindictively with *ad hominem* virulence.

For example, in an interview in January 1976, Hayden, now in the public eye, noted that 'pride in one's racial heritage should not imply separatism either in practice or in theory'.[71] He further stated, 'If I have a missionary zeal about anything, it is this. Technique is very important to me. I've not spent my life as a poet just to put words together in any old way.' In another interview in March 1976 Hayden said that the antagonism over the Black Aesthetic was dying down. He further said that those 'who are critical of my position simply haven't read the work. I've never tried to be anything but what I was.'[72] In still another interview, in September 1976, Hayden referred specifically to the misinterpretations of 'A Ballad of Remembrance', stating that when the controversy first began, he had tried to explain his work, but finally he realized that he had already done that in the poems themselves:

In the 1960s [Hayden said], when it was fashionable to be bitter, people would read 'Ballad' and I would try to explain. Then I got mad. If you read carefully – and I write carefully – you don't have to question me about anything.[73]

In almost every interview the issue would come up, or he would bring it up himself, but always without calling names, always as a point of philosophy and artistic principle, often, I feel, as a blow for freedom for other Black writers so that each artist might be considered as an individual, not as a spokesman for a cause. For example, in an article in 1978 in the *Nashville Tennesseean*, when Hayden was back at Fisk to receive an honorary doctorate, the whole focus of the interview was on this same issue. He was quoted as saying, 'We talk about black poetry and American poetry, when we should just talk about American poetry, or just poetry.' The irony of the fact that the article focused not on his poetry but on his race was enhanced by the article's caption 'Noted Black Poet Sees Race Relations Decline'. Perhaps Hayden sensed the reporter's preoccupation with the fact of his race; consequently, he downplayed his persecution at the hands of the militants: 'I wasn't as bitterly attacked as I might have been because there were people who realized that some of the schemes being talked about had formed the basis of my poetry – that I had used Afro-American history, and had a feeling for the struggle':

Hayden said he believes another reason he was not bitterly attacked by black separatist poets is that, 'The fact I am a Bahá'í and believe in the oneness of mankind became known in the 60s.

'My philosophy, then as now, was that the struggle had to be a human struggle, with blacks and whites cooperating to remove evils as human beings rather than doing it separately as races.'[74]

The issue was not finally resolved until the last day of Hayden's life. He had wanted so desperately to attend the tribute to him by the Center for Afro-American Studies, and anyone close to him, aware of the controversy that had plagued him, could understand why. It signaled that at last what he had said so often, what he had written out in 1948, shouted out at the Fisk conference, and repeated throughout his career was finally being understood, that while he was a Black man and a poetic chronicler of Black history, an eloquent 'dark singer' for justice and human dignity, he was a human being first who refused to be delimited, diminished or enslaved by labels of any sort.

Sixteen years before Hayden's death, Amiri Baraka (LeRoi Jones) had said that Hayden's poetry needed 'a fuller audience'.[75] Sixteen years later in a memorial piece in *Black World*, Haki Madhubuti (Don Lee), perhaps Hayden's most inveterate adversary, also paid tribute to the deceased poet. In magnanimity and in recognition of Hayden's undeniable talent, Madhubuti acknowledges that in spite of their differences he respected both the man and his work:

. . . Robert Hayden is the one with whom I had, in a private and very personal way, the greatest philosophical and ideological differences. However, our differences did not affect my deep respect for the man and his work. In February of this year we, quite unexpectedly, lost Robert Hayden due to an 'apparent heart attack'. Now, at his 'final' calling, our differences don't really seem to matter that much. What does matter is that we have lost a great Afro-American poet (I purposely do not use Black because he didn't view himself as a Black poet, or possibly, even as an Afro-American one).[76]

Madhubuti praises Hayden as a bringer of life, as an unselfish teacher whose 'need to share knowledge with the young was like air and water to him', as a contributor to 'the development of a higher knowledge base among his people'. He concludes by stating, 'His unique presence as well as the towering shadow we all felt of Robert Hayden will be missed; and as only he can say it, '"Mean mean mean to be free."'

Part III

THE CONTINUITY OF HAYDEN'S POETRY I

It has been wisely said that a poet does not choose his subject; his subject chooses him, and I have been fortunate in that some rather important subjects have chosen me.[1]

Robert Hayden, 1976 interview

In an assessment of Hayden's life and career in Scribner's *American Writers* series, Robert Greenberg states: 'Chronological development is not the soundest basis on which to discuss Hayden's work. There is neither the set of philosophical preoccupations nor the persistent subject matter to warrant serial study.'[2] While Greenberg's contention is understandable in light of the numerous problems confronting anyone wishing to pursue such a study, the continuity of Hayden's work makes a chronological analysis both warranted and extremely rewarding.

The most obvious obstacle to a serial study is lack of access to the ten volumes of poetry in the Hayden canon. Presently, only two are currently in print, *Angle of Ascent* (Liveright, 1975) and *American Journal* (Liveright, 1982). Fortunately, these two volumes contain most of Hayden's major poetry. In addition, the poems in these volumes are, for the most part, grouped according to their original appearance in earlier volumes, which were published privately in limited editions or else are long since out of print. However, the current availability of Hayden's poetry does not completely resolve the problem. Since Hayden made many revisions, both in individual poems and in the sequence of groups, one must be carefully guided through these volumes.

But even assuming that one were able to have access to these early volumes, another more crucial problem would await – understanding how Hayden painstakingly orchestrated each volume with regard to theme and then attempting to discover the continuity among the separate volumes. Both Dennis Gendron and Pontheolla Williams have in their respective dissertations attempted a serial study of major portions of Hayden's work, and Gendron in particular has established substantial foundations for seeing in Hayden's volumes a continuity of certain developing themes.[3] Furthermore, a number of more recent studies have analyzed Hayden's poetry with regard to recurring images which suggest some of the major groups of symbols in Hayden's poetry.[4] And yet no one has yet surveyed the progress of Hayden's themes throughout the entirety of these ten volumes to understand the underlying progress and unity which renders these separate works parts of one *magnum opus* whose structure and meaning takes its overall significance from Hayden's beliefs as a Bahá'í.

Part of this continuity among Hayden's works is due to conscious arrangement by the artist as he developed his ideas and techniques. In another sense, this continuity is due to the fact that there were few gaps in Hayden's work so that the sequence of publications reflects the evolution in Hayden's own thinking, which, while not precisely linear in its development, does evince, by Hayden's own admission, a coming to terms with the major issues that for a lifetime pursued him – questions of identity, the function of the artist, the purpose of physical reality and the hope for mankind. This is not to say that by the end of his life Hayden had carefully resolved all the paradoxes and enigmatic questions that he compasses in his verse, but it does imply an ever more expansive treatment of the questions themselves as they became illuminated to him, largely through his study of the Bahá'í Writings.

Some of the poems in one volume may reappear in succeeding works, but there is after the publication of *Heart-Shape in the Dust* in 1940 a steady and consistent output over the next forty years of Hayden's matured style that reads very much like a chronicle of search, Hayden's own *American Journal.*

Hayden produced a new volume approximately every four years, with each volume containing an average of fifteen new poems:

		Title	New Poems	Total Poems
1.	1940	*Heart-Shape in the Dust*	43	43
2.	1948	*The Lion and the Archer*	6	6
3.	1955	*Figure of Time*	14	14
4.	1962	*A Ballad of Remembrance*	22	36
5.	1966	*Selected Poems*	14	41
6.	1970	*Words in the Mourning Time*	16	20
7.	1973	*The Night-Blooming Cereus*	8	8
8.	1975	*Angle of Ascent*	8	73
9.	1978	*American Journal*	13	13
10.	1982	*American Journal*	10	23

The course of Hayden's life over this forty-year period was hardly staid or static, but he did not radically alter his primary beliefs or his essential goals. Unlike what we have come to consider the traditional erratic life of a poet, Hayden remained married to the same woman, conscientious in his duties as a teacher, and faithful to his religious convictions as a Bahá'í. He never altered his aspiration of becoming the best poet he could be. He may not have considered himself more stable or wiser with the passing years, but his poetry does reflect in its themes and, most particularly, in the evolving character of the narrator/persona whose presence frequently guides us through these poems, a coherent and expanding consciousness that makes a serial study warranted and virtually essential to an effective assessment of the scope of Hayden's art.

10. *Heart-Shape in the Dust*
1940

It is time to repeat in descending darkness
The names of those who essayed mountains
and forded torrential waters toward new beliefs.[1]

Robert Hayden, 'What is Precious is Never to Forget'

A study of the continuity of Hayden's poetry might well ignore this first volume, which bears little resemblance to the poetics of anything Hayden wrote after 1940. The collection gathers the young poet's apprenticeship experiments, most of which were pointedly imitative of one or more poets or schools. Understandably Hayden did not like anthologists to use the poems from this volume, nor critics to give much attention to them in assessing his work. The difference in style is so remarkable that even the most casual reader has to look twice to be sure the poems after 1940 are by the same author. And yet the work should not be too easily ignored because in *Heart-Shape in the Dust* one can discern the themes, and even some of the stylistic features of Hayden's later verse.

As Arthur Davis has noted in his discussion of Hayden, one can understand the poet's desire not to have these early poems represent his mature style:

One can understand this reluctance because too many, though not all, of the pieces in *Heart-Shape in the Dust*, are simply dated; others are both dated and repetitious, echoing themes already used too often during the Renaissance years . . . More protest statement than poetry, it no longer pleases modern readers, partly because we are no longer moved by the subjects treated.[2]

But not all the poems in this volume are protest poems; not all are imitating the Harlem poets; and not all the reviews were negative. In *Opportunity* (1941) William Harrison said that Hayden had promise because he 'has something to say, and he knows how to say it'. He noted further:

There is a true marriage of form and content, a happy fusion of mastery of technique with the rough and raw material of life-experience. Among Negro poets only two challengers to Mr Hayden come readily to mind: Sterling Brown and Langston Hughes.[3]

James W. Ivy's review in *The Crisis* (1941) was less enthusiastic, stating that 'Mr Hayden has lyrical ability and his poems are readable though many of them are banal and lacking in real poetic fire'.[4]

Hayden's later view of the work would probably align with Ivy's assessment. He would later characterize the work as 'the usual kind of rhetoric',[5] poems typical of his 'socially conscious' period. As one interviewer remarked, social protest poetry in those years 'became as predictable and poetic as a bottle of beer'.[6]

Most generally the poems in *Heart-Shape* have three obvious failings that set them apart from Hayden's later style. First, the poems are arbitrary in sound effects. Frequently Hayden employed iambic metrics, and rhymed couplets, or else four-line stanzas with an *abab* rhyme. Sometimes the couplets are in the form of alternating rhyme which Hayden has broken into four lines, as in the first poem 'Autumnal':

> Pity the rose
> With death for root
> And bleeding boughs
> Bereft of fruit.
>
> (p. 9)

Second, while there is some use of symbol and imagery, most poems are very obvious and do not force the reader to employ much imagination or thought. This is not to say that the themes are trivial; as Gendron has pointed out in his discussion of the historical backgrounds to the poems, many are based on historical events or on the trying realities of the Depression, especially in the Detroit area.[7] But poetically, they do not require much of us. Thirdly, as Ivy noted, there is little 'real poetic fire'. Because the poet is writing formulaically, choosing subjects that the socially aware poet was supposed to select, using forms and themes that he borrowed from other poets, only a few poems seem deeply felt, though, interestingly, several of these relate importantly to Hayden's later work. This is not to say that Hayden was not personally concerned with the evils he decries or the unity of mankind he implores, but few of the poems themselves are capable of conveying well that feeling. Neither is there apparent logic to the arrangement of the forty-three poems, though the poems can be divided into three main groups – poems imitative of the English Romantics, poems imitative of the Harlem Renaissance modes and poems which reflect the proletariat concerns and anti-war protest.

In only about half the poems is there a clear racial identity to the speaker, and in only three does Hayden employ dialect. Virtually all the racially oriented poems are geared to the plight of the Depression. For example, there are no fewer than five poems which deal with lynching. Two are historically based: 'Gabriel', about the lynching in 1800 of Gabriel Prosser who had attempted a slave revolt in Virginia, and 'Coleman', about a Negro veteran who was lynched by the Black Legion. 'Religioso' employs what had become a traditional device of comparing a lynching to the crucifixion of Christ:

> By every black man burned
> > Upon the lynchers' tree,
> We know, Lord Christ, we know
> > Thine agony.
>
> > > (p. 40)

In 'We Are The Hunted' Hayden conveys fairly successfully panicked flight from 'lantern-eyed hounds' and 'hooded posse' in a rhythm which anticipates somewhat the sound effects of 'Runagate Runagate':

> We run, run, run.
>
> But more relentless than the savage pack,
> The hairy hands of the assassins,
> Our hearts' belief that somewhere just ahead
> We shall find shelter from the black pursuit
> And doors against the tangled, multi-dark.
>
> > (p. 46)

Finally, in 'Diana', a rather sensational exercise, the poet suggests the lynching of a 'black boy' who has come upon Diana bathing, the resulting encounter creating a symbol of the ironic notions of the purity of Southern womanhood and the perverted chivalry of 'southern mythology'. This motif of miscegenation is also handled with a different sort of irony in 'Southern Moonlight', which employs a White woman as speaker:

> That none may see—
> Oh, moon, moon, hide your light—
> That he is black
> And I
> > am white.   (p. 16)

Another thematic group of racially oriented poems portrays the Depression from the point of view of the disenfranchised Negro. Three of these use dialect: 'Shine, Mister?', 'Bacchanale', and 'Ole Jim Crow'. The first uses traditional blues phrasing to portray an unemployed auto-factory worker:

> Ford ain't hirin—
> Shine em up,
> Shine, mister?
> Briggs is firin.

> Man at Cadillac
> Said: Gwan back home.
> Went an played me a number
> But it wouldn't come.
>
> Asked for a shovel
> On a W.P.A.,
> Man said: Uncle Sam
> Ain't handin out today.
>
> (p. 42)

'Bacchanale' likewise portrays the despair of a worker whose 'Factory closed this mawnin', whose woman has left him, and who concludes that his only solace is in getting 'High's a Georgia pine' (p. 44). 'Ole Jim Crow' uses much the same persona to decry the speaker's frustration of dealing with 'Jim Crow', the systematic suppression of the Afro-American through segregation.

By far the best of Hayden's poems on the plight of the poverty-stricken community of Afro-Americans, however, avoids dialect and anticipates both the more detached point of view and fine imagery of his later verses on Paradise Valley. 'Sunflowers: Beaubien Street' depicts the Detroit ghetto and contains some hints of Hayden's later skill at phrasing, imagery, and symbol:

> The Negroes here, dark votaries of the sun,
> Have planted sunflowers round door and wall,
> Hot-smelling, vivid as an August noon.
> Thickets of yellow fire, they hold in thrall
> The cruel, sweet remembrance of Down Home.
>
> O sun-whirled, tropic tambourines
> That play sad juba songs in dooryard loam,
> Recalling chain-gang heat and shimmering pines;
> O sunward cry of dark ones mute within
> The crumbling shacks; bright image of their will
> To reach through prayer, through long belief the sun
> Fixed in the heavens like Ezekiel's Wheel.
>
> Here phonographs of poverty repeat
> An endless blues-chorale of torsioning despair—
> And yet these dark ones find mere living sweet
> And set this solid brightness on the bitter air.
>
> (p. 12)

Perhaps because Hayden is depicting here scenes he has experienced firsthand, this poem has a vitality, a credibility lacking in most of the other poems in the volume. Instead of speaking in dialect to evoke feeling, or depicting emotion too directly, Hayden recalls a specific setting with enough detail to empower our imaginations.

Two other racially slanted poems repeat traditional themes of the Harlem Renaissance. 'Poem for a Negro Dancer', clearly influenced by Hughes' 'For a Nude Negro Dancer' and McKay's 'Harlem Dancer', celebrates Black pride:

> You should live naked,
> Naked and proud,
> Where black skin is neither
> God's curse, nor a shroud.
>
> (p. 41)

'To a Young Negro Poet' employs a traditional Romantic mode of a disembodied voice – presumably a Muse or demi-god – exhorting the poet to his lofty purposes. In this case the 'dark singer' is called to chronicle the history of his people, to become the voice of 'Inarticulate millions', and to create a comforting song 'With hope and the new tomorrow in it'.

Similar to this poem in theme are four poems which demonstrate Hayden's early interest in history. The poems are not so much history poems themselves, however, as they are articulations of the significance of history in the survival and ascendancy of a people. Two of these are similar in statement and title: 'We Have Not Forgotten' and 'What is Precious is Never to Forget'. The first is a tribute to the Afro-American forebears who paved the way for future hope:

> These are the vital flesh and blood
> Of any strength we have; these are the soil
> From which our souls' strict meaning came—where grew
> The roots of all our dreams of freedom's wide
> And legendary spring.
>
> (p. 10)

Coming at the volume's beginning, this piece serves as a sort of preface to the commemoration of Black heroes, whereas the second poem, 'What is Precious is Never to Forget', is one of the last pieces in the volume and thus concludes this theme:

> It is time to call the children
> Into the evening quiet of the living-room
> And teach them the legends of their blood.
>
> It is time to repeat in descending darkness
> The names of those who essayed mountains
> And forded torrential waters toward new beliefs.
>
> This is the spirit's true armament,
> Heart's true program of defence—

> That we remember the traveled roads of our history,
> That in the stream of heroic yesterdays
> We find those spas which shall renew our strength.
>
> (p. 52)

'Dedication' is very similar to both in theme and tone, exhorting the poet, presumably the same 'dark singer' of 'To a Young Negro Poet', to celebrate the faces, the laughter and sorrow of his people:

> Love their faces, O poet, gather unto your heart
>   the living poems of their faces,
> Beautiful in laughter, beautiful in sorrow as wheatfields
>   bending with choric movements in the wind.
> Make radiant your song with the ancient and difficult
>   wisdom of their eyes.
>
> (p. 15)

Finally, 'Essay on Beauty', though also celebrating Black history, relates most strongly to another theme, the relationship of America as symbol of liberty to the condition of the Afro-American, and the irony that these victims of injustice fight for the same land which denies them freedom:

> Know, then, that all your beauty's passionate burning
> Is lusterless beside the blood-bright legends of
> My slave-bound people's valor in a murderous season.
>
> There is no more blood-burning loveliness to me
> Than slaves at Valley Forge fighting for liberty,
> Than Toussaint's freedom-dream, the Douglass memory.
>
> (p. 29)

Interestingly, then, these poems, which set forth the necessity of the 'dark singer' commemorating the heroic past of the Afro-American, importantly anticipate what Hayden himself would soon accomplish with his own history poems. It is as if the poet knows what he wants to do, but as yet does not have the skills to carry it off. Perhaps more accurately, he makes a mistake common among less mature poets of trying to convey a theme by writing in generalities rather than going from particular example or symbol to imply the overall thesis, as Hayden himself would later do with 'Frederick Douglass'.

There are other racially oriented poems which continue this notion of the relationship between America as symbol of freedom and the racism which stifles that freedom. In 'The Negro to America', for example, the speaker states:

> But, oh, my country,
> You are not free
> So long as there's
> A mortgage on
> My liberty.
>
> (p. 26)

This and similar 'proletariat' pieces are probably the weakest poems in the volume, though at the time they may have well been the most impassioned. But because they speak on the conceptual level rather than giving specific images, and because they are pointedly didactic, they appear strained and condescending, and the tone is that of a political rally, not a poem. The same tone is evident in 'Speech', in which Hayden portrays someone giving an oratorical/philosophical pronouncement that the same mentality which taunts the Blacks also taunts the Whites. This call for unity against hatemongers is also set forth in the final poem of the volume in a Whitmanesque 'mass chant' which for eight pages blends the voices of various Afro-Americans in 'These Are My People'. Written during the late thirties when Hayden gave readings of his work at labor union meetings 'and at other public demonstrations, thus earning the unofficial title of Detroit's "People's Poet",[8] this poem anticipates the technique of synthesis Hayden would employ in his more mature poems. Switching from first to third person, from hymnal to modern lyric, the poem has some fine images mixed in with the political rhetoric:

> It's spring, spring, spring
> down in the slums,
> spring that comes
> like a pale mulatto girl,
> thin,
> tubercular,
> wearing a dirty dress,
> singing a song of despair.
>
> (p. 57)

It concludes with the call for America to 'listen to my song', to march together, Black and White: 'Take my hand/ and march with me' (p. 63).

Another group of protest poetry in the volume is the anti-war verse, most of which is effectively devoid of racial overtones but which is no less delimited by the protest mode than are the poems about racial injustice. The most substantial of these is 'Words This Spring', a three-part poem that plays off an epigraph from a news article, stating, 'the war will really get under way with a big offensive in the spring':

> We have lost April from the mind,
> Thinking of hunger, death, and war;
> We read no comfort any more
> In spring's anthology, by woe struck blind.
>
> (p. 19)

'Poem in Time of War', is not nearly so effective; in its sweeping axioms, it is less a poem than a slogan:

> O poets, lovers, eager-lipped young men,
> Say with me now that life is worthy—O give
> It affirmation; bring largesse of living,
> Make urgent now the will to live.
>
> (p. 20)

Without any characters or places, the poem leaves our minds dangling with abstractions – 'life', 'affirmation', 'largesse of living'.

Besides the various poems on racial themes, or on the broader themes of war and unity, almost half the poems in the volume are imitative of the English Romantics in theme and poetics. In these there is no hint of racial identity, no causes. The poems are less didactic, but they are, for the most part, only a little less weak. Again the principal reason for the failure is Hayden's dwelling on generalities and trying to make the reader feel by describing the emotion rather than providing data by which feeling can be induced. For example, several poems take up the Keatsian notion of easeful death, as in 'Monody':

> Better the heart should yield and fall and sleep
> In unremembered earth where blowing grass is deep,
> And strive no more in battle dubious and hard
> Against a foe unworthy of the sword.
>
> (p. 33)

Who is the speaker? Where is he and why is he thus suicidal? Similar questions arise in 'This Grief', where the speaker talks of his depressive state with the determination that he will emerge victorious over it:

> This grief will perish,
> It will pass
> Like hail blown over
> Summer grass.
>
> (p. 34)

But we cannot feel the grief or exult in the speaker's determined transcendence because we are left totally ignorant of the circumstance. The poem 'Sonnet to E.', from which the title of the volume is taken, is a little fuller – the speaker is rescued from his attraction to death by his beloved (Erma in real life), but we are still left ignorant of why he is attracted to death:

Beloved, there have been starless times when I
Have longed to join the alien hosts of death,
Have named death father, friend, and victory
More sweet than any triumph of the breath.
In hours extreme with weeping and despair
That turned my valor's blunted sword to rust
And tore the pennons of my strength from air
To lie crumpled heart-shape in the dust —
Oh, in such hours death has seemed a kind
And balsam-handed lord . . . But not again,
By any gentle mask death has designed,
Shall I be fooled; I see his cunning plain,
Since love with generous wisdom tutors me
To see what hitherto I could not see.

(p. 31)

Despite the fine rendering of a Shakespearean sonnet, an extremely difficult form to use well, the poem still lacks definition and impact – we do not know what he 'hitherto could not see', why death's gentle guise is only a mask, and we must simply take the speaker's word that there has been catharsis because we are not given concrete detail to experience it for ourselves.

But among the lyric poems of the Romantic mode are also some of the best poems in the volume, two elegies about Hayden's foster father which anticipate similar elegiac pieces from his later volumes. The best of these is the brief poem 'Rosemary':

He never lived for us
Until he died;
We never knew him
Till he moved
Beyond the need
Of our too laggard knowing.

(p. 37)

The elliptical quality of this compressed verse is helped by the avoidance of set meter and rhyme scheme. Hayden also hints at his future skills in a brief quatrain that paints an impressionistic verbal picture with subtle grace in the poem 'Old Woman With Violets':

Quiet and alone she stands
Within the whirling market-place,
Holding the spring in winter hands
And April's shadow in her face.

(p. 54)

Likewise, in 'Leaves In The Wind', Hayden's feel for line and image is well foreshadowed in what may be the tightest poem in the volume:

> I shall want this rainy sound of leaves
> In the wind, this breath
> Of aerial song, when winter is unleashed upon us,
> And trees are filigrees of death.
>
> When snow lies heavily upon the bough,
> And the mad wind grieves,
> And wheels creak out the winter's whetted cold,
> I shall long to hear these leaves.

(p. 55)

This fine use of alliteration and assonance, similar in technique to the lyrics of Dylan Thomas, anticipates Hayden's future use of organic sound effects. Also, the less pretentious sentiment here, focusing on a specific emotion, gives the reader something more immediate to grasp, as well as the sensual data wherewith to support that emotion.

Most of the poems in *Heart-Shape in the Dust* are imitative, though the breadth of Hayden's sources implies a young poet who was continually experimenting, who was hardly dominated by interest in one poet or group of poets. The variety of styles and, more important, the consistent reliance on direct expression of abstraction and generalization, also demonstrate clearly a poet who is groping for his own voice. And at the same time, one finds in these experiments the concerns, the raw material which would form the basis for his later work. His Romantic poems, for example, may show his love of Keats, but they also show him looking for a technique which would allow the poet as persona, as character in his own poems, to use his own introspection to advantage. He would later utilize such modes in his intimate reflections on childhood and Paradise Valley. Similarly, in his call for a Negro poet, a 'dark singer' who can celebrate Afro-American heroes, one senses the apprentice poet longing to undertake that task, which indeed he did successfully accomplish almost immediately in the early 1940s with his *Black Spear* sequence that won him the Hopwood award in 1942. Even his most blatant protest poems indicting racism, war and economic injustice foreshadow the themes he would later pursue, because he never lost sight, especially after his conversion to the Bahá'í Faith, of his belief in the perfectibility of man and society.

Almost immediately, and seemingly mysteriously, his poetic voice would change and mature. He would synthesize and consolidate his gains and put aside imitation. He would arrive at a solid understanding of how a poem works. It is all here in this early collection in embryonic form, lurking behind the borrowed modes – his joy in language, his adept metrics and sense of line, the imaginative figurative image. *Heart-Shape in the Dust* anthologizes his beginnings, like a primeval soup into which the protean resources have been stirred, but as yet improperly blended. But to the careful eye, the voice is burgeoning, the dark singer about to unloose his song for the 'Inarticulate multitudes'.

11. *The Lion and the Archer*
1948

> With flourishing panache
> I bow to the applause
> and open danger's door
> while brasses breathe their Ahs
> and set the mood for courage
> that is lionlike; with a crack of my whip I enter the cage.[1]

Robert Hayden, 'The Lion'

There are a number of major observations to make about *The Lion and the Archer* as the next step in the evolution of Hayden's career. Even though eight years had passed since the publication of *Heart-Shape* and Hayden had undergone many personal and professional changes, each poem in this pamphlet is so markedly distinct from anything in *Heart-Shape* that the reader must marvel at the difference in style. It is clear from the prefatory flier which heralded the Counterpoise series that Hayden was well aware of this change and, further, that the theme of the poems themselves was intimately connected with his intent to accomplish something quite different from anything he had done previously. In this sense, *The Lion and the Archer* is Robert Hayden's declaration of independence and the establishment of his theory of poetics. As poems representative of his middle or 'baroque' period, this work is still not the finished Hayden style, though three of the six poems would appear later in the *Angle of Ascent* collection (1975). Whatever else can be noted about this milestone in Hayden's career, it must be said that this publication succinctly marks the beginning of his mature poetics.

A pamphlet of thirteen poems, six by Hayden, seven by Myron O'Higgins, this first number in the Counterpoise series was published privately by Hemphill Press in Nashville in 1948. In spite of limited distribution, the work was well received, and the impact of these poetic experiments is partially to be inferred from the lavish praise in Selden Rodman's review in the *New York Times*:

It is possible that this modest pamphlet, containing thirteen short poems by two young Negro poets, may come to be regarded as the entering wedge in the 'emancipation' of Negro poetry in America . . . The recent books by Margaret Walker and Gwendolyn Brooks were steps in the direction of independence from a limited minstrel quaintness, but they lacked the experimental vigor of these poems.[2]

The review seemed almost a reply to the daring challenge of the Counterpoise flier in which Hayden objected to 'special pleading', to having poetry by Black writers 'overpraised on the one hand by those with an axe to grind, or with a conscience to salve, to having it misinterpreted on the other hand by coterie editors, reviewers and anthologists who refuse us encouragement or critical guidance because we deal with realities we find it neither possible nor desirable to ignore'.[3] In short, Hayden was not only using these poems to demonstrate boldly his independence, he was also daring critical readers to assess his work by the same rigid standards by which all poetry was evaluated.

It is precisely this theme of the poet discovering his own voice that underlies the sequence of Hayden's poems and gives added impact to the individual pieces. The title, for example, takes its meaning from combining Hayden's astrological sign, the lion for Leo (August 4), with O'Higgins' sign, the archer for Sagittarius, but it also becomes a symbol in Hayden's last poem in the volume, 'The Lion', of the poet's psyche or subconscious. The poems in the volume thus delineate symbolically the poet's discovery of his own voice and the indirect process by which the poem implies its meaning. As a sequence, the six poems function as Hayden's *ars poetica*, a preface to all his subsequent work and a statement of his poetic principles.

Stylistically, the poems are not representative of Hayden's fully emerged poetics, though one must be careful not to make too much of these poems as examples of his 'baroque' or middle period. That is, while these poems are ornate, more lavish in imagery, more abstruse, more thickly painted than his later verse, he was during this same period writing other poems, such as the history pieces, which were hardly baroque. Furthermore, Hayden would use this style in some later pieces, such as 'Witch Doctor' and 'The Ballad of Nat Turner'.

In attempting to describe the distinction between the poems in *The Lion and the Archer* and his later work, Hayden stated:

I did go through a period in the forties that I call my Baroque period, a period in which my poems were rather heavily ornamented. But I shouldn't say ornamented, because ornamentation sort of connotes the idea that you don't really need it, you know, that it's something that you can do without. But I'll tell you, the kind of imagery and the kind of texture that I tried to create in my poems was different and was what I call Baroque. It was more involved, for one thing, and more heavily symbolic, I think, too.[4]

The general difference between these poems and Hayden's later work is that these have difficult, sometimes impenetrable surfaces, whereas the later poems are quite accessible on the literal level. Symbolism is at work in both periods, but in these baroque poems, once the surface is penetrated, the meaning is clear. In Hayden's later poems, understanding the surface action is only the beginning of grasping what the poems are really doing. Clearly the later work offers the reader more possibilities, vaster strata of meaning, even though these baroque poems at first seem the more complex of the two styles.

One major reason that these poems are so hard to approach is the language itself. Hayden's breadth of interests and reading provided him with a wealth of allusion and esoteric vocabulary, and in these early poems he flaunts his style with lush phrases: 'the sallow vendeuse/ of prepared tarnishes and jokes of nacre and ormolu'; 'somewhere the laths began to show from underneath/ torn hurdygurdy lithographs of dollfaced heaven'; 'the clawfoot sarabande, the knucklebone passacaglia'; 'Peacock's feather of a boy,/ piebald giraffe (obscurantist creature)'. He further employs exquisitely fashioned figurative images: in New Orleans the 'Tight streets' are 'unfolding to the eye/like fans of corrosion and elegiac lace'; a blues singer intones the song of a woman moaning for her lover 'in sixty-watt gloom'; after the war 'Europe hurts all over from the swastika's/ hexentanz'. In addition to word choice and imagery, the poems are thick with symbolism and a variety of devices all dealing in some way with this theme of the poet discovering his own voice and determining the courage it will require to use that tool effectively.

It hardly merits the effort to note the differences in style between these poems and the verse in *Heart-Shape* – there are few similarities to speak of. There is little if any hint of racial point of view, certainly none of the traditional devices of the Harlem poets, and none of the formulaic modes of the English Romantics. To a certain extent, the poems evidence a marked influence by Pound, Eliot and the whole New Critical orientation towards poetry, as we will see later, but these poems are hardly imitative of Poundian notation or Eliot's allusions except that they require somewhat the same sort of dedication on the reader's part. There is no set pattern of sound effects, no encumbering metrics, as one finds in *Heart-Shape*; nevertheless, the use of sound is truly remarkable as Hayden employs diverse rhythms and patterns of alliteration in coordination with the tone and mood of each poem.

The subjects of the poems, however, are extensions of concerns expressed in the *Heart-Shape* volume. For example, these six poems bestow identity on the 'dark singer', give him his charge and display him beginning to particularize the history and heroes of the Afro-American people. The result is an integration of form with artistic purpose so that while poems allude to the methods the poet must employ to carry out his awesome task, they also demonstrate this technique in action. To carry out this presentation of new poetics, Hayden has grouped the six poems into three pairs. Very simply, the first two poems deal with epiphany and change, the second pair presents two 'singers' and the third pair analyzes the internal mechanism of the poetic process.

The first pair begins with 'Magnolias in Snow' (p. 2), a landscape of clashing symbols. Literally the poem is a first-person description of a southern scene, trees covered in 'startling ornaments of snow, a baroque/ surprise'. Figuratively, the speaker explains that the snow symbolizes and recalls the North, which to him 'means home and friends I walked with under boughs/ of hemlock when the cold of winter/ was a carilloneur that played on china bells', and the Magnolias 'stand for South, as every copy-/reader knows'. The blending of these symbols calls to mind for the speaker the idea of progress or transformation: 'O South, how beautiful is change.' We presume that the speaker, in this case perhaps the poet having moved to Nashville, exhorts the South to become more open racially. But juxtaposed with the second poem 'A Ballad of Remembrance', the poem, more significantly, hints at the personal change that the speaker is about to undergo. On the one hand, the 'snow-shine upon magnolia leaves' reminds the speaker of the freedom he 'must forgo/ if I would safely walk beneath these trees'. And yet the dangerous external circumstances, like the streets of New Orleans in the second poem, are not ultimately so important as the possibilities of internal change which the clashing of these symbols represents.

'A Ballad of Remembrance' (p. 3; *AA*, p. 99) then depicts that epiphany, ushered in by the figure of Mark Van Doren in the poem, but really taking place within the speaker as the result of his agonizing over the issues for some time. On a literal level, the poem is set in New Orleans at *Mardi Gras* where the speaker, surrounded by the gaudy masquerades of festival, feels intensely the unsubtle racial tensions which pervade the atmosphere. The surrealistic images of the 'down-South arcane city with death/ in its jaws like gold teeth and archaic/ cusswords' evoke a mood of tension and warring voices vying for the speaker's allegiance.

The occasion which instigated the poem was a trip Hayden made in 1946 to read his poems at a War Bond rally on the same platform with the noted poet Mark Van Doren:

We wanted to have coffee together in one of the interesting restaurants in the French Quarter, but the segregation laws made it just about impossible for us to do so. We did manage, by a ruse, to have coffee together the following day, however, and then we spent a couple of hours walking around and talking about poetry.[5]

Thus the 'sallow vendeuse/ of prepared tarnishes and jokes of nacre and ormolu' is, we may presume, the waitress. The voices symbolizing the various responses to this injustice are the 'zulu king', who symbolizes accommodation, the 'Afro angels', who symbolize love, and the 'gunmetal priestess', who symbolizes hate and violent recompense:

> Accommodate, muttered the zulu king, throned
> like a copper toad in a glaucous poison jewel.
> Love, chimed the saints and the angels and the mermaids.
> Hate, shrieked the gunmetal priestess
> from her spiked bellcollar curved like a fleur-de-lys:

The voices are the speaker's own confused emotional responses to this bizarre array of pageantry and racism. As the internal struggle intensifies, it becomes a whirling dance 'now among/ metaphorical doors', doors of choice which Hayden had already confronted in his life and in his poems about how to respond to this injustice. But as the pitch of the poem is heightened, there is a sudden break in tone and mood with the arrival of Van Doren, who is 'meditative, ironic,/ richly human'. Though much ado was later made by critics because of the solace a white man provides, in the poetic context, the meaning is clear – in the midst of the 'hoodoo of that dance' and 'the switchblades of that air', Van Doren demonstrates his individual ability to transcend such matters and he thereby becomes 'shore where my heart/ rested, released'. It is not so much a rescue, then, as it is a poignant example for the speaker of human possibilities, an example that releases the speaker from his hate and his inner turmoil. He realizes profoundly that individual spiritual ascent can overcome 'the minotaurs of edict', and the poet can speak with his 'human voice again', not as a Negro or as the advocate of a cause, but simply as one artist to another.

That the poem also signifies importantly this dramatic shift in Hayden's poetic style is clear in a revision that Hayden later made, changing 'human voice' to 'my true voice'. In effect, the politicized voice of *Heart-Shape in the Dust* is not the poet's own voice, but imitations of other people's rhetoric. Now freed from the need to use his art in such a limiting way – to yield to the taunting of the 'zulu king', the 'Afro angels', or the 'gunmetal priestess' – the poet will discover his own voice.

The next two poems show this voice in action by displaying very specific images of poetic figures. The first, 'Homage to the Empress of the Blues', is a remarkable tribute to Bessie Smith, but, more important, a subtle analysis of what it is, exactly, that the blues singer does, as artist, as poetess, to communicate with and comfort her people. The poem begins objectively, with a third-person description of what empowers her songs:

> Because somewhere there was a man in a candystripe silk shirt
> gracile and dangerous as a jaguar and because some woman moaned
> for him in sixty-watt gloom and mourned him Faithless Love
> Twotiming Love Oh Love Oh Careless Aggravating Love;
>   She came out on the stage in yards of pearls, emerging like
>   a favorite scenic view, flashed her golden teeth, and sang.
>
>   (p. 5; *AA*, p. 104)

In the second section of the poem, which, like the first, is one whole sentence, two more subordinate clauses set up the rationale for her song, except that in the last line the objectivity disappears and the speaker includes himself as part of the audience:

> Because somewhere the laths began to show from underneath
> torn hurdygurdy lithographs of dollfaced heaven,
> because there were those who feared alaruming fists of snow upon
> the door and those who feared the riot squad of statistics;
>   She came out on the stage in ostrich feathers, beaded satin,
>   and shone that smile on us and put the lights to shame and sang.

As in a number of poems from *Heart-Shape*, the poet here speaks of injustice and poverty, fear and sadness, but instead of dwelling on generalities, he creates for us a description of the relationship between the blues singer and the audience to whose emotions she gives sensual form in her songs. Some suffer love-loss; others sense the fragile underpinnings of their illusion of heavenly salvation begin to show and the stark reality of their daily lives begin to sunder their hopes. By the end of the poem, she sings the poet's grief and our own because we are in that audience with him.

In addition to the very effective image of this empathetic relationship between singer and audience, then, this poem, especially in the context of this sequence, portrays well the task of the artist to give concrete or sensual form to the abstract emotions, a process that Hayden can only allude to in *Heart-Shape*. It would not be sufficient, in other words, if the singer sang generalities – she gives dimension, specificity, and palpability to unspoken grief and fear, acts it out, gives it a name.

The second poem in this pair, '*Eine Kleine Nachtmusik*' (p. 6) portrays another sort of blues, and Hayden is the singer. Anton, a young student in war-torn Europe, studies by candlelight in the 'groaning after-silence' of war:

> Anton the student hunches in a cold-starred room and reads and hears
> the clawfoot sarabande, the knucklebone passacaglia coming close:

What exactly Anton reads we are not sure – perhaps an account of Europe's glorious past. But by the poem's ending Anton becomes a symbol of Europe's destruction and possible rebirth:

> Now as skin-and-bones Europe hurts all over from the swastika's
> hexentanz: oh think of Anton, Anton brittle, Anton crystalline;
> think what the winter moon, the leper beauty of a Gothic tale, must see:
> The ice-azure likeness of a young man reading, carved most craftily.

This ironic contrast between the sound of Mozart's serenade of the title and the 'siren cries that ran like mad and naked screaming women/ with hair ablaze all over Europe' parallels the contrast between the brittle young man and the rich culture so ostensibly obliterated.

If, as I contend, these two poems are examples of how the artist uses his voice to name the furies that dwell within all of us, then Hayden is attempting to do for Anton what Bessie Smith did for him, to make the fears less awesome by giving them definition. And if, as I further contend, Hayden's six poems are pointedly arranged to portray the birth of a poet, the last two poems summarize that process. Both, interestingly, are highly symbolic, almost visionary in tenor, and both rely on similar vehicles of circus motifs.

The first poem, 'Invisible Circus' (p. 8), concerns the relationship of audience to art, and in particular, the inferential process by which, as the poems in this pamphlet well illustrate, the reader must go from particular image to general induction. In this poem Hayden compares the poet, or the poet's imaginative faculty, to a 'Peacock's feather of a boy', who has a 'sprigged-with-sorrow joy'. This boy, whom I take to be the poet's own unconscious, is perched upon a 'piebald giraffe (obscurantist creature)'. The two are capable of showing us 'jingling marvels', but instead, 'pelting us with subtleties/ make us create our own/ comiques and flying devils'. Thus, just as the poet must infer from his own literal recollections of himself as child, and figuratively from the childlike images he retains, so we must infer from the poet's artifice the reality beyond the images, the 'invisible circus' of our imaginations.

> From their gemglitter stance we must infer
> the clocked and tilting frivols
> of Maximo the Merry
>   on his filament floor.

The poetic images, like memory in the poet's mind, are just what they appear, but they also imply a further symbolic meaning and are, therefore, 'a part/ of the living statuary/ of the three-ring heart'. If we are to recover the poet's meaning, we must use our imaginations to create within us the 'invisible circus' from the materials of the poet's craft – the characters, places and images he creates and pelts us with.

The final poem 'The Lion' focuses on the daring which the poet must have to follow the boy, or in the context of this poem's symbols, to enter the 'gilt and vermilion cage' and make the lion perform. Similar to Coleridge's 'Kubla Khan' in the symbolic division of poetic faculties, this poem distinguishes between the unconscious self, in its primitive anger and uncontrolled raw emotions, and the conscious artist who enters the cage of self to control and channel that raw emotion and insight into intelligible pattern and form. The end result of this courageous act is the ability of the 'archer' to control the beast through his will power:

> As he leaps through circles of fire,
> gold shadow of my will,
>   dire beauty that creates
> and tethers my desire,
>   my soul, the archer said,
> exults and Holy cries. And Holy cries, the archer said.
>
> (p. 10; *AA*, p. 64)

Interestingly, the poem begins with the archer having tried to kill the 'vernal beast', but since he did not have the heart, he caged the lion instead. This may well allude to the suicidal motif in several of the *Heart-Shape* poems, emotions which the poet's conscious mind can now control. In later revisions of the poem, Hayden would omit the reference about having tried to kill the lion. In addition, the archer becomes simply 'he', and the single lion becomes 'lions'. These changes clarify even more exactly the relationship among the central symbols – the speaker, the lions, the cage, the whip, and making the lion leap through fire. But in the revised version, published in 1970 a long time after Hayden's baroque period, the poet is more lenient and leaves less to speculation:

> And in the kingdom-cage
> as I make my lions leap,
>   through nimbus-fire leap,
> oh, as I see them leap—
>   unsparing beauty that
> creates and serves my will,
>   the savage real that clues
> my vision of the real—
>   my soul exults and Holy cries
> and Holy Holy cries, he said.
>
> (*WMT*, p. 56)

The whip is gone, but the will, which the whip symbolizes, is not. Thus there is still a tripartite division between the raw emotion (what Coleridge refers to as the 'primary imagination'), the artistic faculty which is capable of shaping that raw vision into artistic form (Coleridge's secondary imagination) and the will or volition which empowers the speaker to 'open danger's door/ while brasses breathe their Ahs/ and set the mood for courage/ that is lion-like'.

This poetic rendering of Hayden's artistic theory neatly concludes the six-poem sequence, and when coupled with the Counterpoise manifesto, this brief volume becomes the logical beginning point for Hayden's new stylistics, even though he never relinquishes the essential themes he sets forth in the

Heart-Shape volume. The difficulty of these poems is due to the baroque surfaces, and somewhat to the fact that Hayden's art was still evolving. His basic theory would ever remain the same – he would rely on symbols and other figurative devices, and he would always require much of his readers.

12. *Figure of Time*
1955

He is a scythe in daylight's clutch. Is gnomon.
Is metaphor of a place, a time. Is our
time geometrized.[1]

Robert Hayden, 'Figure'

No one has given *Figure of Time* its due, in part because it had meager distribution as the third in the Counterpoise series, and mostly, I suspect, because all but one of the twelve poems reappear seven years later as the first two sections of *A Ballad of Remembrance*. But even though the heavy teaching load at Fisk took its toll, Hayden was not only carefully at work on the history poems and Mexico poems which would constitute the third and fourth parts of *A Ballad of Remembrance*, he also constructed this brief volume with utmost care and artistry. Therefore, even though the poems are incorporated into the structure of his next collection, they have in *Figure of Time* a coherence and structure that give this collection integrity and make it follow logically from the poetic principles he has established in *The Lion and the Archer*. If for no other reason, it is well worth considering this volume separately because it is the first of his collections in which he includes poems that make explicit allusions to the Bahá'í Faith. Furthermore, Hayden used these allusions to Bahá'u'lláh as the climax to the sequence and the resolution of the central problems which the sequence introduces.

Figure of Time attracted little critical notice, in spite of the auspicious beginnings which the *New York Times* review of *The Lion and the Archer* had seemed to presage. The title, taken from the poem 'Figure', a stark, photographic portrait of a lynched Black man as our 'time geometrized', does indeed imply that our age is one of violence and injustice. The title is also a *double entendre*, however, referring not only to the literal figure of the lynched man as symbol of our age, but also to the various figurative images (figures) throughout the sequence which are emblematic of this time.

In general, the sequence presents a collection of settings and characters to connote various times in history, though all poignantly relate to our modern heritage from past times, as well as to our future hopes. In this sense, each character, each setting, becomes a symbol or correlative for a period or an attribute, and as with *The Lion and the Archer*, there is in the arrangement of the sequence a clear indication that Hayden has carefully grouped the poems to present this theme. This technique of orchestrating his poems Hayden discovered early and consistently maintained: 'I discovered that there is a certain design or pattern that manifests itself when I begin to put it altogether, and I try to arrange the poems and put the book together so there is some sense of that pattern.'[2]

In *Figure of Time* there unfolds a natural grouping of four sections. The first three poems depict settings; the next four poems present symbolic or representative characters; the next two poems conclude these figures of our time with a reference to the figure of Bahá'u'lláh; and in the final three poems Hayden returns to mundane images of time, concluding with Lear as a figure of human transcendence.

Individually, the poems are varied in form, tone and point of view – some are objectively narrated portraiture; others are impassioned first-person accounts. For the most part, the literal or surface meaning is much more accessible than with the poems in *The Lion and the Archer*, the style more lapidarian and the developing Hayden proclivity for the ballad tradition, the elliptically told story, more apparent. But there is still evidence of his baroque phrasing, as evidenced in such lush and exotic word-choice as *curveted, jactations, palimpsests, sachems, avuncular, agenbite, brummagems, gelid, cloacal, flounces.*

The continuity of Hayden's work is thus apparent both in the progress of his style and in the succession of theme. *The Lion and the Archer* sets forth the poet's special voice, but *Figure of Time* shows that poetic skill being applied with daring. More significantly, the volume takes the premise implied in *The Lion and the Archer* – that the poet's job is to infer subtleties from the raw emotions he encounters – and uses that technique to portray in thickly applied strokes an impression of our age. It is not a random portrait, though it is precisely varied, because, whip in hand, the poet controls his lions, and thus finds in this gallery of figures the personage of Bahá'u'lláh giving meaning to the seemingly pointless procession of time.

The three poems which initiate this powerful sequence seem intentionally random in selection – a city ghetto, a Southern estate, Coney Island – and yet each scene ingeniously evokes a people, a mentality, an era. The first poem, 'Summertime and the living . . .', immediately brings to mind his poem 'Sunflowers: Beaubien Street', first because it begins with the flower as symbol of these 'dark votaries of the sun' who populate the ghettos and, like the hardy flower, thrive there:

> Nobody planted roses, he recalls,
> but sunflowers gangled there
> sometimes, tough-stalked and bold
> and like the vivid children there unplanned.
>
> (p. 2; *AA*, p. 111)

The summer setting also recalls in Hayden's archival notes his statement that 'It is always summer when he thinks of his life on Beacon Street. The grownups sit on the front porch, taking their ease after the demands and vexations of the day':[3]

> But summer was,
> they said, the poor folks' time
> of year. And he remembers
> how they would sit on broken steps amid
>
> Jactations of the dusk, the dark, wafting
> hearsay with funeral-parlor fans
> or making evening solemn
> by their quietness.
>
> (p. 2)

One of Hayden's finest depictions of this bygone era, this poem conjures up a complete street scene and a more innocent age through his careful selection of detail – the 'wild street-preachers', the 'Elks parades'. It is not a lithesome recollection of happiness – there were 'no vacations for/ his elders so harshened after each unrelenting day/ That they were shouting-angry' (p. 2). But the poem ends with a symbol of hope for a people subjugated by poverty and racism:

> big splendiferous
>
> Jack Johnson in his limousine made all
> the ghetto bloom
> with fantasies
> of Ethiopia spreading gorgeous wings.
>
> (p. 3)

The final allusion to blooming is the blossoming of imaginations, pricked by the dreams that Garvey nurtured of the renaissance of a noble race in a rediscovered homeland in Africa.

Hayden would in several later poems return to scenes from this time and place, Paradise Valley in the 1920s. It becomes in his poetry a complex personal symbol of vitality and charm, of vibrant color and hyperbolic characters all blended with innocent aspirations and spirits harshened by poverty and disdain. Even here it is an ambiguous symbol, made all the more fascinating by

Hayden's third-person treatment of himself as a young boy in the scene, a narrative device he employed frequently with great effectiveness.

Where 'Summertime and the living . . .' recalls the past with mixed emotions, the second poem 'Locus' depicts a setting whose past is more directly evocative, associated as it is with a chronicle of evil and injustice. Here too Hayden has chosen precisely the correct details to bring about in the reader's mind the emotions suggested by a place, and here too the poet begins by noticing the flora and fauna which, by process of association, recall the past:

> Here redbuds like momentary trees
>   of an illusionist;
> here Cherokee rose, acacia and mimosa;
>   here magnolia, totemic flower
> whose redolence wreathes the legends of this place.
> Here violent metamorphosis
>   a look, a word, a gesture
> may engender, with every blossom fanged and deadly
>   and memorial sentinels,
> sabres drawn, storming fire-wood shacks,
> apartheid streets. Here raw-red earth and cotton-
>   fields like palimpsests
> new-scrawled with old embittering texts . . .
>
>   (p. 4; *AA*, p. 45)

The figurative comparison of the earth and fields to relic parchment documents of the past is an apt introduction to the recollected history suggested by this place – De Soto's 'death march' observed by wary Indian scouts, the plantation mansions, 'Symbol houses' which belie the 'brutal/ dream' that slavery upheld. The poem climaxes with the final ironic contrast between the beautiful setting and the sad reality – that inherited guilt and evil yet endure in the descendants of that history:

> Here the past, adored and unforgiven,
> its wrongs, denials, grievous loyalties
>   alive in hard averted eyes—
> the very structure of the bones; soul-scape;
>   terrain
> of warring shades whose guns are real.

The third poem 'from *The Coney Island Suite*' presents two settings charged with connotations – one a Times Square street scene, the other a Coney Island sideshow. In both scenes a third-person observation of a character provides implicit irony. In the street scene it is a prone figure, 'asleep or maybe drunk or merely/ Dead' (p. 6), and at the sideshow it is 'Unique

Original Jemima', an aging Black woman who, by virtue of her race, is equated with a 'Congress of Freaks' (p. 7). In both pieces the speaker is more than observer. Like the other passersby, he dares not 'risk/ the possibility of clues' when he notices the fallen man, and in the figure of the Negro 'mammy' he sees 'someone's notion of themselves/ and me', as part of 'this stale American joke' by which a Black woman and himself 'are made confederates of the snake-skinned man,/ the boy with elephant face' (p. 7). These two settings with their attendant 'figures' connote both place and time, but more importantly, coming forward in history, a mentality at least as dangerous and insidious as the catalogue of past injustices which the first two poems imply.

The second group contains four poems, each of which presents a representative character. The first of these in 'The Burly Fading One' is, like the scenes in 'Summertime and the living . . .', drawn from the poet's personal history, a picture of his Uncle Jed. Studying a fading photograph of Jed 'beside the engine/ holding a trainman's lantern in his hand', the speaker remembers the family legends of this 'Coal miner, stevedore and railroad man' (p. 8). In particular, the narrator/persona recalls how this 'man's man' died not 'in his own/ well-mastered bed' but, so the legend goes, swimming in the Johnstown flood

> To save the jolly girl
> his wife for months had hopelessly wished dead.
> (p. 8; *AA*, p. 105)

Like the ambivalent nostalgia for Paradise Valley, the speaker's 'wintered recollections' of the hearty figure recall an era strangely blended with human virtue and frailty:

> oh how he brawls and loves from Texas clear
> through Illinois, a Bible over his headlong
> heart and no liquor on his breath.

The second character who appears, in 'Incense of the Lucky Virgin',[4] is a mother, implicitly rural and Black, who in despair and poverty methodically commits infanticide rather than see her children 'hungry, daddyless' (p. 9). Like a folk version of the Medea myth, this taut ballad leaves the reader to speculate about her true motivation – whether she murders because she was deserted and not even special herbs or incantations can 'bring him home again', or because she cannot abide watching Garland, Cleola and Willie Mae starve before her eyes (' . . . won't be hungry any more,/ oh they'll never cry and hunger any more').

If the distraught mother figure indicts poverty, the next figure in this brief galley of characters, 'Perseus', more directly drawn from Greek myth, is a subtle portrait of the deluding effects of power. Perseus as first-person narrator confesses, as he recalls his decapitation of the dreadful Medusa, that even as he 'lifted up the head' he 'thirsted to destroy'. Alluding to his power to turn into stone all who looked on the dire trophy he hides in a special wallet, Perseus concludes in a sinister tone:

> none could have passed me then—
> no garland-bearing girl, no priest
> or staring boy—and lived.
>
> (p. 10; *AA*, p. 114)

This symbolic portrayal of the insidious results of using violence to destroy evil may have some reference to the rural Southern attitude about the racial problem as portrayed in the next poem 'Figure', but it also establishes the more generalized applicability of the symbol two poems later in the allusion to the Nazi holocaust.

'Figure' is a remarkably improved treatment of the lynching theme which Hayden had dealt with so often in *Heart-Shape*. Instead of an emotional outcry, however, the narrative voice is restrained and ironically muted in tone. From the dispassionate detail we infer the violence that has occurred – the roped wrists, the 'Stripes/ Of blood like tribal markings', the jeans 'torn at the groin', the body itself set angularly, motionless. In particular, the narrator dwells on the chain which suspends the body 'to the torture tree':

> And the chain, we observe the chain—
>
> The kind a farmer might have had use for or a man with
> a vicious dog. We have seen its like in hardware
> stores; it is cheap but strong
>
> And it serves and except for the doubled length of it lashing
> him to the torture tree, he would slump to his knees, in
> total subsidence fall.
>
> (p. 12)

The poet does not need to tell us the emotion he feels or what we should feel; he does not need to explain the inhumanity and injustice which produced such a travesty. From the masterfully chosen and arranged details the poet has selected, we infer the violence and the mentality that equates a human being with a 'vicious dog'. It is the same mentality which equates a large Black woman with sideshow oddities.

In one sense 'Figure' concludes the array of portraits, summarizes, it might seem, the depravity of our own age, and the next two poems in their allusions to the suffering of Bahá'u'lláh and the incipience of the Bahá'í Revelation give solace and meaning to these previous images. But inasmuch as the first part of 'In Light Half Nightmare and Half Vision' begins with a contemplation of the Nazi holocaust, the bloodshed in Johannesburg and Seoul, it is more logical that halfway through this poem is the conclusion to both of these first two groups of poems:

From the corpse woodpiles, from the ashes and staring pits
    of Buchenwald, Dachau they come—
O David, Hirschel, Eva, cops and robbers with
    me once, their faces are like yours—
from Johannesburg, from Seoul. Their struggles are all horizons,
    their deaths encircle me.

(p. 13; AA, p. 116)

The lynched man and the other images of evil build to a crescendo for the poet in this chronology of even more recent examples of human degradation and the decline of faith. He sees in the concentration camp victims the faces of his childhood playmates and in the racism of South Africa's apartheid and the violence of the Korean war evidence that the evils he has chronicled are neither finished nor peculiarly American.

Figuratively, the speaker is thus chased 'through target streets', attempting emotionally to escape 'what I cannot/ flee', the awareness of human failure. But as he runs, he comes to a cell, 'that cold cloacal dripping place', where suddenly his despair is stopped and his understanding enlightened. It is the Síyáh Chál, the black pit where Bahá'u'lláh 'lies chained in criminal darkness'. The year is 1852 and 'he, who is man beatified/ and Godly mystery', becomes aware that the time has arrived for His ministry to begin. The poem concludes with the very specific reference to the Bahá'í belief in Bahá'u'lláh as the Prophet for this age whose suffering and teaching will enlighten mankind and transform human society. And implicit is the speaker's sudden awareness, or comforting recollection as a Bahá'í, that all the horrors he has chronicled or encountered are but signs or figures of this time in which dramatic transformation will be ushered in:

> The anguish of those multitudes
> is in his eyes, his suffering transilluminates
> an era's suffering.

Clearly it would be impossible for the reader to understand this poem without the recovery of this allusion, or to understand the impact of the sequence without an awareness of the poet's perspective as a Bahá'í. Specifically, the reader necessarily must be aware that Bahá'ís believe Bahá'u'lláh to be the most recent in a succession of Prophets ordained by God to educate mankind through a progressive enlightenment regarding the spiritual principles that govern the affairs of men. Furthermore, the reader must understand basic similarities in the coming of these Figures – that while Each acknowledges the capacity of His teachings to transform mankind, Each readily submits to whatever persecution and rejection inevitably seem to be His lot. In this clear distinction between the sublimity of spiritual station and temporal power, Each thus undergoes hardship and suffering in order to bring His message to mankind.

But in the context of these poems, and even more so in later volumes, it is also essential that the reader know something of the Bahá'í perspective of history as a divine process which takes its meaning from the cycles of the successive dispensations of these Prophets. This concept of Progressive Revelation, somewhat similar to Yeats' notion of the gyre-like progression of history, is essential here because it not only implies that turmoil and injustice will subside; it also means, as the poem implies, that history is guiding man towards an enlightened stage of existence wherein such degraded events will not recur.

Even this early in the continuity of Hayden's poetry, the Bahá'í perspective is essential to anyone wishing to understand the relationship of particular symbols and individual poems to the thematic statement of the entire sequence. Without such insight even the careful student of Hayden's life and poetry is doomed not only to miss the most expansive inferences that these poems provide, but also, as several studies demonstrate, to misunderstand rather drastically what Hayden is describing on the literal level.[5] But lest the reader unwittingly become distracted from the crucial nature of this climax to the sequence, Hayden provides a footnote to explain who the prisoner is. More important, he presents in the next poem an even clearer statement of the Bahá'í perspective of Bahá'u'lláh as the consolation to sufferers and the lightbringer for the world.

In 'The Prophet' (which is entitled in later volumes 'Bahá'u'lláh in the Garden of Ridwan') Hayden portrays Bahá'u'lláh ten years later. It is 1863 in the Garden of Riḍván as Bahá'u'lláh is about to be exiled further from Persia, and He has arranged to meet with His followers to announce what most have already concluded – that He is the Promised Manifestation.[6] The setting of the poem is nighttime. The followers and family are asleep in their tents; figuratively, mankind is in a state of sleep or obliviousness to the impending Revelation and subsequent transformation. Bahá'u'lláh paces in the garden, watches and prays, while even the atoms and energies of the phenomenal world are bestirred in anticipation of the power about to be unleashed:

> Agonies confirm his hour
>   and swords like compass-needles turn
>   toward his vast heart.
> The midnight air is forested
>   with presences that shelter him
>   and sheltering sing
> the sunburst darkness which is God
>   and sing the word made flesh again
>   in him,
>   eternal exile whose return
>   epiphanies repeatedly
>   foretell.

He watches in a borrowed garden,
        prays. And sleepers toss upon
                their armored beds,
half-roused by golden knocking at
        the gates of consciousness. Energies
                like angels dance
glorias of recognition.
        Within the rock what undiscovered suns
                release their light.

                (p. 14; *AA*, p. 117)

Possibly the most purely religious lyric of all Hayden's poems, this crucial work plays a pivotal part here and in its later incorporation into his future volumes. Its power, however, is not due solely to its position in the sequence, but to the fine compression of Bahá'í understanding into succinct images and phrases. In short, the poem reveals a poet who is fully aware of his beliefs, who sees them as empowering and organizing his themes, and who is emphatically familiar with the Bahá'í Writings. For example, the reference to the swords as 'compass-needles' refers to the Bahá'í belief that historically, and ironically, the persecution of the Prophets by the followers of the previous religion has provided one sort of guidance to the identity of the Prophet. The setting itself is taken from a passage in the second volume of Nabíl's narrative:

'One night,' [Nabíl] continues, 'the ninth night of the waxing moon, I happened to be one of those who watched beside His blessed tent. As the hour of midnight approached, I saw Him issue from His tent, pass by the places where some of His companions were sleeping, and begin to pace up and down the moonlit, flower-bordered avenues of the garden. So loud was the singing of the nightingales on every side that only those who were near Him could hear distinctly His voice.'[7]

The allusion in the poem to the 'sleepers' and their 'armored beds' is taken more or less from the several references in *The Hidden Words* and other Tablets, wherein Bahá'u'lláh exhorts mankind to wake from the sleep of ignorance:

How long art thou to slumber on thy bed? Lift up thy head from slumber, for the Sun hath risen to the zenith, haply it may shine upon thee with the light of beauty.[8]

Many a dawn hath the breeze of My loving-kindness wafted over thee and found thee upon the bed of heedlessness fast asleep.[9]

Finally, the last allusion to the 'undiscovered suns' within the rock recalls the passage in Bahá'u'lláh's *The Seven Valleys* which quotes a Persian mystic poem as stating, 'Split the atom's heart, and lo!/ Within it thou wilt find a sun.'[10] It also recalls the statement by 'Abdu'l-Bahá in *Some Answered Questions* that the appearance of a Manifestation reinvigorates the world of being:

. . . the day of the appearance of the Holy Manifestations is the spiritual springtime; it is the divine splendor; it is the heavenly bounty, the breeze of life, the rising of the Sun of Reality. Spirits are quickened; hearts are refreshed and invigorated; souls become good; existence is set in motion; human realities are gladdened, and grow and develop in good qualities and perfections.[11]

Further explication here is not necessary; it is sufficient to note that the strategic placement of this poem, as well as its succinct and potent treatment of Bahá'í themes, illustrates the essential nature of the Bahá'í perspective to this early volume and the requisite awareness of those beliefs for anyone wishing to understand the ample possibilities of theme which this insight reveals.

The last three poems in the sequence come like the falling action in a dramatic plot – they coalesce and conclude the thematic observations, repeat the earlier motifs, and then end on a note of personal triumph. 'On the Maine Coast' (p. 15; *AA*, p. 102), a three-part description set on the Sebasco Estates, seems to allude to the process of the first group whereby history is associated with a place. In this case the setting evokes an *ubi sunt* questioning of who built these structures and paced this ground – what Indians and Puritans.[12] Now they are gone, and over the beach gulls are 'scouting and/ crying', oblivious to the 'dropped gull/splayed/ on sand', as modern man in this time is oblivious to the plight of his fellowman, whether in Times Square or in foreign lands.

In 'A Road in Kentucky' (p. 18; *AA*, p. 103), recalling the gallery of characters in the second group, the narrator draws from his family history another lively figure, this time his foster mother, Sue Ellen Westerfield. As the speaker studies the Kentucky road, he wonders if this is not the same path she had traveled 'to ease the lover whose life she broke', that woman, who in her pride could not forgo her racial identity to stay with Jim Barlow, could not abandon him to die alone.[13]

The volume ends aptly with '"Lear is Gay"', a brief but magnificent lyric image of man's ability to transcend frailty and old age. This final figure of time was inspired by Yeats' line in 'Lapis Lazuli' which says, 'They know that Hamlet and Lear are gay;/ Gaiety transfiguring all that dread.'[14] The figure of Lear in Hayden's poem connotes this 'transfiguring' gaiety, the same resolve and strength that Hayden witnessed in his friend and fellow artist Betsy Graves Reyneau, to whose memory he later dedicated the poem:

When I was writing this, I had in mind my wonderful old friend Betsy Graves Reyneau, who is dead now . . . Betsy was an artist and a gallant human being, in many ways years and years ahead of her time . . . She'd endured much physical suffering but had a rich and exciting life nonetheless.[15]

Hayden stated further that the poem thus becomes a symbol for all people who are old but undefeated, and also for himself:

That gaiety oh
that gaiety I love
has white hair
or thinner or none;
has limbs askew
often as not;
has dimmer sight.

Can manage, can,
in rags, fevers,
in decrepitude.
Is not silenced by
sweet pious rage
against time's
uncontrollable rages.

Can smile and oh
can laugh sometimes
at time
and all we fear from it,
as at a scarecrow
whose hobo shoulders
are a-twitch with crows.

(p. 19; *AA*, p. 70)

Like the resilient sunflowers with which the volume begins, Hayden ends
with this figure who symbolizes transcendence in a time of life, just as, implicitly, the Afro-American people whom the flowers represent exhibit resilience
during this time in their history. But the volume does not end here; Hayden
includes as closing inscription a poetic prayer which alludes to God's
revelation to man throughout history, concluding, 'Let now/ Your love oh
everywhere oh everywhere be our concern' (p. 20).

13. *A Ballad of Remembrance*
1962

There is, there is, he said, an imminence
that turns to curiosa all I know;
that changes light to rainbow darkness
wherein God waylays us and empowers.[1]

Robert Hayden, 'Theme and Variation'

The publication in April of 1962 of Hayden's *A Ballad of Remembrance* attracted little critical attention at the time, even though four years later it would win for him in Dakar the *Grand Prix de la Poésie* at the First World Festival of Negro Arts. Like his previous two volumes, this collection was exquisitely edited and printed, but it was published by Paul Breman in London in only three hundred copies, and Hayden's reputation remained underground. One cannot overemphasize the significance of this collection, however, for it assembles all the poetry Hayden had written from 1940 until 1962, including most of the poems from *The Lion and the Archer* and *Figure of Time*. In addition, the majority of the poems in this volume would become the heart of *Selected Poems* (1966), his first volume by a commercial press, and the concluding section to *Angle of Ascent* (1975), the most complete collection of his poems. But the most significant feature of *A Ballad of Remembrance* is that Hayden's careful arrangement of the poems into four groups advances further the themes he had established in his first two volumes.

In one sense the structure of the volume is simple – Hayden has divided the thirty-six poems into four categories of remembrance. The first two groups, comprised of poems from the previous two volumes, delineate a struggle towards faith and identity, as exhibited first in the external world or macrocosm and, in group two, in the private search of the persona. Group three consists of poems which probe in the Mexican culture outward symbols of a similar inward yearning for a lost or subverted identity as ritualized remembrances from an ancient heritage. The last group of poems on Afro-American history presents a chronology of a people bereft of identity and heritage struggling for transcendence, partially through remembrance but primarily through the ascent towards a new and broader definition of their humanity.

Ostensibly, the work assembles an array of characters, settings, themes all loosely related to the poet's collection of remembrances, personal and historical. In fact, one can discover in this sequence in seminal form most of the major concepts which Hayden would compass and expand in his later volumes – the idea of history as symbol, the relationship between physical and spiritual realities, the idea of a Divine plan empowering human progress, the relationship between faith and action, and various other complex philosophical and theological questions. But there is a continuity underlying the sequence of these four groups which gives a coherence to these disparate themes and enhances the potentialities of the individual pieces by allowing them to interact.

To a certain extent, Hayden has in the first two groups continued and expanded the structure he began in *Figure of Time*. That is, the first group of eleven poems begins with settings, primarily an array of Southern landscapes, and the second group contains some of the characters from his two previous works – 'Figure', 'Perseus', and 'Lear'. But mixed in with the settings of the first group are character pieces – 'Homage to the Empress of the Blues', 'The Burly Fading One . . .', and two new poems 'Witch Doctor' and 'Mourning Poem for the Queen of Sunday'. Likewise, in the second group he includes significant settings in 'Summertime and the Living . . .' and 'Eine Kleine Nachtmusik', as well as a series of brief conceits: 'Weeds', 'The Web' and 'The Anguish'. In short, Hayden has something more complex in mind than what he had done in *Figure of Time*.

The best explanation for these changes is implied in Hayden's shifting of 'Summertime and the Living . . .' to the second group together with two new lyrics that also depict with candor remembrances of the poet's childhood – 'The Whipping' and 'Those Winter Sundays'. The first group consists of settings and characters external to the persona, remembrances of a racial or cultural history, and the second group contains intimate revelations of the persona's private search through his personal history for understanding and, more importantly, for consolation. Both groups thus allude to places and people who represent, besides themselves, a history of grief and struggle, and both conclude with images of religion and religious figures as the implicit solution to the public and private search for meaning. In the first group religion fails in this regard; in the second, its success is imminent.

Group one begins with the title poem 'A Ballad of Remembrance' which serves well as preface to the whole volume as well as to the first group. One infers that while the second group of poems is most obviously personal, the poet/narrator is throughout the volume yearning for understanding and belief, both as an individualized Afro-American Bahá'í who finds reflections of himself everywhere he turns, whether in an alien culture or in the chronicles of his racial heritage, and as an Everyman figure who suffers the same fears that everyone endures and who struggles for the same faith that everyone longs for. Hayden has changed the climax to the poem so that now, after epiphany, he speaks 'with my true voice again'. Thus, the 'schizoid city' of New Orleans in the context of this volume represents not only the South, but also the present state of human society divided against itself in numerous ways. The poet's voice, suddenly detached from those divisions, speaks not as a contestant in these enmeshed quarrels, but as artist, one whose task it is to observe and report back to us in sensual forms how we are doing.

What follows in this group, and really throughout the volume, are the results of that poet's study, and if we peruse his findings carefully, we are the richer for that examination. In this first group, to begin with, we encounter a series of six settings, the first five in the South, the sixth 'On the Maine Coast'. In general, each setting connotes the history of a social evil, most frequently one derived from racial injustice. 'Locus', the second piece, observes that the 'brutal dream' which was the foundation of Southern plantation life still lives in the 'hard averted eyes' of those who have inherited that dream. 'Tour 5', not in his previous volumes, then portrays the Natchez Trace as viewed from an automobile. This historic trail from Nashville to Natchez, Mississippi, was an Indian trail, a military highway in the Civil War and a route for escaping slaves, 'the route of phantoms, highwaymen, of slaves and armies' (p. 9; *AA*, p. 101). And yet the past trauma and iniquity which have haunted the trail still live in the impoverished shacks that line its borders and, more ominously, in the demeanor of the gas station attendant, 'a rawboned man whose eyes revile us as/ the enemy, as menace to/ the shambling innocents who are the thankless/ guardians of his heritage'.

This same background awareness of the persona – that he is an Afro-American and therefore examining the external world with a special perspective – we also note in 'On Lookout Mountain', the next historically charged landscape he examines in this symbolic odyssey through the past. At the site of the historic battle in the war for his people's freedom, the first-person narrator observes with irony that not much has changed, that as the Sunday 'alpinists' search for souvenirs where the frenzied soldiers once grappled for foothold, the 'scions of that fighting' climb other 'hills of war' (in Korea), in yet another 'warfare of our peace' (p. 10; *AA*, p. 46).

Following the Lookout Mountain setting are 'A Road in Kentucky' and 'On the Coast of Maine', two other places that recall for the narrator past struggles or heroism. Then follows in the last five poems of the group a succession of portraits, beginning with Bessie Smith in 'Homage to the Empress of the Blues', Uncle Jed in 'The Burly Fading One . . .' and the distraught mother in 'Incense of the Lucky Virgin'. These figures, who connote a more recent history, represent, in the context of this group, various human responses to this inherited history – the blues singer is comforter; Uncle Jed conveys a sense of fallible vitality; and the mother is a figure of methodical despair. The group concludes with two more characters who represent ironic portraits of religion as traditional responses to this history of injustice and lost identity.

The first of these religious figures is 'Witch Doctor', a charismatic religious charlatan, based somewhat on the figure of Daddy Grace but primarily on the Prophet Jones.[2] Another of his 'baroque' poems, this lavish and critically acclaimed portrait depicts a manipulative egoist totally absorbed in sensuality and materialism. He rides in his limousine, dines alone, reposes 'on cushions of black leopard skin', smokes 'Egyptian cigarettes' as he drives through the park 'that burgeons now/ with spring and sailors' (p. 20; *AA*, p. 107). Hayden portrays in the fourth part of the poem the exorbitant performance of the preacher's artistry, his absolute control of the audience, and then he depicts his descent from the altar in terms reminiscent of Milton's portrait of Satan in *Paradise Lost*:

> He signals: tambourines begin, frenetic
> drumbeat and glissando. He dances from the altar,
> robes hissing, flaring, shimmering; down aisles
> where mantled guardsmen intercept wild hands
> that arduously strain to clutch his vestments,
> he dances, dances, ensorcelled and aloof,
> the fervid juba of God as lover, healer,
> conjurer. And of himself as God.
>
> (p. 22; *AA*, p. 109)

The serpentine imagery and the focus on the preacher's pride introduce another source of evil or injustice, the internal perversion of capacities, almost the antithesis of the blues singer – instead of comforting or empathizing with his fellowman, the preacher deludes and preys upon them.

The final poem in the group, 'Mourning Poem for the Queen of Sunday', is also ironic in its portrayal of an exquisite singer in the Sunday choir who gets gunned down, presumably the result of unreligious behavior: 'Oh Satan sweet-talked her/ and four bullets hushed her' (p. 23; *AA*, p. 110). Employing a toned-down dialect form blended with hymnal refrains, Hayden here narrates the story from the point of view of those perplexed churchgoers who are amazed that the Lord's 'fancy warbler' could 'end that way':

> Four holes in her heart. The gold works wrecked.
> But she looks so natural in her big bronze coffin
> among the Broken Hearts and Gates-Ajar,
> it's as if any moment she'd lift her head
> from its pillow of chill gardenias
> and turn this quiet into shouting Sunday
> and make folks forget what she did on Monday.

But the power of the lyric, and probably the reason Hayden placed it at this crucial point at the end of the first group, is found in the lines,

> Who's going to make old hardened sinner men tremble now
> and the righteous rock?
> Oh who and oh who will sing Jesus down
> to help with struggling and doing without and being colored
> all through blue Monday?

This final question with its image of Jesus descending, returning, God coming down in human form to assist man, sets up exactly the issue that will be reconciled in the second section. The first section ends with ironic portraits of religion, the one force that should be capable of guiding man towards identity and enlightenment; the second section leads the speaker towards consolation through a religious vision.

Like the first group, the second group begins with the recollected past, but this is a scene from the poet's personal history. Still, the objective is essentially the same – to assay the past to determine the origin of those forces and fears presently at work in his struggle toward identity and faith. This process is accomplished with four subsets of poems within the fourteen-poem group. The first three poems are taken from the speaker's childhood, the first of these being 'Summertime and the Living . . .' with its rich portrait of Paradise Valley as the birthplace of the poet's identity. The next two poems are impressions of Hayden's foster parents, touching and revealing glimpses of love curiously blended with anger and loneliness. 'The Whipping', for example, demonstrates at the end of the poem the poet's ability to understand that the mother is beating the child to purge herself, to avenge herself 'for lifelong hidings/ she has had to bear' (p.28; *AA*, p. 112), possibly a reference to her ill-fated love for Jim Barlow. But the powerfully negative impact of the whipping on the young boy is artfully conveyed by the sudden and unexpected shift in point of view halfway through the poem. The narrative begins in the third person – we watch with the speaker from a distance as the 'woman across the way' is 'whipping the boy again'. We hear her accusations, watch his frantic flight and vain pleading as she deftly corners him 'in spite of crippling fat'. In the third stanza these 'woundlike memories' force the poet from his objective point of view, and the narration shifts to first-person:

> my head gripped in bony vise
>   of knees, the writhing struggle
> to wrench free, the blows, the fear
>   worse than blows that cruel
> words could bring, the face that I
>   no longer knew or loved . . .
> Well, it is over now, it is over,
>   and the boy sobs in his room,

Of course it is not over; its lasting effect is still implied in the poet's emotional involvement in recounting the personal remembrance.

But if the speaker recalls the personal injustice, he also recalls the love implicit in the everyday acts of sacrifice and caring which the poet remembers in 'Those Winter Sundays', perhaps Hayden's most anthologized short lyric:

> Sundays too my father got up early
> and put his clothes on in the blueblack cold,
> then with cracked hands that ached
> from labor in the weekday weather made
> banked fires blaze. No one ever thanked him.
>
> I'd wake and hear the cold splintering, breaking,
> and smell the iron and velvet bloom of heat.
> When the rooms were warm, he'd call,
> and slowly I would rise and dress, fearing
>
> the chronic angers of that house, speaking
> indifferently to him, who'd driven out
> the cold and polished my
> good shoes as well. What did I know,
> what did I know of love's austere and lonely offices?
>
> (p. 29; *AA*, p. 113)

The simple acts of love do not erase the negative remembrances, but now at mid-life, assessing his progress through the years –as in the first group he has assessed his people's progress at mid-century – he can appreciate as a father himself the love in those thankless daily chores. If he finds in looking back some sources of turmoil and pain, he also discovers these examples of nobility, of a faith expressed in action, not words alone.

The next three poems which constitute the next part of this group seem incongruous following these intimate lyrics. Each is an impersonally described extended metaphor or symbol. But none is ostensibly related to the speaker's past. 'Weeds' indicts social solutions to injustice by illustrating that when 'the mowers came' to cut the 'invaders down', they 'did not/ spare the ailing flowers' (p. 30), a reference, once again, to the impoverished ghetto dwellers as sunflowers. 'The Web', also an analogy, uses the symbol of the spider's web to represent the internal mechanism of evil as 'a web more darkly intricate,/more fragile and the stronger for/its fragileness' (p. 31). Apparently an image of self-deception of the sort the Witch Doctor exhibits, the poem, though objectively told, can thus be seen as a private symbol. The same holds true for 'The Anguish', an ambiguous short lyric reminiscent in theme of some *Heart-Shape* poems, like 'This Grief', which portrays the speaker's self-defeating search for a place where 'one is always/deathfully alone' (p. 32).

After these succinct equations for negative human qualities, which perhaps betray the speaker's own self-evaluation, Hayden incorporates a series of six characters, four of whom are drawn from his two previous works. Similar to the portrait gallery in *Figure of Time*, these characters represent an array of human possibilities and seem to present the poet reaching outside his personal experience after his introspection. In doing so, he discovers various responses to injustice and change exhibited by these characters, some of whom are victims and others of whom are victimizers.

The first of these, 'The Wheel', establishes in fable form the whole notion of Progressive Revelation which the final poems about Bahá'u'lláh will affirm at the end of this group. In this poem the narrator is the functionary of a devious ruler, not unlike the Witch Doctor, who commands the persona to some sinister errand, presumably the persecution of the coming Manifestation:

> I rose to do his bidding as before.
> And so once more,
> the feckless errand bitterly accomplished,
> I crouch in the foulness of a ditch;
> like traitor, thief or murderer hide
> and curse the moon and fear the rising of the sun.
>
> (p. 33)

The title symbolizes the cyclical interpretation of history, and the persona represents those who, in every age when a Prophet appears, carry out the insidious commands of rulers who feel their power threatened by the coming change. The 'moon' and the 'sun' of the last line clearly refer to the often used symbols in the Bahá'í Writings of the religious luminaries and the Prophet himself; thus the speaker is stating that in his miserable state he hates all light, whether that reflected from the previous Prophet (the moon), or the incipient light of the coming Revelation (the sun).[3]

Besides initiating the gallery of portraits which will conclude with the Figure of Bahá'u'lláh, this poem, though not entirely successful, alludes once more to Hayden's beliefs as a Bahá'í. Specifically, it establishes the idea that those who persecute the Prophet, though they be incited by others, do so through free will. In this sense, the nameless ruler symbolizes the Satanic forces latent in everyone, and the speaker's hatred or dread of light establishes the symbol of light and darkness which Hayden will use repeatedly in his later work.

Following 'The Wheel' are the figures drawn from his previous two volumes – Anton who, like the poet, is struggling against a ghastly historical backdrop; the lynched man in 'Figure' symbolizing 'our/ time geometrized'; Perseus who, though intent on conquering evil, has become enamored of the power he has achieved; and Lear who symbolizes transcendence, whether for the poet/persona over his private history of grief or for Everyman, as represented by the poet/seeker, over the array of ills that plague mankind. The fifth character is perhaps the most significant of these figures. In 'Theme and Variation' Hayden introduces 'the stranger', an interesting sort of Platonic guide who reappears in several later poems. Delivering his brief discourse *de rerum natura*,[4] the stranger makes several observations about reality – that it is in a condition of constant change, that it is only a shadowy reflection of a 'changing permanence', and that empowering this whole system is 'an imminence' 'that changes light to rainbow darkness/wherein God waylays us and empowers':

I

Fossil, fuchsia, mantis, man,
fire and water, earth and air—
all things alter even as I behold,
all things alter, the stranger said.

Alter, become a something more,
a something less. Are the revelling shadows
of a changing permanence. Are, are not
and same and other, the stranger said.

II

I sense, he said, the lurking rush, the sly
transience flickering at the edge of things.
I've spied from the corner of my eye
upon the striptease of reality.

There is, there is, he said, an imminence
that turns to curiosa all I know;
that changes light to rainbow darkness
wherein God waylays us and empowers.
(pp. 40–41; *AA*, p. 115)

As several studies of Hayden's work have observed, this crucial poem presents an essentially Platonic vision of reality. Constance Post attributes the idea to Heraclitus.[5] Dennis Gendron sees this as Hayden's own special synthesis of 'Greek mythology, Plato, Keats, Shelley and Yeats'.[6] Wilburn Williams, Jr., sees these themes in Hayden's poetry 'squarely in the American tradition emanating from Emerson',[7] the whole system of symbolic correspondences as delineated in Swedenborgian neo-Platonism. These and several other critical readers give lip service to the influence of the Bahá'í teachings in this pivotal theme, but since none seems to have extensive knowledge of the Bahá'í Writings, each misses the nature of that relationship, especially as this poem sets up the two poems on Bahá'u'lláh. For example, the notion in the poem of constant change 'Abdu'l-Bahá discusses in *Some Answered Questions* where he states that whether in the physical or the spiritual realm, all things are in motion: 'Know that nothing which exists remains in a state of repose – that is to say, all things are in motion. Everything is either growing or declining, all things are either coming from nonexistence into being, or going from existence into nonexistence.'[8]

Underlying Hayden's poetic reference to the doctrine of physical reality as a metaphorized spiritual reality are numerous passages by Bahá'u'lláh in which He affirms that all physical reality has the capacity to reflect the divine attributes and that this is their essential function without which the physical creation would cease to exist:

Know thou that every created thing is a sign of the revelation of God. Each, according to its capacity, is, and will ever remain, a token of the Almighty . . . So pervasive and general is this revelation that nothing whatsoever in the whole universe can be discovered that doth not reflect His splendor.[9]

The doctrine of God empowering man in 'rainbow darkness' Hayden explains in the two succeeding poems on Bahá'u'lláh, but it is important here to understand that it applies to both the macrocosm and microcosm. That is, the persona in his nightmare vision is chased and chastened by his private vision of horrors, lost identity and remembered fears and furies. Then he reaches the cell where Bahá'u'lláh Himself is imprisoned in 'rainbow darkness', wherein His ministry begins. In 'The Prophet' the world is also pictured figuratively as asleep in darkness, but about to be awakened and empowered.

The reason Hayden describes this process as changing 'light to rainbow darkness' is that light, as a repeatedly used symbol of truth and enlightenment, is when it comes from our own meager efforts, still darkness relative to the enlightenment with which the Prophet empowers us. In addition, this image conveys the sense of 'rainbow darkness' as a state of humility or, in the case of the persona in 'In Light Half Nightmare . . .', a desperation derived from his careful assessment of the condition of mankind. In this state of receptivity God guides us through the teachings and systems of the Manifestation, which are tailored to the special exigencies of this time in history. Thus, the 'rainbow darkness' of 'Theme and Variation' is the 'auroral darkness' of 'The Prophet'. This last poem in the second group depicts in magnificent imagery the stillness immediately prior to the dawning, a darkness in which the entire world senses the imminent change.

The last two groups in the volume are ostensibly separate and unrelated to what seems to be the completed sequence of the first two groups, a problem which Hayden's rearrangement of these groups helps resolve in *Selected Poems* (1966). But even in this volume a closer examination reveals an integral relationship.

Both of the last groups examine the condition of a people struggling for vitality and transcendence: group three examines the Mexican culture and group four the Afro-American culture. As in the first two groups, this outer reality is often filtered through the consciousness and psyche of the poet/persona. In Mexico he is an alien visitor, the 'Gringo' observing and evaluating curious rituals and traditions. In chronicling the history of the African people upon the American shores, the poet is sometimes objective, sometimes an impassioned commentator. In both groups the persona is involved, sees these struggles as reflecting his own, and sees the struggle of each individual culture as related to the emerging, from Hayden's Bahá'í perspective, of a larger collective identity of mankind as members of one integral organism, the planet itself: 'The earth is but one country, and mankind its citizens.'[10]

The seven poems which comprise the Mexico group begin as snapshots of settings, festivals, edifices, all of which become highly charged symbols that imply the curious blending of past with present, of life with death. Aptly titled 'An Inference of Mexico', these poems do not presume to provide objective analysis of the people and setting, but rather impressionistic reflections, remembrances by the poet/persona who observes this strange admixture of brilliant beauty with blighted poverty. The result is the suggestion of a rich heritage and the contemporary dramatization of a desperate longing for revitalization.

The first inference is derived from the curiously blended mixture of Christianity and tribal remembrances in 'Day of the Dead', a poem alluding to the Mexican All Souls Day celebration (*Dia de los Muertos*) in which villagers parade in gaudy masks of Mr Death, and children eat 'skulls of marzipan' (p. 46; *AA*, p. 89). Contrapuntal to the third-person descriptions of this pageantry is the taunting voice of an 'androgynous' young man who 'invites, awaits, obliquely smiles' as he offers the speaker 'pretty girls', while 'Tehuanas in rhythmic jewels of gold/bear pails of marigolds upon their heads/to the returning dead'.

Recalling the Keatsian fascination for death as a vitalizing transcendence, this poem anticipates the explicit references to the ancient human sacrifice in the description of the altar in the third poem 'Idol', in the grotesquely realistic statuary of 'El Cristo' and in the symbolic game of death in 'La Corrida'. Even in the other poems this motif is apparent. In the second poem 'Veracruz', for example, the speaker himself senses the appeal of death as he looks out across the tranquil expanse of sea, so beauteous and serene compared to the 'fly-blown' village. Sensing as well the transcendent reality which lies behind the 'striptease' of reality, the speaker is tempted to leap from the cliffs:

> Leap now
> and cease from error.
> Escape. Or shoreward turn,
> accepting all—
> the losses and farewells,

> the long warfare with self,
> with God.
> (p. 48; AA, p. 92)

Appropriately, the speaker at Veracruz ('the true cross') faces his own crucial decision – to turn shoreward and struggle with his faith and with the crass facade of reality, or to attempt to circumvent that arduous journey by escaping.

The speaker, like Hayden, chooses life and struggle, an act of faith itself, from a Bahá'í perspective. And yet, because religious belief from a Western viewpoint usually implies a blind and unquestioning inductive leap, students of Hayden's work often interpreted this grappling with belief to be a sign of wavering. Hayden himself stated to Gendron: '. . . I am struggling towards belief and faith all the time. I am struggling with my own inner devils all the time . . . But I am struggling, working towards being a believer.'[11] As 'Veracruz' implies, the poet's determination to acquire certitude by working through the inferential process of physical reality is, from a Bahá'í view, a solid example of faith as knowledge in action. As numerous passages in the Bahá'í Writings attest, the Bahá'í concept of belief and faith is that spiritualization is not a one-step process of affirmation, a condition which is either there or not; it is a gradual process of growth through 'warfare with self':

Men who suffer not, attain no perfection. The plant most pruned by the gardeners is that one which, when the summer comes, will have the most beautiful blossoms and the most abundant fruit.[12]

The mind and spirit of man advance when he is tried by suffering . . . Just as the plow furrows the earth deeply, purifying it of weeds and thistles, so suffering and tribulation free man from the petty affairs of this worldly life until he arrives at a state of complete detachment.[13]

At the end of 'Veracruz', after the speaker has made his crucial choice, he concludes with an assessment of reality that seems to repeat the same observations the 'stranger' has made – that for him and for these villagers reality is something quite 'out of reach', only hinted at by these archaic rites and psychedelic settings:

> Thus reality
>   bedizened in the warring colors
>   of a dream
> parades through these
>   arcades ornate with music and
>   the sea.
>
> Thus reality
>   become unbearably a dream

> beckons
> out of reach in flyblown streets
>   of lapsing rose and purple, dying
>   blue.
>
> Thus marimba'd night
>   and multifoliate sea become
>   phantasmal
> space, and there,
>   light-years away, one farewell image
>   burns and fades and burns.
>   (p. 49; *AA*, p. 92)

This enigmatic perception of a star burning (actually only the illusion of light since its apparent fires have long since passed) concludes the pained meditation of the speaker. In succeeding poems he will continue to discover the reality of this culture within the symbolic rites and pastimes, and of himself as a similar victim of a lost culture and history.

In 'Idol' (p. 50; *AA*, p. 93) we imagine with the speaker, as he visits the altar at Coatlicue, the ancient 'sirenscream' as the living heart was excised and burned in praise. We view in 'El Cristo' (p. 51) the 'dentured agony' of the icon to Christ which 'pleads the joy of suffering'. In '*Sub Specie Aeternitatis*' ('under the aspect of eternity') we visit the vacant convent in Tepotzlán where 'The curious/ may walk the cloister now,/ may enter portals barred/ to them no longer', where visitors may meditate 'on/ such gods as they possess,/ as they have lost':

> Hollow cells are desolate
> in their tranquility
>   as relic skulls.
>   Arched windows there
> look toward the firegreen mountain
> resonant with silence of
>   a conquered and
>   defiant god.   (p. 52; *AA*, p. 94)

This culture subverted by the invading White Spaniards is everywhere apparent to the poet's keen eyes. In 'Market' (p. 53; *AA*, p. 95) the 'Fire King's/ flashing mask of tin/ looks down with eyes/ of sunstruck glass' on the 'Ragged boys', the 'barefoot cripple' and other descendants of that once proud culture now begging *turistas* for alms. In 'La Corrida' the same descendants find in this sport a morality play, a 'transfiguring' remembrance of their ancient intimacy with death. The matador thus becomes their temporary savior, appeasing the 'conquered god' and revitalizing the people through human sacrifice:

iii: sol y sombra

From all we are yet cannot be
deliver, oh redeem us now.

Of all we know and do not wish
to know, oh purge us now.

Olé!

Upon the cross of horns
be crucified for us.

Die for us that death
may call us back to life.

Olé!

(p. 57; *AA*, p. 98)

This concluding section, alluding as it does to 'sun and shadow', portrays the unconscious longing of the Mexican people for a revitalization of their former nobility, and yet the past remembrance also recalls their conquering and diminution. Both of these realizations relate strongly to the speaker's awareness that his own remembrances both encourage and defeat him:

I seem always to be aware of the past within the present. And I know that in regard to my own life, I am often painfully conscious of how my experiences as a young person shaped – misshaped? – me, determined my present . . . In Mexico the impact of the past is everywhere dramatically apparent, and it accounts for some pretty startling contrasts.[14]

After his poetic speculation about the origin and present status of the Mexican people's anxiety and aspirations, Hayden concludes this section of remembrances with the attempt to examine the culture of his own people. He does this partially to determine, no doubt, the sources of lost identity and unconscious longings which he as Afro-American has unwittingly inherited, and partially to suggest the nobility of that cultural heritage. The similarities between the two displaced cultures may not at first be apparent, but both have been conquered, subverted by White Western colonialism. Of course, literally yanked out of his physical environment, the Afro-American has less recollection of his culture apparent in the artifacts and rituals of his daily life than has the Mexican. Therefore in these last four poems Hayden attempts to redeem that lost identity by recalling the transition from tribal warrior to slave, to Afro-American.

From this view the poems present a sequence of heroes. Cinquez, the captive African prince, leads the slaves to mutiny in 'Middle Passage'. In 'O Daedalus, Fly Away Home' a Georgia slave clings to his remembrances of

Africa and recalls a myth of his 'gran' who 'spread his arms and/ flew away home'. In 'The Ballad of Nat Turner' Hayden portrays the mystic leader of the 1831 slave revolt in Virginia. Finally, 'Frederick Douglass' is a tribute to the former slave who achieved education and dignity within his adoptive homeland by nobly espousing the cause of emancipation and full civil rights for freed men as well as for women. On a personal level these often celebrated poems parallel the same struggle toward identity which is evident in the personal life of the speaker in the first two groups. Figuratively these poems become a symbol of human progress towards an ever-more expansive understanding of the identity and purpose of humankind.

Hayden himself stated that his interest in Afro-American history began as a young poet with the forthright desire to render an accurate account:

I've always been interested in Afro-American history, and when I was a young poet, since I knew that our history had been misrepresented, I wanted to contribute toward an understanding of what our past had really been like. I set out to correct the misconceptions and to destroy some of the stereotypes and clichés which surround Negro history.[15]

So it is, for example, that the dramatic and powerful 'Middle Passage' is, first of all, a synthesis of historical voices recalling the inhuman cruelty of a people transported as chattel. And yet we must infer that violence from the civilized rhetoric of the court deposition:

> that there was hardly room 'tween-decks for half
> the sweltering cattle stowed spoon-fashion there;
> that some went mad of thirst and tore their flesh
> and sucked the blood.
>
> (p. 62; *AA*, p. 119)

We do not hear the voice of the African captives or their leader Cinquez; any indictment of the slavers comes from our own reaction to the powerful irony of the accusations of the slavers themselves, as is exemplified in the speech by the Spanish emissary from Havana:

> We find it paradoxical indeed
> that you whose wealth, whose tree of liberty
> are rooted in the labor of your slaves
> should suffer the august John Quincy Adams
> to speak with so much passion of the right
> of chattel slaves to kill their lawful masters
> and with his Roman rhetoric weave a hero's
> garland for Cinquez.
>
> (p. 66; *AA*, p. 123)

Assembled by Hayden from historical records, these speeches document the fabric of a society, ostensibly founded on principles of freedom and justice, actually interwoven with threads of racism and injustice:

> Shuttles in the rocking loom of history,
> the dark ships move, the dark ships move,
> their bright ironical names
> like jests of kindness on a murderer's mouth . . .
>
> (p. 64; AA, p. 121)

But just as the ancient identity and beliefs of the Mexican people reassert themselves, so these poems recount the 'timeless will' of a people to struggle for freedom and identity:

> the deep immortal human wish,
> the timeless will:
>
> Cinquez its deathless primaveral image,
> life that transfigures many lives.
>
> Voyage through death
> to life upon these shores.
> (p. 66; AA, p. 123)

The symbolic or figurative implications of 'Middle Passage' will be explained in more detail later, but it is important to note here that in addition to referring to the second leg of a three-part journey of a slave ship (from America to Africa, from Africa to a Caribbean or West Indies port, from there to America) this middle journey implies the middle or transitional stage in the progress of the speaker, of the Afro-American people, and ultimately of mankind upon the shores of physical reality and history. In a most general sense the middle passage thus reflects the sentiments of the Bahá'í burial ring inscription which states that we come from God and return to God.[16] The ascent from slavery symbolizes in broad terms the aspiration toward detachment and certitude for which the speaker longs in 'Veracruz', and which the sleepers anticipate in 'The Prophet'.

In 'O Daedalus, Fly Away Home' there are similar levels of meaning. The poem literally portrays a slave's nostalgia for his homeland. Symbolically Hayden's combining of Greek and African myth employs an image of flight, which becomes in several later poems a figurative expression of a spiritual condition. More specifically flight becomes in Hayden's poetry a symbol of spiritual transcendence and detachment. Significantly, this image of flight is here contemplated during the nighttime:

> Drifting night in the windy pines;
> night is a laughing, night is a longing.
> Pretty Malinda, come to me.

Night is a mourning juju man
weaving a wish and a weariness together
    to make two wings.

O fly away home fly away.
                    (p. 67; *AA*, p. 124)

'The Ballad of Nat Turner' as the third historical piece is a highly successful impressionistic attempt to probe the curious character of Turner who, according to Gendron, represents here depravity and insanity more than the mystic leader he perceived himself to be:

Thus, Hayden, through the character of Nat Turner, vivifies the awful effects of slavery on Negroes during a period of deepest despair [the realization that return to Africa was not possible]. Nat's insanity is the insanity of frustration, and his misreading of the Bible and of 'God's will' stands as an ironic comment with that of his white Christian masters.[17]

Hayden himself having used his research in the forties to compile the factual background for the poem stated that 'I came to see him as a gothic figure, as a rather frightening kind of vengeful mystic whose faith in the Old Testament God of battles was absolute'.[18] In any case, much like the figure of Perseus or John Brown, about whom Hayden was to later write a similar poem,[19] the figure of Turner tells his own story by recalling his several visions, of warring angels, of martyred Ibo warriors, and finally of 'conqueror faces' like his own, which he takes as a sign of his leading slaves to rebellion and freedom. There is ironic power in his speech, as 'newborn' and 'purified' he awaits the time of revolt, which ends, ironically, in disastrous bloodshed.

But if Nat Turner presents an image of a misguided aspiration toward freedom, the concluding poem 'Frederick Douglass' establishes both a literal hero and a model for human transcendence, as an expression of human virtue far beyond the mere loosening of physical restraint. The sonnet thus implies the ultimate goal of human progress:

When it is finally ours, this freedom, this liberty, this beautiful
and terrible thing, needful to man as air,
usable as earth; when it belongs at last to our children,
when it is truly instinct, brainmatter, diastole, systole,
reflex action . . .

                    (p. 71; *AA*, p. 131)

This state of achieved humanity is not an intellectual understanding nor a physical condition, but, the poem implies, the habituation of the human soul, of faith in action. And when humanity achieves this state, the poem goes on to say, Douglass 'shall be remembered' for exemplifying that evolved condition:

> Oh not with statues' rhetoric,
> not with legends and poems and wreaths of bronze alone,
> but with the lives grown out of his life, the lives
> fleshing his dream of the beautiful needful thing.

Just as the persona's search for freedom and identity in the first two groups of poems ends with the example of a man who has fleshed out that promise, so the persona's quest for transcendence ultimately takes him outside himself. By confronting these various images, he is educated, his identity confirmed and his aspirations exemplified. In later volumes he would rearrange the order of these groups, but the essential purposes they imply would remain. In both *Selected Poems* (1966) and *Angle of Ascent* (1975) Hayden concludes with the sequence of poems on Afro-American history and 'Frederick Douglass' as the final symbol of a man grown beyond the bounds of a single culture to represent the limitless possibilities of human ascent.

14. *Selected Poems*
1966

Swam from
the ship somehow;
somehow began the
measured rise.[1]

Robert Hayden, 'The Diver'

Few critics would deny that *Selected Poems* is superior to *A Ballad of Remembrance* – all the strengths of the 1962 collection are retained, weaker poems are deleted, a number of excellent new poems have been added, and the grouping more explicitly delineates Hayden's overall thematic plan for the sequence. Since most critics had not seen *A Ballad of Remembrance*, assessments of the volume were made without awareness of Hayden's previous work. The extremely positive tenor of most reviews, coupled with the winning of the Dakar award after twenty years of drudgery at Fisk and the long-awaited ascent of his 'underground' reputation, made 1966 a propitious year for Hayden's career.

Gwendolyn Brooks, most noted among the reviewers, rightly distinguished Hayden's art from the 'bare-fight boys', poets who pour out raw emotion, their 'wounds like faucets above his page'.[2] She designates Hayden as a type of poet who 'finds life always interesting, sometimes appalling, sometimes appealing, but consistently amenable to a clarifying enchantment via the powers of Art', a poet who has a 'reverence for the word Art'.[3] Her praise of his work is unabashed, terming his varied stylistic approach 'a little school'.[4] She concludes that Hayden 'reaches richly, then molds and resolves with confidence and precision'.[5]

Other reviews were no less praising, though clearly less knowledgeable of Hayden's talents: Robert Spector exalted Hayden's work, but too easily classified it as 'Black poetry'; he noted Hayden's 'sensitive recording of the simple language of black men', 'a poetry nurtured on the bittersweet milk of the blues'.[6] David Galler, the only critic to react negatively to the work, viewed the poems strictly from a racial point of view, harshly condemning Hayden for trying to write outside his perspective as a 'Negro': 'The subject matter is inescapable – and if one is a Negro, he will not wish to escape it.'[7] After further criticizing Hayden's use of the Bahá'í Faith in his poetry, Galler concluded that while Hayden is 'as gifted a poet as most we have', he does not have a solid 'frame of reference'.[8] As I hope to show, Hayden's frame of reference is solid and consistent throughout his poetry, and clear to anyone willing to take the trouble to discover it.

In other reviews the matter of Hayden's racial origin was considered as less important than the quality of his work. After decrying his previous obscurity, the review in *Choice* stated that *Selected Poems* 'reveals the surest poetic talent of any Negro poet in America; more important, it demonstrates a major talent and poetic coming-of-age without regard to race or creed'.[9] But while this and other reviews recognized Hayden's talent, not one noted the deeper symbolic possibilities of the individual pieces or the thematic unity of the whole structure.

Perceptive and articulate students of Hayden's work have since recognized in *Selected Poems* the full power of this collection. Pontheolla Williams has observed how it 'repeats the themes of the earlier volume'.[10] Dennis Gendron stated that Hayden believed this to be the 'definitive edition of the *Ballad* and *Figure of Time* poems',[11] and Gendron's study attempts to analyze the structure and deeper significances of this volume. What no one has adequately assessed, however, is the distinction between *A Ballad of Remembrance* and *Selected Poems*. For while the majority of poems in *Selected Poems* are retained from *A Ballad of Remembrance*, and while Hayden also maintained the basic integrity of the four groups as he had constructed them in the previous volume, *Selected Poems* is nevertheless a substantially changed work.

To begin with, Hayden has in this collection added a substantial fifth group which he has placed first in order. These are his newest poems and they add significantly to the impact of the volume. Hayden has placed the 'inference of Mexico' group of poems before the other three groups from *Ballad* so that the persona, in effect, examines another culture before he examines the images from his personal history. In addition to the lead section of ten poems are three other new poems, two in the Mexico group and one in the final section of Afro-American history poems. Finally, Hayden has deleted eight poems: 'El Cristo', 'Locus', 'On Lookout Mountain', 'Weeds', 'The Anguish', 'Eine Kleine Nachtmusik', 'Figure' and 'Lear is Gay . . .'

Considered individually, there changes may not have seemed terribly weighty to those reviewers who happened to be familiar with his work. Thus assembled, the revisions are clearly substantial. Statistics alone hint at the magnitude of the difference: with an addition of thirteen poems and a deletion of eight, a total of twenty-one individual changes from the thirty-six poems in *Ballad*, there is a revision in fifty-eight percent of the book. This is not to say that the heart of the volume is totally changed; it still relates a pilgrim's narrative of a quest for definition and direction. But in the light of these individual changes, and considering Hayden's reordering of groups, it is well worth our while to note the impact of these revisions if we are to understand accurately the continuity of Hayden's art and his final intentions for this sequence.

Clearly the most significant of these changes is the addition of the ten new poems which constitute the first group. This section begins with 'The Diver', a highly symbolic poem which most critics consider crucial to Hayden's major themes. The poem is quite enigmatic and, consequently, there are various opinions as to what exactly is being represented by this highly imagistic piece, but it is clear to every serious reader that it prefigures the spiritual journey that Hayden presents in this first section and in the volume as a whole.

On a literal level, the poem presents a first-person description by a scuba diver of his descent, his near-fatal experience with nitrogen narcosis ('rapture of the deep'), and his 'measured rise' to the surface. Symbolically, the work has been variously interpreted as implying a death wish,[12] as depicting a sublimated desire for sexual union with a person of 'another color',[13] as implying a desire to escape from racial prejudice through subterfuge,[14] or simply as a figural treatment of a personal depression.[15] Similarly, it has been deemed influenced by or having parallels to Keats' 'Ode to a Nightingale', Yeats' 'Sailing to Byzantium', Dunbar's 'We Wear the Mask', Ellison's *Invisible Man*, and Hayden's own 'Veracruz', as well as his later poem 'For a Young Artist'.

Hayden himself wisely refused to ascribe a specific value to the x-factor in this correlative, remarking that: '. . . the act of diving and the temptation the diver feels to let go, to yield to death, really represent, are symbolic of, something very personal. The entire poem is actually a metaphor.'[16] He further commented to Gendron that, though born out of personal concerns, the poem 'is about the nature of reality and "the very thin line" between the real and the fanciful':[17]

> The Diver
> Sank through easeful
> azure. Flower
> creatures flashed and
> shimmered there—
> lost images
> fadingly remembered.
> Swiftly descended
> into canyon of cold
> nightgreen emptiness.
> Freefalling, weightless
> as in dreams of
> wingless flight,

plunged through infra-
space and came to
the dead ship,
carcass that swarmed with
voracious life.
Angelfish, their
lively blue and
yellow prised from
darkness by the
flashlight's beam,
thronged her portholes.
Moss of bryozoans
blurred, obscured her
metal. Snappers,
gold groupers explored her,
fearless of bubbling
manfish. I entered
the wreck, awed by her silence,
feeling more keenly
the iron cold.
With flashlight probing
fogs of water
saw the sad slow
dance of the gilded
chairs, the ectoplasmic
swirl of garments,
drowned instruments
of buoyancy,
drunken shoes. Then
livid gesturings,
eldritch hide and
seek of laughing
faces. I yearned to
find those hidden
ones, to fling aside
the mask and call to them,
yield to rapturous
whisperings, have
done with self and
every dinning
vain complexity.
Yet in languid
frenzy strove, as

one freezing fights off
sleep desiring sleep;
strove against the
cancelling arms that
suddenly surrounded
me, fled the numbing
kisses that I craved.
Reflex of life-wish?
Respirator's brittle
belling? Swam from
the ship somehow;
somehow began the
measured rise.

(pp. 11–12; *AA*, pp. 75–6)

Most critics agree that the diver's rise from the depths is a positive thing, a return to life, a decision like that of the persona in 'Veracruz' to participate in reality. Only Wilburn Williams, Jr., however, agrees with my own inclination that the diver's mystical encounter with 'those hidden ones' is not a longing for death, but 'a profound intensification of life'.[18] Like the artist entering the cage to confront and control his lions, the diver's desire to 'fling aside the mask' is an aspiration for enlightenment, not obliteration. Therefore, the ascending diver rises 'possessed of a deeper, more disciplined capacity for experience'.[19]

The poem is ambiguous about the cause of the diver's ascent, but it is very clear about the appeal of the underwater realm. Like the instant metamorphosis that leaping from the cliffs at Veracruz could provide, staying in this transcendental state would enable the diver to 'have/ done with self and/ every dinning/ vain complexity'. The voice at Veracruz, which occurs in the second section of this rearranged sequence, beckons the speaker to *'cease from error'*, to forgo *'the long warfare with self'.*[20]

The interpretation of both conditions (the vision and the rise) as affirmative states establishes thematically the journey of the persona which immediately follows the poem – he too descends through images of horror until his mystical vision of Bahá'u'lláh, after which, we infer, he rises consoled and confirmed. The final group of history poems then parallels that process by chronicling the descent of man into slavery and his 'measured rise' to freedom of body and spirit. This interpretation also lays the groundwork for major parallels to this process of transformation as depicted in the Bahá'í Writings and in the Platonic allegory of the cave, both of which become increasingly important unifying themes in Hayden's poetry.[21] For example, while the Bahá'í Writings exhort one to 'turn away from thyself',[22] to focus on the essentially spiritual nature of life, they also ordain that faith be expressed in deeds, through working daily in the physical world.[23] These concepts thus parallel the vision and the return.

Platonically, 'The Diver' lends itself to two appropriate interpretations. On the one hand, the descent into mystical vision could represent the ascent from the dark cave in the Platonic allegory.[24] In both analogies, the speaker as true philosopher or aspirant to enlightenment returns to the 'real' world possessed of insight and understanding and, therefore, better able to utilize the physical metaphor. Or the descent may represent the diver as true philosopher come down to the mundane from the transcendental contemplation of the 'forms'.[25] Significantly, the diver carries with him a flashlight with which to probe the dark reaches of the wrecked ship, an appropriate analogue for the cave world of shadow and image in Plato's conceit. The diver's desire to remain in the nether world would then represent the temptation of the aspirant to spiritual transformation to yield to sensual desire and the other enticements of the phenomenal world, a notion which the sensual imagery of the underwater realm seems to corroborate.

But whether the poem is simply a rejection of a death wish or a more complex symbol, the diver's rise clearly affirms the phenomenal world as necessary and appropriate, and, therefore, the poem works through either interpretation to introduce both the first group of poems and the entire sequence of five groups. For example, there is a descent by the persona, an awesome, sometimes terrifying descent into darkness wherein he examines images, both personal and universal, of a world of perverted faith, inherited evil, lost identity, and spiritual longing. And yet, like the diver, the persona emerges from despair and grief to the hope of reconciliation and resolution. Importantly, it is only a hope at this point in the persona's life and at this time in history – it is a middle part of the journey.

What follows this prefatory poem is, figuratively speaking, the persona's descent into darkness and his subsequent probing of images of a lost and destitute age with the accurate beams of his lantern art. Hayden emphasizes in the imagery of this first group, and in the added poems in the other four sections, the universal symbols of light and dark. The ten poems in section one establish both of these motifs with the declining faith and spiritual tone among these poems and with the transition from light (the 'fire' of faith exhibited in 'Full Moon' and 'Dawnbreaker') to the darkness of the final poem in this first group ('Night, Death, Mississippi', which represents human perfidy and degradation). Structurally, this group sets up the examination in the next three groups of the search for spiritual identity and transformation, a quest which is finally rewarded with a vision of future ascent as foreshadowed in the poems on Bahá'u'lláh and in the 'measured rise' which is implied in the history poems of the last group.

But in addition to this general rationale for the arrangement of poems in this first section there are two other apparent explanations for viewing this as an introduction to the other poems. First, most of these ten poems anticipate particular poems in the other groups, just as 'The Diver' anticipates 'Veracruz'. For example, 'Electrical Storm', 'Full Moon' and 'Dawnbreaker' as affirmations of religious faith foreshadow 'From the Corpse Woodpiles, from the Ashes' (formerly 'In Light Half Nightmare and Half Vision') and 'Bahá'u'lláh in the Garden of Ridwan' (formerly 'The Prophet'). 'The Rabbi', the fifth poem, is a negative image of institutionalized religion similar to, but milder than, 'Witch Doctor'. 'Belsen, Day of Liberation', like 'From the Corpse Woodpiles . . .', alludes to the Nazi deathcamps. 'Approximations' and 'Snow' are similar in elegiac mood to 'Those Winter Sundays'. 'The Ballad of Sue Ellen Westerfield' as a story of Sue Hayden's star-crossed love for Jim Barlow sheds light on 'The Whipping' and also utilizes the same ballad tradition as 'The Burly Fading One'. Finally, 'Night, Death, Mississippi' is a lynching poem, the best and last Hayden ever did, and replaces 'Figure' as the archetypal symbol of inhumanity and evil.

Another structuring device among these ten new poems is the explicit pairing of poems which is reminiscent of Hayden's technique in *The Lion and the Archer* volume. Combined with the idea of the group as a succession of descending images, this pattern best explains how these poems work individually and as integral parts of the entire sequence. For example, paired with 'The Diver' is 'Electrical Storm', also about a persona escaping death, though in this case it is through implied divine intervention when a friend saves the speaker and his wife from downed power lines.

But if the nature of the speaker's revived faith is left ambiguous in these first two poems, the second pair of poems clarifies the basis for faith. 'Full Moon', a much more sophisticated treatment of the idea of history as cyclical than Hayden had concocted in 'The Wheel', implies the ironically changing symbology of this celestial body. Once revered, the moon now connotes a potential arms base, a 'livid sector' (p. 15; *AA*, p. 79). Yet the light it emits 'burned in the garden of Gethsemane' and in this age 'spread its radiance on the exile's path' of Bahá'u'lláh.[26] Here again Hayden employs the symbolism of a light shining in darkness as an allusion to progressive revelation: 'the full moon dominates the dark'. Paired with this objective symbol is 'Dawnbreaker', the impassioned description of the martyrdom of Ḥájí Sulaymán Khán, a poem which also employs fire and light as symbols of renewed faith.[27] The title, which designates the early followers of the Báb, the Prophet-Herald of the Bahá'í Faith, signifies those first believers who recognized the dawning light. The candles burning in the wounded flesh of this courageous man, intended as grievous torture, become in the context of the poem a symbol of his ignited faith, for after the candles were placed in his flesh this early believer danced through the streets singing God's praise until his death:

> Ablaze
> with candles sconced
> in weeping eyes
> of wounds,
>
> He danced
> through jeering streets
> to death; oh sang
> against
>
> The drumming
> mockery God's praise.
> Flames nested in
> his flesh
>
> Fed the
> fires that consume
> us now, the fire that
> will save.
>   (p. 16; *AA*, p. 80)

The use of the future tense in the final line importantly signifies here that the ultimate transcendence of the speaker and mankind is something anticipated, something vitally in progress, but not yet achieved. Hayden has placed this assertion of incipient change and the growing flame of belief early in the sequence, almost as if to indicate that the dark images he is about to parade before us are but symbols of the auroral dark which immediately precedes the dawning.

The third pair of poems are bonded by virtue of a shared perspective – both are from a child's point of view – and the fact that both are concerned with the Jewish identity, but in quite different ways. The first of these, 'The Rabbi', plays off the theme of religious conviction exemplified in the previous pair, but with an ironic twist. Where the previous poems portray religious faith as a positive response to enigmatic questions and injustice, in 'The Rabbi' religious identity becomes a source of division. As the poet recalls the relationship between the Jews and Blacks in his neighborhood, he notes that while the grownups were aware of the easy generalizations, he and his playmates in their childlike innocence were oblivious to such prejudicial distinctions:

> Hirschel and Molly and I meanwhile
> divvied halveh, polly seeds,
> were spies and owls and Fu Manchu.
>   (p. 17; *AA*, p. 81)

The boy is awed by the rites and the mystery of the synagogue inside which he cannot see, but when the neighborhood changed, 'the synagogue became/

New Calvary./ The rabbi bore my friends off/ in his prayer shawl'. From this terse observation we infer the irony that later will be made blatant in 'Witch Doctor' – that these institutions of religious instruction can become sources of discrimination and division by which the clarity of the child's perspective is clouded by cruel indoctrination. In effect, what should be a source of humanization and harmony becomes another means by which 'The ceremony of innocence is drowned', as Yeats described the decline of faith in 'The Second Coming'.[28]

This capacity of man to pervert benign institutions is even more forcefully implied in the second poem in this pair, 'Belsen, Day of Liberation'. Alluding to the liberation of the Nazi deathcamps by Allied soldiers, this poem is also concerned with the enlightening clarity of the child's perspective. A young girl whose parents have been executed; her 'childhood foreclosed', watches the 'golden strangers' marching in:

> Afterwards
> she said, 'They were so beautiful,
> and they were not afraid.'
> (p. 18; *AA*, p. 82)

Succinctly, the child summarizes the difference between these faces and the maimed visages she has daily observed. This same mechanism of prejudice which separated the 'schwartzes' from 'Jew Baby' in the Paradise Valley of 'The Rabbi' has here even more hideously darkened the aspect of civilization.

The next pair of poems is not so obviously a further descent into darkness. Playing off the death of the girl's parents, 'Approximations' and 'Snow' are brief impressionistic elegies that connote mourning and silent grief. 'Approximations', a series of four images in the haiku tradition, originally inspired by the death in 1957 of Hayden's mother, utilizes the same symbols of light and dark which Hayden has consistently employed to designate the search for identity and understanding:

> Darkness, darkness.
> I grope and falter. Flare
> of a match.
> (p. 19; *AA*, p. 83)

The simple act of igniting a match implies here some volitional effort on the speaker's part to find his way – a prayer, perhaps, or some other release from his sense of loss. The last haiku, however, implies not triumph over grief, but the somber equation at dawn of the crated coffin with waiting sacks of mail:

> On the platform at
> dawn, grey mailbags waiting;
> a crated coffin.

Likewise, the second poem 'Snow' then approximates the speaker's mood as the weather in the macrocosm seems to mirror his own sadness.

Again by association the final pair of poems play off the speaker's thoughts about his mother's death in 'The Ballad of Sue Ellen Westerfield', a narrative about Hayden's foster mother, and 'Night, Death, Mississippi', a lynching poem portraying the full extent of inherited prejudice. 'The Ballad' alludes to Sue Ellen's love for a white man (Jim Barlow) and her inability to override the forces of racism which disallow their love. She refuses to 'forfeit what she was' and 'forswear her pride' by living as 'fugitives whose dangerous only hidingplace/ was love'. And yet, as Hayden implied in several interviews, she never forgot this man:

> They kissed and said farewell at last.
> He wept as had her father once.
> They kissed and said farewell.
> Until her dying-bed,
> she cursed the circumstance.
>   (p. 21; *AA*, p. 85)

The 'circumstance' in 'Night, Death, Mississippi' is more contemporary and more severe. As Hayden uses Frederick Douglass as a symbol of human virtue which has become habituated, instinctive, Hayden uses a family of lynchers in this poem to illustrate the reverse – the possibility of inherited evil becoming 'diastole, systole,/ reflex action'.[29] Returning home at night after mutilating Black men, this rural father jovially relates to the mother how it went:

> Then we beat them, he said,
> beat them till our arms was tired
> and the big old chains
> messy and red.
>   (pp. 23–4; *AA*, p. 88)

In dehumanized logic, the lyncher analyzes the thrill he experiences from this debased act:

> Christ, it was better
> than hunting bear
> which don't know why
> you want him dead.

The invocation to Christ here ironically recalls the crucifixion, and the whole tone of the narration implies that this sanctioned perversity is, like the mentality at the death camp, a reversal of affirmative conviction and a clear index to the depth of the diver's descent into darkness.

Hayden's ability to probe the psyche of even the most perfidious of human-kind, to find there the mechanism of evil, is skillfully interlaced in the fabric of the verse by means of three italicized lines (presumably the poet's voice which can no longer be stilled): '*O Jesus burning on the lily cross*'; '*O night, rawhead and bloodybones night*'; and '*O night betrayed by darkness not its own*'. Significantly, this last line occurs after the mother has told the children to 'fetch Paw/ some water now so's he/ can wash that blood/ off him'. The parental instruction here recalls the implicit lessons which separate the children in 'The Rabbi', and thus the darkness of this night is not its own, but a darkness passed down from generation to generation, though now the preju-dice is sheared of the veneer of legalized purposes and Roman rhetoric which characterize the trial in 'Middle Passage'. This does not exculpate the perpetrators, but it does demonstrate that the decline of humanity, like the ascent, is a collective endeavor achieved incrementally.

With the shift of the Mexico group to the second position, this theme of light and darkness, of lost and perverted faith is continued. The 'Hollow cells' of the convent, the strange mixtured Christian and tribal rites, the desperate longing of the people for rejuvenation all play off the idea in the first group of the poet probing images in darkness. In this context his despair at Veracruz is not so much a sense of personal failure as it is a logical extension of the despair that we too feel in considering what man has become. This tone is then sustained as the speaker probes more personal and intimate settings and figures in groups three and four until he finally flees down 'target streets', coming at last to the 'cold cloacal cell' where Bahá'u'lláh resides, 'His pain/ our anguish and our anodyne' (p. 60; *AA*, p. 116).

But this ray of hope in the 'auroral' dark is not Hayden's final vision of a revived and ascended humanity – these are, after all, only images of incipience and hope, not a *fait accompli*. It is in the final group of history poems that Hayden demonstrates that process of ascent in sensible form as symbolized in the ascent of the Afro-American people. Appropriately, this evolving identity was changing in the 19th century simultaneously with the major historical events of the Bahá'í Faith. 'Bahá'u'lláh in the Garden of Ridwan', for example, is set in 1863 during the height of the American Civil War and the most crucial period in the quest for freedom by the Afro-American (the Emancipation Proclamation went into effect on January 1, 1864). Yet, while these final poems particularize the ascent of one culture, they do not represent a narrowing of purposes, because the struggle of this one people clearly symbolizes in Hayden's poetry the aspiration of all mankind.

To enhance and strengthen the effect of this symbolic chronology, Hayden has added 'Runagate Runagate'. The penultimate poem in the volume, this piece follows Nat Turner's revolt in time and portrays the Underground Rail-road, which in the middle 1800s aided slaves to escape north to freedom via a secret network. Led by Harriet Tubman and traveling mostly at night, the slaves would rely on navigation by stars, such as the 'drinking gourd' (the Big Dipper constellation which incorporates the North Star).

Rhythmically, the poem captures the mood of frantic flight of a 'runagate' (a *renegade* or escaped slave):

> Runs falls rises stumbles on from darkness into darkness
> and the darkness thicketed with shapes of terror
>
> (p. 75; *AA*, p. 128)

Obviously playing off the whole symbolic implications of this period in history as a time of darkness, Hayden uses the journey northward (upward on a map) as a figural expression of incipient spiritual ascent. Just as the speaker has, after his descent, journeyed through the dark to discover the 'hidden ones' and his own means for escape and enlightenment, so this poem uses the physical journey to symbolize that spiritual pilgrimage.

But the journey is not an easy one; like the diver or the persona at Veracruz, the escapees are tempted to give up, until they are prodded into action by the indomitable heroine Harriet Tubman:

> And fear starts a-murbling, Never make it,
> we'll never make it. *Hush that now,*
> and she's turned upon us, leveled pistol
> glinting in the moonlight:
> Dead folks can't jaybird-talk, she says;
> you keep on going now or die, she says.
>
> (p. 76; *AA*, p. 129)

As in the final poem 'Frederick Douglass', the journey here is at midpoint and true freedom is a vision of the future, but these heroic figures, especially in the context of the Bahá'í perspective of history, substantiate that vision and flesh out the dream: 'Mean mean mean to be free' (p. 77: *AA*, p. 130).

Part IV

THE CONTINUITY OF HAYDEN'S POETRY II

I think that today when so often one gets the feeling that everything is going downhill, that we're really on the brink of the
abyss and what good is anything, I find myself sustained in my
attempts to be a poet and my endeavor to write because I have
the assurance of my faith that this is of spiritual value and it is a
way of performing some kind of service.[1]

Robert Hayden, *Conversations with Writers*, 1977

It would seem from the events in Hayden's life that his career, like John Brown's life as Hayden described it in verse, had 'the symmetry/ of a cross',[2] and that 1966 was the crucial turning point in that career. Before 1966 Hayden was largely unknown, despite the bright promise of his early accomplishments and recognition, and his first five volumes had attracted relatively little attention. After 1966 his reputation soared, his career as poet and teacher changed remarkably and his second five collections of verse were, one and all, critically acclaimed.

Part of this change some biographers have attributed to his winning of the Dakar award; others to his publishing with a commercial press. Pontheolla Williams attributes this change to a shift in Hayden's poetics. She states that his poetry after *Selected Poems* represents a shift away from apprenticeship, experimentation, unevenness and occasional 'flamboyance' in using 'symbolism for its own sake' to poetry which she characterizes as possessing 'a new economy and a surer command of the poetic device in service of the subject'.[3] Dennis Gendron also notes a change in Hayden's career after 1966, but in theme, not poetics: 'If *Selected Poems* focuses on Hayden's personal identity, *Words in the Mourning Time* tries to establish an identity for contemporary America'.[4] He also notes the shift from an emphasis on the historical past to a concentration on contemporary history.

The year 1966 may represent a turning point in Hayden's career, but it was not really a breach in the continuity of his stylistics or his unrelenting pursuit of the lofty questions which both haunted and intrigued him. For if, as Williams contends, the poems in *Words in the Mourning Time* are less obviously symbolic, the poems in succeeding volumes are much more symbolic, a return, in some cases, to the baroque mode, the extended conceits and the 'objective correlative'.[5] In addition, the poetry of the first half of his career, which *Selected Poems* assembles and organizes, was not abandoned or left behind. This same sequence of poems is included as the fourth and concluding section in Hayden's *Angle of Ascent,* the most comprehensive collection of his work. Furthermore, *American Journal,* which effectively closes his career, responds to the same essential questions about man's identity, about the function of art, about the relationship of physical experience to spiritual enlightenment, about the progress of history as a process of human metamorphosis and 'transillumination'.

In short, in the second half of his career, Hayden continued his unrelenting drive for excellence and 'high seriousness'.[6] The span of years between volumes lessened, his output increased, and his experiments with poetics became even more innovative. Because his poetry inevitably reflected his own sincere and ceaseless efforts at examining the human condition and the most meaningful response to the enigmas of that condition, there is a discernible continuity to his art, partly natural and partly the result of his conscious artistry. For as he assembled his work for these last five volumes he could see the intricate relationships among the poems within them, and from volume to volume. He cleverly exploited this natural continuity by meticulously assembling his work, especially in *Angle of Ascent* and in the second version of *American Journal*. The end result is a startling unity of purpose around the most weighty themes that confront us in this age of violent change.

15. *Words in the Mourning Time*
1970

I bear Him witness now:
towards Him our history in its disastrous quest
for meaning is impelled.[1]

Robert Hayden, 'Words in the Mourning Time'

One might expect that following the hint of human transformation at the conclusion of *Selected Poems*, Hayden's succeeding volume might explore details of that ascent. Instead, *Words in the Mourning Time* provides a more ample study of the Bahá'í concept of history as divinely guided and a more detailed analysis of this particular time in history as a strategic milestone in that process. In particular, Hayden conveys in this four-part sequence the paradoxical nature of the Bahá'í perspective about this period – it is a time of unleashed energy, incredible change and unfathomed promise, but it is also a time of mourning, the blackest night preceding the dawning. Often the persona in these poems, unlike the usually objective diver of *Selected Poems*, frequently abandons the distance between himself and the images of man before him. In this volume the diver is in the dark recesses of the wrecked ship looking out, often unaware of light or hope, until it breaks through the dark to remind him of the divine guidance impelling human history.

Like Hayden's previous volumes, this collection is tightly structured and orchestrated, a major collection of fifteen new poems (one of which has ten parts), plus three poems from *Figure of Time*, one from *A Ballad of Remembrance* and one from *The Lion and the Archer*. Pontheolla Williams largely dismisses the work as 'transitional',[2] though in reality it is a very even, very solid and dramatic collection of poems *about* 'transition'. But as with certain poems in Hayden's previous collections, it is necessary to know something about the relationship of Hayden's perspective as a Bahá'í to these poems in order to understand many of the individual pieces, as well as the thematic integrity of the sequence as a whole. In particular, to recover the central allusions of this volume, one must have some notion of the Bahá'í concept of history as the purposeful education of man on this planet.[3]

As has already been mentioned briefly, from a Bahá'í view mankind is ordained to advance spiritually and materially by the assistance of divinely guided Prophets, whom Bahá'ís term 'Manifestations', figures such as Abraham, Moses, Christ, Muḥammad and, most recently, Bahá'u'lláh. Each of these successive Teachers reiterates the eternal verities, the unchanging spiritual concepts, and advances the physical and social ordinances to reflect man's expanded spiritual understanding and the changed exigencies of the phenomenal world. In this sense history is cyclical; dispensations succeed as one day follows another. As the potency of the previous revelation declines into darkness, so begins the search in that darkness for the first rays of light to herald the dawn of a new day and another Prophet. From such a view, the significant history of mankind is the chronicling of these successive Teachers, all of Whom are in accord with regard to Their crucial purposes.

However, history from a Bahá'í perspective is not only cyclical; it is also progressive. Each Prophet or Manifestation is able to build on what the previous Teacher accomplished so that, like students in a classroom, mankind receives an ever-expanding education. And yet, just as there are milestones in the progress of an individual, so there are in the cycles of progress on this planet certain quantum leaps forward. According to the Bahá'í Writings, the transition which mankind is currently experiencing is the most significant transformation he will ever undergo, equivalent, by analogy, to an individual's *rite de passage* from adolescence to adulthood. This transition to maturity necessarily involves the abandonment of archaic systems and attitudes, the attendant loss of identity, and the acquisition of insecurity and trepidation, even though the ultimate outcome of that transition will be a radically advanced, refined and fulfilled organism.

From this perspective of history as divine process, then, one has the bountiful expectation of a changed world consciousness about man's essential identity and purposes, as well as the hope for the cessation of active hostilities and the eventual establishment of a world civilization which shall not decline. At the same time the Bahá'í Writings foretell a necessarily terrible period of transition which will usher in that dawning, inasmuch as religious and political leaders rejected the opportunity to seize upon the devices for implementing easily a spiritually oriented world commonwealth.[4] Therefore, the imminent turmoil is not divine retribution so much as it is the logical consequence of mankind's stubborn adherence to archaic points of view (nationalism, selfishness, prejudices): 'The dust of sedition hath clouded the hearts of men, and blinded their eyes. Erelong they will perceive the consequences of what their hands have wrought . . .'[5] Nevertheless, in spite of these ominous warnings, the tenor of the Bahá'í Writings regarding this period is positive. Indeed, this is portrayed as the time of fruition and fulfillment which all the Prophets of the past have longingly awaited:

Great indeed is this Day! The allusions made to it in all the sacred Scriptures as the Day of God attest its greatness. The soul of every Prophet of God, of every Divine Messenger, hath thirsted for this wondrous Day. All the divers kindreds of the earth have, likewise, yearned to attain it.[6]

At the same time, no Bahá'í can be oblivious to the dire nature of the tribulations which, because of the refusal of religious and political leaders to respond earlier to the guidance outlined by Bahá'u'lláh, are now ushering in the transformation of human society. According to Shoghi Effendi, Guardian of the Bahá'í Faith, a bewildered humanity can perceive neither the origin nor the destiny of the vast changes currently sweeping the planet:

A tempest, unprecedented in its violence, unpredictable in its course, catastrophic in its immediate effects, unimaginably glorious in its ultimate consequences, is at present sweeping the face of the earth. Its driving power is remorselessly gaining in range and momentum. Its cleansing force, however much undetected, is increasing with every passing day. Humanity, gripped in the clutches of its devastating power, is smitten by the evidences of its resistless fury. It can neither perceive its origin, nor probe its significance, nor discern its outcome.[7]

Well versed as he was in the Bahá'í Writings, Robert Hayden was painfully aware of this paradoxical vantage point from which the Bahá'í must needs view contemporary history, and his poetry reflects this admixture of hope and dread. In *Words in the Mourning Time* Hayden catalogued images of this formidable transition as foreshadowed in the tumult of the 1960s: the racial violence in American cities, the assassinations of benign leaders, the war in Vietnam, the bloodshed in Biafra. The persona in most of these poems is, therefore, this Bahá'í voice, immersed in the throes of violent change, intellectually aware of the ultimately propitious direction of history, but feeling, nevertheless, the legitimacy of grief in this time of mankind's mourning.

Hayden's allusions in this volume to the Bahá'í concept of history are thus inescapable and essential to a proper assessment of the work. Without it, the enunciation of love and hope seems naive and desperate, or at least without rational foundation. In his interview with Hayden, John O'Brien implies as much when he asks the poet why the title poem concludes with an affirmative perspective:

The first few sections [of this ten-part poem] catalogue the madness of our age, particularly that of the 1960s. Yet love enters the last section and restores what appeared to be a hopeless condition, I'm not sure how you move from the vision of the evils to one of love.[8]

Hayden's response to this important question not only referred the interviewer to the Bahá'í perspective; it succinctly described the theme of *Words in the Mourning Time* as communicating the Bahá'í concept of history:

The final poem [in the ten parts of 'Words in the Mourning Time'] is the culmination, the climax of the sequence. For me, it contains the answers to the questions the preceding poems have stated or implied. If I seem to come to any conclusion about injustice, suffering, violence at all, it's in the lines about man being 'permitted to be man'. And it's in the last poem, written originally for a Bahá'í occasion.[9] Bahá'u'lláh urged the absolute, inescapable necessity for human unity, the recognition of the fundamental oneness of mankind. He also prophesied that we'd go through sheer hell before we achieved anything like world unity – partly owing to our inability to love.[10]

One does well, therefore, to read this volume with a clear distinction in mind between the poet as creator and the persona as Everyman, but Everyman with this special point of view, a Bahá'í voice crying out in the midst of transition. Without such an understanding, the reader is likely to reach the same conclusion as Robert Greenberg who states that 'when, as in "Words in the Mourning Time", he [Hayden] bears witness to Bahá'u'lláh as a figure to redeem our age, a lapse of judgment occurs. Since the general audience doesn't share Hayden's sentiments about this prophet, his faith seems undemonstrated in the poem, an imposition on the reader'.[11] Indeed, Hayden could not have expected his readers to agree with his acceptance of Bahá'u'lláh, but he could expect that they might have the capacity to recover these allusions to the Bahá'í point of view. In short, one must know something about Bahá'í beliefs in order to understand the dramatic perspective of the first-person speaker as a sensitive human being reacting to contemporary events, sensing where 'our history . . . is impelled', yet recoiling at the present violence and promised turmoil that such a vision entails.

For Greenberg, Williams and some other critics, the Bahá'í allusions in this volume are shortcomings, especially since they feel that while Hayden professed the Bahá'í Faith, his 'poetry deals with/fluctuations of viewpoint, ambivalences explored, uncertainties succumbed to, despair lived to the bottom'.[12] Their misapprehension results from two sources – their failure to understand the Bahá'í definition of faith as a struggle towards growth, not a blind adherence to dogma, and the mistaken notion by some that the Bahá'í Faith was something Hayden inherited from Erma rather than a system of belief he studied, pursued and accepted.

To understand properly this volume is to appreciate the speaker as a character struggling, not to believe, but to confront the complexity of emotional responses which his belief incurs. Unfortunately, not one of the reviews acknowledged this theme or perspective. William Wallis stated that while none of the poems has the caliber of 'Frederick Douglass', 'the briefer lyrics contain a brilliance of reality'.[13] Daniel Jaffe alluded to the persona's emotional references to the Bahá'í view as understandable flaws, but he praised the volume as indicative of Hayden's vast talent: 'When his poems fail, they fail in the most human way, as he cries out importances. His best poems merit wide distribution and not only in collections intended to celebrate the achievements of blacks'.[14] Jerome Cushman also applauded Hayden's capacity to surmount the racial point of view and praised the literary quality of his verse.[15]

But it was Julius Lester's review in the *New York Times* that exalted the poet beyond the scope of any other review. Lester's assessment sacrificed in-depth evaluation of the poetry to focus instead on Hayden the man. The result was an astounding tribute to a poet 'who honors language',[16] 'one of the most underrated and unrecognized poets in America'.[17]

Some critics have since noted the careful organization of the volume, but not one has asserted the primacy of the Bahá'í relationship in this structure. Dennis Gendron, for example, has stated that the work 'tries to establish an identity for contemporary America' and depicts in a consciously arranged sequence 'Hayden's outrage over our violent society': 'Like *Selected Poems, Mourning Time* is a very carefully organized book. Hayden himself attests that it was "a kind of design or pattern book from the beginning", that the pattern "was very carefully done", and that "there is a thematic arrangement there".'[18] But while Mr Gendron's subsequent discussion of the volume is consistently enlightening, alluding at times to the relationship between Hayden's beliefs as a Bahá'í and individual poems, he does not explain the integral relationship between this 'pattern book' and the Bahá'í assessment of this period in history, a relationship which an examination of the volume will readily confirm.

On the most basic level, the structure of *Words in the Mourning Time* is obvious. The first section contains seven poems which treat the problem of identity and loneliness, though in a more explicit fashion than previous poems from *Ballad.* The second section contains five settings which are pointedly arranged to communicate our contemporary dilemma. The third section, containing the four parts of 'El-Hajj Malik El-Shabazz' and the ten parts of 'Words in the Mourning Time', forcefully rejects violence as a solution to evil and injustice, noting particularly the irony in the assassinations of those who would lead us to the realization of our humanity. The fourth and final section contains six poems which deal variously with the theme of human resilience and transcendence during times of severe testing.

In this general sense of structure, the volume follows somewhat the same pattern of resolution as *Selected Poems.* The persona experiences a loss of identity, examines external images of that loss in characters and settings, and becomes totally submerged in his grief and despair. At the end of group three he is philosophically consoled by the certitude of his belief in Bahá'u'lláh, and in the final group he discovers existential assurance in examples of human resolve and rebirth. But all is not quite so simple.

The first section of the volume is a carefully planned analysis of the human response to displacement and lost or shattered identity. In general, the seven poems in this group form a composite portrait of 'Humanity, gripped in the clutches' of violent change, unable to 'discern its outcome', but the individual poems do not necessarily treat figures who literally represent this age. Instead, Hayden analyzes in these poems several different effects that result from problems of identity and then several ways of responding to these problems.

This first group of seven poems begins with 'Sphinx', an enigmatic and philosophical poem that establishes the thematic premise for this first section and, like 'The Diver' in *Selected Poems*, for the whole volume:

> If he could solve the riddle,
> she would not leap
>   from those gaunt rocks to her death,
> but devour him instead.
>
> It pleasures her to hold
> him captive there—
>   to keep him in the reach of her
> blood-matted paws.
>
> It is your fate, she has often
> said, to endure
>   my riddling. Your fate to live
> at the mercy of my
>
>   conundrum, which, in truth,
> is only a kind
>   of psychic joke. No, you shall
> not leave this place.
>
>   (Consider anyway the view from
> here.) In time,
>   you will come to regard my questioning
> with a certain pained
>
>   amusement; in time, get so
> you would hardly find
>   it possible to live without
> my joke and me.

(p. 11; AA, p. 35)

The cynical tone of the poem's conclusion and the mysterious 'conundrum' have led several critics to speculate how this dire riddle related to the poet's life, when the most significant impact of the poem clearly relates to larger implications of the work. In Greek myth the riddle of the Sphinx asked, 'What has one voice and walks on four legs in the morning, two at noon, and three in the evening?'[19] The failure of Theban wayfarers to solve the riddle meant death at the hands of the vicious beast. Since the Sphinx in the poem still taunts the passerby, and us, we can presume the poem is set prior to Oedipus' resolution of the riddle and the Sphinx's subsequent self-destruction, or perhaps the 'him' in the poem is Oedipus. Regardless, the answer to the riddle is man, who crawls as an infant, walks on two legs when matured and needs a staff in old age.

The riddle thus establishes the whole issue of identity, implying that a clear perception of what man is and how he develops will prevent the seemingly arbitrary violence that results from a lack of self-knowledge. However, the poem seems to invert the question to ask, 'What is man?' It further plays off the symbolism of the periods of the day, alluding to the Bahá'í concept that this period in history is the dawn of a new day and, further, that it is also a period of transition from adolescence to adulthood when mankind will assume the noontime or upright position.

Therefore, the cynical assumption by the Sphinx – that man needs the 'psychic joke' – is erroneous, from Hayden's viewpoint, the result of a failure to understand the essential distinction between man and a miscreant monster like the Sphinx, who assumes that man, like her, subsists on contention and bloodshed. Importantly, however, the riddle in the context of the poem is not yet solved, and man does not yet know that being aware of his own identity will stop the violence. In this way, Hayden uses the poem to pose the question, to ask the riddle, and uses the rest of the poems in the volume to approach the answer to the question. As the title *Words in the Mourning Time* implies, however, the poet in this volume is more concerned with conveying powerfully the effects of the reign of the Sphinx than he is with giving easy answers to the riddle. Because what becomes clear by the volume's end is that it is not enough for one hero, like an Oedipus, to discover the identity of man; the riddle must be resolved by all men before the Sphinx will leap to her death, even though heroic figures, like Douglass in the previous volume, can guide us to a common awareness of the solution.

The six poems in this first section which follow 'Sphinx' all concern the response of six different characters to the effects of the Sphinx's reign of terror. In general, the major effects are injustice, displacement, desperation, loneliness. The responses to these effects range from suicidal retreat into a world of fantasy to a stoic endurance and noble transcendence. In this sense, each poem can be seen as emphasizing a particular aspect of this composite portrait of mankind's lost identity and offering a slightly different solution, though all are quite similar in their surrealistic, dreamlike quality.

The first of these six poems, 'The Dream', for example, is set in 1863, the year of the Emancipation Proclamation, and depicts the reaction of a slave, Sinda, to liberation at the hand of 'Marse Lincum's soldier boys'. Structurally the poem switches from the poetic narration of her fevered thoughts to the prose excerpts from her brother Cal's letter about his experiences as a Federal soldier. Thematically the poem focuses on the contrasts between her longtime dream of freedom and the unexpected reality of that emancipation:

> How many times that dream had come to her—
> more vision than a dream—
>> the great big soldiers marching out of gunburst,
> their faces those of Cal and Joe
>> and Charlie sold to the ricefields oh sold away
> a-many and a-many a long year ago.
>
> (p. 12; AA, p. 36).

Instead of following 'Marse Lincum's soldier boys' and 'their ornery/ funning, cussed commands', she hides, stays behind, 'Fevered, gasping'. The dying woman then struggles across the yard where she fights 'with brittle strength to rise', so that she might 'welcome Joe and Cal and Charlie' (p. 13; *AA*, p. 37).

Gendron insightfully compares Sinda's struggle to rise with the diver's rise, concluding that, unlike the diver, Sinda is 'unable to reject her fantasy world and so dies enthralled by the cancelling images from which the diver escapes'.[20] Yet it is hardly a willful death, since Sinda is not committing suicide; she is dying from disease. Thus the idea that Sinda's beguiling dream of freedom prevents her from accepting the reality of freedom is not totally in accord with the facts of the poem, and yet this contrast does relate well to the distinction between the long-awaited vision of the spiritual transformation of man and the wrenching transition to that reality as portrayed in this volume.

The remaining five poems in this first group similarly portray a variety of characters all of whom have the problem of lost, ill-defined, displaced or shattered identities. The only common cause they share is that each is human and, to some degree, the angst of each is caused by the human condition, as if Hayden is posing a new version of the Sphinx riddle – what is it in this period that must struggle with its identity? But the catalogue is not haphazardly arranged – each character has a specific response to his plight, a solution which each pursues with determined vigor, and by the group's end we sense Hayden's assessment.

The second poem, for example, '"Mystery Boy" Looks for Kin in Nashville', relates impressionistically the confused fragments of recollected past in the mind of an amnesiac who is searching for his name. Inspired by a local Nashville newspaper article, the poem obviously parallels Hayden's own anxiety and confusion at discovering he was not Robert Hayden. The tension in the poem thus revolves around the desperate search for that 'disremembered time' and 'the name . . . he never can repeat' (p. 14; *AA*, p. 38).

In the third poem, 'The Broken Dark' is the character of the poet himself, or at least the persona/presence that is dramatic stand-in for Hayden, as he lies at night in a hospital room contemplating his own mortality. Listening to the groaning of a 'Man with his belly slashed,/ two-timing lover', the poet/ persona watches the 'shadows of a flower and its leaves/ the nightlight fixes like a blotto/ on the corridor wall':

> Shadow-plays
> of Bali—demons move to the left,
> gods, in their frangipani crowns
> and gold, to the right.
> Ah and my life
> in the shadow of God's laser light—
> shadow of deformed homunculus?
>
> (p. 15; *AA*, p. 39)

This simple but symbolically packed image alludes at once to two major themes he has established in previous poems. By referring to the cave-like darkness of the room and the 'Shadow-plays' on the wall as distortions of reality, he recalls the whole Platonic allegory of the phenomenal world as a distorted reflection of a spiritual reality. And by alluding to 'God's laser light' which breaks the dark, he calls to mind the consistent use of these same symbols in 'Bahá'u'lláh in the Garden of Ridwán' and 'The Diver'. The persona's dilemma, then, is that in this confused and cavelike darkness he is no longer the diver with light probing the wreck; he is inside looking out toward the light, trying to determine exactly what life is: 'Death on either side,/ the Rabbi said, the way of life between.' Amid the groaning and the terrifying shadows, his 'death still/ a theorem to be proved', the speaker cannot be philosophical but instead calls out in prayer, 'Alláh'u'Abhá. O Healing Spirit!/ Thy nearness our forgiving cure.'

The tone of this conclusion is ambiguous. At first it seems to be a desperate prayer of a frightened soul. But the line is not an exclamation. Furthermore, *'Alláh'u'Abhá* is praise of God (this version of 'The Greatest Name' translates 'God of the Greatest Glory'),[21] and the rest is a paraphrase of a Bahá'í prayer for healing:

Thy name is my healing, O my God, and remembrance of Thee is my remedy. Nearness to Thee is my hope, and love for Thee is my companion. Thy mercy to me is my healing and my succor in both this world and the world to come. Thou, verily, are the All-Bountiful, the All-Knowing, the All-Wise.[22]

In this context the speaker's words seem a statement of belief and resolution, an acknowledgment that his hope, and by implication the hope of mankind, is that God will penetrate the darkness with his 'transilluminating' light of nearness.

In the succeeding poem, 'The Mirages', we meet 'the stranger' once again who has his own solution to the problem of identity. He continues his axiomatic observations about reality which he began in 'Theme and Variation', that the physical world is but shadow play of mirages. And yet, unlike the persona in 'The Broken Dark' who prays for transilluminating guidance, the stranger tells us he has 'often/ changed [his] course/ and followed them' in order to be 'Less lonely, less/ lonely then' (p. 16). The poem does not seem to criticize the stranger's decision, however; with a universal symbol for the alienation and loneliness of modern man, Hayden describes the stranger in a state of 'Exhaustion among rocks/ in rockfall sun'. The stranger may be aware, in short, of the illusory nature of the sensual world, but at times his existential needs outweigh the dictates of his philosophical understanding.

Loneliness seems the lot of man when he exists in two worlds at once, on the tenuous path with 'Death on either side', but it is handled differently by the drug addict in 'Soledad'. Playing off the Spanish word for 'solitude' and the name of a prison in California, the poem portrays the 'prisoner' comforted not by a lover, or God, or by following 'mirages', but by complete withdrawal from reality through drugs and music:

> Naked, he lies in the blinded room
> chainsmoking, cradled by drugs, by jazz
> as never by any lover's cradling flesh.
> > (p. 17; *AA*, p. 40)

There is communication of sorts, similar to the common bond between Bessie Smith and her audience in 'Homage', but here music does not aid in enduring so much as the voice of Billie Holliday (herself an addict) confirms his desire to escape from the unbearable reality of 'His fears and his unfinished self':

> He hides on the dark side of the moon,
> takes refuge in a stained-glass cell,
> flies to the clockless country of crystal.
>
> Only the ghost of Lady Day knows where
> he is. Only the music. And he swings
> oh swings: beyond complete immortal now.

Ironically, the 'clockless country' to which the crystal methadrene takes him is only a mirage, and the pills that provide his temporary escape become his 'treacherous jailers'.[23] The term 'unfinished self', used here to imply the addict's particular plight as well as his identity as an Afro-American, also alludes forcefully to all the problems with identity, the conundrums which, according to the Sphinx, are a natural ingredient in man's existence.

The last poem in this catalogue of human responses, 'Aunt Jemima of the Ocean Waves', portrays Hayden's own mythological figure of resilience. Extending the character from the second part of 'From The Coney Island Suite',[24] Hayden uses the figure of Jemima as an archetypal symbol of the displaced Afro-American identity. The woman's lengthy narrative recounts her adventures from her days as the 'Sepia High Stepper' in Europe, to her present status in a sideshow as a 'fake mammy to God's mistakes' (p. 20; *AA*, p. 43). As he listens to her intriguing narrative of 'High-stepping days', the persona finds in her a beautiful image of survival and strength, in spite of her 'unfinished' or fake identity born from the original displacement of the culture:

> An antique etching comes to mind:
>
> 'The Sable Venus' naked on
> a baroque Cellini shell—voluptuous
> imago floating in the wake
> of slave-ships on fantastic seas.[25]

If the group of poems portrays the confused identity of man in this time of mourning, the second section points to another symptom of this period as inferred from a series of five settings. The first two of these, 'Locus' and 'On Lookout Mountain', Hayden had used previously in *A Ballad of Remembrance,* but in this section the poems establish clearly the idea of the violence which belies the guise of tranquility during this time. Arranged in chronological order, these poems have in common ironic contrasts between appearance and reality, between the myth of stability and serenity and the bloodshed which these settings disclose or threaten.

In 'Locus' the contrast is between the natural beauty of the landscape and the violent past which the land has witnessed. More important, there is the contrast between the idyllic 'symbol houses' (the Southern mansion) and the 'brutal dream' which created them in a land where the past is still 'adored and/ unforgiven' (p. 25; *AA*, p. 45). The tranquil setting not only disguises the violent history; it becomes a 'soulscape' which connotes present violence and injustice as a continuing heritage of evil. In 'On Lookout Mountain' there is a similar clash between appearance and reality, the symbols of freedom (the battlefield itself and the 'stuffed gold eagle') and reality: that the freedom for which the soldiers died is yet unfulfilled; that the 'Sunday alpinists' are oblivious to the symbol's meaning; and that 'A World away' the 'scions of that fighting' (p. 26; *AA*, p. 46) are still dying.

'Kodachromes of the Island' presents more subtle contrasts, yet the end result is a more contemporary image of the same theme, the violence and harsh reality that belie the bright beauty of this Mexican island. Each of the three parts functions as a photograph from which we can infer the contrast between the 'colors teemed/ in thronging sunlight' (p. 27; *AA*, p. 47) and the poverty of the islanders. In the first picture, for example, we see the multicolored flowers and birds juxtaposed with the 'young beggar' with 'fingerless hands', who chants, *'Dios se lo pague'*(May God repay you). In the second picture we find the tranquil image in the background of Indian fishermen casting their 'mariposas' (butterfly-shaped fishing nets) on the water while in the foreground on the shore women toss the guts of cleaned fish to squealing piglets as a butterfly lights on the 'offal'. Finally, the speaker watches 'Black turkeys children/ dogs' playing under drying fishnets while 'Vendors urged laquerwork/ and glazed angels/ with candles between their wings' (p. 29; *AA*, p. 49). Like Yeats (in the poem 'The Circus Animals' Desertion'), the poet/persona searches for a theme to all this, though the contrasts have created the theme for him.[26]

Where in 'Kodachromes . . .' Hayden has switched from past to present settings, 'Zeus over Redeye' presents a contrast between the present and the future. As in the first three poems, the natural beauty that once pervaded this setting at the Redstone Arsenal is contrasted with the manmade 'sacred phallic grove' of readied rockets:

> Radar corollas and Holland tulips
> the colors of Easter eggs
> form vistas for the ironist.
> Where elm, ailanthus, redbud grew
> parabola and gantry rise.
>
> (p. 30; *AA*, p. 50)

This inversion of procreative imagery – an array of rockets that are 'totems of our fire-breathing age' – forms 'new mythologies of power':

> I feel as though invisible fuses were
>
> burning all around us burning all
> around us. Heat-quiverings twitch
> danger's hypersensitive skin.
> The very sunlight here seems flammable.
> And shadows give
> us no relieving shade.
>
> (pp. 30–31; *AA*, p. 51)

This contrasts the reassuring 'partial answers' of the guide with the future holocaust hovering in abeyance. For the speaker, and us, this evokes an image of the 'tempest' which Shoghi Effendi seems to be describing, a violence from which there is no 'relieving shade', not in the shadows of this reality, not in the stranger's mirages.

The final poem in this group is also futuristic in tenor, though lighter in tone. 'Unidentified Flying Object' is the humorous anecdotal narrative of Mattie Lee's supposed abduction by alien visitors, as recollected by Will, who saw it all (p. 32; *AA*, p. 52). The poem is related by an unnamed neighbor who speculates as to whether 'Will's tale' is not a cover-up for what many of Mattie Lee's friends suspect. From the contrast between appearance and reality, between myth and the violence the myth symbolized in the previous poems, the reader is almost forced to concur with what 'some are hinting' – that behind Will's quaint myth is a violent reality. Will's account is thus little more assuring than the insane logic of the guide at the arsenal, and the tenor of this time as an age of violence (past, present and future) is sustained throughout.

The third section, clearly the dramatic climax to the volume, combines the theme of identity of the first group with the issue of violence in the second to portray two characters who struggle for insight, identity and the proper course of action in a time of violence. In both 'El-Hajj Malik El-Shabazz' and 'Words in the Mourning Time' the characters achieve identity and, at least for themselves, solve the riddle, though it is still clear by the section's end that until mankind is in accord regarding the solution, the Sphinx as symbol of bestiality – a violence at odds with man's true nature – will continue to feed on the wayfarer through this life.

'El-Hajj . . .' is a four-part chronology of the life of Malcolm X, beginning with his childhood in Detroit and ending with his assassination after his rejection of the Black Muslim movement. Affected strongly by Malcolm X's autobiography, particularly the evidence of this man's sincerity and growth, Hayden wrote this portrait in the third person, concentrating, as the title implies, on the changing names as index to an evolving philosophy.

In part one he is 'Dee-troit Red', a man ensnared by the 'violence of a punished self/ struggling to break free', but though he 'fled his name', 'his injured childhood bullied him' (p. 37; *AA*, p. 55). In part two, as '"Satan" in The Hole', he escapes his Calvinist background and converts to the Black Muslim movement, relishes his 'prideful anger', but cannot escape 'the odors of the pit' (p. 38; *AA*, p. 56). In part three he becomes Malcolm X, exhorts his people to vengeance, becomes 'their scourger who/ would shame them, drive them from/ the lush ice gardens of their servitude' (p. 39; *AA*, p. 57). Finally, on pilgrimage to Mecca, he assumes his final name, 'El-Hajj Malik El-Shabazz', when he transcends his racial point of view:

> He fell upon his face before
> Allah the raceless in whose blazing Oneness all
> were one. He rose renewed renamed, became
> much more than there was time for him to be.
> (p. 40; *AA*, p. 58)

The implicit praise of Malcom X results from this ascent from ghetto, through anger, to a love of mankind, a pilgrim's journey which Hayden could well understand and appreciate. As a symbolic figure in the context of the volume, Malcolm X represents free will in action, a figure who follows the highest light he perceives penetrating the darkness. He has no illusions about changing the hearts of men or the course of history in this 'The martyr's time', but in searching for his personal identity he discovers the full extent of human identity – that mankind is one.

The second poem in this section, 'Words in the Mourning Time', is a mingling of voices, poetic forms and modalities. But unifying the ten parts of the poem (which become three parts in *Angle of Ascent*) is the impassioned voice of the persona who struggles towards catharsis and epiphany. The voice obviously articulates Hayden's own feelings to an extent, but no critic has heretofore understood that the persona, though a Bahá'í, is a character whom Hayden the artist employs here for dramatic effectiveness. That is, just as the life of Malcolm X in the previous poem presents a progress from anguish, guilt and fear to insight and transformation, so the character here progresses from grief in part I:

> For King, for Robert Kennedy,
> destroyed by those they could not save,
> For King for Kennedy I mourn.
> And for America, self-destructive, self-betrayed.
>
> (p. 41; *AA*, p. 59)

to cynical anger in part II:

> Killing people to save, to free them?
> With napalm lighting routes to the future?
>
> (p. 42)

to repulsion at the grotesque inhumanity of the Vietnam war in part III:

> He comes to my table in his hungry wounds
> and his hunger. The flamed-out eyes,
> their sockets dripping. The nightmare mouth.
>
> (p. 43)

to philosophical musings in part V:

> Our world—
> this violent ghetto, slum
> of the spirit raging against itself.
>
> (p. 45)

to the guiding voice of Martin Luther King, Jr., in part VII:

> Oh, master now love's instruments—
> complex and not for the fearful,
> simple and not for the foolish.
>
> (p. 47)

to fearless resolve in part IX:

> We must not be frightened or cajoled
> into accepting evil as deliverance from evil
> We must go on struggling to be human,
> though monsters of abstraction
> police and threaten us.
>
> (p. 49)

to his final perspective as a Bahá'í that ultimately this mourning time will have meaning only through the guidance of Bahá'u'lláh's Revelation:

> I bear Him witness now—
> mystery Whose major clues are the heart of man,
>   the mystery of God:
>
> Bahá'u'lláh:
> Logos, poet, cosmic hero, surgeon, architect
>   of our hope of peace
>
>   (p. 50; *AA,* p. 61)

The final resolution at the end that 'towards Him our history in its disastrous quest/ for meaning is impelled' is not a surprise. In the initial section the speaker states essentially the same thesis which, in no uncertain terms, is the theme of the entire volume:

> I grieve. Yet know the vanity
> of grief—through power of
> The Blessed Exile's
> transilluminating word
>
> aware of how these deaths, how all
> the agonies of our deathbed childbed age
> are process, major means whereby,
> oh dreadfully, our humanness must be achieved.
>
>   (p. 41; *AA,* p. 59)

Yet even though a Bahá'í and aware of history as a divinely ordained process towards a 'Most Great Peace',[27] the speaker cannot ignore suffering, his outrage at violence and injustice, his grief at the loss of noble leaders, or his fear at what additional agony man will undergo before we reach a consensus about our common identity and the Sphinx leaps to her death.

The poem thus arrives at a resolution of sorts – the speaker realizes emphatically the importance of his perspective in this transitional 'deathbed childbed' age, this 'auroral dark'. And yet, as these oxymorons imply, the tone is hardly one of elation or peace. As the poem ends, the speaker recites his beliefs as he might recite his daily 'Obligatory Prayer' on which the last section is based[28] – as a reminder of God's ultimate ascendancy regardless of whatever else ensues. The result in the final section is the most powerful expression in Hayden's poetry of the relationship between his beliefs as a Bahá'í and the quest for peace and human fulfillment:

> *and all the atoms cry aloud*
>
> I bear Him witness now
> Who by the light of suns beyond the suns beyond
>   the sun with shrill pen

revealed renewal of
the covenant of timelessness with time, proclaimed
advent of splendor joy

alone can comprehend
and the imperious evils of an age could not
withstand and stars

and stones and seas
acclaimed—His life its crystal image and
magnetic field

I bear Him witness now—
mystery Whose major clues are the heart of man,
the mystery of God:

Bahá'u'lláh:
Logos, poet, cosmic hero, surgeon, architect
of our hope of peace.

wronged, exiled One,
chosen to endure what agonies of knowledge, what
auroral dark

bestowals of truth
vision power anguish for our future's sake.
'I was but a man

'like others, asleep upon
My couch, when, lo, the breezes of the All-Glorious
were wafted over Me . . .'

Called, as in dead of night
a dreamer is roused to help the helpless flee
a burning house.

I bear Him witness now:
towards Him our history in its disastrous quest
for meaning is impelled.

      (pp. 50–51; *AA*, pp. 61–2)

 The last section of the volume lends itself to various interpretations because the six poems which constitute this finale are so varied, but in general the poems seem to respond to two implied questions: How do we comfort ourselves in the meantime, and what can the artist do to assist us? The implicit answer to these questions are six poems which intermingle characters epitomizing transcendence and rebirth with poems that examine how the artist helps us confront our fears and become likewise transcendent.

The first poem, 'Monet's "Waterlilies"', like Auden's 'Musée des Beaux Arts', examines the effect that the painter's art has on the poet. Specifically, Hayden states how Monet's impressionism transports him from the harsh chronicle of violence and decay which 'poisons the air like fallout' to 'that world/ each of us has lost' (p. 55; *AA*, p. 63). The escape which the artist provides, however, is more significant, it seems, than the temporary indulgence the mirages provide the stranger. With his painting Monet has given concrete form to a time of innocence, stability and serenity with such skill that 'the eye of faith believes'. Here in the 'shadow of its joy' the poet is comforted and refreshed, not by illusion, but by calling up within him the exquisite emotions that are possible, that the poet recalls or else longs for. By reminding us of human possibilities, by giving us this faith that dignity can exist, the artist exhorts us to strive for such beauty.

'The Lions', a revision of the poem from *The Lion and the Archer*, continues this analysis of the artistic process by going beyond the apologia for art as a practical aid to human existence; instead, it explains the relationship between the artist and his primary resource, his own emotions. The extended conceit compares the artist to a lion tamer who in his daring opens 'danger's door' and 'in the kingdom-cage' (p. 56; *AA*, p. 64) makes his lions perform. In general Hayden seems here to allude to the 'courage leonine' with which the artist tears aside the mask of illusion, asks the awesome questions, and confronts the apparent ironies. More important, Hayden states that this daring analysis reveals 'the savage real that clues/ my vision of the real'.

But if the artist can provide understanding and comfort by giving sensible form to these hard-won insights, so can well-lived lives. That is, as we witness the human capacity for overcoming unexpected difficulties, we begin to believe in ourselves and in the possibility of human ascent in general. In 'October' Hayden uses various symbols to represent the triumph of the human spirit, but the central symbol is the poet's daughter Maia, who, after many difficult emotional and physical battles as a young woman, became for Hayden an example of human transcendence:

> I write this
> for your birthday
> and say I love you
> and say October
> like the phoenix sings you.
> (p. 58; *AA*, p. 66)

The poem is more than an occasional piece; in the four parts of the poem Hayden uses a series of symbols to represent triumph over unexpected tribulation, and yet, like the month itself, these symbols also imply that before the final rebirth of spring a further mourning time of winter must come. The autumn leaves are falling, dying, and a 'surprising snow' in part four breaks the branches, but the brilliant colors of the leaves 'set/ the snow on fire'. The 'chiming/ and tolling/ of lion/ and phoenix/ and chimera/ colors' represent a dying, a decline, but it is a 'deathless/ dying', a decline which promises rebirth. Of course, from a Bahá'í perspective this may refer to life after death, as well as the ability of someone like Maia, or the poet himself, to overcome temporal adversity, but it also clearly refers to the eventual ascent of mankind in history after the transitional period of mourning is done, a new life instigated by the dying of the old, like branches crashing to the snow.

'The Return', inspired by Hayden's reading of Pasternak's *Doctor Zhivago*, seems to recall the scene in the novel when Zhivago has returned to his now-shattered family home, and in the icy darkness of the once happy structure he tries to write his poetry. As he sits amid the 'spiderwebs of snow and ice' and the 'wolf-wind gloom', he remembers the elegant past:

> Faces, voices, books we loved.
> There were violets in Chinese bowls.
> And, ah, the dancers—
>
> (p. 61; *AA*, p. 69)

As with Monet's painting, the poet's mind recalls a time of innocent joy, which now seems like a dream, a life someone else lived:

> We lived here—when?—under a spell.
> We have awakened. We are here.

Like Hayden in the museum being briefly comforted by 'the serene great picture that I love', we cannot live long under the spell, but recalling it somehow assures us that joy is real, is possible. And like the picture, and the decaying edifice, like the poet's daughter, the figure of Lear in the next-to-last poem provides us with another image of human transcendence over adversity, 'in fevers, rags,/ decrepitude' (p. 62; *AA*, p. 70). As in the *Figure of Time* volume and the second group of *A Ballad of Remembrance*, '"Lear is Gay"' here effectively concludes these final images of muted consolation, muted because the time of mourning is not yet completed. But it is the final poem, 'A Plague of Starlings', which concludes the volume as a whole, recalling those lives sacrificed so that the period of mourning might be lessened, the transition be made less severe, and the Sphinx's 'blood-matted paws' be rendered lifeless. This concluding piece also foreshadows the Platonic themes which were to dominate Hayden's next volume.

On a literal level the poem is a first-person account of a professor's concern about the 'workmen' who fire shotguns into the magnolia trees at night on the Fisk campus to kill the bothersome starlings. But the powerful image of their death in the second stanza implies a deeply serious tone:

> Their scissoring
> terror like glass
> coins spilling breaking
> the birds explode
> into mica sky
> raggedly fall
> to ground rigid
> in clench of cold.
>   (p. 63; *AA*, p. 71)

The speaker himself gives us a clue to the symbolic meaning of the poem when he compares the spared birds who return to 'chitter and quarrel/ in the piercing dark/ above the killed' to the 'choiceless poor' returning to a 'dangerous/ dwelling place'. Here again darkness becomes a symbol of this mourning time, and the dark birds (once used in racist cartoons of Afro-Americans) become a very serious allusion to the assassinations discussed earlier in the volume. In the fourth stanza the speaker threads his path 'past death's/ black droppings' the next morning on the way to class, trying to avoid the 'troublesome' bodies. In the final stanza he states in an ironic tone that he must be careful not to

> tread
> upon carcasses
> carcasses when I
> go mornings now
> to lecture on
> what Socrates,
> the hemlock hour nigh,
> told sorrowing
> Phaedo and the rest
> about the migratory
> habits of the soul.

What Socrates told Phaedo in that precious time of mourning before the execution was that the 'true philosopher' desires to 'get away from the body and to turn to the soul'.[29] Therefore, in the *Phaedo* Socrates argues that the true philosopher looks at death not as an ending but as a liberation of the soul from its physical restrictions:

In this present life, I reckon that we make the nearest approach to knowledge when we have the least possible intercourse or communion with the body, and are not surfeited with the bodily nature, but keep ourselves pure until the hour when God himself is pleased to release us. And having thus got rid of the foolishness of the body we shall be pure and hold converse with the pure, and know of the clear light everywhere, which is no other than the light of truth.[30]

It is important to note that this dialogue, like Hayden's poem, is told after the philosopher's death as Phaedo recalls for others what Socrates had said in his last moments. What Phaedo then relates is a lengthy discourse on immortality, on knowledge as recollection of understanding what once was experienced in a previous existence, of physical reality as a transient shadow of what is truly real – all the major themes of Hayden's volume. The allusion to metempsychosis occurs when Socrates humorously introduces the idea that some souls return to the corporeal realm in a form befitting their previous life – tyrants into wolves or hawks, for example. But this surface humor, both in the *Phaedo* and in Hayden's poem, belies the serious nature of the statement. Here the speaker in Hayden's poem remarks that he must tread carefully since the dead bird may have been an incarnate human soul. Figurally, he is alluding to the historic deaths which he must not 'tread upon' or disregard, the sacrifices of those slain leaders.

But the discussion of the 'migratory/ habits of the soul' in the Socratic dialogue hardly concludes with the explanation of metempsychosis. It focuses instead on the ephemeral, though purposeful, nature of corporeal reality and the more substantial spiritual reality which awaits the true philosophers, thus accounting for Socrates' detachment in facing death. This is the real impact of what Socrates tells sorrowing Phaedo in that mourning time, what Phaedo in the dialogue recalls the philosopher saying, that for one truly aware of what is real and rewarding, death is a release from confinement, not a reason to mourn.

Perhaps Hayden, like Phaedo recalling the words of Socrates, recalls the voice of Martin Luther King, Jr., in the poem 'Words in the Mourning Time'; apparently aware of his own impending 'execution', he exhorts people to 'master now love's instruments':

> I who love you tell you this,
> even as the pitiful killer waits for me,
> I who love you tell you this.

> (p. 47)

Perhaps Hayden, as speaker/persona in this piece, also recalls the teachings of Bahá'u'lláh, that mourning is vain because death is, when understood properly, a release:

I have made death a messenger of joy to thee. Wherefore dost thou grieve?[31]

Death proffereth unto every confident believer the cup that is life indeed. It bestoweth joy, and is the bearer of gladness. It conferreth the gift of everlasting life.[32]

How far to take this allusion to Socrates and the symbolism of the poem as it relates to the time of mourning and to the relationship between the physical life and the spiritual realm is difficult to say, but with the more explicitly

Platonic allusions of Hayden's next volume all speculation is put to rest.

Clearly the tone of this volume is elegiac, darker and possibly more unre-solved than one might expect from a poet who is firm in his religious convictions. Since he is examining this period of darkness prior to dawn, and since, further, he is exploring in this volume the terrifying solitude and anxiety of those not possessed of insight into the course of history, the negative tone is understandable and valid. There is some resolution, even beyond the stoic endurance of a Maia, or Lear or Jemima, beyond the sacrificial deaths of Malcolm X, Kennedy and King. In the darkness of prison, of cave or ship-wreck, the light breaks the dark night of despair, guiding the dwellers in this nether region to ascend in a measured rise, to attain an ampler understanding of their unfinished selves beyond this time and place:

> Reclaim now, now renew the vision of
> a human world where godliness
> is possible and man
> is neither gook nigger honkey wop nor kike
>
> but man
>
> permitted to be man.

(p. 49)

16. *The Night-Blooming Cereus*
1973

> But I can see none of it clearly, for
> it all takes place in semi-dark.
> A scene one might recall
> falling asleep.[1]
>
> Robert Hayden,
> epigraph from *The Night-Blooming Cereus*

A brief collection of eight poems, *The Night-Blooming Cereus* was published by Paul Breman in commemoration of the tenth anniversary of the Heritage series of poetry collections, which Hayden's own *A Ballad of Remembrance* had initiated in 1962. The twentieth in that series, this limited publication of 150 copies received little attention until its re-publication in 1975 as the second section of *Angle of Ascent*, from which Hayden deleted only one poem in this sequence, 'Ballad of the True Beast'.

The strategic importance of this volume in the progress of Hayden's art, however, far outweighed any considerations of length or distribution. Not only did this volume contain several of the best poems Hayden wrote – such as 'Richard Hunt's Arachne', 'The Night-Blooming Cereus' and 'The Peacock Room' – it also continued and encapsulated most of the major themes which had for thirty years pursued Hayden. His own comment about the volume in 1973 very clearly estimated its status. He called it 'my favorite book up to now. Writing it released me, also confirmed ideas and feelings I'd had before, but distrusted. I began to move in a new direction and to consolidate my gains . . .'[2] Viewing the poems in that light is one method of understanding the logic of the subjects and styles assembled here – each poem can be seen as a powerful crystallization of a major theme from previous volumes: the idea of the individual's search for identity, the concept of history as a divinely guided process, the belief that this period is a point of crucial transition in the progress of man's spiritual evolution, the sense of this immediate time as the wrenching grief in the auroral dark preceding even greater pangs of birth that will usher in the new day. But overriding and coordinating all these themes in this volume is the strategic emphasis on the Bahá'í/Platonic cosmological belief, as implied by the Platonic allusion in the epigraph that the physical experience, individually and collectively, is but a dramatization of a higher, more 'real' spiritual existence. In addition, this idea, introduced earlier in such poems as 'Theme and Variation' and 'The Mirages', dictates that the process of human advancement is inextricably linked to our ability to infer from these metaphorical relationships the spiritual verities that animate the phenomenal realm. Such a view, from Hayden's perspective as a Bahá'í, does not mean that the goal of human progress is a mystical detachment from the crass symbols of a loftier reality. Having understood the concept, the idea or attribute which has been given concrete or sensible form, the individual, or mankind collectively, is then obliged to reverse the process and reincorporate insight into action. In this sense – and this is the most powerful overriding consideration in *The Night-Blooming Cereus* – physical reality is comprised of artifacts and we must develop our poetic faculties in order to discern the messages this vast classroom has to impart.

At the time the book was published, students of Hayden's poetry were only beginning to understand these lofty principles which permeate all of his work.[3] Consequently, the review which appeared in *Black World* has totally out of touch with what Hayden was attempting at this climactic point in the continuity of his poetry. Written by Angela Jackson, herself a poet of substantial credentials, the review praised Hayden's overall poetic technique, the 'frankly studied' tone, but because the volume has no racial context Jackson scathingly denounced it.[4] She stated that the work is 'never at the center of Black/ activity in this world; it dwells along the periphery, coreless'.[5] The *non sequitur* – that the work is 'coreless' because this Black poet makes no allusions to racial utterance – shows that even at this date in 1973 Hayden's work was being judged according to the special criteria of the Black Aesthetic. Therefore, when the reviewer states that she does not 'hear a heart' in these lines, that the poems are a 'trick-or-treat for the intellect',[6] she is clearly examining the poems from the narrow confines of the requisites for Black poetry and totally misses the more encompassing themes it treats, as well as the crucial relationship between this volume and the continuity of Hayden's art.

But we certainly do not need to take Hayden's word for the important relationship between the poems in this brief collection and the major themes they 'consolidate'. Right off, the poet in his epigrammatical allusion to the Platonic allegory of the cave lets us know what is coming – scenes and images like visions 'one might recall/ falling asleep'. And the ambiguous 'it' ('I can see none of it clearly') has the same antecedent as the 'it' in the concluding poem 'Traveling through Fog':

> Looking back, we cannot see,
> except for its blurring lights
> like underwater stars and moons,
> our starting-place.
>
> <div align="center">(p. 15; <i>AA</i>, p. 32)</div>

And yet the 'starting-place', which may encompass the individual past as well as the collective history of man, is not all that the speaker hazily perceives:

> Behind us, beyond us now
> is phantom territory, a world
> abstract as memories of earth
> the traveling dead take home.

This idea of the present tense as wedged between abstractions, phantom worlds, clearly recalls the whole theme of life as a middle passage with 'death on either side', as well as the Bahá'í notion captured in the passage, 'We all come from God and unto Him do we return.'[7] But the conclusion of this final poem unmistakably relates these shadow images in the dark to the cave allegory, thus encapsulating the sequence in Platonic allusion:

> Between obscuring cloud
> and cloud, the cloudy dark
> ensphering us seems all we can
> be certain of. Is Plato's cave.

If all we can be certain of is the notion that phenomenal experience is a metaphor of a world 'abstract as memories of earth', if eternal verities and spiritual reality are only hazily perceived by those of us ensphered in this dark cave of the physical realm, then why, one might ask, should one struggle for knowledge? The answer to this question is partially contained in the rest of the analogy, that ascent is possible, even if, in this world, only to a limited or relative extent. But the epigraph and the final poem imply only the overall attitude, that knowledge and understanding are limited in this life. In between the two are seven poems which give voice to some of these relatively understood verities that have pursued the persona (and us with him) throughout seven volumes of verse.

The first of these observations in 'Richard Hunt's "Arachne"' is, as in previous poems, conveyed through the persona's study of a work of art which itself offers analogic possibilities. In this case the persona studies Richard Hunt's statue of Arachne being transformed from woman to spider by Athena, who had taken pity on her. The sculpture, which we can see clearly through Hayden's lucid description, is an image of terror, not because the woman must become a spider, but because in that instant of discomfiting transition which the sculptor has frozen in time (as the Grecian urn in Keats' poem immortalizes the moment in the lovers' lives[8]) the woman is totally without identity. The resulting poem is a curious blend of aesthetic distance, of almost scientific analysis of 'the moment's centrifuge of dying/ becoming', a portrayal of the internal aspect of instant and total metamorphosis:

> Human face becoming locked insect face
> > mouth of agony shaping a cry it cannot utter
> > > eyes bulging brimming with horrors
> > > > of her becoming
>
> > > > Dazed crazed
> > > > > by godly vivisection husking her
> > > gutting her
> cutting hubris its fat and bones away.
>
> > > > > > > > (p. 5; *AA*, p. 23)

The neutral 'it', neither woman nor spider at this frozen moment, has totally lost identity but is beyond simple loneliness; being exactly in between, she is simultaneously amazed and terrified.

Mythologically, the story alludes to Arachne's hubris in her contest with Athena – she illustrated the amorous adventures of the gods and hanged herself when angry Athena destroyed her work. Analogically, 'cutting hubris its fat and bones away' alludes importantly, as does the whole poem, to the chastening of mankind in the transition to maturity. Like Arachne, mankind, from a Bahá'í perspective, is not aware of its destiny, what it is becoming; therefore, the 'godly vivisection' is all the more awesome. More than anything else, Hayden uses Richard Hunt's statue to symbolize the starkest fears and utter confusion of transformation. The poem is hardly a polemic, then, but a sympathetic examination of why such change devastates us – we cannot cry out; our old identity no longer suffices, but our new self is not yet attained. What we are left with in the meantime, as Hayden has noted in so many previous poems, are lost, displaced or fake identities, unfinished selves. But rather than portraying directly the various manifestations of this dilemma as he has in his previous catalogue of human struggle, he relies here on a simple but effective 'objective correlative' for the whole array of crises.

The second poem in the sequence is 'The Night-Blooming Cereus', the first poem ever commissioned by the Phi Beta Kappa chapter at the University of Michigan. Like the first poem, this anecdotal narrative serves as analogue for metamorphosis and transition, but the image suggests incipience, a joyful anticipation of fruition and fulfillment. The tone is, therefore, sometimes ecstatic, sometimes whimsical, sometimes reverent, awed.

The poem depicts the speaker and his wife keeping watch over the exotic bud, awaiting its blossoming:

> And so for nights
> we waited, hoping to see
> the heavy bud
> break into flower.
> (p. 6; *AA*, p. 24)

As they wait, the individual personalities of the couple are reflected in their different responses to the 'bud packed/ tight with its miracle', which sways as if 'impelled/ by stirrings within itself'. The speaker is both attracted to and repulsed by the strange bud; as a poetic soul he imagines it as 'snake,/ eyeless bird head,/ beak that would gape,/ with grotesque life-squawk'. While the wife 'conceded less to the bizarre/ than to the imminence/ of bloom'.[10]

The couple jokingly agree 'to celebrate the blossom,/ paint ourselves, dance/ in honor of/ archaic mysteries/ when it appeared'. These 'archaic mysteries' are a serious allusion to a sense of ancient religious faith which parallels their own awareness of 'rigorous design' and the 'focused/ energy of will' in the flower's process of becoming. As they wait in the darkness there is a 'belling of/ tropic perfume' (p. 7; *AA*, p. 25) which heralds the event:

> We dropped
> trivial tasks
>
> and marvelling
> beheld at last the achieved
> flower.

The remainder of the poem concentrates on the transitory beauty of the 'moonlight/ petals', 'recessing/ as we watched':

> Lunar presence,
> foredoomed, already dying,
> it charged the room
> with plangency.
> (p. 8; *AA*, p. 26)

But lest the applicability of this literal event to the Bahá'í theme of incipience seem strained, the poet makes the allusion himself in the next-to-last stanza:

> older than human
> cries, ancient as prayers
> invoking Osiris, Krishna,
> Tezcátlipóca.

The couple, in reverent awe at the event ('We spoke/ in whispers when/ we spoke/ at all . . .'), are aware that they are in the presence of a vital connection to an eternal ordering, much as the succession of Prophets (Osiris to ancient

Egyptians, Krishna to East Indians, Tezcátlipóca to the Aztecs) likewise reflects divine ordination in human history.

If one applies the analogy exactingly, if the flower is Bahá'u'lláh, then in what sense is that blossoming already dying? The expectancy, the understanding that archaic mysteries are still alive, all parallel the emotions of a Bahá'í aware of the incipience of mankind's fulfillment. The bloom of the flower may indeed represent the appearance of the Prophet Himself, who throughout His ministry cautioned His followers to adhere to His guidance since He would be with them in person only briefly.[11] But regardless, the final focus is on the simultaneous and unifying insight on the part of both husband and wife regarding the feeling of beauty, power and reverence which this event inspires. The appearance itself is 'Lunar' (fleeting and in the nighttime), but the effect it has on the observers, we infer, will be lasting. For this reason Hayden has written the poem in the past tense to indicate the lasting impact this epiphany has had on their lives.[12]

The third poem, 'The Performers', is on the surface a curiously light poem to be in this collection, an unrhymed sonnet in which the persona watches from his office as window washers walk 'along/ the wintry ledge' (p. 9; *AA*, p. 27). In the octave[13] the persona watches these 'two minor Wallendas' as they 'almost matter-of-factly' go about their routine, while the speaker is awed by the terror of such a feat and imagines himself tumbling from the perch 'through plateglass wind onto stalagmites below'. In the sestet the workers 'end their center-ring routine/ and crawl inside', as the speaker remarks in appreciation of their daring, 'A rough day . . ./ for such a risky business. Many thanks.' One of the workers replies 'Thank *you*, sir', and the poem ends.

As a brief lyric it might be sufficient that the poem communicates human empathy and simple kindness. But symbolically the poem clearly alludes to the 'courage leonine' with which the artist pursues his own awesome task, takes his own risk of falling 'onto stalagmites below'. In this sense artists are also 'high-edge/ balancers' who perform their 'center-ring routine' just as the speaker in 'The Lions' makes his lions 'leap, through nimbus-fire'. Also like these workmen, the artist cleanses the windows of our perception and, too often, receives little appreciation for or understanding of his work. The artist pursues his task with or without accolade, but when someone does take note, his spirits brighten.

If 'The Performers' hints at the thankless courage that art requires, 'The Peacock Room' which follows it deals directly and forcefully with an even more crucial issue regarding the relationship between art and the artist, and between art and life. Certainly one of Hayden's most allusive and splendid works, 'The Peacock Room' requires a great deal of us if we are to decipher the answer it implies to the question it poses initially:

Ars Longa   Which is crueller
Vita Brevis   life or art?

(p. 10; *AA*, p. 28)

or to the questions it leaves us with in the final stanza:

What is art?
What is life?
What the Peacock Room?

(p. 11; *AA*, p. 29)

This poem clearly necessitates some recovery of allusion before its total impact can be gleaned, though Hayden himself provided this background information in several interviews.[14] Dedicated to the memory of Betsy Graves Reyneau, the poem unfolds the associational pattern of thoughts evoked by the persona entering the lavishly ornate museum room. Begun in 1876 by Tom Jeckyll for art connoisseur Frederick Leyland, the room was completed, to everyone's displeasure, by James Whistler, who satirically decorated the fine Cordova leather with gaudy gold peacocks trampling gold coins. This vengeful act resulted in Whistler's ejection from the home and, according to various accounts, Jeckyll's insanity and death weeks later. The room itself was preserved, transported from London to the Detroit home of the Freer family in 1892 and finally to the Freer Gallery of the Smithsonian museum in 1923. As a child of twelve Betsy had been given a birthday party in the room when it was still in Detroit, a fact to which the poet alludes in stanza four, followed by Hayden's allusion in stanza five to Mrs Reyneau's request that her body be donated to science when she died.

The structure of the poem, then, literally evolved out of Hayden's reflections on visiting the museum room (as drafts of the poem in the following chapter illustrate),[15] and the structure, consequently, is arranged so that each stanza embodies a complete thought sequence and also sets up the next stanza until all the associations merge in the last stanza. In the first stanza, for example, the speaker is in the room, briefly sheltered from the external world by its *fin de siècle* environment that recreates another era, as Monet's painting does in a previous poem. As if entering another world, the speaker feels secure from macrocosmic terror, just as he did in the glow of the rose-shaped lamp his mother lit at night sometimes 'to keep/ Raw-Head-And-Bloody Bones away'.[16] In the second and third stanzas the speaker feels the irony of this 'lyric space', this 'Triste metaphor', which, in spite of its obliviousness to the sad progress of man outside the museum walls ('Hiroshima Watts My Lai'), also recalls its own sad history – Whistler's 'arrogant art', his 'vengeful harmonies' which drove Jeckyll mad. In stanza four the persona imagines Whistler's pitiful rival cowering in a corner, shielding his face 'in terror of/ the perfect malice of those claws', but the persona also recalls another visitor to this time machine, Betsy Graves Reyneau on her twelfth birthday, a recollection which quickly recalls her passing. Consequently, in the fifth stanza the persona grotesquely imagines her bodily remains:

> pickled in formaldehyde,
> who was artist, compassionate,
> clear-eyed. Who was belovéd friend.
> No more. No more.

This *ubi sunt* plaint dovetails with all these various associations, funnels them succinctly into the enigmatic theme – What is art that it should endure while these subtle, lofty human qualities disappear? The question, made now more poignant by the poet's own demise while the room yet remains, is abstrusely answered with a final mystic, almost oriental response:

> What is art?
> What is life?
>   What the Peacock Room?
> Rose-leaves and ashes drift
> its portals, gently spinning toward
>   a bronze Bodhisattva's ancient smile.

The smile of the nearby Bodhisattva, an avatar who has delayed his entrance to Nirvana in order to assist others, is captured in bronze by an ancient artist, just as Whistler has given sensible form to an era, as well as to the anecdote of the room's creation. But the ancient smile precedes in time the room and hints at a meaning that empowers the ostensible transience of human life and the permanence of art, as symbolized here by the rose leaves and ashes, remnants of past life and fleeting beauty. The initial question is not finally answered, though there is the hint that an answer exists – that in spite of the cruelty of life's transience and art's haunting capacity to remind us of our own mortality and losses, there is a larger meaning which transcends both life and art, a meaning towards which these images are spinning.

This magnificent elegy alludes once again to the Bahá'í consolation of an 'ever-advancing civilization',[17] a progressive revelation which structures all history and ultimately shears away the veils of irony and mourning, but it is an incomplete consolation here. The symbolic remains spin 'gently', subtly, almost unperceived toward meaning. The speaker ultimately finds solace only in the enigmatic smile on a statue fashioned hundreds or thousands of years before by another artist who had sensed hope in the wisdom of the avatar's benign face. Just as the rose lamp as artifact provided a comforting light to the poet during his childhood, so the room's glow now provides him with shelter, comfort, wonderment and the final sense that beyond the enigmatic ironies of life is an ancient wisdom which resolves these questions.[18]

To a certain extent these questions are more specifically answered in the next two poems of the sequence which examine in remarkably tight imagery the relationship between life and art. 'Smelt Fishing' and '"Dance the Orange"', alike in their imagistic compression of thought, are as close to imagism of the New Critical School as anything Hayden wrote. There is no persona, no biographically based anecdote, only the barely perceptible images which, to the casual or untrained eye, conceal the symbolic possibilities they offer. Put another way, without being aware of Hayden's conscious artistry and symbolist technique, one might pass over these as difficult and finely sculpted images, but nothing more. Coming as they do in the midst of this precisely shaped sequence, these poems are well worth the effort they require.

The first poem, 'Smelt Fishing', consists of three haiku, each with the traditional caesura separating the two parts of the metaphoric equation:[19]

i

In the cold spring night
the smelt are spawning. Sportsmen
fevered crowd the lake.

ii

Thin snow scatters on
the wind, melting as it falls.
Cries for help for light.

iii

Who is he night-
waters entangle, reclaim?
Blank fish-eyes.

(p. 12; *AA*, p. 30)

The natural image in the first part of each stanza is equated with the human image in the second part until the third stanza where the two are mingled, as, implicitly, the fisherman himself is entangled and reclaimed by nature.

The cries in the second stanza, which if heeded are apparently unsuccessful, lead Gendron to speculate that the poem is about man's inhumanity to man,[20] but such an inference has no real basis in the poem. Instead, the images focus on man as 'sportsman' trying to fish in the night, with the waters as a subaltern of Nature taking the human life back to the waters from which man evolved. Since Hayden has consistently used night and darkness to symbolize this period in history prior to man's reclamation by God's Revelation, it seems logical that the cries, which fade in the night like melting snowflakes, are unheeded not because the other fishermen are heedless but because they are 'fevered' and because there is no light.

The 'nightwaters' are the deadening forces that permeate the darkness of declining faith, the same decline which Arnold and Eliot lamented.[21] The spawning fish recall Yeats' own symbol of a world caught up in 'sensual music' in 'Sailing to Byzantium', a country from which the persona wants to flee:

> That is no country for old men. The young
> In one another's arms; birds in the trees,
> —Those dying generations—at their song;
> The salmon-falls, the mackerel-crowded seas,
> Fish, flesh, or fowl, commend all summer long
> Whatever is begotten, born, and dies.[22]

There is no persona in Hayden's poem to reject the image of sensuality, but the implicit equation of spawning smelt and fevered sportsmen establishes a negative image of man as degraded to the level of fish, and, like the drowned man, as returned in the dark to an unevolved spiritual state. The man with 'Blank fish-eyes', then, symbolizes all who in this period of darkness have become spiritually dead, as Bahá'u'lláh cautions those entangled in sensuality in *The Hidden Words*: 'Were ye but to open your eyes, ye would, in truth, prefer a myriad griefs unto this joy, and would count death itself better than this life.'[23]

'"Dance the Orange"' is similar to 'Smelt Fishing' in stylistics, containing highly compressed images which do not easily relinquish the meanings they imply:

> And dance this
> boneharp tree
>
> and dance this
> boneflower tree
>
> tree in the
> snowlight
>
> miming a dancer
> dancing a tree
> (p. 13; *AA*, p. 31)

To a certain extent, deciphering the poet's intent here depends on knowing that it is inspired by Maria Rilke's *Sonnets to Orpheus* from which the title is taken, a work which deals thematically with fragmentary images from life, images which the artist's imagination unifies and from which he discerns 'new beginnings, signs, metamorphoses'.[24] Like Baudelaire's 'Correspondences', Rilke's sonnets collect images from nature, and from them the poet suggests human emotion and higher significances:

Stay . . . that tastes . . . Already in flight.
. . . A scrap of music, a stamping, a humming—:
Maidens, warm, maidens, mute,
dance the taste of experienced fruit!

Dance the orange. Who can forget her,
how, drowning into herself, she struggles
against her sweetness. You have possessed her.
In her exquisite windings turns your proselyte.[25]

The affirmative, joyful tone of Rilke's verse, like the simple beauty of Hayden's images, exhorts the dancer as artist (indeed, the human being as sensate interpreter of feeling) to translate intimations from nature into artistic form or physical action. In effect, Hayden here established a causal analysis of the artistic process similar to what Wallace Stevens does in 'Peter Quince at the Clavier' – Peter Quince tries to translate his desire into music:

Just as my fingers on these keys
Make music, so the selfsame sounds
On my spirit make a music, too.

Music is feeling then, not sound.[26]

In the same way the speaker exhorts the dancer to 'dance this boneflower tree' which appears in 'snowlight' as if the tree itself were a dancer dancing a tree. The succession of causality hints at the whole Romantic theory which Hayden avowed – that the artist by studying the images around him discovers in them their correspondences, their veiled and hidden meanings, very much as the Platonic philosopher ascends the cave walls by inferring the higher reality implied in the dark images, a notion succinctly concluded in the final poem 'Traveling through Fog'.

The poem before that concluding piece, in spite of Hayden's deletion of it from *Angle of Ascent,* is very important as a consolidation of his previous poetic observations regarding the nature of evil in human society. The poem is a parable, a ballad about a village plagued by a beast which the villagers believe to be

Enormous and greedily vicious. Four
snapping heads. Reptilian
body exuding ichor of evil.

(p. 14)

One day at dark 'the Stranger', Hayden's twice-used fictive persona, and a friend encounter the beast. Surprisingly, the beast is 'child-like,/ vaguely charming', 'just as frightened/ as we were'. Unfortunately, when the stranger and his friend return home, the villagers do not believe them and taunt them.

In their rumors they make the beast even worse than before, and the villagers' prejudices affect the friends:

> But worse, much worse, the Stranger
>
> said—we ourselves, this friend
> and I, fell to quarreling
> over what each of us had seen—
> and soon were bosom enemies.

The poem is too pat, perhaps, too didactic, but it conveys, albeit in a light-hearted tone, Hayden's very serious belief as a Bahá'í that evil is not external, not an objective force, that it is essentially nonexistent:

This evil is nothingness; so death is the absence of life. When man no longer receives life, he dies. Darkness is the absence of light: when there is no light, there is darkness. Light is an existing thing, but darkness is nonexistent.[27]

From such a view, virtue, guidance, humanity, goodness are like beams of light in the darkness, the means for guidance, growth and progress. Evil results from man's willful rejection of this light.

The parable also portrays dramatically the mechanism of the scapegoat, racism and similar forms of misdirection (witchhunts, lynching, genocide) which Hayden has catalogued in his previous volumes. Quite obviously the poem relates strongly to the whole Platonic motif as well, demonstrating that the villagers, like the night-fishing sportsmen, are rejecting the light of knowledge, of insight, and remain entrapped in the cave of shadowy fantasies of reality, not reality itself. It is also important here that the same fallible Stranger who sometimes followed mirages also becomes a victim of this illusion.

The overall effect of this sequence is to leave the reader with a powerful symbol or analogue for almost every major Hayden theme. It is as if the previous volumes contained the data from which the poet induces the climactic statement of principle in this volume: images of history, of personal struggle, of transition, expectation, inherited evil, injustice and lost identity. It is logical, then, that the poet concludes the volume with the overriding and unifying vision of the Platonic allegory; like the themes they reflect, none of the poems presumes to draw these conclusions with dogmatic clarity. The light in this darkness is perceived with difficulty and hazily, 'like underwater stars and moons'.

The concluding image of understanding in 'Traveling through Fog' is thus an expression of the poet's humility with regard to what he knows. What he observes are 'blurring lights' in this middle passage 'Between obscuring cloud/ and cloud', between our hazily perceived 'starting-place', and the 'phantom territory' that lies before us. All we can be certain of is that there is a reality which our perceptions can reveal if we are daring enough to confront them with total honesty:

Looking back, we cannot see,
except for its blurring lights
like underwater stars and moons,
our starting-place.
Behind us, beyond us now
is phantom territory, a world
abstract as memories of earth
the traveling dead take home.
Between obscuring cloud
and cloud, the cloudy dark
ensphering us seems all we can
be certain of. Is Plato's cave.

(p. 15; *AA*, p. 32)

17. *Angle of Ascent*
1975

silken rustling in the air,
the angle of ascent
achieved.[1]

Robert Hayden, 'For a Young Artist'

The publication of *Angle of Ascent,* together with Hayden's election to the American Academy of Poets and the appointment as Consultant in Poetry to the Library of Congress, made 1975 a climactic year in Hayden's lifelong struggle for his own ascent. Finally he was being published by a major house, Liveright, now a division of W. W. Norton, and his work could receive the distribution and recognition that critic after critic had deemed so long past due. It was only logical and fitting that the volume should contain, in addition to his new work, the best of his past work as well. Consequently, Hayden included the best of his poetry from *Selected Poems* (1966), *Words in the Mourning Time* (1970), *The Night-Blooming Cereus* (1973), in addition to twenty pages of his recent work.

The result was that in *Angle of Ascent* Hayden assembled all of the poetic groups thus far delineated, and arranged them according to his thematic purposes. For the first time students of his poetry could appreciate the unity, the coherence, the logical thematic progression of Hayden's life's work. He would publish two more important volumes, but this collection represented all of the major poetry from *Heart-Shape in the Dust* (1940) until 1975.

The importance of this work is still being assessed, because except for those few scholars who had studied his work before 1975,[2] relatively little in the way of major scholarship had been done on Hayden's poetry before this time. After the publication of *Angle of Ascent* numerous articles began to appear, exulting in his symbols, probing his themes, marveling at his meters and craftsmanship. Ironically, the poet would have only five years to relish this adulation and recognition. Only the year before he had told Dennis Gendron in an interview that he did not consider himself 'in the first rank of poets – and

I wish I were'.[3] Now he was, knew he was, and so did everyone else. Not that
it changed his life much, except to make him fair game for those who would
intrude upon his time. He still pursued his art as he always had, giving it
primacy, trying to do more, never feeling he had done enough, never resting
on his belated laurels.

Quite naturally the reviews of his new volume were numerous and glowing.
His friend and fellow poet Michael Harper reviewed the book for the *New
York Times*, praising him in well-turned phrases that became repeated many
times over. He called Hayden 'the poet of perfect pitch',[4] and he noted that
Hayden's solution to the desire for spiritual transformation 'is to find
transcendence *living among the living*'.[5] To my knowledge the only slightly
negative review appeared in *Poetry* by William Logan, who found it 'discon-
certing to find the older poems last'[6] in the volume, and who felt that
Hayden's newer poems 'have not matched' the 'singular performance'[7] of
'Middle Passage'. Logan lauded 'The Dream', 'The Ballad of Sue Ellen Westerfield' and the 'stunning' 'Middle Passage', but found the newer poems less
moving, lacking in 'first-rate metaphors' or Hayden's 'dramatic narrative
mode'.

This review illustrates yet again that the failure to view the symbolic possibilities in Hayden's work still obtained – everyone adored his emotionally
charged narratives about the stark horror of placing human beings in the hold
of a ship 'spoon-fashion' like 'sweltering cattle', but few critics had yet
examined such themes as the Platonic imagery in 'The Diver' and 'Veracruz',
or the larger applications of the history narratives as a figural portrait of
mankind's progress. Except for Gendron, none had done any sort of justice to
the Bahá'í perspective. It was understandable – no one wants to invest valuable creative energy in deciphering imagery unless he is relatively sure that the
search will yield fruit. With the work of a Yeats, an Eliot, a Pound, of poets
already established and proved worthy of such study, the reader is happy to
speculate. But few critics previous to this volume had taken Hayden at his
word, that he was a symbolist poet whose poems' quiet surfaces conceal the
deep waters beneath.

With this background in mind, one can more adequately appreciate the title
of Harper's *New York Times* review – 'A Symbolist Poet Struggling with
Historical Fact'. In such a brief space Harper could barely hint at the particular
examples of this important quality of Hayden's verse, but he ably assessed
Hayden's capacities that are showcased in this collection – his 'singular
achievements' with the ballad form, his narrative bent, his focus on Black
themes without allowing his poems to become politicized. Other reviews were
even more lavish in their praise. Richmond Lattimore in the *Hudson Review*
called Hayden a 'temperate warm wise and cultured man' whose 'themes
never degenerate into hysteria or propaganda', a poet 'skilled in language and
line'.[8] He further observed Hayden's universal application of symbols which

transcends issues of race and evidences an 'irony and compassion' which 'belong only to a master poet moved by such feelings'.[9] James Cotter in *America* insightfully noted that the lack of early fame may have protected this fine poet whose new volume should 'bring him the fame his talent deserves . . .'[10] Praising both the longer narratives as well as the more compressed pieces, Cotter concluded by saying that Hayden's poems 'tell us of the journey we all hear in the heart beyond the color of our skin or the applause of the crowd'.[11] A review in *Choice* called *Angle of Ascent* a 'rich book of poems' which evinces a 'sheer delight of the revelatory possibilities of language which reminds one of Wallace Stevens . . .'[12]

Later there would be more intensive studies of the work: Lewis Turco's 1977 assessment of this collection as transcending Stephen Henderson's definition of Black poetry in *Understanding the New Black Poetry*;[13] Wilburn Williams' 1977 study of symbolism in *Angle of Ascent*;[14] Howard Faulkner's 1977 analysis of the themes of transformation in *Angle of Ascent*.[15] In short, the assessments of Hayden's talent, and of this volume in particular, were, with few exceptions, unhesitantly enthusiastic, and the volume set in motion a groundswell of recognition and serious study of Hayden's work.

But while the publication of *Angle of Ascent* finally provided an ampler audience with access to most of Hayden's poetry, to those aware of the previous continuity of his poetry the volume presented at least one major problem. As Logan correctly noted, one must wonder at Hayden's rationale for having placed the newer poems in the first section so that the whole structure of four groups presents us with a reverse chronology of Hayden's work: I. 'Angle of Ascent' (the new poems); II. 'The Night-Blooming Cereus'; III. 'Words in the Mourning Time'; IV. 'A Ballad of Remembrance' (the sequence as presented in *Selected Poems*). For example, if *The Night-Blooming Cereus* poems consolidate and conclude his prior themes, why are these poems in the second position? Furthermore, what relationship do the new poems have to the continuity of theme that they should be in the first position?

The simplest explanation for the whole structure was offered by John Wright who in his 1982 review of *American Journal* stated that *Angle of Ascent* 'recapped the work of the previous fifteen years':[16] therefore, the more recent works come first in order. Upholding such a contention is the fact that the sequences within the four groups are substantially unchanged from their previous arrangement: from 'The Night-Blooming Cereus' section Hayden has deleted only 'The Ballad of the True Beast'; from the 'Words in the Mourning Time' section Hayden has deleted 'The Mirages' and seven of the ten parts from the title poem; from 'A Ballad of Remembrance' he has deleted only 'The Web' and 'The Wheel'.

But these changes, minor though they be, do show that the volume was carefully scrutinized by Hayden who was too conscientious at arranging and orchestrating his volumes to neglect this propitious opportunity at a definitive structuring of these thematically related groups of poems. Certainly he did not intend that we read the volume backwards. Put another way, if he had no qualms about shifting the Mexico group from its third position in *A Ballad of Remembrance* to its second position among the five groups in *Selected Poems,* we can safely infer he would have had the daring to assemble the groups howsoever he wished in this final edition of what was then his life's work, especially since most readers were not even familiar with the earlier editions of the poems. But a brief examination of the relationship among these groups is the simplest way to become convinced of Hayden's purposes in organizing the volume.

To begin with, it is not surprising that the new poems are first, because, as I intend to demonstrate, these poems serve well to introduce in an indirect manner and softer tone the overriding themes of the later sections – questions of identity and origin, the artist's relation to society, the search for spiritual guidance, the desire for revitalization and transformation. It is also logical that 'Words in the Mourning Time' would come between the introductory poems and the careful working toward resolution which I have earlier delineated as occurring in section four, 'A Ballad of Remembrance'. That is, because the poems in 'Words in the Mourning Time' are generally the darkest images, it makes sense that the submergence into mourning and grief would occur before reconciliation and consolation take place. The sole problem remaining, then, is why section two, 'The Night-Blooming Cereus', a sequence he described as a consolidation of his previous work, would precede those poems in this volume.

In a sense the answer to this dilemma is obvious; though *The Night-Blooming Cereus* volume was published after the poems in the third and fourth sections, it contains powerful and compressed images of what those poems particularize. Therefore, while the *Cereus* poems may have represented to the poet a 'consolidation' and confirmation of his previous poetry, they also function quite well as powerful introductions to those particular images.

The end result is that the structure of *Angle of Ascent* retains the basic pattern of consolation as implied in *Selected Poems,* but this journey of ascent (concluding with the Afro-American history poems) is first established in section one by the general and largely impersonal equations for those issues. Thus, the first section of new poems employs indirect symbols from nature, myth and history. The crucial themes are hinted at, but very obliquely. The second section reiterates most of these same themes, but more subjectively, more directly, more clearly, and encapsulated in relation to the perspective of life as a spiritual journey toward enlightenment and transformation. The third section then examines contemporary society in terms of the violence and sacrifice endemic to this time of mourning. Finally, in the concluding section the poems switch from the macrocosm to the internal struggle of the persona who climaxes his search with epiphany and consolation, first through his mystical encounter with Bahá'u'lláh, and finally through the fleshing out of that prophetic vision in Afro-American history.

This careful structure, together with the weighty themes these poems approach, make this work a superb collection of Hayden's poetry, a *magnum opus* whose worth is only beginning to be assayed. Perhaps uniquely in contemporary poetry, this collection examines themes appropriate to the scope of a *Commedia Divina* or *Paradise Lost,* but without becoming trite or doctrinaire. Not only does Hayden attempt to justify the ways of God to man; he also explains through poetic images how that justice is wrought in history and in each individual life. The 'angle of ascent', therefore, indicates the transcendence of the artist as well as the individual's emergence from cave-like darkness; it also implies the ascent of humankind from myopic fear to an all-embracing world vision. To analyze properly the full impact of this orchestration of Hayden's thirty-five years of work would require more space than is here appropriate. What is more beneficial for the purposes of assessing the continuity of Hayden's work is to understand how the new poems in the first section introduce this theme of ascent as it is played out in the succeeding sections.

Like the poems in *The Night-Blooming Cereus,* the eight poems in the first section of *Angle of Ascent* have no clear sequential arrangement. One can discern a loose grouping of thematic concerns inasmuch as the first two poems deal with the poet's past, 'Beginnings' and 'Free Fantasia: Tiger Flowers', both being romanticized nostalgia for Paradise Valley. Similarly, 'Stars' and 'Two Egyptian Portrait Masks' – the fourth and fifth poems – are alike in their use of celestial bodies (sun and stars) to symbolize divine guidance in general and progressive revelation in particular. The next two poems, 'Butterfly Piece' and 'The Moose Wallow', are similar in elucidating certain human traits by demonstrating ironically man's response to natural beauty. Finally, the last poem, 'Crispus Attucks', though ostensibly another history poem, alludes powerfully to the symbolism of flight and falling as established in the third poem, 'For a Young Artist', a parable about the artist and society.

Coming at the beginning of the volume, these poems could also be seen as organized around the objective of establishing in the reader's mind the personality of the poet/narrator. That is, having established his origin in the first two poems and his objective in the second (to attain his 'angle of ascent' via the wings of his art), the persona then seems to examine randomly a variety of images from the particular perspective of his personality. In studying the stars he finds paradox; in viewing the golden Egyptian portrait masks he thinks of the response of these historical figures to the search for spiritual truth; while seeing the pinned butterflies he marvels at the human desire to possess abstractions; at the moose wallow he notices his own mixed emotions of fear, awe and anticipation; in the figure of Crispus Attucks he considers the ironies of Afro-American history as it relates to human progress.

But while such inferences may indeed create for us a mental picture of the personality who will serve as guide through this complex journey of the human spirit, these initial poems have their most powerful significance in establishing with the subtle skills of an illusionist the major themes interwoven throughout the other three sections. In these simple, detached images are the seeds of that growth, the faint refrains that will build with increasing momentum to a crescendo and climax in section four.

In 'Beginnings', for example, Hayden presents a five-part chronology of family characters who played a part in fashioning the poet's emotional heritage. Generically, the five parts anticipate 'The Burly Fading One', 'Summertime and the Living . . .', 'The Whipping' and 'Those Winter Sundays'. It starts with a simple list, a catalogue of names. Not all are blood kin, but all play a major role in shaping the perspective of the artist/guide.

> Plowdens, Finns,
> Sheffeys, Haydens,
> Westerfields.
>
> Pennsylvania gothic,
> Kentucky homespun,
> Virginia baroque.
>
> (p. 1)

Part two alludes to Joe Finn (whom Sinda thinks about in 'The Dream') who survives the battle at Gettysburg but then disappears, so far as the family knows. Part three succinctly describes 'Greatgrandma Easter' who could still 'chop and tote firewood' at age ninety. Part four delightfully recalls great-aunt Sally, great-aunt Melissabelle and Sarah Jane as vibrant and daring young ladies who 'Sold their parlor chairs to go/ to Billy Kersands' minstrel show' (p. 4). After the upbeat account in rhymed couplets and dance rhythms of these lively ladies Hayden ends the poem in part five with Pa Hayden's lament for Floyd Collins' entrapment in Crystal Cave:

> Poor game loner
> trapped in the rock
> of Crystal Cave, as
> once in Kentucky coal-
> mine dark (I taste the
> darkness yet)
> my greenhorn dream of
> life. Alive down there
> in his grave. Open
> for him, blue door.
>
> (p. 5)

The simple anecdote implies essentially the same humanity in this characterization of Pa Hayden that Hayden will reveal in 'Those Winter Sundays'. Pa Hayden recalls the feeling of that darkness, and prays for Collins' relief from that wretched darkness.

Of course, one cannot help anticipating here Hayden's use later in the volume of the Platonic allegory, though someone approaching the poem unaware of what succeeds it might hardly suspect the allusion. But a careful reading will take the reader back to this poem to see in that final plea a cry 'for help for light'[17] which is a spiritual as well as a physical longing.

The second poem anticipates later portraits of Paradise Valley and that era which Hayden portrays in later poems with elegiac nostalgia. For example, 'Free Fantasia: Tiger Flowers' recalls the characters and era depicted in 'Summertime and the Living . . .', but with its closing allusion to Rousseau's painting *The Virgin Forest* (and by implication the concept of the 'noble savage'), 'Free Fantasia' poignantly establishes the theme of innocence and vitality which Paradise Valley represented to Hayden. It is not a naive idealization of the era or of Tiger Flowers as hero: it is a 'scuffler's/ paradise of ironies' where the speaker runs errands 'for Miss Jackie/ and Stack-o'-Diamonds' Eula Mae', though '(unbeknownst to Pa)' (p. 6). The poem alludes to the 'bluesteel prowess' of the Black prize fighter who was an 'elegant avenger', and it refers to his untimely death in an auto wreck as having a dramatic impact on the speaker: 'I'd thought/ such gaiety could not/ die.' There is, then, with the closing allusion to Rousseau's painting, which the speaker chooses 'now as elegy/ for Tiger Flowers' (p. 7), a sense of past nobility which Hayden particularizes later in the volume.

The third poem is perhaps the most crucial of these new pieces – certainly it has been the most discussed. Inspired by the short story 'A Very Old Man with Enormous Wings' by Nobel Prize-winning author Gabriel Márques, this narrative forms a parable from which the volume's title is derived. In the context of this volume the poem introduces the theme of the artist's relation to society and to his art, the same theme which becomes particularized in section two with poems like 'The Peacock Room' and '"Dance the Orange"', in part three with 'Monet's "Waterlilies"' and 'The Lions', and in part four with 'A Ballad of Remembrance' and 'O Daedalus, Fly Away Home'. As Howard Faulkner notes in his study of Hayden's theme of transformation, images of flight and ascent appear several times in Hayden's work as symbols of or analogues to spiritual metamorphosis, just as the achievement of flight and ascent is always 'threatened in these poems: by the danger or lure of falling, by the necessity of fleeing, by the seductiveness of stasis'.[18]

Literally, the narrative begins *in medias res* with a winged man 'Fallen from the August sky' being kept on a farm in a pigsty. To the rural onlookers this alien creature fascinates and repels as 'he twists away/ from the cattle-prod, wings/ jerking', regards them all 'with searching eyes':

> Neither smiles nor threats,
> dumbshow nor lingua franca
> were of any use to those
> trying for clues to him.
>
> They could not make him hide
> his nakedness
> in their faded hand-me-downs.
>
> (p. 9)

The third-person narrator describes the onlookers as 'Humane, if hostile and afraid', an important description since we can assume that Hayden's sympathies are clearly with the winged man who seems to allegorize the artist in society. The man cannot use their gifts of 'Leftovers' nor appreciate the 'Carloads of the curious' who pay to get a look at this 'actual angel? carny freak?' On his pallet in the chicken-house he eats sunflowers and 'the lice crawling his feathers', pays little heed to the people who 'crossed themselves and prayed/ his blessing;/ catcalled and chunked at him'.

Later, alone in the dark, the man begins to try his heavy wings, though at first he is unsuccessful:

> In the dark his heavy wings
> open and shut, stiffly spread
> like a wooden butterfly's.
>
> He leaps, board wings clum-
> sily flapping, big sex
> flopping, falls.
>
> The hawk-haunted fowl
> flutter and squawk;
> panic squeals in the sty.
>
> (p. 10)

Finally gathering his strength, the seemingly awkward creature tries again:

> He strains, an awk-
> ward patsy, sweating strains
> leaping falling. Then—
>
> silken rustling in the air,
> the angle of ascent
> achieved.

As an allegory the poem is appropriate to this beginning section since it is hardly a complete or final analysis of the poet's relationship to society. The poem is concerned with the mixed feelings of awe and fear with which society regards the poet, and with the desire of the artist to transform himself from his ostensible awkwardness into something beautiful, a 'silken rustling in the air' achieved by the wings of his art. The poem thus calls to mind one part of Coleridge's own allegory of the artist, 'Kubla Khan':

> And all should cry, Beware! Beware!
> His flashing eyes, his floating hair!
> Weave a circle round him thrice,
>   And close your eyes with holy dread,
>   For he on honey-dew hath fed,
> And drunk the milk of Paradise.[19]

Like Cassandra whose prophetic art was doomed to be scorned, the artist in these poetic parables must endure the misunderstanding of society which perceives his art as ridiculous, unpragmatic and his 'nakedness' (his frank portrait of life) as offensive. The onlookers are interested, probe the creature as they would a strange animal, but finally resort to persecuting what they cannot understand.

It may seem strange that Hayden characterizes these people as 'humane', but the poem is not aimed at condemning those who do not understand the function of art and the artist; the poem conveys the perspectives of each. To the people the artist is interesting but asocial; he nourishes himself on strange food (sunflowers which symbolize light and strength), disencumbers himself of anything which would interfere with the working of his art (the lice). They cannot get him to respond, cannot communicate with him and he cannot fly until he is alone in the dark. Even then his flight is achieved only with great effort after several failures, and he is still awkward, a 'patsy', until the instant he is airborne, at which time, one infers, the beauty and value of his art are apparent.

The poem does not condemn society or praise the artist as savior – it simply introduces the ironies and enigmas of the artist and his art in relation to pragmatic society. In later poems Hayden continues this theme, questioning the value of art and extending the imagery of flight and falling, with regard to art and the philosophy that ascent and falling imply, in such poems as 'The Diver', 'The Performers' and even in the final poem of this first group, 'Crispus Attucks'.

The fourth poem 'Stars' is also a major new poem. Like 'Beginnings' it is divided into five parts with a hint of chronology and with allusive symbolism. Often discussed by critics because of its explicit allusion to the Bahá'í Faith in part five and because of its symbolic possibilities, the poem is, like all of these in group one, quiet and indirect. With finely honed images, it introduces into the volume the notion of light as guidance.

The first part of 'Stars' alludes to the ancient literal worship of Orion, perhaps by Hayden's African forefathers or by the Greeks:

> Stood there then among
> spears and kindled shields,
> praising Orion.
>
> (p. 11)

The Greeks praised this constellation as symbol of the hunter. As Constance Post points out, as 'the lover of Eos, the Greek goddess of dawn, he [Orion] represents, in a larger sense, those who love the dawning of this new manifestation of God'.[20] But the first section also implies the theory which is explained in the second part: the starlight which man follows is a paradox, a light that is not really there when it provides guidance:

> Abstract as future yesterdays
> the starlight
> crosses eons of meta-space
> to us.
>
> Algol Arcturus Almaak
>
> How shall the mind keep warm
> save at spectral
> fires— how thrive but by the light
> of paradox?
>
> (p. 12)

This paradox, that we study and use as guidance light that is no longer there, 'spectral fires', parallels the other paradoxes that we must abide – that we are essentially spiritual beings seeking transformation in a material world. And yet Hayden may also be hinting at another meaning to 'the light/ of paradox'. Light, as so often with Hayden, symbolizes knowledge, enlightenment or a means of enlightenment. Paradox thus becomes guidance itself, teasing the mind out of complacency and imitation. Also, the use of stars in this poem clearly alludes to Bahá'u'lláh's own statement regarding the symbolic use of celestial bodies in the Holy Scriptures:

Thus, it hath become evident that the terms 'sun', 'moon', and 'stars' primarily signify the Prophets of God, the saints, and their companions, those Luminaries, the light of Whose knowledge hath shed illumination upon the worlds of the visible and the invisible.[21]

Therefore, the starlight which guides us years after that light has been shed parallels the guidance given by the Prophets years after their physical appearance on earth, coming to us through the 'meta-space' of history.

The third section alludes to an escaped slave, Isabella Van Wagener, who called herself 'Sojourner Truth' and lectured on abolition. Hayden here describes her as following the stars out of slavery (the 'drinking gourd' or Ursa Major which guided escaping slaves northward to freedom):

III

(Sojourner Truth)

Comes walking barefoot
out of slavery

ancestress
childless mother

following the stars
her mind a star
(p. 13)

Here then is another paradox which warms the mind – a 'childless mother'
who follows a star and who is herself a star of guidance. The image also utilizes
the literal journey to physical freedom as a symbol of guidance into a spiritually enlightened state, recalling Christ's often cited exhortation to the Jews, 'If
you continue in my word, you are truly my disciples, and you will know the
truth, and the truth will make you free.'[22]

In part four Hayden shifts from the mid-nineteenth century to contemporary scientific attempts to use stars as guidance in trying to decipher the
radio waves emitted from outer space, as if spiritual guidance could be
discovered through the same technology with which an equation is resolved:

Cosmic Ouija,
what is the
mathematics of your message?

The final section entitled '(The Nine-Pointed Star)' answers this question:

fixed star whose radiance
filtering down to us lights mind and
spirit, signals future light.
(p. 15)

As Constance Post notes, the nine-pointed star is a symbol of the Bahá'í
Faith, but it comes to be used as a symbol by Bahá'ís partly because it represents the nine extant world religions.[23] Here it is used most obviously to allude
to the guidance of God through Bahá'u'lláh; therefore, the nine-pointed star is
not a variable star or spectral fire. It is a 'sun star in the constellation/ of the
nuclear Will'. But it is also a symbol of the continuity of guidance throughout
history by means of the succession of Prophets.

By alluding to the primacy of the Bahá'í teachings in particular, and
progressive revelation in general, 'Stars' thereby establishes early in the
volume the importance of the Bahá'í perspective in understanding Hayden's

intent for the entire sequence. The poem not only anticipates the other allusions to the Bahá'í Faith in such poems as 'The Broken Dark', 'Words in the Mourning Time', 'Full Moon' and 'Dawnbreaker'; it also sets in motion the theme of divine assistance in the persona's search, which ultimately climaxes in the poem 'Bahá'u'lláh in the Garden of Ridwan'.

'Two Egyptian Portrait Masks', the fifth poem in the first group, continues this same theme. Like stars, the faces of Nefert-iti and Akhenaten peer through the fog of history into the poet's eyes. From these artifacts the poet infers two thoughts: the one, which he will amplify in 'The Peacock Room', has to do with the capacity of art to preserve beauty, to freeze it in time; the other echoes the 'spectral fire' of past religious vitality by alluding to Akhenaten's revolutionary understanding of monotheism.[24]

'Nefert-iti' seems at first to have little religious allusion; her mask is a 'memory/ carved on stelae of/ the city Akhenaten built for God', but the beauteous face in sculpture seems to represent primarily the capacity of art to keep her 'burntout/ loveliness alive in stone', 'like the fire of precious stones' (p. 16). But with the second poem Hayden clearly focuses on this ancient Pharaoh's attempt to institute a monotheistic religion with Aten (the sun disk) as the symbol of that God. In the poem Hayden alludes to God speaking to the Pharaoh, inspiring him to institute the religion:

> Upon the
> mountain Aten spoke
> and set the spirit moving
>
> in the
> Pharaoh's heart: O Lord of every land
> shining forth for all:
>
> Aten
> multi-single like the sun
> reflecting Him by Him
>
> reflected.
> Anubis howled. The royal prophet reeled
> under the dazzling weight
>
> of vision,
> exalted – maddened? – the spirit moving
> in his heart: Aten Jahveh Allah God.
>
> (p. 17)

The last line clearly refers to the Bahá'í concept of progressive revelation, implying the succession of religion from Akhenaten's belief in Aten, to the Jews' and Christians' belief in Jahveh (Jehovah), to the Moslem belief in Allah, to the Bahá'í belief that all of these appellations designate God. The mask of the Pharaoh thus recalls that continuity vividly, and the artist's function has been made sacred by his giving concrete form to the reality that histories can only chronicle and by corroborating from the past the assurance of God's continued guidance.

There are more than these inferences to be gleaned from these companion pieces. According to some histories, Akhenaten not only 'reeled/ under the dazzling weight/ of vision', he later recanted and went back to the old gods. Also in some accounts it is speculated that Nefert-iti remained faithful to the new religion and, for this reason, was later discarded by him, though two of her six daughters became queens of Egypt.[25] Thus, the exaltation of her beauty in the first poem assumes a deeper, more spiritual significance – hers is a spiritual as well as physical beauty:

> Fair of face   Joyous with the Double Plume
> Mistress of Happiness   Endowed
> with Favor   at hearing whose Voice
>
> one rejoices   Lady of Grace
> Great of Love   whose disposition cheers
> the Lord of Two Lands—

The last three poems in the section seem to focus on a single clear irony or mind-warming paradox: in 'Butterfly Piece' that the 'Wild beauty' is 'killed, sold to prettify' (p. 18); in 'The Moose Wallow' that the speaker both fears and hopes to see 'the tall ungainly creatures/ in their battle crowns' (p. 19); and finally in the four-line tribute to 'Crispus Attucks' that the 'Name in a foot-note' is 'propped up/ by bayonets, forever falling' (p. 20). But each piece ties into the sequence importantly and, like the other poems in the group, establishes in very broad terms issues which later poems examine in detail.

'Butterfly Piece', at once a lush literal image of mounted Brazilian butter-flies and an allusion to man's attempt to seize crassly the outward vehicle of beauty, to possess it literally rather than grasp its metaphorical value, is also playing off the positive use of artifact in the previous poem:

> Colors so intense I imagine them heavy enough
>   to have broken the live wings—as human
> colors in our inhuman world burden, break.
>
>   (p. 18)

The irony that color in nature is perceived by human beings as beauteous whereas color in human beings is perceived as a defect is compounded by the negative results of each: both butterfly and African natives are captured and sold. The paradox that our human world is 'inhuman' is metaphorized by the notion that color (an abstraction) burdens both nature and man when it should embellish and glorify each. The poem also recalls the bright colors, the 'psychedelic flowers' of the Rousseau painting which Hayden uses as symbol of the flashing lights of Paradise Valley in 'Free Fantasia'.

'The Moose Wallow', though less serious in tone, focuses on the persona's ambivalence as he enters this dark abode of these 'ungainly creatures'. The mixture of fear and hope which the speaker feels sets up well the poems later in the volume which will describe that same ambivalence with regard to this age of transition – this time of dawning and mourning:

> I felt their presence
> in the dark (hidden watchers)
> on either side.
>
> (p. 19)

The 'hidden watchers' in the dark woods parallel the 'hidden ones' in the underwater wreck of 'The Diver', just as the speaker's enchantment with this danger foreshadows the diver's desire to 'fling aside/ the mask and call to them . . .'[26] This scene also anticipates the dark of the hospital room when the persona senses 'Death on either side',[27] or, in a more positive vein, the excitement and anticipation the characters feel awaiting the bloom in 'The Night-Blooming Cereus'. Naturally, all these images blending a hope and fear sensed in the dark prefigure the larger symbolic implications of mankind awaiting transformation in the 'auroral dark' of history's centrifuge, as described directly in 'Words in the Mourning Time' and as implied in the structure of the entire volume.

The final poem 'Crispus Attucks' is a deceptively simple reference to the runaway slave who was the first American to die in the Revolutionary War. His death, only a footnote in accounts of the 1770 Boston Massacre, thus becomes symbol both of the American spirit and, paradoxically, of the Black nationalist:

> Name in a footnote. Faceless name.
> Moot hero shrouded in Betsy Ross
> and Garvey flags—propped up
> by bayonets, forever falling.
>
> (p. 20)

The poem obviously keys on 'falling', a word which, like the wings broken by color in 'Butterfly Piece', recalls the symbolic use of 'flight' and 'ascent' established in 'For a Young Artist'. As the volume's title implies, flight is a key symbol for the whole work. Here the falling is purposefully ambiguous – it signals both the literal death of the man, which becomes his only importance in history, and the figurative negation of flight or ascent. This figurative descent anticipates the persona's individual descent as diver probing the wreck, followed by his eventual ascent as believer, as Bahá'í. It also prefigures the historical treatment in later poems of the Afro-American descent into slavery and the envisioned journey towards freedom as traced and heralded in the last five poems of the volume: 'Middle Passage', 'O Daedalus, Fly Away Home', 'The Ballad of Nat Turner', 'Runagate Runagate' and 'Frederick Douglass'. Finally, this compressed image may also allude to the even more expansive implications of the descent and ascent of mankind through the cycles of progressive revelation.

As with the previous volumes such a cursory examination of the poems can hardly unleash their artistic fire or do justice to this magnificent collection. But here we can see that the grouping within the volume is logical and that the new poems serve importantly to establish unobtrusively but effectively the themes which the poet treats forcefully and directly in succeeding poems. There is emotion in this first group, but it is restrained – none portrays the emotions of the persona. Only two use the poet/persona at all ('Beginnings' and 'The Moose Wallow'), and even these relate to images outside the immediate first-hand perception of the persona.

The effect of this structure is a dramatic progression from the subtle indirection of the first group to the powerful, but also largely objective, images in the 'The Night-Blooming Cereus' group, to the intimate, personal, groping journey of the persona as he descends into mourning and searches for his 'true voice', his human identity. He wends his way back up in a 'measured rise' empowered from within by free will, his 'courage leonine, and assisted from without by Bahá'u'lláh's 'transilluminating word', just as the Afro-American people and mankind in general are similarly empowered and impelled.

The symbolic use of flight to represent human ascent works on every level, from the personal struggle of the persona as poet and as Bahá'í to the struggle of mankind in history towards promised fulfillment and enlightenment. The wings which aid in that flight may thus symbolize the poet's art or mankind's understanding, but in the continuity of Hayden's poetry these wings are two in number because they symbolize a two-fold process – knowledge and faith (knowledge in action). As 'Abdu'l-Bahá states: 'Regarding the "two wings" of the soul: These signify wings of ascent. One is the wing of knowledge, the other of faith, as this is the means of the ascent of the human soul to the lofty station of divine perfections.'[28]

Of course, this figurative image relates to other expressions of the Bahá'í and Platonic themes that unify the volume – images of light and shadow, of appearance and reality. But clearly most important is Hayden's use of ascent or flight to symbolize the ascent of mankind in history. Thus the falling Attucks in the first section is succeeded in the last section by the ascent of Frederick Douglass, and the flight of the old winged man prefigures the transcendence of man over violence and over himself. And while, the poet implies, that flight itself has not yet been achieved, the angle of that ascent has been.

18. *American Journal*
1978

charming savages   enlightened primitives   brash
new comers lately sprung up in our galaxy   how
describe them   do they indeed know what or who
they are   do not seem to[1]

Robert Hayden, '[American Journal]'

The title poem from *American Journal* purports to be the critical report of an alien visitor to his superiors about his assessment of the American people and really of the human race in general. As the final evaluation of a parting guest, this poem, together with the volume it represents, effectively closes Hayden's career, concludes his own journal. But of the two collections of poetry by Hayden under this title the second is clearly the most indicative of this theme, since it contains many poems written by Hayden after he had become aware that he had cancer, whereas this first was published in conjunction with the American bicentennial commemoration.

The relationship between the 1978 Effendi Press publication *American Journal* and the 1982 Liveright publication by the same title is very much like the relationship between *A Ballad of Remembrance* (1962) and *Selected Poems* (1966). The Effendi Press version was published privately and limited to one hundred bound and one thousand paperback copies, whereas the 1982 edition by Liveright has received substantial publicity and distribution. But more importantly the Liveright version of this collection contains ten new poems (out of a total of twenty-two poems) and is divided into five structural groups. To an extent the new poems amplify the purposes of the Effendi Press publication, because Hayden has scattered the additional poems throughout the sequence to flesh out the themes and to form the structural groups within the volume. Thus, just as *A Ballad of Remembrance* establishes the fundamental theme of personal search which is the heart of *Selected Poems*, so the Effendi Press *American Journal* lays the foundation for Hayden's final collection.

At a glance, the poems in the Effendi Press *American Journal* seem to be more of the same themes Hayden had treated throughout his career – Black heroes (Matthew Henson, Phillis Wheatley and Paul Laurence Dunbar); images of Paradise Valley; questions of identity; analogues of our modern quest for enlightenment. But there are important differences here in style and theme. There is no radical departure from Hayden's usual lyric modes, but in many poems there is a substantially heavier reliance on image and a return to his focus on dramatic characters. Thematically, the poems are solidly yoked together by the specific notion of an alien visitor taking leave of his temporary abode. In other words, the Platonic motif picks up where *Angle of Ascent* left off – the 'true philosopher' descends, re-enters the cave after his ascent, probes the dark from his new perspective and then departs the physical class-room. The end result is a unified statement about the artist's function in society.

The book was well received despite its limited distribution. It was reviewed in the *New York Times* by Michael Harper and received a nomination for the National Book Award. Harper's review notes Hayden's 'precision and economy'[2] and the organization of the poems in the sequence. He cites a major theme as 'the contrast between the celebration of ancestral rituals and the damage to our spiritual lives wrought by a materialistic world'.[3] Harper closes by stating: '[Hayden's] poems promise a blossoming evident in the continu-ous journal of an America he has both named and penetrated.'[4] Robert G. O'Meally in *Book World* observed how Hayden in these poems 'draws characters of stark vividness as he transmutes cardinal points and common-places of history into dramatic action and symbol'.[5] He concludes by describing the book as consisting of 'unforgettable images of America and her people, a prayerful report from one of our most hauntingly accurate, and yet hopeful, recorders'.[6] Reginald Gibbons in the *Ontario Review* noted that while Hayden had not produced the quantity of verse that some poets have, his 'delicacy and care with which he takes the common tongue' override this concern.[7] More particularly, he notes the 'thoughtful organization' of the volume, the artistic restraint, and the powerful use of irony in assembling accounts of 'explorers' from various times and places.[8]

This structural motif which both Harper and Gibbons note is at once subtle and yet, for most readers, more accessible than the thematic structure of Hayden's previous works because the volume is a catalogue of aliens. Some are literally explorers to alien places (astronauts and arctic travelers); some are simply misfits. There is also a hint of chronology in the arrangement of these figures. It begins with the 1773 letter of Phillis Wheatley and ends with the alien's futuristic report. But overriding any strict concern for chronological sequence is the sheer variety of points of view which Hayden's catalogue provides.

For example, among the aliens commemorated or recreated are the Black poet Dunbar, who penned his lyrics in a 'broken tongue'; the 'rag man', who has 'rejected all/ that we risk chills and fever and cold/ hearts to keep'; the poet/persona, who visits the prison cell of a 'lifer' and an idyllic Caribbean island; Matthew Henson, who, in addition to being the first explorer to reach the North Pole, lived for a while among the Greenland Eskimos; and finally the astronauts, who probe the lunar wastes.

Only a few poems do not seem to relate obviously to this unifying theme – 'The Point', 'Killing the Calves' and 'Zinnias'. Two others, 'Elegies for Paradise Valley' and 'Names', partake symbolically of this theme of alienation by alluding to the poet/persona as Afro-American and by implying that the artist as a sensitive spirit is alien to this world, just as mankind in a refined state is alien to, or at least uneasy with, physical reality. Furthermore, as with most of Hayden's previous volumes, there is an internal order to the sequence. Specifically, Hayden arranges the poems in three successive pairs, followed by two groups of three poems, with '[American Journal]' as a concluding poem for the whole volume.

The first pair of poems, 'A Letter from Phillis Wheatley' and 'Paul Laurence Dunbar', concern two Black poets whom Hayden greatly respected. The first poem which Hayden described as a 'psychogram',[9] is an epistolary form of a dramatic monologue in which the former slave writes to her friend Obour during a visit to London in 1773. With wry humor she relates her encounter with a young chimney-sweep who, observing her dark skin, asks, 'Does you, M'lady, sweep chimneys too?' She also notes the hissing scorn of 'would-be Wits' who 'murmur of the Yankee Pedlar/ and his Cannibal Mockingbird', a phenomenon she refers to as the 'Serpent' in idyllic England's Eden.

The equally restrained lyric 'Paul Laurence Dunbar' concerns the dead poet's worth. The persona lays 'roses on his grave' and speaks 'sorrowfully of him/ as if he were but newly dead', recalling Dunbar as the 'Poet of our youth', 'his "cri du coeur" our own'. When the bequeathed roses 'flutter in the wind', the speaker weights them down with stones, symbolizing, no doubt, a determination not to neglect either of these poetic pioneers, just as a much younger Hayden had written in the poem 'We Have not Forgotten' over forty years before:

> And if we keep
> Our love for this American earth, black fathers,
> O black mothers, believing that its fields
> Will bear for us at length a harvesting
> Of sun, it is because your spirits walk
> Beside us as we plough; it is because
> This land has grown from your great deathless hearts.[10]

The second pair of poems are autobiographically based reflections, the first of which, 'Elegies for Paradise Valley', is a sequence of eight childhood scenes that imply both an attitude and a story. The most lavishly praised of any poems in the volume, the sequence begins with the poet's first intimations that he is himself an alien:

I

My shared bedroom's window
opened on alley stench.
A junkie died in maggots there.
I saw his body shoved into a van.
I saw the hatred for our kind
glistening like tears
in the policemen's eyes.

(p. 25)

In part two the speaker describes the 'Godfearing elders, even Godless grifters' as 'Rats fighting in their walls' (p. 26). The ambiguous 'their' could refer here to the ghetto landlords, more often White than Black, thus implying that the persona and his people must struggle to survive in dwellings not their own, or, more inclusively, that the Black populace is viewed by the rest of the citizenry as an unwanted nuisance in the walls of the city edifice.

The child's awareness of himself as alien and of the human mechanism of prejudice which creates such a status develops further in part seven as the persona recalls his parent's lore about Gypsies. They 'kidnap you', they had said, and he 'must never play/ with Gypsy children' who 'all got lice in their hair'. But the as yet unconditioned psyche of the child suggests the ironic process at work when his own people ascribe to the Gypsies the same alien status they have themselves:

Zingaros: Tzigeune: Gitanos: Gypsies:
pornographers of gaudy otherness:
aliens among the alien: thieves,
carriers of sickness: like us like us.

(p. 31)

In a more general sense the poem catalogues the rich assortment of characters who populated the child's world and filled his imagination with a pageantry of human possibilities. In part five Hayden resorts to a delightful list of baroque characters succinctly captured by one-line epithets in the traditional mode of an *ubi sunt* elegy:

And Belle the classy dresser, where is she,
who changed her frocks three times a day?
    Where's Nora, with her laugh, her comic flair,
    stagestruck Nora waiting for her chance?

Where's fast Iola, who so loved to dance
she left her sickbed one last time to whirl
in silver at The Palace till she fell?
    Where's mad Miss Alice, who ate from garbage cans?
    Where's snuffdipping Lucy, who played us 'chunes'
on her guitar? Where's Hattie? Where's Melissabelle?
    Let vanished rooms, let dead streets tell.

                              (p. 29)

Uniting these elegies throughout the eight sections is the elliptically told story of Uncle Crip who is murdered by Uncle Henry. It is Uncle Crip's laughter we hear enjoying Bert Williams on the victrola; it is his voice that wisely points out to the boy that the Gypsies grieve as 'bad as Colored Folks', and 'Die like us too'. It is Uncle Crip who dances with the boy to 'Jellyroll/ Morton's brimstone/ piano on the phonograph' (p. 30). Ultimately, however, the poem focuses on the sense of 'guilt/ and secret pain' evolving in the psyche of the young boy who, in spite of his rigorous Baptist training, is charmed and enchanted by Uncle Crip's boisterous ways:

> We'd dance there, Uncle
> Crip and I,
> for though I spoke
> my pieces well in Sunday School,
>
> I knew myself (precocious
> in the ways of guilt
> and secret pain)
> the devil's own rag babydoll.
>
>   (p. 32)

Paired with 'Elegies' is 'Names', another poem which yields clear insight into the persona's sense of alienation and lost identity. This brief lyric alludes to Hayden's discovery in his early forties that 'my name was not my name', an indignity reignited by his discovery in his last decade that legally he was still Asa Bundy Sheffey, not Robert Hayden:

> I felt deserted, mocked.
> Why had the old ones lied?
> No matter. They were dead.
>
> And the name on the books was dead,
> like the life my mother fled,
> like the life I might have known.
>
>   (p. 35)

The reference here to his mother's flight from poverty (and him) forcefully ties the poem to these allusions, and yet, elliptical though the narrative may be, one can infer the whole story from the last lines:

> You don't exist—at least
> not legally, the lawyer said.
> As ghost, double, alter ego then?
>
> (p. 35)

The young boy who had sensed his alien status in the policemen's eyes now discovers that he is less substantial still, nonexistent, only a ghost, possibly the same 'formal ghost hovering behind his lines'[11] that Gibbons describes in his review.

This poignant and unusually personal revelation (for Hayden) anticipates well the final poem in the volume where the ghostly alien's visit to this planet parallels Hayden's own odyssey. As outsider the poet also is an assayer, an observer who travels about, sometimes as a participant in the society of man but usually as an analyst, a reporter reflecting back to us the images of our world and ourselves.

The third pair of poems continues the theme of the alien in society, except that both of these characters are misfits, asocial, anti-social, outcasts. The persona in these poems shifts from his point of view as alien to become society's representative, or at least an intermediary between society and these figures. In both 'The Rag Man' and 'The Prisoners' there is implicit criticism of the society in the interplay between these symbolic figures and the world they reject.

'The Rag Man' is a simple portrait, matter-of-factly recounted about one who walks 'the winter streets' rejecting materiality and haunting the speaker's conscience:

> Where is he going or coming from?
> He would not answer if we asked,
> refusing our presence as he would
> our brief concern. We'd like to buy
> him a Goodwill overcoat, a bowl of soup;
> and, yes, we'd like to get shut of the sight of him.
>
> (p. 17)

But beyond the ironic and revealing ending, the poem is full of connotations that elevate the portrait beyond the obvious. The Rag Man is a 'noted stranger', an epithet which, in the context of Hayden's poems, at once recalls the Stranger/persona who in 'Theme and Variation' sensed the spiritual reality beyond the 'striptease' of the phenomenal world. The Rag Man disdains the cold, which, the speaker implies, society perceives so severe as to be 'a punishment/ for our sins—a dire warning at the very least'. Thus, the materiality which society risks 'chills and fever and cold/ hearts to keep' does not control the Rag Man; the cold does not affect him. But the message which his transcendence implies is not one the speaker, as a member of society, wants to hear. For even though he is sufficiently incisive to observe the ironic grating which the Rag Man's rejection of materialism causes among the passersby who try to ignore him, the speaker, like them, is also caught up in following the mirages which apparently the stranger has now ceased to follow.

In 'The Prisoners' the speaker is also a representative of society observing an outcast, but here the persona sheds his aloof pretense and attempts to establish a meaningful communication with the alien, in whom the persona recalls his own status. Based on an effort by Hayden and other Bahá'ís to share the Bahá'í teachings with inmates at Jackson State Penitentiary,[12] the poem depicts the speaker reading to a prisoner from Bahá'u'lláh's *Hidden Words*, a collection of poetic expressions of spiritual verities 'revealed by the Godlike Imprisoned One, whose crime was truth' (p. 18). The persona also reads his own 'poems I hoped were true' to the prisoner who, like himself, is 'dispossessed', possibly a victim of circumstance. The poem climaxes with the hint of communication between the poet as alien, as ghost, and the one who is literally imprisoned in an alien environment: 'It's like you been there, brother, been there,/ the scarred young lifer said'.

The next group of three poems seems unrelated to what has gone before. 'The Point' describes a memorial park at Stonington, Connecticut, where American Revolutionists repelled the British in 1775. 'Killing the Calves' alludes to a topical story of farmers slaughtering their own calves and throwing them into a ditch 'to fatten the belly of cost' (p. 42). 'Zinnias' is a description of a flower which has 'bravura/ persistence', 'wine/ colors' and 'hardy élan', but not something one would present 'to Nureyev/ or Leontyne Price'. What unifies these pieces is that slightly beneath these simple surfaces are important implications about human attributes which we derive in each poem from the interaction between man and nature. Hayden has obviously employed these images to exemplify qualities of the composite American personality, though the images point beyond the American traits (as do most of the poems in the volume) to the best and worst of human capabilities.

'The Point' and 'Zinnias' both praise the literal beauty of nature – the one depicting 'Land's end', wild swans crossing in 'translucent flight', the terns gathering, the sunbathers 'on the lambent shore', the other noting the zinnias' hardy beauty, much like the sunflowers in his previous poems. The natural beauty of the former battlefield, the speaker observes, seems a better tribute to the sacrifices made by the 'dead patriots of Stonington' than any literal memorial in bronze or stone. But, more significantly, the speaker himself as a poet who has ascended from ghetto to Consultant in Poetry to the Library of Congress is a memorial to the principles for which the soldiers died; therefore, he states, 'we are for an instant held in shining/ like memories in the mind of

God' (p. 45). The durable zinnia likewise becomes a symbol of the American character – persistent, brightly colored, enthusiastic, but hardly elegant.

Sandwiched between these two positive images of the American spirit is 'Killing the Calves', a sinister portrait of man's nobler instincts being subverted by the same material concerns the Rag Man has indicted. For even though 'the killing is "quick and clean"', it flies in the face of 'the terrible agony of the starving/ whom their dying will not save', and visually the slaughter recalls the Nazi deathcamps and

> men women children
> forced like superfluous animals
> into a pit and less than cattle
> in warcrazed eyes like crazed cattle slaughtered.
>
> (p. 42)

Following these three images of the American personality is another group of three poems which tie together the poetic portrait of the American character with the theme of the alien in a foreign land. Each of the three poems has as its central characters American explorers – the poet himself, Matthew Henson and astronauts on the moon – and in each poem the character's reaction to being in an alien environment elicits a revealing portrait. Specifically, all three poems focus on the American pioneer spirit as an index to the human desire to explore the limits of this life.

The first of these is 'The Islands', a poem inspired by Hayden's exhilarating visit to St Thomas in the Virgin Islands.[13] The lapidarian lyric of ten three-line stanzas conveys a mood usually not found in Hayden's autobiographic poetry, a simple sensual joy untainted by too much cerebration. The speaker does note the acquired mercantility of the natives with their 'promises of rum' and 'bargain sales'. But he is clearly caught up in the warmth and tropic beauty of the place, its 'Flamboyant trees', the 'Flame trees', the 'intricate sheen of waters flowing into sun'. He cannot totally relinquish his serious probings; he observes that the cheerful Jamaican cleaning woman is full of 'raucous anger' because she is 'called alien by dese lazy/ islanders'. Likewise, he notes as he tours the ruins of a sugar mill that 'More than cane/ was crushed' within these broken walls. But unlike so many poems where his potential for untarnished joy in nature is stained by historical connotation (as in 'Locus', 'On Lookout Mountain' and 'Tour 5'), the poet/persona here refuses to become enmeshed in his usual moral assessments and considerations:

> But I am tired today
>
> of history, its patina'd clichés
> of endless evil.
>
> (p. 47)

Divesting himself temporarily of his analytical task as poet, the speaker joys in the emotional release:

> I wake and see
> the morning like a god
> in peacock-flower mantle dancing
>
> on opalescent waves—
> and can believe my furies have
> abandoned for a time their long pursuit.
>
> (p. 48)

This uplifting tone, so uncommon among the usually ironic and serious themes of Hayden's work, sets up by antithesis 'from *The Snow Lamp*', a poem which also portrays an alien visitor to an evocative natural setting. This three-part fragment of what was to be an extensive epic treatment of Matthew Henson's travels utilizes three distinct poetic forms and three different points of view (somewhat similar in variety to his previous experiments in 'Middle Passage' and 'Words in the Mourning Time').[14] Hayden himself in his prefatory notes to the volume states that the title comes from an Innuit folk tale, and the first section 'attempts to suggest the spirit and mode of an Eskimo song-poem'.[15]

Phrased as though chanted in the imagery and tone of a tribal folk epic, the poem honors 'Miypaluk' (their name for Henson) 'who returned to us/ bringing festive speech', who is hunter, 'handler of dogs', 'who came/ from the strange-/ness beyond the ice', but who returned 'to his people', though 'not knowing one of us' (p. 52). This notion of Henson, an alien in his own country, bringing light to the Eskimos not only recalls 'The Prisoner' and the poet as bringer of light, but alludes once more to the Platonic cave allegory. This notion is borne out in part two of 'from *The Snow Lamp*' wherein the third-person narrator describes 'the lunar wastes of wind and snow' as in a 'darkness dire/ as though God slept/ in clutch of nightmare' (p. 53). It is a 'chimera's land/ horizonless/ as outer space', 'desolate/ as the soul's appalling night'. Ironically, it is the place 'Furthest North', the direction of freedom in images of escaping slaves in Hayden's history poems, but here as stark abstraction it terrifies because without human context freedom itself is meaningless.

In the third part of the poem we hear the voice of Henson in the prose narrative of a diary entry describing how they fester in the 'Demonic dark that storms/ the soul with visions none visionless can bear' (p. 54). Starving, 'verminous', the alien visitor struggles 'against the wish to die', uses 'Eskimo women to satiety' to sense himself still alive and not 'ghosts', an image that immediately recalls the poet's observation in 'Names' about being a nonentity. This struggle against the wish to die also recalls similar internal combat in

'Veracruz', 'The Diver' and other settings in the illusory dark where the persona must exert the full force of his will to reject the temptation to '*Leap now/ and cease from error./ Escape.*'[16] But like the persona at Veracruz who turns shoreward, or the diver who rises, or the old man who attains flight, Henson survives to become a symbol of strength and courage to the Eskimos, even though he is only a stranger, a visiting alien.

'Astronauts', the final poem in this group, uses similar imagery. These explorers literally probe 'lunar wastes', and 'Armored in oxygen,/ faceless in visors', they are childlike as they explore this 'Absolute Otherwhere':

> Risking edges, earthlings
>   to whom only
> their machines are friendly
>   (and God's radar-
> watching eye?), they
>   labor at gathering
> proof of hypothesis;

(p. 55)

The possibility of God's watchful eye in this remote region recalls 'God's laser light' in 'The Broken Dark',[17] except that this poem does not end with the affirmation of divine protection but with enigmatic questions: 'What is it we wish them/ to find for us?' 'Why are we troubled?/ What do we ask of these men?/ What do we ask of ourselves?'

The answer to these Sphinx-like riddles Hayden has implied all along in his successive volumes. What we wish from these 'antiheroes' is the same thing the people in 'La Corrida' ask of the matador, some insight into our own identity which will bring us back to life. At the same time, we are discomfited by this exploration because we do not know what this new identity will demand of us. In effect, we are threatened as we have been throughout history by explorations which disturb our complacency, just as the church was threatened by the explorations of Galileo, Copernicus and Darwin.

But despite the distrust that seems to typify the human response to aliens and explorers, the final poem '[American Journal]' does not conclude that Americans (or, by extension, humankind in general) are necessarily timid, narrow or doomed. The alien visitor's report does note the noise, the 'ignorant pride', the 'squalid ghettos in their violent cities/ paradox on paradox' (p. 59). But overriding these negative observations is the visitor's impression of the people's 'hardy élan'.

> here among them   the americans   this baffling
> multi people   extremes and variegations   their
> noise   restlessness   their almost frightening
> energy   how best describe these aliens in my
> reports to The Counselors

The visitor describes the people as 'charming savages   enlightened primitives   brash/new comers lately sprung up in our galaxy' (p. 57). They are
'wastefully ingenious', and the Counselors believe them a decadent people. He
acknowledges the hypocrisies, the injustices, 'a divided/ people seeking
reassurances from a past few understand and many scorn' (p. 59). But in a
passage paralleling the Stranger's observations in 'Theme and Variation' the
alien visitor calls America 'an organism that changes even as i/ examine it' (p.
60). And like the Stranger attracted to materiality in the poem 'The Mirages',
the Visitor confesses he is 'curiously drawn' to the people, though he doubts
that he could 'exist among them for/ long however   psychic demands far too
severe':

> much violence   much that repels   i am attracted
> none the less   their variousness their ingenuity
> their élan vital   and that some thing   essence
> quiddity   i cannot penetrate or name
>
> (p. 60)

His appreciation of this zinnia-like 'élan' cannot offset the visitor's difficulty
in living among 'crude neophytes like earthlings everywhere' (p. 60). And
while one should not align Hayden's personal perspective too neatly with this
fictive one, it is true that the poet himself was most disturbed by the increasing
violence which he saw invading society, and to which he could never become
inured.

But beyond this general figural possibility of the poet as alien explorer is the
more explicit continuation and conclusion of the Platonic parable. For if the
early volumes delineate this age as a maelstrom of anguish immediately prior to
humankind's transformation and metamorphosis, and if *Angle of Ascent*
coalesces those themes into a statement of individual ascent and future collective ascent, *American Journal* portrays the post-ascent stage, or what Robert
Stepto has called the 'post hibernation' stage, of spiritual transformation.[18]
Discussing 'Elegies for Paradise Valley', Stepto compares the persona in his
search poetically for the figures that peopled his childhood world to Ralph
Ellison's hero in the *Invisible Man*:

In his epilogue the Invisible Man declares, 'Step outside the narrow borders of what
men call reality and you step into chaos . . . or imagination.' Paradise Valley, like the
Harlem vibrating above Ellison's hero's head, is unreal because it is for the most part
unseen. After hibernation, as Ellison and Hayden tell us, the unseen must be not only
seen but also imagined.[19]

Put another way, in his artistic manifesto in 1948 Hayden had stated that
'poetry has humanistic and spiritual values not to be ignored with impunity'.[20]
He further stated his belief in 'the importance of the arts in the struggle for
peace and unity'.[21] I have noted that throughout his poems Hayden portrays

the poet, the artist in general, as a courageous explorer of human boundaries and capacities, a mission that takes Hayden's persona through the chronicles of history, into the uncharted depths of his own experience and renders him naked. And yet time and time again, after ascent on the wings of his art, after flight, after contemplation of the verities behind the 'striptease' of reality, after dwelling in the ether, after hibernation, the artist/persona returns to the cave, sometimes wittingly and willingly, sometimes by falling. But upon his return, the artist, like the visitor to the literal prisoner in this volume, is obliged to inform us what he has discovered, to name the names, to shed light upon our own identity. As in Plato's allegory, the cave dwellers may not believe what seem to be lunatic ravings; they may attack him, catcall and chunk at him, as the rural folk do to the winged man.[22] Such is the necessarily lonely task of the true artist, Hayden seems to say.

19. *American Journal*
1982

It is too late
for any change
but death.
I am I.[1]

Robert Hayden, 'The Tattooed Man'

Not published until nearly two years after Hayden's death, the manuscript for the Liveright version of *American Journal* had been carefully structured by Hayden and 'hand-carried to his publisher'.[2] By this time he knew he had cancer and sensed that this was the last volume of his poetry he would assemble. As a result, there are in section four of the volume nine poems which one reviewer, Fred M. Fetrow, has deemed as 'closest to the deliberate and forthright statement of personal lyric', poems penned in a voice which 'often derives straight from the confessional heart'.[3]

Certainly the tone of these poems, and of many of the other pieces in the volume, confirms Fetrow's assessment, and yet, as in *Words in the Mourning Time,* Hayden never relinquishes here that artistic distance he had maintained so rigorously throughout his career. Even in 'Ice Storm' and '"As my blood was drawn"', lyrics clearly evoked by his moments of deepest sadness, he is an artist watching himself, gauging those emotions, studying how his own grief relates to a grieving age. Another reviewer, friend and fellow poet, John Wright, observed that even here Hayden was not a confessional poet, that 'with words at least, he wore the mask, and won in wearing it the detached control and objectivity without which poetic marvels like his most widely acclaimed poem, "Middle Passage", would not have been possible'.[4]

The line between a poem in the confessional mode and one which uses autobiographical material but is not, is often a thin one, sometimes an indistinguishable one. With Hayden's poetry, Wright's observation is based on the manner in which the poet has employed personal history and himself as character, not to inform us about Robert Hayden, but always to get at something else, something larger than a single individual, something which affects us all. Clearly Hayden's style represents a middle ground between the purely confessional mode, which presumes that the intimate emotions of the poet and the mechanisms of his microcosm are sufficient goal, and the totally impersonal tropes of some New Critical imagists. But that is the most important distinction one can make in approaching Hayden's poetry, especially these last poems which are often so powerfully charged with a personal emotion so clearly urged by his private circumstances.

It is obviously too early to determine what impact *American Journal* will have on critical estimations of Hayden's career, but it should be considerable. It consolidates and organizes all of Hayden's poetry from 1975 until his death. Coupled with *Angle of Ascent,* which is also still available through Liveright, *American Journal* provides the student of Hayden's work with access to all his major poetry, something that was never possible during his life. Containing sixty pages of verse, this final volume compares in length with *Selected Poems* (78 pages) and *Words in the Mourning Time* (64 pages).

Both Fetrow and Wright see as the major themes of this work Hayden's concluding statements about the artist in relation to society and the nature of evil in relation to the individual and society. But both also use the occasion of reviewing *American Journal* to render a general appraisal of the continuing thematic concerns of Hayden's career and the distinguishing characteristics of his stylistics. Fetrow, for example, states that Hayden has a 'narrative versatility, a range in modality perhaps unmatched among contemporary poets'.[5] He further notes that Hayden's 'ultimate significance in American letters may be as chronicler of American culture, because he subsumed and then transcended his personal and cultural "roots" in order to address inclusive human concerns': 'As a minority in race, religion, and artistic calling, as one whose life fleshed out the prototypal American search for personal identity in an amalgamated yet fragmented society, Hayden literally lived the American dream in both its nightmarish and aspirational aspects.'[6]

Wright also traces the progress of Hayden's themes and techniques, noting that Hayden's definition of the purpose of poetry as stated in the McClusky interview ('poetry is one way I have of coming to grips with both inner and external realities . . . a prayer for illumination, perfection'[7]) is exceeded by the definition implicit in his life's work:

The fuller answer, if more oblique, is projected, of course, in the body of his work. There Robert Hayden the time-keeper, Robert Hayden the symbol-maker, Robert Hayden the believer, Robert Hayden the wrestler with language and form, all voice in concert 'the deep immortal human wish' that man be 'permitted to be man', that injustice, suffering, and violence must yield, along with the inability to love on which they feed, to what Hayden's Baha'i prophet, Baha'u'llah, envisioned as the absolute, inescapable necessity for recognizing the fundamental oneness of mankind.[8]

Wright describes *American Journal* as focusing on the heroic, particularly with regard to the artist in society as symbolized most powerfully, perhaps, in 'The Tattooed Man'. But the thrust of Wright's review is as tribute to the whole poetic career, how Hayden's stylistics developed from the apprenticeship in *Heart-Shape,* through the influence of Auden and the New Poetry movement, to his own variety of perspectives and techniques, and how his themes devolved from his personal search for 'names' and identity to his assessment of mankind's own longing for definition.

But as extensive as these reviews are, they only hint at the workings of the five poetic groups in *American Journal.* For example, Fetrow points out that group one acknowledges 'the pervasive presence of evil in the world'[9] and group two catalogues victims of that evil, 'victims of the world's failure to understand or appreciate "difference"'.[10] What he fails to note is the central issue of the artist as alien among aliens, whether exemplified through instances of racial injustice, the artist in society, Hayden as persona in this age of transition, or mankind in phenomenal reality. In short, what one needs in order to understand Hayden's arrangement of groups and the impact the added poems provide is a more thorough examination of the groups and the interplay of the new poems within them.

Overall, the organization of *American Journal* has a parallelism provided by the relationship between groups one and two and between groups three and four, with group five as the conclusion to this volume and Hayden's career. The first group asserts the evil and injustice in society, 'the cussedness/ of the human race' as Hayden puts it in 'Theory of Evil', the third poem in group one. The first two poems in the group – 'A Letter from Phillis Wheatley' and 'John Brown' – serve to set up this hypothesis by showing two distinct responses to injustice: Phillis Wheatley endures it with dignity and forbearance; John Brown, like Nat Turner before him, attempts a bloody purge. Group two then provides a catalogue of five characters, three of whom are artists, as they too respond to evil and injustice, though one clearly infers here that evil is essentially manmade, as Hayden has earlier implied in 'The Ballad of the True Beast'. Each of the five poems in group two thus implies that art, or an artistic point of view, suggests a creative response to some crucial societal issue – Dunbar and Robeson to racial injustice, the Rag Man to materialism, the poet to the prisoner, and the Tattooed Man to his paradoxical desire to have acceptance and love but retain his independence as artist and human being. In the same way, groups three and four go from theory or origin of evil to response and reconciliation to evil, but as exemplified in the intimate personal life of the poet/persona, not in society at large. Group three consists of the eight parts of 'Elegies from Paradise Valley', which, as I have already noted, portray the poet's recollections regarding his first awareness of himself as an alien in society and, more particularly, of his guilt at feeling himself an alien sinner among those Godfearing elders. The fourth group then catalogues that theme of identity, guilt and alienation in an associationally patterned but magnificently arranged group of personal lyrics. The eleven poems in this group begin with the literal question of identity posed in 'Names', and then proceed by process of association to examine the poet's reaction to societal evil as it has 'invaded my body's world'. But the depressive, almost desperate, tone of the first seven poems is followed by the hope expressed in 'The Year of the Child' and the implied reconciliation of the poet as he relinquishes his analytical perspective in 'The Islands'. The final group – 'from *The Snow Lamp*', 'Astronauts' and '[American Journal]' – has the same effect as it has in the Effendi version of the sequence. It takes leave of the physical experience by implying that the task of all men, like that of the artist, is to explore human possibilities, though as aspirants to human transcendence and spiritual perfection each of us is in an alien atmosphere. Once aware of these lofty purposes, Hayden implies, each individual must struggle on this 'darkling plain' (as Arnold termed it) to use well the physical experience and not disregard or neglect this vehicle by which transcendence is attained.

His parting assessment of the American people, and of mankind in general, is therefore an optimistic one – that, though in a relatively primitive stage of spiritual evolution, mankind has a potential and impelling energy which is not easily quashed by evil, whether intrinsic or extrinsic. In spite of his avowed Romanticism, this final portrait is not a Rousseauistic affirmation of natural goodness; nor is it, conversely, a condemnation of an inherently depraved creation bent on its own destruction. The poet, like the departing alien, like Socrates to sorrowing Phaedo, decries injustice, but observes in the raw materials of human capabilities the seeds of future growth, providing these instincts are sustained and nurtured.

Unlike Socrates, the persona in this volume is hardly calm or unwavering in his assurance. Like the dying man he is, the persona in section four experiences a condensed panoramic view of his own emotional history and his personal response to evil and injustice. As a result, we witness a range of emotions from anger to denial, from nostalgia to hope and finally to reconciliation. And yet even in what critics consider his most personal lyrics in the fourth group, as well as in the sequence throughout, one should not view this solely as a touching insight into Hayden's final struggle. As with *Words in the Mourning Time*, where the speaker cries out against injustice and finally to Bahá'u'lláh for assistance, the speaker here is clearly based on Hayden's own situation as a cancer victim, as an artist, as a Bahá'í, but the character has as well an objective existence all his own. For example, the range of emotions which Hayden gives to the persona in part four is remarkably parallel to the five emotional stages of a terminally ill patient as observed by Elisabeth Kubler-Ross: (1) denial and isolation, (2) anger, (3) bargaining, (4) depression and (5) acceptance.[11] But such conscious patterns occur in the other groups as well, and it is valuable to see how Hayden has incorporated the newer poems into a working relationship with poems from the Effendi Press volume by forming these five thematic groups.

In the first group Hayden has added 'John Brown' and 'Theory of Evil' to the psychogram 'A Letter from Phillis Wheatley' to establish the idea that evil seems fundamental to human society, though we can react to it in a variety of ways – with noble restraint or by overt warfare against injustice. Clearly Hayden's contention all along been that the most effective response to injustice is not violence, not to 'Bleed' society or 'return evil for evil', but to elevate ourselves through education and personal transformation, through love, and through God's guidance in history in the teachings of His Manifestations. But the third poem in this first group, 'Theory of Evil', seems to conclude that human 'cussedness' is inherent, not, as Hayden has implied in 'The Ballad of the True Beast', solely a rejection of goodness. In the context of the volume as a whole, however, this group serves as a statement of problem, not a solution or final insight. And even within this first group Hayden's affirmation of human goodness is evident.

After the subtle and sophisticated observations implied in 'A Letter from Phillis Wheatley' Hayden presents the five parts of 'John Brown', a poem commissioned by the Detroit Institute of Arts.[12] It is a biographical sketch, partly third-person and partly first-person, which is similar to Hayden's 'The Ballad of Nat Turner' in portraying a character who in his deluded, mystical calling attempts a bloody and vengeful war against injustice. The portrait begins with the poet/persona viewing a picture of the man, questioning what he was – 'Axe in Jehovah's/ loving wrathful hand?' (p. 5). Part two switches to John Brown's point of view to answer that question: he was 'Doing The Lord's work', 'Bleeding Kansas' (p. 6). Brown follows this medical image with a justification for the bloodshed as 'poison meat for Satan's/ maw':

> I slew no man but blessed
> the Chosen, who in the name
> of justice killed at my command.

Alluding to his own son killed at Harper's Ferry, Brown then observes:

> I am tested I am trued
> made worthy of my servitude.
>
> Oh the crimes of this guilty
> guilty land:
>   Let Kansas bleed.

That this is Brown's assessment and not Hayden's is made clear, of course, in the volume, but also in the remaining parts of the poem. In part three Brown's stream of consciousness continues as he relinquishes his assured tone and muses on the enigmatic nature of his calling, which he depicts in oxymoronic

terms as 'angelic evil' and 'demonic good' (p. 7). These paradoxical figures of
speech hint at the internal torment of one whose 'hands/ are bloody who
never wished/ to kill wished only to obey/ The Higher Law' (p. 7). He ends
this section with a final oxymoron regarding the 'Fury/ of truth, its enigmas/
its blinding/ illuminations'. The fourth section of the poems shifts narrative
mode again and alludes to the events at Harper's Ferry, presumably as Brown,
about to be hanged, recalls the event:

> Fire harvest: harvest fire:
>
> spent forlorn colossal
> in that bloody light
> death-agonies around him
> Gabriel and Nat
> awaiting him:
>
> I have failed:
>
> Come, Death, breathe life
> into my Cause, O Death.

The final lines here, recalling the ritualistic longing implied in 'La Corrida',
are, in context, questionably noble. In part five the narrator speaking in the
present tense ponders the 'mordant images' on the museum wall that allude to
this heroic anti-hero and his enigmatic life. Appropriately, the poem makes no
final assessment other than to note the accuracy of Brown's prophetic vision:

> Hanged body turning clockwise
> in the air
>   the hour
> speeding to that hour
> his dead-of-night
> sorrows visions prophesied:
>   (p. 9)

The body twisting like a timepiece foreshadows future violent transformation.
The succeeding poems, however, respond to Brown's assessment of the
'guilty/ guilty land' and how best to respond to its evil.

The final poem in this first group, 'Theory of Evil', ponders the 'cussed-
ness/ of the human race', implying the hypothesis that evil and injustice are an
inherent characteristic of man. This is not, however, Hayden's theory, but a
theory belonging to the historical tradition that the Natchez Trace recalls. The
setting is contemporary; the persona travels with companions down this
ancient trail from Nashville to Jackson, Mississippi, as he had in 'Tour 5',
recalling the legends of this ancient trek, of 'Big Harpe [and] Little Harpe' (p.
10) who attacked innocent wayfarers and who represented 'mystic evil's face'.

From the poem we infer that, having been captured, Big Harpe was killed and his head nailed to a sycamore tree as a warning to the iniquitous and righteous alike:

> It crooned in its festering,
> sighed in its withering—
> Almighty God
> He fashioned me
> for to be a scourge,
> the scourge of all humanity.
>
> (p. 11)

In one sense, then, the theory Hayden cites here is the notion of primal sin, the same sort of theology which in the heyday of Calvinism encouraged the persecution of so-called demonic people in Salem. But it is also the same theology which in Southern Protestantism allowed for persecution of Blacks as somehow inherently inferior or satanically possessed. If the theory and observations are Hayden's own at all, it is in the sense that evil, or evil in human action, is a 'scourge', a means by which humanity is stirred out of complacency, tested and taught. In effect, such a theory would imply that because the rejection of good has consequence in society, brings about negative results, man is impelled to act.

Hayden himself explained some of the symbolic implication of this trail in a discussion of 'Tour 5':

Once it was a pathway through the wilderness, and it became a dangerous and sinister road used by escaped criminals, highwaymen, murderers – 'the devil's highway' as I called it in a poem about the Trace I never finished [this one]. Travelers were often robbed and killed there. It was a lurking place for evil. But it was also used by fugitive slaves.[13]

From this comment in 1972 about the poem in its then unfinished state, one infers more easily the notion that the pathway of the slave, the pathway toward freedom, is fraught with evil, with highwaymen and injustice, but the real threat, the important evil, is not external but internal where we are truly scourged and chastened.

The second group of poems in the volume is a catalogue of figures all of whom are outcasts of one sort or another, all aliens to society because of their art or their social attitudes, and all respond in various ways to this theory, to the evils and injustices encountered on that path toward freedom. In addition to the poems on Dunbar, the Rag Man and the Prisoners which he carried over from the Effendi Press edition, Hayden has included the brief elegy 'Homage to Paul Robeson' and an allegory of the artist in society, 'The Tattooed Man'. All of these poems depict responses which are distinct from that of the persona, as if he were assaying the attitudes of others before turning the 'laser light' on himself.

The highly elliptical 'Homage to Paul Robeson' alludes to Robeson's advocacy of communism as a response to social injustice: he traveled to the Soviet Union, was blacklisted during the McCarthy hearings, and was thoroughly ostracized in spite of his incredible list of accomplishments as actor, singer, Phi Beta Kappa graduate of Rutgers, valedictorian of his class, All-American football player, and law school graduate of Colombia University.[14] Though Robeson's legal rights were restored by the Supreme Court in 1958, his reputation yet suffers because of his political stand. But it is on Robeson as artist that the poet here focuses his attention:

> Call him deluded, say that he
> was dupe and by half-truths betrayed.
> I speak him fair in death,
> remembering the power of his
> compassionate art. All else fades.
>
> (p. 16)

One should not infer from this eulogy that Hayden deemed art as license; rather Hayden implies that Robeson, like Malcolm X, was struggling, exploring boundaries. But most clearly the high regard is based on Robeson's 'compassionate art', just as in the succeeding poems, 'The Rag Man' and 'The Prisoners', Hayden focuses on the artist as becoming compassionate through his art. In 'The Rag Man' the poet as artist surpasses compassion and comes to admire the outcast, and in 'The Prisoners' the poet attempts to use his art as a means of communicating identity and understanding.

But it is the final poem in this group, 'The Tattooed Man', which conveys Hayden's most comprehensive assessment of the artist's role, as well as his plight as alien. A remarkable dramatic monologue, this allegory reveals a sideshow freak (like the compassionate 'Aunt Jemima') who, like Hayden, is 'Born alien,/ homeless everywhere', who chooses this life of 'bizarrity,/ having no other choice' (p. 19). Clearly tying together previous symbols of the artist, Hayden portrays this intriguing character as gazing from 'a gilt/ and scarlet cage' reminiscent of the 'gilt and vermilion cage' in which the archer's lion performs.[15] Like the old winged man in 'For a Young Artist', the tattooed man acknowledges that

> Hundreds have paid
> to gawk at me—
> grotesque outsider whose
> unnaturalness
> assures them they
> are natural, they indeed
> belong.
>
> (pp. 19–20)

In depicting this alien, this 'grotesque outsider', the poem obviously anticipates the childhood recollections of 'Elegies of Paradise Valley' in group three.
But perhaps most poignant of the speaker's observations is the anxiety he feels
because of the conflict between his desire for love and acceptance and his
determination to live for his art:

> Oh to break through,
> to free myself—
> lifer in The Hole—
> from servitude
> I willed. Or was
> it evil circumstance
> that drove me to seek
> in strangeness strange
> abiding-place?
>
> (p. 19)

This question of whether the artist is born alien or chooses his lot in order
to examine reality and to comfort man is left open, though having achieved his
station as artist, the speaker acknowledges that to continue in his condition
involves pain, the images acquired by needles here symbolizing the agony with
which all artists bring forth their labors:

> Da Vinci's Last Supper—
> a masterpiece
> in jewel colors
> on my breast
> (I clenched my teeth in pain;
> all art is pain
> suffered and outlived);
>
> (p. 20)

As Wright notes, for Hayden the artist's imagination is not a retreat, a place of
refuge, but 'a danger zone . . . because art is both cruel and mysterious'.[16]

The symbolic possibilities of this poem are vast and embrace so many of
Hayden's other poems and symbols that a neat summary of its function in the
sequence is impossible. But besides examining the agony of the artist as
comforter, the poem also concludes with the revealing insight that the
tattooed man could become normal, could dare 'the agonies/ of metamorphosis', could 'endure caustic acids,/ keenest knives', but he has accepted his
alien status too long:

> And I—I cannot
> (will not?) change.

It is too late
for any change
but death.
I am I.

(p. 21)

As a summary to the catalogue of artists in society in group two, the implication in this final phrase is clear, that the determination of the artist to choose
this path of art as a reaction to 'evil circumstance' is a more benign, more
courageous, and ultimately more effective response to evil than the violent
answers of John Brown or 'Them Harpes'.

Having probed external images of the artist's response to evil and injustice,
Hayden reviews the origin of his own response, first by probing in the 'Elegies
for Paradise Valley' his first pangs of alienation and guilt, of love and death,
the origin of his own theory of evil. Then in the fourth group he assembles
diverse and sundry personal lyrics which review at this crucial time in his life
how he has responded to these forces. The resulting sequence is, as I have
noted, a powerful series of emotional associations, beginning with his lost
identity in 'Names' and ending with the implicit resolve and acceptance of his
past in 'The Islands'. After 'Names', with its recalled anger and present feelings of being a 'ghost', the speaker in 'Double Feature' remembers how as a
boy he would go with friends to the local theater for an interlude to escape 'the
bill-collector's power' and to ride 'with the exotic sheik/ through deserts of
erotic flowers' (p. 36). Ignoring 'the rats and roaches we/ could not defeat', the
youngsters would revel in the hero's 'noblest wrath' as he defeated 'weakéd
men':

Oh how we cheered to see the good we were
destroy the bad we'd never be.
What mattered then the false, the true
at Dunbar, Castle or Arcade,
where we were other for an hour or two?

(p. 36)

This childhood fantasy of desiring to be 'other', never bad or alien, is immediately followed by 'The Dogwood Trees', an allusion to 'an evil time' when
'crooked crosses flared', when 'shrill slums/ were burning' and the speaker
dared a 'comradeship' with a white friend. This recollected courage, however,
is then followed by an enigmatic 'Letter', a sonnet to an unnamed person who
has 'risked pain' and is 'yet compassionate' because of the persona's anguish
that 'rends my spirit like beast-/angel, angel-beast' and who has 'for/ a lifetime nurtured and tormented me' (p. 38). The sonnet, both in its structure and
content, recalls immediately the 'Sonnet to E.' in *Heart-Shape* wherein the
poet praises Erma whose 'love with generous wisdom tutors me/ To see what

hitherto I could not see'.[17] Whether or not the poem here alludes to a specific anguish or the artist's love-hate relationship with life is not important – if it were, we can be certain Hayden as a careful artist would have given us more clues. Like the 'conundrum', the 'psychic joke' in 'Sphinx', the speaker has been scourged by this evil, has been tormented and impelled to create. Like the Tattooed Man, however, the speaker is 'desperate still' but has resolved that he 'will no longer ask for more/ than you have freely given or can give' (p. 38), realizing that coming to terms with the paradoxes of his life can meet with only limited success.

This same theme continues with the next two poems in the group, almost as if this were one continuous lyric. In 'Ice Storm' the speaker is unable 'to sleep, or pray' and stands in the dark at the wintered windows observing 'moon-struck trees a December storm/ has bowed with ice' (p. 39). Perhaps representing the third or 'bargaining' stage in his emotional response to the cancer which the next poem will reveal more explicitly, the speaker here notes that the trees 'will survive their burdening,/ broken thrive', and asks rhetorically, 'And Am I less to You,/ my God, than they?'

'As my blood was drawn' then enunciates more clearly than any other poem in the volume Hayden's own theory of evil as well as the premise of the volume itself. In keeping with the depressive phase of the Kubler-Ross paradigm of the terminal patient, the speaker alludes to the cancer as metaphor of the infested body of mankind. The speaker observes that as his 'blood was drawn,/ as my bones were scanned' the evil events in the macrocosm seemed to parallel his own deterioration:

> the People of Bahá
> were savaged were slain;[18]
>
> skeletons were gleaning
> famine fields,
> horrors multiplying
> like cancer cells.

> (p. 40)

He goes on in an apostrophe to address the personified world as a cancer patient, asking if this external evil has not infected his internal world:

> World I have loved,
> so lovingly hated,
> is it your evil
> that has invaded
> my body's world?

The speaker's condition further parallels the 'sickness' of the external world in the ostensibly terminal nature of the disease – as the 'surgeons put/ me to the knife,/innocents/ were sacrificed' and 'As spreading oilslicks/ burned the seas,/ the doctors confirmed/ metastasis'.

As an artist whose primary function it is to observe, to explore rather than to 'make things happen', the speaker ultimately has only one response to this realization that the world body politic, like himself, is cancer-ridden; he calls upon 'the veiled/ irradiant One' and, at the end, 'the irradiant veiled/ terrible One'. Like the prayerful plea in 'The Broken Dark', the impassioned affirmation in 'Words in the Mourning Time', and the consoling encounter with Bahá'u'lláh at the end of his panicked flight in '"From the Corpse Woodpiles, from the Ashes"', this desperate cry connotes the somber assessment of contemporary events as well as his own hopeless medical condition. However, it is not indicative of a loss of faith. Bahá'u'lláh Himself often described the Manifestation as the Divine Physician: 'The Prophets of God should be regarded as physicians whose task is to foster the well-being of the world and its peoples, that, through the spirit of oneness, they may heal the sickness of a divided humanity.'[19] And in one particularly appropriate passage Bahá'u'lláh cautioned that the failure of world leaders to utilize the remedies ordained by God through his Prophets was causing the world to approach a stage of terminal illness: 'Its sickness is approaching the stage of utter hopelessness, inasmuch as the true Physician is debarred from administering the remedy, whilst unskilled practitioners are regarded with favor, and are accorded full freedom to act.'[20]

But Hayden's grave tone in this poem is not the concluding attitude of this fourth group, and certainly not of the volume, but before the perspective changes, Hayden includes another dire image of this age in 'Killing the Calves'. Reflecting upon the harsh ironies which abound in a world not aware of its own disease, the speaker observes the irony that one part can afford to kill cattle to 'fatten the belly of cost' while the bellies of starving children are empty in another part of the same world. Recalling the intentional inhumanity of the concentration camps, this unwitting cruelty results from the failure of mankind to understand its changed identity, that it has become a world community. As Bahá'u'lláh noted in still another use of medical imagery, an important part of healing the body of mankind and the attendant social ills that plague the patient is to recognize the unique requirements of this new identity:

The All-Knowing Physician hath His finger on the pulse of mankind. He perceiveth the disease, and prescribeth, in His unerring wisdom, the remedy. Every age hath its own problem, and every soul its particular aspiration. The remedy the world needeth in its present-day afflictions can never be the same as that which a subsequent age may require. Be anxiously concerned with the needs of the age ye live in, and center your deliberations on its exigencies and requirements.[21]

In 'The Year of the Child', the eighth poem in the group, the tone changes from the depressive outlook of a terminally ill patient in a terminally ill society to a prayer-filled hope for the future recovery of a diseased world as foretold in the Bahá'í Writings and as hinted at throughout Hayden's poems. Dedicated to Hayden's grandson and composed in commemoration of the United Nations Year of the Child,[22] this poem incorporates a Navaho Indian prayer chant and an allusion to 'The Most Great Beauty' (Bahá'u'lláh) in a series of expressed wishes for all mankind:

> May you walk
> with beauty before you,
> beauty behind you, all
> around you, and
> The Most Great Beauty keep
> you His concern.
>
> (p. 44)

Besides the possible allusion to the Socratic notion of 'The Beautiful' as representing the combined attributes of 'the Good' or 'God',[23] the poem more directly expresses the hope that what the speaker and his generation of fellow artists and fellow Bahá'ís have longed for may, in his grandson's time, become a reality:

> What we yearned
> but were powerless to do
> for them, oh we
> will dare, Michael, for you,
> knowing our need
> of unearned increments
> of grace.
>
> (p. 44)

The last three poems in this fourth group – 'The Point', 'Zinnias' and 'The Islands' – are retained in order from the Effendi Press edition and complete this tone of consolation. But in the context of this amplified sequence in the fourth group the focus is on the personal and internal reconciliation of the persona. On this most personal level the poems thus complete the five stages delineated by Kubler-Ross with the stage of acceptance. The setting in 'The Point' is of quiet beauty and human lives as fitting tribute to noble deeds, as 'memories in the mind of God' (p. 45), just as the speaker's art has attempted that same memorializing of human aspiration. Likewise 'Zinnias', in addition to symbolizing the 'hardy élan' of the American people, becomes here a personalized symbol of an accolade the poet would wish for himself – not the sort of award for a Nureyev or a Leontyne Price, but for this escapee from Paradise Valley a suitable way 'of exclaiming / More More More/ as a gala/ performance ends' (p. 46). As an appropriate conclusion to this intensely emotional series of lyrics 'The Islands' neatly and touchingly demarks the poet's departure from his elaborate and serious theme of human progress. He is tired of history, its lessons, its symbolic meanings. He has completed his task as best he could and is content to luxuriate in the lush beauty of the morning time (another allusion to the incipience of medicinal change) and to 'believe my furies have/ abandoned for a time their long pursuit' (p. 48).

The final group, images of explorers, takes us back outside the persona's situation and his internal struggle, and returns us to the larger perspective, which, as I have already discussed, becomes a summary statement of human aspirations and capabilities. It is not totally a positive perspective – the dark wastes in 'from *The Snow Lamp*' are at least as powerfully negative as the Natchez Trace. And yet the emphasis in the poem is not on the horizonless arctic landscape, so reminiscent of the imagery of 'Traveling through Fog', but on resolute Miypaluk who fights the wish to die and determines to retain his sense of humanity, 'knowing ourselves men, not ghosts' (p. 54). Neither is 'Astronauts' a completely affirmative view of the human desire for exploring definitions and boundaries, though the 'heroic antiheroes' who are 'Risking edges' are touchingly childlike as they sing and exult in this uncharted terri-tory. The image as a mixture of pioneering heroism and hubristic aplomb anticipates significantly the impressions of the alien visitor in the final poem '[American Journal]'. In both poems the Americans rely too heavily on 'machine made gods' (p. 57), and yet in both there is a sense of Americans as 'charming savages', as 'enlightened primitives', as 'brash new comers'.

The rationale for this fascinating narrative device in Hayden's final poem is clear: were this final assessment of humanity from the poet/persona's view-point, we might attribute the observations to the emotional context of the speaker. But since the speaker is from another world we accept as accurate the report of our alien visitor, his praise and his criticism. The dominant impression of this report, consequently, is an optimistic one, a people and a civilization full of promise, of hope, in the process of becoming, and yet it is a hope significantly tinted with fear, the possibility of violent failure. Further-more, the visitor in his more evolved state confesses that while attracted to this baroque people, he doubts he 'could exist among them for long' (p. 60).

Of course, one cannot and should not avoid the unsettling ironies evoked by the parallel between the poet and the visitor. Both have 'passed for an american', though really both are aliens, as Hayden has noted in 'Elegies for Paradise Valley'. Both have as central purpose the assessment of this world, its history, its people, its potential. Both have since departed, but both have bequeathed to us the accurate and challenging journals of their arduous explorations.

As a Bahá'í with the paradoxical perspective of expectation and dread in this time of auroral dark which he helped illuminate, Robert Hayden left us in his continuous chartings of our progress towards transition and transforma-tion a rich sourcebook. With his own compassionate art he informed us of our origins and defined the basis for our confusion and anxiety as we struggle toward a new identity, towards our own angle of ascent.

Part V

THE POET OF
PERFECT PITCH

Basic style – as mode and strategy, as pattern and plan-of-attack – is a necessary condition of artistic creation. It never exists as such in a poem, or even in a poet's whole work. Rather, it is immanent there, always implicit, even as it is latent in the life of the culture in which the poet works. And the historian, knowing that it exists in a pure state only in his mind, as a historical construct, must try to make it explicit, thus to recount how poems have been integrally part of the life of a culture.[1]

Roy Harvey Pearce, *The Continuity of American Poetry*

The earliest English poets were called *sceops*, a word derived from the Anglo-Saxon word *scieppan* meaning 'to shape' or 'to fashion'. In the tribal courts these word-smiths had a place of honor, dignity and importance.[2] Fashioning heroic narratives and elegiac plaints from his rich word hoard in this pre-literate society, the *sceop* was custodian of the past, guardian of the people's memory. As he chanted their victories and failures, catalogued heroes as well as the killers of close kin, the poet called to mind the highest ideals and the most dreaded sins. With a skill at once original and part of an ancient tradition passed down from father to son, from age to age, he cautioned against pride, exhorted warriors to feats of courage, to qualities of generosity and fidelity. His verse recited around the hearth in the evening was integral to successful living because he alone held the promise of immortality and offered hope through the omnipresent turmoil, through terror-filled days and darksome nights.

Well over a thousand years later, as he received his Nobel Prize for literature in 1949, William Faulkner exhorted writers everywhere to aspire to that same lofty tradition. He stated that when the poet pursues his craft without 'the old universal truths' he produces nothing worthwhile; 'He writes not of love, but of lust, of defeats in which nobody loses anything of value, of victories without hope, and worst of all, without pity or compassion. His griefs grieve on no universal bones, leaving no scars. He writes not of the heart but of the glands.'[3] Faulkner went on to say that it is the poet's duty to extol the human spirit, to glorify the spiritual achievements of man:

The poet's, the writer's duty is to write about these things. It is his privilege to help man endure by lifting his heart, by reminding him of the courage and honor and hope and pride and compassion and pity and sacrifice which have been the glory of his past. The poet's voice need not merely be the record of man, it can be one of the props, the pillars to help him endure and prevail.[4]

Despite such noble beginnings and the subsequent exhortations reflecting that same heritage, we presently have as a society no clear or lofty vision of what a poet is or what he can do for us. More often than not he is perceived as a misfit, a delicate soul who, unable to cope with the real world, resorts to an esoteric art. At best he is deemed a cultural embellishment; at worst, an outcast visionary against whom we must guard ourselves.

Robert Hayden's vision of the poet was as a noble explorer constantly probing the relationship of art to the mundane life of the individual and society. This concern is reflected in many of his poems, in most of the interviews he gave and in the various paragraphs he penned on poetic theory and stylistics. Because he was, in addition to being a poet, an excellent teacher and scholar his comments often demonstrated his ample awareness of other poets and critics, and he often acknowledged the influence of particular individuals and schools of thought. In his vision of the poet he followed in the tradition of the English Romantics and the American Transcendentalists. Many of his thematic concerns, early and late, were in accord with the strains of the Harlem Renaissance poets. In his basic approach to poetics he was most closely akin to the stylistics of the New Critical poets. In the most expansive application of his symbols and themes he was clearly influenced by his perspective as a Bahá'í.

Hayden's craftsmanship ultimately reflects these and other attitudes and traditions in a special combination that becomes his own distinctive style. In fact, long before the recent recognition of the thematic unity and patterns of imagery in his poetry numerous critics had extolled his exquisite poetics. The noted Roy Harvey Pearce called Hayden 'a first-rate poet',[5] and 'a very sophisticated poet formally'.[6] As with any first-rate poet his style is best understood in the experience of his poems themselves, because one can hardly separate theme from style, the method from the message. Hayden acknowledged this inextricable relationship between stylistics and theme in his interview with Paul C. McClusky:

Very often students feel that when they know what a poem is about, when they've grasped the 'message', theme, they've experienced the poem. But what a poem says is really not more important than *how* it makes its statement. And the how, the method, the manner, is a very significant part of the special kind of experience a poem provides.[7]

Having examined the continuity of Hayden's work as it emerged from the continuity of his own life and thought, we can now better understand the particulars of the means by which he effected those themes in his art, for as Emerson noted, 'The thought and the form are equal in the order of time, but in the order of genesis the thought is prior to the form.'[8] It is hardly a simple task with Hayden's poetry. In spite of the ease of his lines and images, the lapidarian quality of his finely polished verse, his style employed a varied and complex synthesis of modes, perspectives, and traditions to compass the array and range of themes that pursued him.

There are many fruitful methods of assaying the relationship between

Hayden's style and theme, and a number of recent studies have begun to plow this fertile ground with exciting results. But logically the place to begin is with the shaping of the literal subject into poetic form through narrative point of view, through structural form, through the fine-tuning in endless revisions to achieve the desired tonal qualities. The literal and figurative imagery which results from this careful craftsmanship pricks our senses, evokes those thoughts and feelings which the poet, as the guardian of our hopes and fears, has explored. The end result of studying the methods of his inquiry into the human condition is a better appreciation of his accomplishments and an expanded awareness of how his findings, revealed to us in the patterns of his images and themes, can enlighten our own auroral darkness as we gather at night to discover our past and search out where we choose to go.

20. The Poet and the Poetic Process

This is an age of overanalysis as well as overkill, and we've analyzed poetry and the poetic process to a point where analysis has become tiresome, not to say dangerous for the poet. And for all our investigation, mysteries remain. And I hope they always will.[1]

Robert Hayden in *Interviews with Black Writers*

Discussions of poetic theory and style are perhaps more eagerly pursued by scholars than poets. Hayden himself distrusted theories, stating that 'you're dealing with unknowns': 'It's still a mystery, and a thing of the spirit. It combines everything and grows out of everything you are – It's not entirely cerebral. It's on a line between the known and the unknown.'[2] My own mentor in poetry criticism, John Crowe Ransom, once told me that in discussing a poem with a class he was often tempted to lower his wire-rimmed spectacles, gaze out of the window and sigh, 'Now isn't that fine!' Sometimes he did just that because a poem, after all, is written to be experienced, not dissected. With some poets, however, a study of their stylistics enhances understanding and appreciation of their art, especially symbolist poets like Hayden.

Discussions of poetry are usually concerned with the lyric tradition, which according to most textbook definitions is a thoroughly subjective art form. Therefore, observations about stylistics are usually inferred from a particular poet's performance, not from prescriptive rules, even though many theorists have wielded great authority in their time. But because a lyric poem implies no set structure, metrical pattern or thematic content, the best definition I have found is the barebones statement in *A Handbook to Literature* which describes the lyric as a 'brief subjective poem strongly marked by imagination, melody, and emotion and creating for the reader a single unified impression'.[3] It concludes that 'Strict definition is impossible' because the '*lyric* has naturally been different things to different people at different times'.[4]

Hayden actively avoided extensive definition of what a poem is or should be, stating simply that 'a poem, like any other form of art, establishes its own laws and fails or succeeds in direct proportion to the poet's ability to carry them out'.[5] But while he had 'very little patience with poetic theories',[6] he also revealed in interviews, in the classroom and ultimately in his own work a thorough awareness of poetic traditions and even the most esoteric of scholarship on the subject. From these conversations and from his verse we can elicit a fairly complete understanding of Hayden's fundamental beliefs about what a poet is, how the poetic process takes place, and how he could best apply these principles in his own practice of his profession as a lyric poet.

Generally speaking, Hayden viewed the poet as someone who loves language. He stated, 'I studied music but I didn't love music the way I loved using words. I enjoyed painting and drawing, but I never dreamed of being a great artist as I dreamed of being a great poet.'[7] The source of this affinity for language Hayden could never fully define, except to repeat that it was a mystery and that to be a poet 'is to have a special kind of awareness, a particular quality of mind, imagination. And these can't be acquired.'[8]

This notion of the poet as having an innate sensibility which others do not have, or else have not developed, is quite in keeping with Hayden's fondness for the Romantic tradition. For example, Coleridge stated that because the poetic process is inextricably linked to the poet's special capacities, one cannot discuss the two separately: 'What is poetry? is so nearly the same question as What is a poet? that the answer to one is involved in the solution of the other.'[9] Hayden emphasized this point when he noted that one cannot become a poet by an act of will:

What is it that makes one a poet? What are you doing when you write a poem? What is poetry? The feeling of mystery is no doubt intensified because you can't deliberately set out to be a poet. You can't become one by taking courses in creative writing. You are born with a gift, with a feeling for language and a certain manner of responding to life.[10]

This notion of the poet as possessing an inherent gift is perhaps best exemplified by the several metaphors which Romantic theorists used for the poet. In most of these the poet is portrayed as a passive instrument. For example, both Coleridge and Shelley compared the poet to an aeolian harp, an instrument whose music is caused by breezes vibrating strings. In Coleridge's poem 'The Eolian Harp' the speaker calls his 'indolent and passive brain' a 'subject Lute' whereon play 'Full many a thought uncall'd and undertain'd/ And many idle flitting phantasies'.[11] In his essay 'In Defence of Poetry' Shelley uses the same metaphor: 'Man is an instrument over which a series of external and internal impressions are driven, like the alternations of an ever-changing wind over an Æolian lyre, which move it by their motion to ever-changing melody.'[12] The transcendentalist Emerson used the metaphor of a lightning rod to portray essentially the same quality of passivity on the poet's part.[13] In my own classroom discussions about the Romantic theory, I use the contemporary metaphor of the television receiver, partly because it is more familiar, but also because it explains the ability to translate abstraction into concrete form, the unseen signal into the seen picture.

As Shelley notes, the origin of this active force playing on the passive instrument can be internal or external. The internal source is the poet's unconscious, his deepest emotions – Hayden's 'lions' and 'furies'. To most Romantics the external source was some form of divine mystery, but clearly a power beyond and greater than the poet himself. In other words, Romantic theory implies an 'outer mystery'[14] which accounts for universal order and employs the poet as an agent for guiding mankind to truth. In his own special blending of Swedenborgian neo-Platonism and Hindu mysticism, Emerson termed this external source the 'Oversoul', a transcendental spiritual essence from which the poet intuits his themes.[15] For other Romantics the source of insight was the spiritual attributes metaphorized in the phenomenal world. Discussed in the theological doctrine of 'correspondences' of Emanuel Swedenborg, this theory is reflected in Baudelaire's famous poem 'Correspondence':

> La nature est un temple où de vivants piliers
> Laissent parfois sortir de confuses paroles;
> L'homme y passe à travers des forêts de symboles
> Qui l'observent avec des regards familiers.[16]
>
> [Nature is a temple where living columns
> at times yield confounding words;
> There man passes through forests of symbols
> which observe him with fond gazes.]

The hint of pantheism in the poem is partially attributable to poetic license, but the idea of nature as a divinely instituted classroom is clearly derived from the Platonic doctrine of 'forms' as portrayed in the parable of the cave in Book VII of the *Republic*.[17] This Platonic analogy also introduces another metaphor for the poet and an alternative view of his capacity; the poet is the 'true philosopher' who with effort is able to detect the increasingly higher levels of reality. From such a view the poet is no longer a passive instrument. He struggles from the darkness of the cave into the light of knowledge by discerning reality in the symbolic images cast on the cave wall. In the words of Baudelaire's poem, he attunes his ear to the *'confuses paroles'* which are murmured in the forest of symbols that is temporal reality.

This vision of the poet as a more willful agent does not discount the belief in his innate capacity, but it begins to introduce the concept of the process by which that capacity is utilized, and is in keeping with Hayden's concession that 'maybe everyone is *potentially* a poet'.[18] For example, in his seminal study of the poetic theory of the Romantics, M. H. Abrams explains that unlike the neoclassicists who perceived the poet as a mirror reflecting nature, the Romantics construed the poetic faculty as a lamp, a 'candle of the Lord' which throws 'its beams into the external world'.[19] More akin to the doctrines of Plotinus than Plato, this theory perceives the poet as an active explorer of the Platonic cave, shining the lamp of his poetic insight onto the wall of dark shadows.

This perception of the poet as a bringer of light accords with Hayden's poetic images of the artist, but it also relates to another attribute or definition of the poet as stated in Emerson's appellation for the poet as 'Namer':

... the poet is the Namer or Language-maker, naming things sometimes after their appearance, sometimes after their essence, and giving to every one its own name and not another's, thereby rejoicing the intellect, which delights in detachment or boundary ... For though the origin of most of our words is forgotten, each word was at first a stroke of genius . . .[20]

This idea of the figurative or symbolic value of etymology reflects Platonic doctrine as well as the theory of correspondences,[21] but it also relates to two weighty aspects of Hayden's perception of the poet. First of all, Hayden discussed the value of the poet as namer in relation to seeking his own name or identity, and in the more basic struggle to identify or name those 'furies' which dwell within:

As a young poet, poetry was for him no doubt an escape, a release. It was a way of discovery, discovery of self and the world. It was the magic power of words. It was too, he often thought when older, the exorcism of personal demons who must leave the spirit when the tormented unwilling host to them learns to say their names.[22]

Second, the idea of poet as namer relates significantly to Hayden's beliefs as a Bahá'í. As I have earlier noted, Bahá'u'lláh confirms the Platonic assertion that physical reality is essentially symbolic or metaphoric, 'that every created thing is a sign of the revelation of God'.[23] Furthermore, the use of the epithet 'Namer' for one who recognizes that spiritual essence in creation is described in the Koranic version of the Adamic myth: Adam as a Prophet of God is sent to bestow on creation its names, each of which, Muḥammad implies, represents a spiritual virtue.[24] This notion, then, of the poet as also having the capacity to recognize the spiritual value in the phenomenal world and then to reincorporate that insight into artistic form that others may share that perception – this is at the heart of Hayden's lofty regard for the station of the poet. Therefore, the view of the poet as perceiver of and maker of symbols and metaphors is the most encompassing of all Hayden's definitions of the poet, because it gets to the heart of poetry as an attempt to interpret the world. In fact, Louis Simpson has stated that the metaphorical process is at the heart of the definition of poetry and of human learning:

Metaphor is a process of comparing and identifying one thing with another. Then, as we see what things have in common, we see the general meaning they have. Now, the ability to see the relation between one thing and another is almost a definition of intelligence. Thinking in metaphors – and poetry is largely this – is a tool of intelligence. Perhaps it is the most important tool.[25]

Thus, according to Hayden, when the poet probes either his internal world or the external world he is involved in a spiritual process, 'a form of prayer for illumination, perfection'.[26] More specifically, Hayden related the poet's use of symbols and metaphors to the teaching techniques of the Prophets:

Poetry is very close to religion, and I might say tangentially that when we speak of the Prophets, and Bahá'u'lláh in particular, as being poets, in a sense this is very true, because the Prophet uses symbols, speaks in parables, uses metaphors, and all the devices we associate with poetry.[27]

The relevancy of this definition of the poet to the perception in the Bahá'í Writings of 'veiled' language is therefore crucial and relates directly to Hayden's statement that possibly 'everyone is *potentially* a poet'.[28] That is, not only do the Bahá'í teachings ascribe to temporal reality the capacity to metaphorize spiritual attributes; they portray every man's principal goal in his physical experience as the discerning of spiritual meaning in phenomenal reality and the subsequent incorporation of that insight into deeds. For example, Bahá'u'lláh states that the Prophets used poetic imagery, what He calls 'veiled' language, as a test of man's spiritual understanding:

. . . so that whatever lieth hidden in the heart of the malevolent may be made manifest and their innermost being be disclosed . . . None apprehendeth the meaning of these utterances except them whose hearts are assured, whose souls have found favour with God, and whose minds are detached from all else but Him.[29]

This discussion of the relationship of poetic sensibility to spiritual insight and development is not unique with Bahá'u'lláh. Christ was discussing the same capacity when He distinguished between those who understood His parables and those literal-minded Pharasaic Jews whose legalistic approach to religious truth barred them from grasping His themes. Quoting from the Prophet Isaiah, Christ chided their loss of this poetic ability:

> You shall indeed hear but never understand,
>   and you shall indeed see but never perceive.
> For this people's heart has grown dull,
>   and their ears are heavy of hearing,
>   and their eyes they have closed,
> lest they should perceive with their eyes,
>   and hear with their ears,
> and understand with their heart,
>   and turn for me to heal them.[30]

Most probably it is this practical application of poetry which caused

Bahá'u'lláh to ascribe to the arts the epithets 'wings to man's life' and a 'ladder for his ascent'.[31] This is also the essence of Shelley's meaning when he describes the capacity of poetry to enlighten not only the poet, but all who use the art to exercise this crucial faculty: 'But poetry acts in another and diviner manner. It awakens and enlarges the mind itself by rendering it the receptacle of a thousand unapprehended combinations of thought. Poetry lifts the veil from the hidden beauty of the world . . .'[32]

In addition to this view of the poet as having an acutely developed sensibility common to all human ascent, Hayden shared with the Romantics, and the New Critical poets as well, the vision of the poet as historian. As I have earlier noted, in Hayden's very first volume he included a number of poems which delineate the duty of the 'dark singer'[33] to exalt the noble deeds of his Afro-American ancestors who had laid the foundation for any future ascent of the Black race in America. In his later history poems Hayden attempted to fulfill the original goals of his *Black Spear* sequence – 'to correct the misconceptions and to destroy some of the stereotypes and clichés which surrounded Negro history'.[34] As I have also speculated, one of Hayden's primary goals as poet was to give artistic form to the historical perspective of this era as a period of vital transformation and transition. In both of these contexts Hayden seems to fulfill Emerson's assessment of the poet's function: 'The poet has a new thought; he has a whole new experience to unfold; he will tell us how it was with him, and all men will be the richer in his fortune. For the experience of each new age requires a new confession, and the world seems always waiting for its poet.'[35] T. S. Eliot says much the same thing when he observes that since 'every poet starts from his own emotions',[36] it follows that 'The great poet, in writing himself, writes his time'.[37] While Eliot's point is focused primarily on the necessity of the reader's understanding of the historical context in which a work is produced, it is clear that he also views this process as working in reverse. The poet bespeaks the tenor of an age, just as Eliot himself captured the spirit of the modern age by devising poetic images for the decline of faith and spiritual vitality.

There are other particulars I could cite concerning Hayden's perception of the poet and his calling, but I think the sense of his vision is clear – the poet has an inherent capacity to use a common sensibility to perceive unity in diversity, the abstraction in the concrete. Poetry is not the sole art which involves that faculty, nor is the poet necessarily possessed of spiritual insight; all physical activity, from Hayden's Bahá'í perspective, is capable of revealing mysteries. But the poet, if he exercises his natural skills, is especially adept at this process. In short, Hayden's vision of the poet accords with that of the Romantics and with the Platonic notion of the 'true philosopher', but it also accords with the ancient oral formulaic tradition of the poet as a *sceop*, a bard who reiterates the folk ideal, recalls the tribal heroes and charts the people's progress towards their avowed destiny.

Given Hayden's perception of the poet's fundamental capacity and lofty potential, how does he believe this power is unleashed? The answer to this basic question seems to involve Hayden, and by implication the Romantic theorist with him, in a major paradox. If the poet is born, then how did Hayden account for his need for apprenticeship or his acknowledgment that for him 'no poem is ever finished, only abandoned'?[38] Hayden believed that one cannot become a poet solely by an act of will, just as Shelley before him had stated, 'Poetry is not like reasoning, a power to be exerted according to the determination of the will. A man cannot say, "I will compose poetry."'[39] Emerson also implied that the act of poetic creation is an innate capacity, a spontaneous act, requiring no revision, almost a process of revelation. Wordsworth seemed to imply much the same thing with his dictum that 'all good poetry is the spontaneous overflow of powerful feelings'.[40]

Hayden saw no contradiction between his view of the poet and his view of the poetic process. He resolved this conflict by distinguishing between the capacity, the gifts, the sensibility and the application and development of that talent: 'Once you discover you're a poet – and you have to find out for yourself – you can study the art, learn the craft, and try to become a worthy servitor. But you cannot *will* to be a poet.'[41] More specifically, Hayden delineated this process by noting that once aware of his skill, the poet must acquire knowledge: 'To be a poet one must *know* something. It's not a matter of freely expressing oneself, but a way to work toward the truth . . .'[42]

Correctly understood, Hayden's total theoretical paradigm of the poetic process reflects and corresponds to the Bahá'í concept of human transformation and the underlying intent of the Romantic theorists. First, as I have noted, the Bahá'í view is that spiritual advancement involves the exercise of the poetic sensibility in each of us. But the Bahá'í view of exactly how that process is enacted is spelled out to include a three-part process: 'The attainment of any object is conditioned upon knowledge, volition and action.'[43] Similarly, the acquisition of faith itself is defined as 'first, conscious knowledge, and second, the practice of good deeds'.[44] Bahá'u'lláh likewise describes spiritual growth as the inextricable link between knowledge and action.[45] These statements seem to imply that the process of human ascent involves first knowing the spiritual attribute, understanding its nature, then determining to incorporate that quality into one's daily actions and, finally, habituating that quality through a kind of self-actuated behavior modification.

I do not mean to imply here that Hayden derived his theory of poetics from this process analysis of human spiritual development, but clearly such observations confirmed and upheld his belief that the poet was involved in an essentially spiritual enterprise, as well as his assertion that the poet, though inherently gifted, must first acquire knowledge and then willfully persist in the exercise of his craft. And in spite of the traditional view of the Romantic theory as implying spontaneity in the poetic process, the Romantic theorists, properly understood, enunciated a similar process. Emerson confessed that on only one occasion did he actually write a poem spontaneously.[46] Coleridge, though affirming that he penned 'Kubla Khan' spontaneously,[47] described in *Biographia Literaria* a poetic process which involves the exercise of volitional energy. In this essay Coleridge distinguished between the 'fancy' and the 'imagination', or between the 'primary' and 'secondary' imagination.[48] The first of these (the 'fancy' or the 'primary' imagination) represents the inherent gift; the second (the 'imagination' or the 'secondary' imagination) designates the acquired skill for translating abstract insight into poetic form. Clearly the insight must come first – the poet must know something – but without the determined pursuit of excellence, the thought lies fallow in the furrows of the poet's brain. Coleridge describes the development of this 'secondary' faculty as the sharpening of the poet's skill at employing figurative devices:

This power [of the 'imagination'], first put in action by the will and understanding, and retained under their irremissive, though gentle and unnoticed, control . . . reveals itself in the balance or reconciliation of opposite or discordant qualities: of sameness, with difference; of general, with the concrete; the idea, with the image; the individual, with the representative . . .[49]

This same volitional aspect of the poetic process is also part of the 'spontaneous overflow', which, Wordsworth goes on to say, occurs only after the poet has thought 'long and deeply'.[50] Wordsworth further states that poetry is not produced in the midst of emotion, but 'takes its origins from emotion recollected in tranquillity: the emotion is contemplated till, by a species of reaction, the tranquillity disappears'.[51] Hayden described much the same process when he made the distinction between his earlier verse, as exemplified in the *Heart-Shape* volume, and his growing awareness of the need to distance himself from emotionality in order to deal with the emotion itself:

At first, I was emotionally involved with my subject, but as I continued working I began to feel detached. I might very well have produced nothing but sentimental twaddle otherwise. I know we can't safely generalize about the poetic process, but I believe, from my own experience, that it's one whereby the expression of a strong emotion becomes the means of release from that emotion.[52]

T. S. Eliot made a similar distinction when, in commenting on Wordsworth's dictum about emotion being 'recollected in tranquillity', he stated, 'Poetry is not a turning loose of emotion, but an escape from emotion; it is not the expression of personality, but an escape from personality.'[53]

How Hayden distanced himself from the emotion and his poems from his personality is by far the single most important aspect of Hayden's poetics, not as theory only, but as clue to the special power latent in his poetry. From our historical perspective, the shift from his earlier subjective, imitative mode to his post-*Heart-Shape* poetics is a sudden dramatic change in his perception of the lyric itself. Theoretically, it signals the marked difference between his theoretical alignment with the Romantics regarding the station and function of the poet and the poetic process, and his fundamental accord with the New Critical poets regarding poetic practice. Specifically he arrived at the New Critical conclusion that, as Eliot put it, poetic thought and emotion should have 'its life in the poem and not in the history of the poet', that the 'emotion of art is impersonal'.[54]

The New Critical Movement had its birth in the early 1900s when a group of poets, led principally by Ezra Pound and influenced by the French imagists, advocated a mode of lyric which was objective rather than subjective, a lyric based strongly on figurative image and symbol. In the 1915 preface to *Some Imagist Poets* are listed the six principles which served as a manifesto for this poetic theory:

1. To use the language of common speech, but to employ always the exact word.

2. To create new rhythms.

3. To allow absolute freedom in the choice of subject.

4. To present an image.

5. To produce poetry that is hard and clear, never blurred nor indefinite.

6. Finally, most of us believe that concentration is the very essence of poetry.[55]

For others New Criticism was keyed on other characteristics. To Empson it was ambiguity;[56] to I. A. Richards, the psychological implications of connotative language;[57] to Brooks and Warren, the complete microcosm that each poem creates;[58] to Eliot, the process of creating 'objective correlatives' or formulae for emotions.[59] But whatever the disagreement with regard to emphasis, these and other proponents of New Critical stylistics agreed that 'a poem ought to be allowed to speak for itself',[60] and that a poem 'is never mere self-expression, but an experience which has an existence apart from the poet'.[61] Taken to the extreme, the theory sometimes had the unfortunate implication, as Louis Simpson states it, that 'any expression of the poet's life as it appears in the poem, or of his ideas, is irrelevant': 'To such critics, a poem is a machine without emotion, and the reader another machine constructed to have no emotions. This way of thinking about poetry is not only boring, it is impossible.'[62]

Some of Hayden's 'baroque' lyrics in the early 1940s, which occasionally rely on obfuscated tropes and super-erudition, reflect this tendency, but by and large the influence of the New Critical movement is manifested more benignly in two crucial features of Hayden's poetic practice. The first of these regards Hayden's recognition of the New Critical verity that a 'poem is not a personal letter from one individual to another, but a composition in which the writer ceases to exist as such and becomes the medium of an experience that belongs to all who can read and understand'.[63] This was hardly a radically new idea; Keats had implied as much in his idea of 'negative capability',[64] a doctrine that the poet should not speak *ex-cathedra* but create a fallible narrator who thus has life as a character in the poem. In order to achieve this objective quality the New Critical poet 'creates characters or employs the *persona* or mask . . .'[65]

Hayden thus ceased declaiming as proletariat warrior and employed this narrative device. Sometimes he would use the third person in order to establish objectivity:

By writing in the third person I could be a little more objective, exteriorize up to a point. I could get a perspective and be both inside and outside of the poem at the same time. And, too, I was looking at another self – seeing myself in a different time dimension. You know the feeling you get when you see pictures of yourself as a child.[66]

On other occasions Hayden would use the first-person narrative point of view but employ the persona: 'Frequently, I'm writing about myself but speaking through a mask, a *persona*.'[67] When critical evaluation of Hayden's work fails to notice his reliance on these devices, it diminishes his poetry by viewing his autobiographically based poems as beginning and ending with the facts of his life. From such a perspective Hayden's poems become no more than biographical insight or else explication of these poems becomes dependent on discovering the biographical basis for the poem's creation. Neither result is what Hayden had intended.

The second manifestation of New Critical influence in Hayden's poetic practice is Hayden's reliance on symbolism. As a part of Hayden's overall perspective on poetics his reliance on symbol and image results from his belief that the poem should create an experience, not simply recount or allude to one. Poetry should provide 'an *intensification* of reality', as Hayden once described this quality; it should make the readers 'see things in ways they hadn't seen before; look at things they don't want to look at; face realities they would sometimes rather ignore'.[68] To amplify this belief, Hayden once alluded to a contemporary popular poet whose volumes sell in the millions: 'He's not acclaimed because his poetry gives his readers a new experience; he's acclaimed because his poems give them what they already know – they don't have to do any work; they don't have to think.'[69]

Dennis Gendron attributed part of Hayden's reliance on symbolism to the influence of the seminal essay by James Weldon Johnson in the preface to his 1922 edition of *The Book of American Negro Poetry*.[70] Exhorting the Black poet to transcend the worn-out subjectivity of Black dialect to express racial themes, Johnson states:

What the colored poet in the United States needs to do is something like what Synge did for the Irish; he needs to find a form that will express the racial spirit by symbols from within rather than by symbols from without, such as the mere mutilation of English spelling and pronunciation.[71]

Wilburn Williams, Jr., discussed Hayden's symbolism as reflecting Emerson's doctrine of correspondence:

Viewed as a theory of poetics, Hayden's characteristic method of composition will hardly strike anyone as unique. His preoccupation with the relationship between natural and spiritual facts puts him squarely in the American tradition emanating from Emerson; we are not at all amazed, therefore, when we find correspondences between his work and that of figures like Dickinson and Melville.[72]

Like Dudley Randall I feel that this aspect of Hayden's craft is more the result of the New Critical influence, particularly regarding the poem as an equation.[73] Hayden's use of symbolism and imagery, his overall attempt to create this objective experience, this poetic microcosm, all reflect Auden's axiom (which Hayden so often cited as the foundation of his poetics) that the best poetry is algebraic. In what Auden termed 'arithmetic' poems the reader is required to do little more than add up the poetic statements which the poet has dictated. If he feels anything, it is the result of the poet's having added effective adjectival embellishment to the recounting, or else the reader is reminded of a similar emotion. With algebraic poems the reader is forced to participate because the poet has not told the reader what to think or feel but has instead created something to examine, an experience, an image, a sequence of tropes which become the formula for emotion. The poem thus becomes a process by which the reader works to discover that x factor for which the poetic image is the equivalent. Eliot describes this process as follows:

The only way of expressing emotion in the form of art is by finding an 'objective correlative'; in other words, a set of objects, a situation, a chain of events which shall be the formula of that *particular* emotion; such that when the external facts, which must terminate in sensory experience, are given, the emotion is immediately evoked.[74]

As I have tried to demonstrate earlier in this study, Hayden employed a variety of correlatives – symbols, metaphors, characters, settings. In fact, his frequent reliance on biographically based anecdote as correlative led Lewis Turco to state that Hayden's poetic equivalents for 'the American Black's experience and situation' might be better termed the 'subjective correlative'.[75] Hayden's usual application of this principle is indeed distinct from the allusive imagery in Eliot's work, but the capacity of Hayden's poems to create a complete experience and reach beyond themselves and Hayden's life is, nevertheless, the most expansive quality of Hayden's art.

This fundamental objective of art to find the equivalent of emotion and thought was not an invention of the New Critical Movement. It is essentially the same yearning the speaker feels in 'Kubla Khan' as he contemplates the 'damsel with a dulcimer' and longs to 'revive within me/ Her symphony and song'.[76] But the clarification and restatement of this process by the New

Critics provided for aspiring poets like Hayden a useful insight into how a poem gives concrete form to abstract emotion, how, as Pound put it, poetry ceases to be an intimate note from poet to reader and assumes instead an objective reality like a mathematic equation: 'Poetry is a sort of inspired mathematics, which gives us equations, not for abstract figures, triangles, spheres, and the like, but equations for the human emotions.'[77]

As Simpson noted, the poet's life and ideas are still relevant to his poetry. In fact, it is an essential requisite of the student of Hayden's poetry that in solving for that x factor the reader recover the allusions to his perspective as an Afro-American and, even more importantly, his perspective as a Bahá'í and a human being. This is not a failing any more than is the requirement that we learn something of the Elizabethan perspective before understanding Shakespeare, or Milton's theology in order to grasp *Paradise Lost*, or the mythology documented in Eliot's footnotes before pursuing 'The Wasteland'. As George Williamson observes, information external to the poem cannot by itself create poetic effects, but it can become a necessary tool in completing the poetic equation:

If awareness of an allusion is necessary, the poem will make it evident in some way. Dependence on notes for the recovery of learning is acceptable in reading poetry, but not dependence on notes for effects not realized in the poem . . . Recovery of the allusions may enrich but not replace the poet's meaning; it may also pervert it.[78]

The reader unwilling or unable to recover Hayden's allusions to topical and biographical fact no doubt misses some of the richness latent in his poetry, but the failure to comprehend his allusions to his perspective as a Bahá'í conceals the x factor itself.

The conclusions we can draw regarding Hayden's poetics, then, while relatively few in number, are significant as a prelude to assaying his style. It should be noted as well that while his view of the poet and the poetic process are Romantic and his basic approach to stylistics New Critical, his thematic orientation is distinctly his own. In his view of incipience and transformation, of human ascent and Divine renewal Hayden is markedly distinct from the modern view of the decline of faith. For in the sense that Eliot, Yeats and other modern poets present the climax to the theme which Arnold initiated in 'Dover Beach', Hayden was post-modern, believing that the 'sea of faith' is once more gathering 'at the full'.[79]

However, the term 'post-modern' generally designates that contemporary art which has as its principal theme the meaninglessness of Western values. Stylistically it has come to represent the abandonment of traditional aesthetics and the reassertion of total subjectivity in art. In poetry it is characterized by glorying in solipsism. Gerald Graff describes this assertion of a 'post-modern breakthrough' in his work *Literature Against Itself*: 'From the perception enforced by science that literature has no objective truth, one moves to the conclusion that this is for the best, since objective truth is merely factual, boring, and middle-class.'[80]

The quality of Hayden's craftsmanship has warded off criticism that might have otherwise resulted from this post-modern abhorrence of a doctrinal moral perspective. But such subjective criticism has also severely limited the full scope of what Hayden is doing in his poetry. He is hardly judgmental, condescending or didactic in tone or intent, but clearly he is at odds with the vogue critics who denounce poetry which presumes a moral objective: 'From the perception that "poetry makes nothing happen", as Auden in our century has said, we move to the imperative that poetry *ought* to make nothing happen, and finally to the axiom that it is not real poetry if it aims at practical effect.'[81]

Hayden early learned the detrimental effect of using poetry as propaganda and courageously withstood the later onslaught of those who wished him to contrive verse as ideological slogan. At the same time, Hayden was always fully in accord with Faulkner's exhortation and the richest tradition of the tribal singer. In response to the so-called revolutionary tendencies to diminish his chosen profession, Hayden stated that 'the truly revolutionary poets are always those who are committed to some integrative vision of art and life. Theirs is an essentially spiritual vision which leads to the creation of new forms and techniques, to a new awareness.'[82] Even more pointedly, Hayden affirmed the essential relationship between poetry and man's desire for transcendence: 'If there exists a "poetry of despair" and rejection, there is also a poetry that affirms the humane and spiritual. Our attempts at the present time to achieve a new, a larger vision of God, man, civilization, give substance to the work of many outstanding poets.'[83]

21. Shaping the Poem

> For it is not metres, but a metre-making argument that makes a poem,
> – a thought so passionate and alive that like the spirit of a plant or
> animal it has an architecture of its own, and adorns nature with a new
> thing.[1]
>
> Emerson, 'The Poet'

Naturally any stylistic analysis of Hayden's poetry will imply a systematic
creative process which, as Hayden often noted, belies the mystery and special
circumstances that surround each poem. This is the essence of Pearce's observation that stylistics is largely a fiction for critics who in retrospect attempt to
discover the rationale for a process that is, at heart, beyond logic.[2] But done
wel and applied properly, such *ipso facto* analysis rewards us with insight into
what happens in the poems, if not what happened in the poet, and we emerge
with a richer encounter with the poems themselves.

Thus, while the good poet does not write by formula, our own analysis can
make effective generalizations by pursuing the natural sequence of answers to
fundamental questions we have about every poem, regardless of the circumstance of its creation: What is being described? Who is describing it? What are
the clues to the poet's ulterior purposes? The sequence of these questions
justifiably implies that it would be sane to begin a stylistic assessment by
reviewing the literal subjects of Hayden's poems, especially since these surface
descriptions become the resources from which he fashions his symbols and by
which he guides us to his themes. Of course, each surface is filtered through a
narrative perspective and framed in a structural pattern to give us further clues
as to why the poet has chosen to show us this character, this setting, this
emotion or experience.

The characters and experiences which are the raw materials, the essential
building blocks from which Hayden's poems are fashioned, are striking in
their variety. Catalogued and categorized, they reveal a man intrigued with
people, places, with history and art, but above all, a man acutely sensitive to
the anguish of others.

In the O'Brien interview Hayden said that he was 'more interested in
people than in things or in abstractions', especially in 'heroic and "baroque"

people' and in 'outsiders, pariahs, losers'.[3] Statistically his poems bear him out since most of them focus on characters. He drew these figures from history, from his own family, from Paradise Valley, from myth and art. As a poet with a flair for drama Hayden had an uncanny ability to invade the psyches of these characters and study the human mechanism at work. It mattered not if they were lynchers or window washers, vagrants, prisoners or mystics, whether heroes, sycophants, spiritual leaders or simply survivors.

From Afro-American history he took his portraits of Cinquez, the fictional Daedalus, Sojourner Truth (Isabella Van Wagener), Nat Turner, Harriet Tubman, Crispus Attucks, Frederick Douglass, Matthew Henson, Malcolm X and Martin Luther King, Jr. From his Afro-American cultural heritage he took Phillis Wheatley, Paul Laurence Dunbar, Bessie Smith, Billie Holiday, Tiger Flowers and Paul Robeson. From his own family history he portrayed Pa Hayden, Sue Hayden, Uncle Jed, Uncle Crip and Sinda. From the rich resources of his own imagination he constructed the Rag Man, Aunt Jemima, the 'mystery boy', the 'Queen of Sunday', the tattooed man, 'the stranger', the alien visitor, the diver and the astronauts. From myth and literature he borrowed Lear, Perseus, Márques' 'old man with enormous wings', Arachne, the Sphinx, Daedalus, Akhenaten and Nefert-iti. Of course, most engaging of all his characters is the persona himself. In such lyrics as 'The Broken Dark', 'Words in the Mourning Time' and 'The Peacock Room' we come to know him well as we trace his struggle towards identity and transformation.

Another frequently used subject in Hayden's poems is setting. Here too the great variety of places betokens the variety of symbolic uses they serve. In classifying these places, however, one finds that they form several distinct clusters which indicate the sources for some of Hayden's inspiration. The natural settings predominate, sometimes a landscape, sometimes a powerfully evocative place. In 'Kodachromes of the Island', 'The Islands', 'The Point', 'Veracruz' and 'Gulls' Hayden focuses on detailed seascapes. 'Snow', 'October' and 'Ice Storm' contain seasonal landscapes. 'The Diver' contains elaborate underwater imagery and 'The Mirages' contains a succinct but effective desert image.

Possibly the most prominent source of settings was Hayden's association with the South and the ironic contrasts he felt between the pastoral beauty of the countryside and the violence and racial injustice that the places connoted, both in the past and in the present. 'Locus', 'Tour 5', 'Theory of Evil', 'Magnolias in Snow', 'A Ballad of Remembrance' and 'Night, Death, Mississippi' all focus on Southern settings as symbols of inherited evil. Likewise, Hayden's portrait of the Redstone Arsenal in 'Zeus over Redeye' contrasts the floral beauty of Alabama with the lethal weaponry of modern ballistic missiles, just as the relic battlefield in 'On Lookout Mountain' ironically recalls the principles for which that war was waged, as present wars are yet being fought for freedom and justice.

Rooms are another major subject for Hayden's poetry. Prison cells are important as subject and symbol in 'Soledad', 'The Prisoners', 'Belsen, Day of Liberation' and '"From the Corpse Woodpiles . . ."' In 'The Return' and 'Those Winter Sundays' a homestead plays a major part in evoking philosophical reflection, as do the hospital room in 'The Broken Dark' and the museum room in 'The Peacock Room'.

A number of poems focus on depictions of Paradise Valley. 'Elegies for Paradise Valley', though a character study, relies importantly on setting, as does 'Double Feature', 'Free Fantasia . . .' and 'Summertime and the Living . . .', possibly the most detailed of these poems. The literal subjects in most of the Mexican poems are also focused on setting – 'Mountains', 'Veracruz', '*Sub Specie Aeternitatis*', 'Market' and 'La Corrida' all function as poetic snapshots from which the poet constructs 'An Inference of Mexico'.

In keeping with the Hayden symbology of light versus darkness, a number of poems with strong negative connotation are set at night, among them 'Night, Death, Mississippi', 'Ice Storm' and 'The Ballad of Nat Turner'. Several others are set at night, but portray the light of renewal and hope piercing the dark, though not all of these are strictly focused on setting *per se*. In 'The Broken Dark', 'The Night-Blooming Cereus', 'Full Moon', 'Stars' and 'Traveling through Fog', the nighttime setting is only the backdrop against which more important concerns are discussed, but setting is a necessary part of the symbolism in each poem. Setting is also vital in any number of other poems. In 'Middle Passage' each narrative voice is importantly placed in a dramatic context – in the ship's hold, in the officer's cabin, in the courtroom. Likewise the depiction of the desolate wastes in 'from *The Snow Lamp*' and 'Astronauts' are essential in the interplay between character and environment, as is the sideshow context for the tattooed man and Aunt Jemima, and the barnyard for the winged man.

There are a few other discernible groups of subjects – the use of animals in 'The Moose Wallow', in 'The Lions' and in the 'El toro' section of 'La Corrida'. In each of these the animal is only vaguely characterized, since with each usage the poet is primarily interested in the quality the animals characterize. In this sense these poems function much as did the ancient lyric tradition of the *Physiologus*.[4] Likewise in several poems Hayden uses flowers (zinnias, the night-blooming cereus, the sunflowers), and here too he has used the literal image to evoke immediately the symbolic implication, just as he has done in 'Gulls' and 'Butterfly Piece'. Hayden also uses literal references to celestial bodies as the subject of several poems, again with immediate symbolic value: the moon in 'The Wheel' and 'Full Moon', the stars in 'Stars' and 'Runagate Runagate'. But clearly the most important and frequently recurring literal subjects in Hayden's poetry are the array of characters and settings which he has chosen as his principal correlatives.

After subject, our attention in Hayden's poems naturally focuses on the perspective from which the images are presented to us, the narrative point of view. Of course, often the speaker and subject are the same in his first-person narratives, and sometimes, like a clear mirror, the speaker is transparent, an objective reporter of fact. But always these three ingredients of reader, subject and narrator are in some important relationship, and like a camera lens the narrative point of view determines how we view that interplay.

In much of Hayden's poetry we are aware of the evolving persona who guides us through his world of thought and experience. In his dramatic mono-logues we forget the persona and concentrate on the fictive voice of a dramatic character who always reveals much more than he is aware. But unlike many poets who when they find an amenable narrative technique, hold fast to it, Hayden employed numerous voices and narrative devices. To begin with he employed the first-person point of view with a number of variations. As I have noted, in the 1982 *American Journal* he has a group of poems that seem clearly personal, almost confessional in tone. In 'Names' he describes directly his anguish over discovering he was not legally Robert Hayden. In 'As my blood was drawn' he seems to give vent to his fear and sadness at discovering the ominous progress of his disease. In one sense these poems are little different from his earlier personal poems like 'The Whipping' and 'Those Winter Sundays', 'Electrical Storm' or 'The Night-Blooming Cereus', all of which are mostly first-person narratives about the poet's life. But in the later poems, in 'Elegies for Paradise Valley' for example, the subject seems to be biographical insight into Robert Hayden, whereas 'The Whipping' concerns Sue Hayden, 'Those Winter Sundays' concerns Pa Hayden as a symbol of parental love, 'Electrical Storm' focuses on Divine intervention and 'The Night-Blooming Cereus' on the flower.

It could be well argued that even in these later first-person poems our interest goes beyond Hayden the individual to Hayden the Bahá'í viewing his own death as evidence of the world's painful transition, and I think this is true. With virtually no poem I am aware of is the poet's primary goal to present himself as an individual. As Wilburn Williams, Jr., noted in his study of *Angle of Ascent*, Hayden had the capacity to 'objectivize his own subjectivity. His private anguish never locks him into the sterile deadend of solipsism; it impels him outward into the world'.[5]

Hayden's most frequent use of the first-person viewpoint involves his consistent use of the persona. It is sometimes a thinly guised mask, a fact which has led many critics to view his work as amplifications of biographical fact rather than to consider them as tropes for larger concerns. The continuity of Hayden's poetry demonstrates that one can trace the progress of the persona as he struggles for identity and his own voice in poems like 'A Ballad of Remembrance', as he flees from his furies in 'The Broken Dark' or from the world's turmoil in '"From the Corpse Woodpiles . . ."', as he becomes dis-pirited in 'Words in the Mourning Time' or reconciled in 'October'. These poems also focus on the first-person poet/persona, his experiences and feelings, but more obviously as a character, as a representative of a particular historical perspective, a Bahá'í struggling in a period of wrenching transformation.

Another use of this same persona involves the speaker's recollection of himself in relation to something else – another character, an experience, a work of art, a powerfully evocative setting. All of the Mexico poems have this perspective – the speaker is involved, is affected by what he sees. But while we key on his reaction, our primary concern is with the symbolic materials he encounters – the ritualistic celebrations, the marketplace, the bull-fight. Likewise in 'The Night-Blooming Cereus' or 'Monet's "Waterlilies"' or 'The Peacock Room' we are interested in the speaker's personal reaction to these external objects; we learn about him from the relationship, but our primary attention is on the objects themselves as he reflects them to us.

A substantial part of this effect is Hayden's use of tenses. 'The Peacock Room' and 'Monet's "Waterlilies"' are narrated in the present tense and have immediacy, a feeling of emotional action taking place, whereas 'The Night-Blooming Cereus', narrated in the past tense, displays before us the speaker and his wife in relation to the flower, but also the speaker remembering himself – we infer that he has learned something by remembering his reaction. 'The Moose Wallow' and 'Electrical Storm' are also in the past tense as the narrator recalls himself as a character in the remembered anecdotes, whereas 'A Plague of Starlings' and 'Full Moon', which are in the present tense, have a more uncertain tone, since the persona is in the midst of experience, not reflection.

One of Hayden's most celebrated usages of the first-person persona point of view is in his childhood recollections. 'Those Winter Sundays', which Karl Shapiro called 'a fine example of the "pure lyric"',[6] is perhaps the best example, though most of the recollections of Paradise Valley are similar in mode and narrative construction. 'Elegies for Paradise Valley', 'Free Fantasia: Tiger Flowers', the middle portion of 'The Whipping', 'The Rabbi' and 'Double Feature' all have more or less the same intent. The persona is not overwhelmed with nostalgia – these scenes do not flow naturally or easily before him. The persona dredges up some with pain, guilt, anguish; others he recalls with a sense of loss, but all of these scenes imply a persona willfully attempting a panoramic review of his beginnings in order to understand the mechanisms of the present – his lost identity, his guilt, his need for love, his appreciation of colorful characters.

In yet another use of the first-person narrative technique Hayden wrote a number of poems where the speaker focuses on something not so pointedly related to his own life or emotional response. In 'The Prisoners', for example, the poet/speaker is certainly involved with the inmate, reads to him and ultimately is moved by the prisoner's reaction to the heartfelt attempt at

communication, but the reader's attention is primarily on the prisoner himself
as a symbol for our own condition, not on the speaker or the speaker's
response. Likewise in 'The Performers', 'Homage to Paul Robeson' and 'The
Rag Man' the 'I' is important, if only because we view the exterior world
through his biased perspective. The resulting impressionistic portraits do
indeed give us added information about this artist/companion who guides us
through his life, but here too our primary focus is on the external world, the
window washers, Paul Robeson's career, the philosophical implications of the
street scene in 'The Rag Man'.

Certainly the most dramatic distance between the poet and the poem with
first-person narratives occurs when Hayden creates complete and complex
characters who tell their stories. One of the most powerful of these is 'The
Ballad of Nat Turner', in which Turner himself recounts his vision for his
'brethren'. This remarkable use of the dramatic monologue portrays Turner's
mystic vision and, more importantly, Turner's interpretation of that experience:

> In scary night I wandered, praying,
>   Lord God my harshener,
> speak to me now or let me die;
>   speak, Lord, to this mourner.
>
> And came at length to livid trees
>   where Ibo warriors
> hung shadowless, turning in wind
>   that moaned like Africa . . .
>   (*AA*, p. 125)

Hayden similarly creates the character of Daedalus who recalls how his 'gran'
'flew back to Africa', and who chants his longing to escape his slavery. Likewise a good portion of 'John Brown' is in the form of a dramatic monologue,
though the narrator's voice takes us in and out of that first-person narrative, in
the same way that he does with the figure of Aunt Jemima. But in both poems,
the heart of the narrative is the first-person recounting of lives by the
characters themselves.

There are other minor examples of the dramatic monologue in earlier
poems – Perseus, the speaker in 'The Wheel', the bereft Medea figure in '"Incense of the Lucky Virgin"'. But in his last volume Hayden created some of his
most powerful examples of this effective narrative device. 'A Letter from
Phillis Wheatley' is an epistolary dramatic monologue, and the last section of
'from *The Snow Lamp*' is also presented as the written log entry of Henson's
experience. Hayden's most powerful uses of this narrative technique in *American Journal*, and perhaps in his career, are the monologue of the speaker in
'The Tattooed Man' and the journal of the alien visitor in '[American

Journal]'. In fact, the emphatic use of the dramatic monologue in this last volume caused Fred Fetrow in his review of the work to observe that Hayden's 'narrative versatility' is one of his most distinguishing qualities as a poet:

In retrospect, Hayden's final poems appropriately exhibit his deft talent for creating diversified voices. Indeed, as partially indicated in *American Journal*, a significant element of his unique voice derives from his narrative versatility, a range in modality perhaps unmatched among contemporary poets.[7]

Hayden's uses of the third-person narrative point of view are no less varied or innovative. Most of the poems which focus on anecdotes and elliptically told stories in the ballad tradition are presented in the third-person point of view. Among these are 'The Ballad of Sue Ellen Westerfield', 'The Ballad of the True Beast', 'Unidentified Flying Object', the more elaborate 'For a Young Artist' and 'El-Hajj Malik El-Shabazz'. Likewise most of the character pieces are presented in the third person, though in various forms. There is the formal sonnet 'Frederick Douglass', the richly ornate portrait in 'Witch Doctor', the tightly imagistic sketch of the drug addict in 'Soledad', the surreal impression of the distraught boy in '"Mystery Boy" Looks for Kin in Nashville'. In some of these the third-person narrator is faceless, a dispassionate reporter, a clear mirror, as in 'Kid' or '"The Burly Fading One"', whereas in 'Frederick Douglass' or 'Bahá'u'lláh in the Garden of Ridwan' the narrator makes no pretense at objectivity.

This same distinction holds true for Hayden's use of the third-person point of view in presenting settings. Sometimes the narrative voice objectively presents a place, from which we infer symbolic implications. There may be some tonal qualities in presentation as clues to thematic intent, but the narration itself does not imply that the setting is being filtered through a personality. 'Mountains', 'Stars' and 'Locus', for example, are presented through a keen-eyed but essentially objective point of view, even though we have some sense of that narrator. In pieces like 'Magnolias in Snow', 'Figures' or 'Market' the narrator, though unidentified, charges the portrait with his personal emotions, whereas in the highly compressed imagistic pieces, Hayden uses a dispassionate third-person narration. In such poems as '"Dance the Orange"', 'Smelt Fishing' or 'Snow' we are not only unaware of the narrator; we are also left largely without tonal clues to guide us to the poet's meaning.

A variation on the third-person presentation occurs in several poems which are, strictly speaking, first-person narrations – there is a reference to an 'I' or 'we', but the focus is so importantly on the subject that we are really oblivious to the narrative point of view. In 'Kodachromes of the Island', for example, we are until the end of the poem concentrating on the photographic images of the setting. Likewise, in 'Theory of Evil' the only hint of the first-person speaker is in the lines 'We think of that/ as we follow the Trace' (*AJ*, p. 11). The rest of the poem focuses on the legend of the trail and the story of 'Them Harpes'. The most weighty use of this narrative approach occurs in 'Homage to the Empress of the Blues'. In this poem Hayden presents a third-person portrait of the singer Billie Holiday on stage before an assemblage of entranced onlookers. Our view of this, like the camera's perspective in cinematography, is objective; we watch this interplay between performer and audience until the final line when the poet inserts a simple personal pronoun to suddenly place him there in the audience, and us there with him: 'She came out on the stage in ostrich feathers, beaded satin,/ and shone that smile on us and sang' (*AA*, p. 104).

The analogy of narrative point of view to cinematography is a useful one, for just as we see only what the camera can see so in poetry we view the literal imagery from a certain narrative perspective, and it is often crucial to discern the nature of that point of view, whether the lens is clear and whether the camera angle is distorting reality. Likewise, the camera sometimes presents the world as the character sees it, and sometimes it stands apart, above or beyond the character to show his relationship to the world. But always there is the artist controlling what that camera sees; therefore we must always be aware of what that camera eye represents.

Nowhere is this component of style more apparent than in variation of the third-person point of view in 'The Whipping'. The poem begins in the third person with the narrator viewing objectively the 'old woman across the way' who is 'whipping the boy again'. Then, after three stanzas of describing the boy who is vainly trying to flee, the poem suddenly shifts in the fourth stanza to the first-person perspective as the narrator becomes the boy: 'My head gripped in bony vise' (*AA*, p. 112). Halfway through the fifth stanza, when the whipping is over, the poem shifts back to the third-person point of view. The effect, ostensibly a violation of narrative logic, is incredibly effective, implying among other things that the poet can be objective in recounting his past until the scene recalls 'woundlike memories' and he instantly loses that analytical perspective.

A similarly powerful use of this shift occurs in 'Night, Death, Mississippi'. Interspersed with the last three of the poem's nine quatrains are italicized lines which apparently belong to the narrator. Until this point the poem is the gruesome narrative in the third person of the inhuman torture and mutilation of a lynching victim. But, similar to the use of an intervening narrative voice in 'Middle Passage', the poet can no longer contain his reaction. Alluding to his childhood symbol of utter terror (rawhead and bloodybones), the speaker implies that this vision of reality fulfills the darkest possibilities of his childhood dread:

O Jesus burning on the lily cross

*   *   *

O night, rawhead and bloodybones night

*   *   *

O night betrayed by darkness not its own
(*AA*, p. 88)

Another variation on the third-person narrative point of view is a reversal of the technique used in 'Homage to the Empress of the Blues', where the poem is ostensibly in the first person, but through a phrasal attribution we are aware that the narration is being filtered through a character's perspective. In '"Summertime and the Living . . ."' the attribution occurs in the first line: 'Nobody planted roses, he recalls.' (*AA*, p. 111) Later in the poem there is 'he remembers', but we are virtually oblivious to this 'he' and accept the account, like Hayden's own unfinished autobiographical sketch (also in the third person) as a first-person account. The same holds true for 'The Lions'. The lion tamer explains throughout the poem how he makes his beasts perform, but in the first and last lines appears 'he said' to distance the poem from the poet himself. Clearly it is a narrative device used to create a more objective poetic image, to ensure that we treat the speaker not as Hayden or a thinly guised mask for the poet, but as an independent character with possibilities of perspective and meaning quite beyond the biographical fact of the poet's life. It is precisely the same technique that Hayden employs when he introduces the character of the Stranger as narrator in 'Theme and Variation', 'The Mirages' and 'Ballad of the True Beast'. Naturally we need to ponder this illusive 'he'. We need to consider whether it is an artist, the winged man, a wise Platonic guide or possibly the alien visitor who in Hayden's last poem takes leave of our company. Regardless, it is well worth noting the important effect of this simple shift in narrative point of view.

Hayden's most adept handling of narrative to achieve poetic effect is his synthesis of voices and points of view. He employs this technique infrequently, though most effectively in his epical account of the slave revolt in 'Middle Passage'. In this magnificent poem he combines the voices of the crew, strains of Methodist hymnody, the voice of poet/persona and the speeches of litigants at court in a symphonic structure of theme and variation. As the authors of *Black Poetry in Ameria* note:

Myriad voices speak, indeed, in 'Middle Passage'. Hayden, a careful, painstaking, deliberate workman, sensitive to the infinite possibilities for the management of form in poetry, close student of the poetic mode approved by the New Critics, and, like Tolson, an esteemed teacher as well as a dedicated poet, may be adjudged in his performance in 'Middle Passage' virtually the artist whom he hopes to be in his conception of the ideal poet.[8]

Often compared in technique to Eliot's synthesis of voices in 'The Wasteland', this poem has been widely praised in its use of narrative point of view as providing immediacy, dramatic credibility, and a quality of objectivity. Hayden himself enumerated the variety of poetic voices, citing the voice of the poet as moral commentator, 'the traders, the hymn-singers, and perhaps even of the dead'.[9] Hayden used a similar synthesis in 'Runagate Runagate' when he blended the third-person narration with the nervous voices of the escaping slaves, quotes from wanted posters, from Negro Spirituals and the authoritative commands of the 'General' herself, Harriet Tubman. Likewise, in the original version of 'Words in the Mourning Time' we hear several different voices, though most sections represent the changing emotional reactions of the speaker. But clearly 'Middle Passage' is the best example of this innovative use of narrative point of view, and it demonstrates more than any other of Hayden's poems the shaping of subject into poem which this basic tool can effect.

Closely akin to, sometimes inseparable from, Hayden's shaping of subject through narrative point of view was his organic approach to poetic structure. Hayden's contention that each poem 'establishes its own laws'[10] was hardly an original observation – it reflected the New Critical affirmation of organic art and the theory, if not the practice, of Emerson and the English Romantics: Coleridge had observed that each poem must 'contain in itself why it is so and not otherwise',[11] and Shelley had insisted that a poem 'contain the principle of its own integrity'.[12] But in upholding a 'close relationship between form and content'[13] Hayden was implying more than the abandonment of the arbitrary use of traditional patterns of rhyme, metrics and stanzaic form. By an organic relationship between subject and structure Hayden was designating the lyric mode as well as the literal shape of the verse on a page. As with his varied and innovative use of narrative techniques, the array of lyric structures which results from this approach is remarkable.

As I have previously noted, even a cursory survey of Hayden's work in *Angle of Ascent* or *American Journal* reveals a veritable anthology of lyric forms. In 'Approximations' and 'Smelt Fishing' he has employed the Haiku tradition. He does not abide by the exact metrical requisites for this oriental structure,[14] but he has utilized the compressed equation between tenor and vehicle or between symbol and referent, and he has used the three-line format with the caesural break to set off the two components of the equation. With 'Frederick Douglass' he has used the formal structure of the sonnet (excluding rhyme scheme) to convey the oratorical tone of this tribute. In poems such as 'Those Winter Sundays' and 'Paul Laurence Dunbar' he has employed the elegy, and in the longer poems 'The Peacock Room' and 'Words in the Mourning Time' a good number of the standard ingredients for the pastoral elegy, including the attendant philosophical questions about life and death and the concluding consolation of philosophy. In a number of poems, such as 'The Ballad of Nat Turner' and 'The Ballad of the True Beast' he has skillfully managed the elliptical storyline endemic to the ballad tradition. In 'Crispus

Attucks' and 'Homage to Paul Robeson' he pens what are essentially epitaphs. In a number of poems he employs the dramatic monologue to effect characterization. In 'Middle Passage' he even plays off the traditional ingredients of the epic.[15]

One could profitably assess how Hayden has utilized each of these traditional poetic structures, but for the purposes of reviewing the Hayden style it is more beneficial to catalogue the basic methods by which Hayden incorporated the outward form into the inner purposes so that structure becomes a major index to poetic intent. For example, Hayden has poems which are structured around one compressed image. These are usually visual, and frequently some of Hayden's most difficult poems. With '"Dance the Orange"', 'Smelt Fishing', 'Gulls' and similar lyrics the unembellished compression of thought requires much of us and recalls the statement that for the imagist poet 'concentration is of the very essence of poetry'.[16] Robert Greenberg describes these brief Hayden poems as '"hard" lines without sentiment or generalization; total dependence on image for emotional and intellectual content: haiku-like concentration'.[17]

Related to this structure, but more drawn out in language and style, are other poems which focus on one image. Settings like 'Locus' and 'The Point', like '"Summertime and the Living . . ."', 'Richard Hunt's "Arachne"' and 'Monet's "Waterlilies"', are similar in the imagistic portrait of a single vision and a corresponding thought or feeling. But instead of compressing these images the poet expands them, explores them so that we are aware of their subtle implications and the personality who is studying these visions frozen in time by the artist's skill. This same structural technique is used in 'The Rag Man', 'Two Egyptian Portrait Masks', '"Lear is Gay"' and 'Figure', where there is the same sort of one-shot image and its figural implications, but an image filtered through the persona's imaginative eye.

Related to the character portraits are Hayden's elliptical biographies. These are not compressed or focused on one thought, but often contain a number of parts, a summary of years and actions. Most notable among these are 'Witch Doctor', 'El-Hajj Malik El-Shabazz', 'Aunt Jemima of the Ocean Waves', 'John Brown' and 'from *The Snow Lamp*'. These are not all exactly alike in structure – some focus on one event or one point in a life, whereas others actually attempt to summarize the whole biography. But all possess the same quality of presenting an elaborate insight into a character as a representative of some human attribute.

Another category of Hayden's structures is that group of poems which focuses on literal action, on plot. These are not necessarily more complex than the life studies – often the plots are quite implicit, and even more frequently the literal action is less important than the persona's mental examination of that plot. In 'Electrical Storm', for example, the speaker recalls his narrow escape from death, but the poem begins with the action completed, and the plot itself seems less significant than the persona's speculation about what it meant. In 'The Whipping' there is literal plot, but it is secondary to the speaker's emotional response. Likewise in 'The Night-Blooming Cereus' or 'The Performers' there is action, but the plot itself focuses on the mental action of the persona/observer. In a good many poems, however, the literal action does structure the poem. In 'The Ballad of Sue Ellen Westerfield', '"Incense of the Lucky Virgin"', 'Night, Death, Mississippi', 'The Dream' there are the essential ingredients of a complete story.

A related but more elaborate structure which implies a plot sequence are those several important poems which, though essentially contemplative, portray a complete sequence of emotions, from exposition to falling action. The most elaborate of these are 'Words in the Mourning Time', 'The Peacock Room' and 'Veracruz', but there are a number of other pieces similarly structured. For example, 'A Ballad of Remembrance', '"From the Corpse Woodpiles . . ."', 'The Broken Dark' and 'As my blood was drawn' are also prime examples of this internal pattern of consolation and reconciliation which forms these mental plot structures.

In most of these there is a noteworthy similarity between Hayden's reconciliation of his faith and the same pattern of plot which George Herbert uses in his famous poem 'The Collar'.[18] The persona in Herbert's poem is, like Herbert himself, a priest, and at the outset of the poem he chaffs at the restraint of his holy vows:

> I struck the board and cried, 'No more;
> I will abroad!
> What, shall I ever sigh and pine?'[19]

The speaker grows more fierce, more determined in his resolve to forsake his calling and recover his 'sigh-blown age', but the ranting climaxes and concludes when the speaker regains his perspective and becomes reconciled:

> But as I raved, and grew more fierce and wild
> At every word,
> Methought I heard one calling, 'Child!'
> And I replied, 'My Lord.'[20]

Hayden's persona does not rebel against the demands of his faith, but he does struggle to reconcile his observations of human injustice with the dictates of a faith in progressive revelation and in the eventual triumph of man's spirituality. In several poems this reconciliation is not the result of an intellectual understanding so much as it is an emotional catharsis similar to the implied experience of Herbert's persona. Often this emotional pitch coincides with the persona calling out in prayer. In 'The Broken Dark' he ends with the line, 'O Healing Spirit,/ Thy nearness our forgiving cure' (*AA*, p. 39). In 'Words in the Mourning Time' the speaker concludes by reciting a paraphrase of the

Bahá'í Short Obligatory Prayer: 'I bear Him witness now.'[21] In '"As my blood was drawn"' he calls upon 'the irradiant veiled/ terrible One' (*AJ*, p. 41) ('terrible' here used interestingly in the sense that God's Omnipotence induces awe in anticipating what consequence will succeed man's folly). And, of course, '"From the Corpse Woodpiles . . ."' concludes the speaker's panoramic survey of contemporary evil by affirming that the pain and suffering of the Manifestation are 'our anguish and our anodyne' (*AA*, p. 116).

Structured around this pattern of consolation, these are at once some of the most complex and important poems Hayden wrote, but they are not the only poems which follow this structural pattern. A number of Hayden's recollections of Paradise Valley are similarly structured around the person's contemplation of fundamental questions. 'Beginnings', 'Elegies for Paradise Valley' and, to a lesser extent, '"Summertime and the Living . . ."' and 'Free Fantasia' all portray a purposeful contemplation of the past aimed at resolving major questions: What was so vital about that era? What is the origin of the persona's emotional outlook, his sense of guilt, his quest for a meaningful identity?

Finally, there are several poems which are virtually mini-dramas, which delineate a complete story-line. They are few in number and do not necessarily represent the most complex poems structurally, but they are among the most important poems Hayden produced. Most obviously one would include in this category 'Middle Passage' with its complicated assemblage of voices and modalities. There is the diary prose of the ship's log:

> Blacks rebellious.   Crew uneasy.   Our linguist says
> their moaning is a prayer for death,
> ours and their own.
>
> > (*AA*, p. 118)

the hymnal refrain:

> Jesus   Saviour   Pilot   Me
> Over   Life's Tempestuous   Sea
> > (*AA*, p. 118)

the comments of the Old Salt in a ballad quatrain:

> Aye, lad, and I have seen those factories,
> Gambia, Rio Pongo, Calabar;
> have watched the artful mongos baiting traps
> of war wherein the victor and the vanquished
>
> Were caught as prizes for our barracoons.
> > (*AA*, p. 120)

the rhymed refrain alluding to Shakespeare's Tempest:

> Deep in the festering hold thy father lies,
> the corpse of mercy rots with him,
> rats eat love's rotten gelid eyes.
>
> (*AA*, p. 121)

the rhetorical oratory of the Spanish emissaries from Cuba:

> Now we
> demand, good sirs, the extradition of
> Cinquez and his accomplices to La
> Havana.
>
> (*AA*, p. 123)

Finally, less awesome in complexity but no less complete in plot are Hayden's treatment of Márques' short story in 'For a Young Artist', the powerful monologue in 'The Tattooed Man', the incomplete epical treatment of Matthew Henson in 'from *The Snow Lamp*', and his intriguing narrative from the alien's report in '[American Journal]'.

No doubt there are alternative methods of classifying Hayden's lyric structures, but regardless of how one presents these fundamental ingredients of style, there is an important benefit derived from reviewing Hayden's sources for poetic images, his manipulation of perspective through narrative point of view and his several methods of organizing these raw materials into poetic form. This benefit is a rudimentary appreciation of the scope of Hayden's talent stylistically. If a traditional lyric mode would work, he used it. If he needed something unusual, he discovered it or invented it, whether the telegraphic prose of the alien's report or the Eskimo song-chant in 'from *The Snow Lamp*'. He seemed equally comfortable with a sonnet, a mystical vision, compressed tropes after Rilke, whatever was appropriate. He had learned his craft sufficiently well that he was never limited by his technique as to what themes he could approach or how he could present them. To his readers, understanding this breadth of capacity is important because it means that nothing in his poems happens by chance, that even the fundamental elements of his style are vital clues to internal significance.

22. Image and Symbol

> We are symbols and inhabit symbols; workmen, work, and tools, words and things, birth and death, all are emblems; but we sympathize with the symbols, and being infatuated with the economical uses of things, we do not know that they are thoughts. The poet, by an ulterior intellectual perception, gives them a power which makes their old use forgotten, and puts eyes and a tongue into every dumb and inanimate object. He perceives the independence of the thought on the symbol, the stability of the thought, the accidency and fugacity of the symbol.[1]
>
> Emerson, 'The Poet'

With a symbolist poet like Hayden there is a special challenge in examining the relationship between form and idea because there is often a vast disparity between what the poem is ostensibly portraying and what the poem means. This distinction between subject and theme is ubiquitous in Hayden's poetry. He may be describing butterflies but on another level decrying man's insensibility; he may be describing Mardi Gras in New Orleans, but asserting his own identity; he may be portraying a museum room, but contemplating the enigmas of life and art. So it is that to appreciate the relationship between poetic structure and thematic meaning we are obliged in examining Hayden's art to begin with the surface meaning, the literal image which contains the keys to the larger symbolic values, 'the savage real that clues/ my vision of the real' (*AA*, p. 64), the formulae for thought and feeling.

Thus, 'The Diver' is first off a well-wrought literal image of a dramatic experience – a scuba diver struggling against the intoxicating effects of nitrogen narcosis. But even as we mentally recreate that adventure we are feeling the poem's symbolic or metaphoric weight, wondering what else it means. This use of the term *image* to designate the total correlative of the poem often becomes the poetic process itself, the translation of abstraction into perceptible form, into thought that is felt. But we can also discover the various components of this imagistic process and thereby have a more effective understanding of Hayden's technique. We can distinguish between image and symbol or between literal and figurative image.

On the most basic level the term *image* designates the poet's capacity to effect a mental picture in the reader's mind.[2] There are two basic methods of accomplishing this – directly through literal images or indirectly through figurative images. In Hayden's poetry we find both used abundantly and effectively. Most of Hayden's poetry is first concerned with direct or literal image, but in the process of creating the surface impression Hayden uses both sorts of imagery. His direct or literal imagery is usually achieved by two methods – the careful selection of detail and the application of adjectival embellishment to flesh out the object. Both methods of creating the literal image test the poet's mettle, and Hayden was rarely found wanting.

In the opening lines of 'Elegies for Paradise Valley', for example, we infer an entire setting from the sparse but powerful selection of details:

> My shared bedroom's window
> opened on alley stench.
> A junkie died in maggots there.
> I saw his body shoved into a van.
>
> (*AJ*, p. 25)

From this simple list of factual observations we infer the child's perception, whereas the lush catalogue of flora in 'Locus' represent quite another use of literal imagery to imply a different perspective:

> here Cherokee rose, acacia, and mimosa;
> here magnolias—totemic flowers
>   wreathing legends of this place
>
> (*AA*, p. 45)

The speaker's emotions and point of view are also effectively implied in the literal observations in 'Veracruz':

> At the seaward end,
> a pharos like a temple rises.
> From here the shore
> seen across marbling waves
> is arabesque ornately green
> that hides the inward-falling slum,
> the stains and dirty tools of struggle;
>
> (*AA*, p. 91)

Poem after poem Hayden demonstrates his gift for discovering the precise details of character or setting to make vivid portraits in our minds, whether it be the witch doctor 'Reposing on cushions of black leopard skin' (*AA*, p. 107) or 'The Point', where 'sound and river come/ together, flowing to the sea' (*AJ*, p. 45).

Hayden's use of imaginative adjectives to revive within us what he sees is even more remarkable, demonstrating the kind of effect that most poets reserve for figurative images. We hardly notice them *en passant*, which is as it should be; we notice only that we see and hear and feel. But out of context these simple phrases reveal the poet's supple skill. Some are ostensibly simple words, but coupled with the substantives they modify they create powerful effects: *well-mastered bed, refracting tears, no relieving shade, archaic mysteries, elegant avenger, famine fields, unearned increments of grace, compassionate art, brutal dream, thronging sunlight, lyric space, layered light.*

In other instances Hayden concocts adjectives which have an eyecatching originality, power-packed constructs which, beyond the basic sensual perception, contribute a precise tone and mood to the literal portrait: *goggling terror, blazonry of farewell scarlet, cloacal dark, splendiferous Jack Johnson, the gaudy mumbojumbo of politicians, totemic flowers, frangipani crowns, paleocrystic ice, lambent shore, warcrazed eyes, moonstruck trees, jazzbo strutting of a mouse, elegiac lace, auroral dark, glaucous poison jewels, coruscations of laughter, metaphorical doors, great gelid mass.*

Sometimes Hayden creates literal imagery with imaginative nouns: *plangency, venduce, passacaglia, jactations, decrepitude, the belling of that tropic perfume, cussedness.* On other occasions Hayden creates his own nouns from word compounds: *soulscape, lifesquawk, Absolute Otherwhere, mimosa's fancywork.* But whether simple or baroque, whether with adjectival embellishment or selection of detail, Hayden's direct or literal imagery is so effective that many readers have been ensnared by these intriguing surfaces and have failed to notice the deeper value of these images.

Besides literal imagery Hayden's poems abound in equally well-fashioned figurative or indirect imagery. Figurative imagery in Hayden's poetry is accomplished by a variety of analogical devices – by oxymoron, metonomy, personification, and most frequently by simile and metaphor. While the simile is explicit and the metaphor implicit, both establish the same analogical process whereby two essentially dissimilar things are compared. According to I. A. Richards' effective updating of Aristotle's description of these devices, a figurative image contains three parts – the *tenor* (that which is being described), the *vehicle* (that which is being compared to the *tenor*) and the *meaning* (that area of similitude they share, which Richards terms 'the lynchpin tying together two sharply different contexts').[3]

These devices can be simple or complex. For example, in a simple simile Hayden describes the impact of a policeman's disdainful look:

> I saw the hatred for our kind
> glistening like tears
> in the policemen's eyes.
>
> (*AJ*, p. 25)

Here the vehicle 'tears' is commonplace, but the imaginative comparison of the tears to a look of hatred is uncommon and powerful. Similarly in '*Sub Specie Aeternitatis*', when Hayden compares the vacant convent to 'relic skulls' (*AA*, p. 94) we are not greatly challenged to catch the visual aspect of that simile, but the more we contemplate how many ways that image can work, the more meaning we derive and the more we understand how much energy went into the selection of that vehicle.

This is the key to good figurative imagery and it is the trademark of Hayden's work, the degree to which the reader is challenged to examine the 'lynchpin'. In a trite or commonplace figurative image like 'cold as stone' or 'green as grass' there is no effective image created because the vehicle offers no resistance. If we imagine the reader's thought process as being like the flow of electrical current through a circuit, we could compare the effective figurative image to a resistor. If it is working, the current slows down when it passes through that resistance, just as the reader must pause to examine with his mind and senses the clashing of these dissimilar contexts. Before the current completes the circuit, or the reader's thought is completed by solving for x (that missing ingredient of similitude), the resistance must be overcome. With a trite or otherwise ineffective image, the thought passes directly to meaning without pausing, without reflecting or feeling; there is a shortcircuit and no image is experienced.

In Hayden's more imaginative conceits the reader must sometimes ponder long and hard how the tenor and vehicle are related. For example, in 'Bahá'u'lláh in the Garden of Ridwan' it is hardly obvious why swords are likened to compass-needles:

> Agonies confirm His hour,
>   and swords like compass-needles turn
>   toward His heart.
>
>   (*AA*, p. 117)

To solve for x here, one must recover the allusion to Bahá'í history and the reference to the Bahá'í view of progressive revelation to understand how the persecution of the Prophet is one sign of His station.

As I have already made clear, the most challenging algebra for the reader of Hayden's poetry is in discovering the most expansive use of simile and metaphor as the poems themselves become vehicles. But before approaching those systems of analogue and symbol it is valuable to see Hayden's figurative imagery at work within the process of constructing the literal image itself. For example, Hayden has an unrivaled capacity for creating metaphoric adjectives which are veritable poems in themselves. As with the literal imagery, some of these are fashioned from simple words as if they were easily plucked from the poet's word-hoard: *briary light, wintered recollections, lunar solitude, target streets, icy evil, flame trees, thorny meagerness*. Somewhat more complex are his compound adjectives that also have amazing metaphorical power: *sixty-*

watt gloom, sunwhetted morning, blueblack cold, belltongue bodies, salt-frosted lie, swaybacked jetty, stained-glass cell, plateglass wind, cutglass dark. Some of Hayden's phrasal metaphors are often the focal point of a poem: *weeping eyes of wounds, riot squad of statistics, bony vise of knees, striptease of reality, centrifuge of dying, alarming fists of snow,* the *belly of cost, switchblades of that air.*

But if these phrasal metaphors convince us of Hayden's prowess, his expanded figurative images are even more impressive. '"Lear is Gay"', for example, concludes with an image which is at once visual, emotional and completely convincing:

> And oh can laugh
> sometimes
>
> at time as at
> a scarecrow whose
> hobo shoulders are
> a-twitch with crows.
>
> (*AA*, p. 70)

In 'A Plague of Starlings' Hayden contrives an uncanny image to capture the sound of the shotgun blast killing the unwanted birds:

> Their scissoring
> terror like glass
> coins spilling breaking
> the birds explode
> into mica sky
>
> (*AA*, p. 71)

In 'The Islands' Hayden describes the morning as being 'like a god/ in peacock-flower mantle dancing/ on opalescent waves' (*AJ*, p. 48).

These images are effective because they transcend perception; they imply attributes beyond the senses. In 'Homage to the Empress of the Blues' Hayden begins: 'Because there was a man somewhere in a candystripe silk shirt,/ gracile and dangerous as a jaguar . . .' (*AA*, p. 104). The animal image itself is hardly remarkable, but the phrasing of it in this context implies the total appearance and personality of this 'Twotiming Love'. Likewise, when Hayden describes the drug addict in 'Soledad' he uses an image which visually implies an anguished, contorted figure in a fetal pose, but he also implies the reason for the addiction with the same metaphor: 'cradled by drugs, by jazz/ as never by any lover's cradling flesh' (*AA*, p. 40). The same complexity of image occurs in 'Traveling through Fog' when the speaker compares 'Looking back' to see the 'blurring lights' with watching 'underwater stars and moons', a metaphor which employs the very symbols essential to the whole Platonic theme of the poem.

In addition to his effective use of literal and figurative devices Hayden also employed symbolism to establish the poetic image. Like the figurative image the symbol points beyond itself to another object or idea, but traditionally the symbol is based not on a process of similitude; according to most theorists the symbol is capable of evoking directly the referent.

This distinction does not always work, especially since a powerful metaphor can become a symbol, but it is a useful and valid one all the same. Thus, the cross may symbolize a religion, the flag a country, without two things being compared. But there is always a reason for the process, a rationale for the symbol having the power to evoke the referent, and in Hayden's poetry it is usually important for the reader to ponder that relationship. There is with the symbol, in other words, a three-part process similar to that of the figurative image because, according to I. A. Richards, there is no direct relationship between symbol and referent: 'Between the symbol and the referent there is no relevant relation other than the indirect one, which consists in its being used by someone to stand for a referent. Symbol and Referent, that is to say, are not connected directly.'[4]

Richards explains that between the two is 'an act of reference', a process by which the reader recovers the symbolic relationship by assuming 'an attitude which will, according to circumstances, be more or less similar to the act and the attitude of the speaker'.[5] By discovering the symbolic relationship, the reader can arrive at the same referent or symbolic value and thereby recover the speaker's emotions. In short, while some metaphors become symbols and some symbols have metaphoric possibilities, the focus of the symbol is in discovering what the symbol refers to and why, not what it is similar to.

In general there are two broad categories of symbol – the particular or 'tied' symbol and the universal or 'free' symbol. The universal symbols are those which could be readily recognized outside the poetic context. For example, in 'Runagate Runagate' Hayden portrays the stars as guiding the escaping slaves, the same universal symbol of guidance he employs in the poem 'Stars'. The particular symbols are those which have symbolic value in a poetic context. So it is that 'rawhead and bloodybones' in 'Night, Death, Mississippi' and 'The Peacock Room' symbolizes unknown terror because of the symbolic value Hayden has invested in this image.

The universal symbols occur most frequently in those poems relating to Hayden's religious themes. In 'Bahá'u'lláh in the Garden of Ridwan' darkness represents man's spiritual decline and unenlightened state. The light, particularly the early morning light as symbolized in the appellation 'Dawnbreaker', symbolizes the faith of the first to understand and follow the light of knowledge, and the Dawnbreaker's faith is signaled by the universal symbol of fire which literally burns his flesh, 'the fire that/ will save' (*AA*, p. 80). In addition to being universal symbols, however, many of Hayden's religious tropes apply the same symbolism found in the Bahá'í Writings, as is evidenced in

'Abdu'l-Bahá's explanation of the importance of distinguishing between the literal and the figurative or symbolic in studying the sacred texts:

So the symbol of knowledge is light, and of ignorance, darkness; but reflect, is knowledge sensible light, or ignorance sensible darkness? No, they are merely symbols . . . Then it is evident that the dove which descended on Christ was not a material dove, but it was a spiritual state, which, that it might be comprehensible, was expressed by a sensible figure. Thus in the Old Testament it is said that God appeared as a pillar of fire: this does not signify the material form; it is an intellectual reality which is expressed by a sensible image.[6]

Several other universal symbols in Hayden's poetry also parallel similar symbols in the Bahá'í Writings. His use of flight and ascent as tropes for spiritual transformation correspond to the numerous usages in the Bahá'í Writings of the bird as a symbol of the spirit[7] and the equally frequent use of 'ascent' as a symbol of spiritual transcendence.[8] Similarly, Hayden's repeated use of *sun, moon* and *stars* as symbols of divine guidance accord with Bahá'u'lláh's lengthy exposition on the symbolic use of these images in the prophetic passages of scripture. Bahá'u'lláh states that these celestial bodies may represent the Manifestations,[9] the 'saints, and their companions',[10] the 'leaders of religion'[11] and even the laws and teachings which the Prophets institute.[12]

Hayden has used other universal symbols not so pointedly related to the Bahá'í Writings, such as the shore in 'A Ballad of Remembrance', 'Middle Passage' and 'Letter', or the illusions in 'The Mirages'. But a good illustration of his skillful manipulation of the free symbol is in his use of the phallic imagery in 'Veracruz' and 'Zeus over Redeye'. In 'Veracruz' the pharos (light-house) rises like a temple at 'the seaward end', thus becoming both a procreative symbol and a symbol of light and guidance. As a warning of treacherous shore, as well as the division between land and sea, it symbolizes in the poem the division between the phantasmal expanse of water and the stark reality of the village, or, more importantly, the division in the speaker's mind between the dream world of illusion and the harsh reality of the real world. In 'Zeus over Redeye', however, the rockets stand like a 'phallic grove', not as symbols of guidance and life, but as inversions of procreation, as ironic symbols of man's perversion of the light of knowledge.

Hayden's particular or 'tied' symbols are no less effective. In some poems he borrows symbols from other contexts. From Greek myth he uses the Sphinx as a symbol of arbitrary or capricious torment and trial. The speaker in 'The Peacock Room' observes how Whistler has employed traditional Christian symbolism in depicting peacocks trampling gold coins, a symbol for Christ's chasing out the moneychangers, just as Whistler may have presumed he was purging the connoisseur's philistinism.[13] From the historical context of the Civil War, Hayden uses a northward direction as a symbol of freedom in 'Runagate Runagate' and 'from *The Snow Lamp*'.

But clearly Hayden's most imaginative symbols are those which are purely his own invention. For example, the night-blooming cereus, the sunflowers and the zinnias have as flowers inherent symbolic meaning, but in the context of Hayden's poems they assume particular values. As a mysterious flower that appears infrequently in the night, the night-blooming cereus is a marvelous correlative for the long-awaited appearance of the Manifestation, and for Bahá'u'lláh in particular. In '"Summertime and the Living . . ."' the sunflower as a bold, bright, hardy flower that can bloom with little nourishment amid the city's squalor, becomes a powerful symbol of Afro-Americans like Hayden and Malcolm X who bloomed in the midst of austere circumstance. The zinnias have a similar value – a bright blossom with 'bravura persistence', they seem to designate the sort of bouquet appropriate to the poet's own performance.

Two good examples of Hayden's ironic use of particular symbols are the trees in 'Ice Storm' and the butterflies in 'Butterfly Piece'. Ostensibly the trees, burdened with ice in the December storm, represent hope because in the spring they will mend and emerge ascendant from their winter trials. To the persona in the illness of his winter years the trees' renewal contrasts with his own temporality, and he asks rhetorically, 'And am I less to You,/ my God, than they?' (*AJ*, p. 39). In the midst of his despair the speaker cannot appreciate that, according to his own beliefs, he too will be renewed. The butterflies have this same sort of dual symbolic value in 'Butterfly Piece'. In their brilliant colors they symbolize nature's craft and wonder. But as the persona observes that the creature's color caused its demise, he also thinks how human color, which should also be a sign of beauty and wonder, becomes a burden, a reason for persecution.

Of course, virtually every character-piece and setting is invested by Hayden with symbolic value. Malcolm X and Frederick Douglass clearly symbolize man's capacity for willed transcendence over external circumstance. Lear and Jemima symbolize human resilience. The Witch Doctor represents the volitional perversion of human capacity. The tattooed man and the winged man represent the artist in relation to society. Artists such as Billie Holiday, Monet and Hayden himself symbolize the existential comforters of mankind. Nat Turner and John Brown, among other things, symbolize the dangers of mysticism.[14] But while these and other character pieces focus on human attributes, none is limited by that quality. Hayden has done more than render poeticized versions of character types.

The settings work much the same way symbolically. They connote stories, rich tapestries of history, but each also is pointedly geared to serve as a symbol of a human attitude or condition. The Natchez Trace is a variable symbol of a pathway to freedom, the abode of highwaymen, an erroneous theory of evil, a reminder of the inherited evil of racism. The Peacock Room is a symbol of art's enigmas, the transience of life, the hope of man in history. Less complex symbolic settings might be the movie theater in 'Double Feature', which represents the desire for escape from a negative identity, or the dark forest in 'The Moose Wallow', which symbolizes the subtle admixture of anticipation and fear in the presence of mysterious power. And the various prison settings allude to the Platonic allegory for the physical experience.

Clearly Hayden's rich use of symbolism within his poems offers a resource that defies simple catalogues, and no doubt future studies will bring to light some of the hidden gems which Hayden benignly concealed in his life's work. But even in a cursory summary such as this I feel impelled to note two of my favorite symbols. The first is a simple trope tucked away in one of Hayden's quiet lyrics, 'Those Winter Sundays'. This poem, which has moved so many, captures the father's expression of love in simple ways: he gets up on his day off to prepare his son for Sunday school, polishes the boy's shoes, and stokes the fire. The principal image in the poem is the sensual perception of the fire warming the house: 'I'd wake and hear the cold splintering, breaking./ When the rooms were warm, he'd call,/ and slowly I would rise and dress,/ fearing the chronic angers of that house' (*AA*, p. 113).

The house is figuratively cold – there are 'chronic angers' and no communication; the boy speaks 'indifferently to him,/ who had driven out the cold' (*AA*, p. 113). It is only years later in middle age that the speaker recognizes the symbolic gesture – the father was incapable of being openly warm or communicating his affection with words, but he expressed his inward feeling with outward symbols by giving literal warmth and by tending to the boy's spiritual needs. Now as a parent and remote in time from the emotional turmoil of the house, the grown man recognizes those simple acts of drudgery as symbols of 'love's austere and lonely offices' (*AA*, p. 113).

A second symbol I especially appreciate is Hayden's use of his own disease as a symbol of the world's condition in '"As my blood was drawn"'. As I have noted, this symbol plays off the numerous passages by Bahá'u'lláh that also refer to the deterioration of the world's spiritual condition in terms of a sick patient. But the tone here is not of hope, detachment and reassurance. The speaker accuses the external world, denounces the world's evil for invading his microcosm and infecting him with a lethal disease. At first he can reflect on the ironic parallels between the progress of the cancer in his body and the progress of the evil in the external world – the martyrdom of Bahá'ís, the starving multitudes, the neglected children, the drowning of the Cambodian refugees, the pollution and contamination of the environment. But at the end the relationship reverses, and the speaker observes not a parallel process but a causal relationship – the external sickness is 'luxuriating' in his 'body's world'.

These internal uses of image and symbol to effect meaning within poems critics began to recognize relatively early in Hayden's career, in the early 1950s when it became apparent to some that he could not be easily chucked into a 'literary ghetto'.[15] But the external application of imagery, the patterns of metaphor and symbol which reach out beyond the individual poem, which cluster with other poems and delineate his themes, this critics began to recognize only in the early 1970s, and as yet the surface has only been scratched. In his 1975 dissertation Dennis Gendron discussed how the theme of appearance and reality is borne out by the patterns of imagery in *Words in the Mourning Time* and *The Night-Blooming Cereus*.[16] Several other critics in the late 1960s and early 1970s commented on Hayden's figural use of Afro-American history.[17] In her 1976 study 'Image and Idea in the Poetry of Robert Hayden' Constance Post discussed Hayden's clustering of images around symbols of divine guidance and human transformation,[18] and Howard Faulkner in 1977 studied the images of flight as symbols of spiritual ascent.[19] In 1977 Wilburn Williams, Jr., attempted a more comprehensive analysis of Hayden's symbolism in *Angle of Ascent* by showing Hayden's relationship to the 'American tradition emanating from Emerson'.[20]

As Hayden's reputation increases, which it does daily, these studies will grow in number and variety as students of his work begin to understand that it is in these larger applications of Hayden's symbolism that the richest rewards abound. My own opinion is that truly comprehensive studies of Hayden's imagery and symbolism can only occur as more scholars begin to understand the essential relationship between Hayden's patterns of images and his beliefs as a Bahá'í.

In their studies of Hayden's imagery Gendron and Post allude to Donald Stauffer's study of patterns of imagery in Yeats' poetry.[21] Both critics aver that such images as light and shadow, flight and falling, are repeated throughout Hayden's poetry, just as Yeats repeatedly used such symbols as the 'gyre' and the swan. Whether or not these images are 'obsessive' with Hayden, they are repeated, but in a discernible pattern which, I am quite convinced, Hayden was coordinating and controlling. No doubt some of the patterns result from the organic relationship between his evolving art and his own growing awareness of the relationship between his religious belief and his observations about the external and internal world. But an overview of how those patterns work reveals more a conscious artistry than an unconscious or obsessive reliance on similar tropes.

Probably the most noticeable pattern of imagery is formed by the persistent use of darkness as a symbol of lost faith and ignorance, a period in history when, as Yeats symbolizes it, 'The falcon cannot hear the falconer'.[22] In a good many poems this condition is portrayed directly with literal images of violence and lost identity. In fact, fully a third of Hayden's poems are focused on man's inhumanity to man, and in 'Names', '"Mystery Boy" Looks for Kin . . .' and 'El-Hajj Malik El-Shabazz' the search for identity is explicitly portrayed. As I have noted, many critics have found it difficult to reconcile Hayden's religious beliefs with these negative images, but in fact this time of darkness is quite in keeping with his Bahá'í perspective, as he often tried to explain:

'Our view', says Hayden, 'is that there is a divine plan for the universe. We believe that all kinds of changes are going to take place. Bahá'u'lláh prophesied this period – a time of great upheaval. But he also prophesied that out of this turmoil would come a new society, a new social order characterized by justice for all, a new vision of mankind. If all of us had a humane vision of each other, we could bring about these changes without violence.'[23]

It is appropriate, therefore, that while in over twenty poems Hayden used an image of night or darkness to represent this period, in only two is there no light, no glimmer of hope. In 'Night, Death, Mississippi' the poet depicts a family completely devoid of meaningful humanity, and the poet understandably refers to it as the realization of his childhood fantasies of a terror without hope or logic. In 'Smelt Fishing' there is a cry 'for help for light', but we infer that it is unheeded or unsuccessful.

In the other images of darkness there is light, sometimes as present comfort, sometimes as future hope. In some of these images the light directly alludes to Bahá'u'lláh or the Bahá'í Faith. In '"From the Corpse Woodpiles . . ."' the light is the poet's personal vision of Bahá'u'lláh in the Síyáh-Chál; in 'Bahá'u'lláh in the Garden of Ridwan' 'undiscovered suns/ release their light' (*AA*, p. 117), signaling that nature is already aware of the incipient mystery. In 'Words in the Mourning Time' Bahá'u'lláh's 'transilluminating word' lights the darkness of this 'deathbed childbed age' (*AA*, p. 59), and in 'Full Moon' the speaker in contemplating this variable symbol notes that while the moon is now a target for scientists, it also 'spread its radiance on the exile's path/ of Him who was The Glorious One,/ its light made holy by His holiness' (*AA*, p. 79). In 'The Broken Dark' the fearful speaker prays as he feels himself 'in the shadow of God's laser light' (*AA*, p. 39), and the Astronauts are protected by the unseen light of 'God's radar-/watching eye' (*AJ*, p. 55). Finally, the concluding symbolic value in 'Stars' is 'the Nine-Pointed Star' (the Bahá'í Faith), which 'lights mind and/ spirit, signals future light' (*AA*, p. 15).[24]

A related source of light in the darkness is human presences who give comfort and guidance to those encumbered by night. It may be the subtle and indirect help of a blues singer who 'shone that smile on us' (*AA*, p. 104), or the more direct guidance of Harriet Tubman as she follows the stars and 'jack-muh-lanterns' (*AA*, p. 128) leading slaves to freedom. In 'Stars', part three, Sojourner Truth is following 'the stars/ her mind a star' (*AA*, p. 13). In the 'Electrical Storm' it is the neighbor's warning that saves the persona from 'the archetypal dangers of the night' (*AA*, p. 78). In 'The Peacock Room' the speaker compares the emotional shelter this work of art provides to the 'glow . . . of the lamp shaped like a rose/ my mother would light/ for me some nights to keep/ Raw-Head-And Bloodybones away' (*AA*, p. 28). In 'Double Feature' the cinematographer's fantasy on the screen becomes a ray of hope to the ghetto children who view in the Saturday morning fare their own triumph over evil in this special darkness 'where we were other for an hour or two' (*AJ*, p. 36).

In other poems light as hope or comfort is symbolized by natural objects: the nighttime trees in 'Ice Storm', which are spotlighted by the moon as if to attract the beleaguered speaker's attention. In 'The Night-Blooming Cereus' the flower's 'moonlight petals' symbolize the long-awaited renewal of the 'archaic mysteries' (*AA*, p. 25).

As I have already explained, this light in the darkness is, in Hayden's poetry, hardly a naive hope or a blind leap of faith; it represents the poet's well-considered belief in the Bahá'í analysis of history as a divinely ordained and logical process. To convey the notion of this era as a transition to an expanded identity, to mankind's maturity, Hayden used two patterns of imagery. The first is the ample treatment of the journey by the Afro-American from slavery to freedom. The present condition of that process is the middle or transitional stage, just as mankind is currently passing through a 'middle passage' in order to attain both literal and spiritual freedom. Thus, the middle passage of the slave ship in Hayden's poem refers figuratively to this transition, 'to the unfinished odyssey of a people'.[25] Similarly, the various stages in Afro-American history which Hayden demarks, primarily with his catalogue of heroes, symbolize the stages in the growth of mankind towards spiritual enlightenment.

A second pattern of imagery involves a more expansive treatment of this same theme – physical reality itself as a middle or transitional stage in the life's pilgrimage. In part this image is implied in the portrayal of the persona as an everyman-pilgrim whose quest introduces him to an array of places and characters. But the pattern of imagery which most clearly conveys this notion is found in the blatantly Platonic poems that depict physical reality as a mirage. In several poems the entire poetic image focuses on establishing this relationship. In 'The Mirages' physical reality is a desert journey full of diverting illusions; in 'Theme and Variation' the stranger describes the 'striptease of reality' (*AA*, p. 115); in 'Traveling through Fog' life's journey is also a dreamily recalled experience, as is the recollected past in 'The Return'. In other poems life is portrayed as dreamlike. In 'Monet's "Waterlilies"' the painter has captured a world 'beheld as through refracting tears' (*AA*, p. 63); in 'Veracruz' 'reality' becomes 'unbearably a dream' (*AA*, p. 92); and, in 'The Dream', Sinda disdains the reality of freedom in favor of her dream of freedom.

Simultaneous with Hayden's view of this life as dream, as shadow, is his equally firm belief in the necessity of using the symbols of this reality to acquire spiritual understanding and development. To convey this concept of spiritual ascent, Hayden created several different patterns of images to reflect the explicit stages of the process: the exploration of the cave-like physical world for clues to spiritual verities, the resulting ascent from the darkness into the light of understanding, and the descent back into darkness to assist others towards transformation.

The images of the struggle for ascent are most prominently conveyed through the portraits of literal explorers – Astronauts, Matthew Henson, the diver. But other figures who symbolize the artist also 'probe detritus for clues' (*AJ*, p. 55) – the matador dares death to 'call us back to life' (*AA*, p. 98), the tattooed man has endured the pain of needles for his art; and the lion tamer dares to enter 'danger's door' to make his lions leap and to observe 'the savage real that clues/ my vision of the real' (*AA*, p. 64).

As the explorer uncovers the hidden mysteries, he ascends from darkness, a process which Hayden symbolizes with images of light and literal rising. Obviously the most forceful image of this struggle for flight is the allegory in 'For a Young Artist' when the winged man struggles in the night to attain his 'angle of ascent' (*AA*, p. 10). Daedalus, as a symbol of the displaced African in 'O Daedalus, Fly Away Home', can only dream of flight as he recalls the legend of his 'gran' who 'flew back to Africa' (*AA*, p. 124); he himself has become bereft of the wings for his ascent. Likewise, the disenfranchised folk in Paradise Valley in ' "Summertime and Living . . ." ' sit on broken steps (shattered means of ascent) and ponder their 'fantasies/ of Ethiopia spreading her gorgeous wings' (*AA*, p. 111). Sinda, clinging tenaciously to her dream of ascent, 'fought with brittle strength to rise' (*AA*, p. 37), and the poet/persona in 'Those Winter Sundays' would slowly 'rise and dress,/ fearing the chronic angers of that house . . .' (*AA*, p. 113).

After flight, after proximity to light, there is a duty for the artist, as a sort of Platonic emissary, to descend, to re-enter the cave and use his skills to guide others to the heights. Sometimes the descent is willful, like the diver's descent to probe the dark wreck with his flashlight; sometimes the descent is the result of mishap, like the birds in 'A Plague of Starlings' who 'explode/ into mica sky/raggedly fall' (*AA*, p. 71), or the 'dropped gull' in 'Gulls' whom the other birds in flight ignore as they scurry over the 'mica'd/ fall of the sea' (*AA*, p. 102).

Once in the cave, the artist must work with the materials at hand. In 'The Prisoners' the speaker as artist shows the inmate his poems, together with sacred scripture appropriately entitled 'Hidden Words'.[26] Richard Hunt as artist/guide reflects to us the image of our own agonizing transition; Monet translates into visual correlatives our longing for stability and elegant beauty; the Peacock Room confronts us with the enigma of life's transience and art's enduring truth; the two Egyptian portrait masks reach down through time to confirm the persona's belief in Progressive Revelation.

As Socrates states in Plato's *Republic*, this divinely empowered emissary is not always welcome nor his vision deemed the light of guidance. Coming so suddenly from sunlight to shadow, the artist may appear clumsy, awkward, a strange alien to those who have never left the cave:

Coming suddenly out of sunlight, his eyes would be filled with darkness. He might be

required once more to deliver his opinion on those shadows, in competition with the
prisoners who had never been released, while his eyesight was still dim and unsteady;
and it might take some time to become used to the darkness. They would laugh at him
and say that he had gone up only to come back with his sight ruined; it was worth no
one's while even to attempt the ascent.[27]

Clearly Hayden's image of the artist as alien complies with Socrates' observations. As I have already noted, Hayden makes frequent use of this image in
poems like 'A Letter from Phillis Wheatley', 'For a Young Artist', 'The Rag
Man', all of which portray figures disdained or persecuted for the message
they would reveal.

His task completed, the artist as 'true philosopher', as spiritual explorer and
guide, takes flight again, winging his way to the ethereal world of light and
spirit, just as the alien in '[American Journal]' is about to do, just as Hayden
himself, an alien 'among the alien' (*AJ*, p. 31), has done. And yet there is an
even larger application of these patterns of imagery. In addition to the unity
among these clusters of imagery there is the clear hint of several images that
give an overriding unity to these patterns. There is, as I have already noted, the
Platonic model of spiritual growth as symbolized or allegorized in the cave
analogy. Secondly, there is the Platonic image of the 'ladder of love' in *The
Symposium*, a metaphorical or symbolical explanation of much the same
process by which one ascends to successively higher levels of spiritual insight
and development by starting with the metaphorical substances of this life.[28]
Thirdly, there is Bahá'u'lláh's intricate analogy in *The Seven Valleys* wherein
spiritual advancement is depicted in terms of traversing successive valleys –
search, love, knowledge, unity, contentment, wonderment, true poverty and
absolute nothingness.[29] Fourthly, there is the pattern of a spiritual pilgrimage
which, though incumbent upon everyone, is delineated in Hayden's poems by
the progress of the everyman/persona.

In short, the symbolism and imagery in Hayden's poetry offers a vast array
of interpretations and applications. It recalls for me in its range of possibilities,
its levels of meaning and applicability, the 'Four Senses of Interpretation', a
process formerly used 'in interpreting Scriptural and allegorical materials'.[30]
To distinguish among the successive levels of meaning in symbolic or figurative writing, critics recognized four basic strata: the literal, the allegorical, the
moral or tropological, and the spiritual or anagogical. No doubt it would be
tedious, and somewhat mechanical and arbitrary to apply this exacting process
to Hayden's work, but his systems of symbolism are sufficiently consistent
and firmly grounded in Bahá'í theology that such a process might very well
prove useful.

23. The Finishing Touch

To cite his themes, however, is to point to only part of Hayden's triumph as a poet. His chiseled language, his precision, and economy control his themes and give them their enduring quality.[1]

John O'Brien, *Interviews with Black Writers*

John Crowe Ransom affirmed that 'science is for us in our overt or gross practical enterprises, but poetry ministers directly to the delicate needs of the organism'.[2] In turn it requires a deft and instinctive hand to minister to the delicate needs of the poem, especially in the final stages of refining the completed structure to a condition where image, sound and tone are blended into the guise of effortless grace. This process of fine-tuning a poem probably occupies a greater percentage of the competent poet's time than any other activity, except, perhaps, for the time spent staring at the blank page searching for correlatives.

The sensitivity to the sound, the weight and color of words, to the pacing and phrasing of lines is not something that can be taught, nor do most poets think about the rationale for the hundreds of subtle changes that are usually a part of this final stage in crafting a poem. There is a reason for each change, and if one could look over the artist's shoulder, stop him in mid-change, the poet might be able to explain each move. But for the professional poet, for the artist who has become 'a worthy servitor', this ability has become 'truly instinct, brain matter, diastole, systole,/ reflex action' (*AA*, p. 131).[3]

The ostensible mystery behind this ability, actually the product of hours and years of practice, accounts in part for the poet's sensation of doing something instinctive. It is not that he is unaware of what he is doing when he strives for a certain rhythm or alliteration or tone, but the overall process of revising is much like the seemingly effortless ease with which a ballerina gives form to emotion or an expert athlete demands from his body an animal grace. The raw talent must be there first, the capacity of the dancer's body to be trained, but the ease and flow of movement belie the drudgery, the unobserved hours of thankless solitude that are the bulk of any artist's life. As

Gerard Manley Hopkins said in 'The Windhover', 'shéer plód makes plough down sillion/ Shine . . .'[4]

Among the processes involved in the final revision, the most discernible result is the interplay between sound and meaning. Certainly this is true in Hayden's poetry, because he was acutely aware of sound effects, as he noted in the McClusky interview:

I hear my lines as I write them. I'm almost as much concerned with the way my poems sound as I am with what they say. I think of the two elements interacting. I'm sensitive to the textures, weights of words, to vowel and consonant values. I'll allow a poem to have harsh sounds – dissonances – if they contribute to the effect I'm after. Rhythm obviously determines tonality too. And repetition is a tonal as well as rhetorical device.[5]

Because Hayden was so aware of the organic relationship between sound and meaning, he early abandoned the arbitrary restrictions of set meter and rhyme scheme after the publication of *Heart-Shape in the Dust*, using such patterned sound afterward only when the poem required it. For example, he employed the basic sonnet structure in 'Frederick Douglass' and slant rhyme in the couplets of 'Snow', but in both cases sound is integral to thematic purpose. In fact, the alternating rhyme in the quatrains in one of his last poems, ' "As my blood was drawn" ' (*abcd*), is actually reminiscent of his similar poetics in his first volume, *Heart-Shape*, where he would form a four-line stanza from brief lines that are, in reading, actually couplets. A comparison of a stanza from ' "As my blood was drawn" ' and 'Gabriel' will illustrate what I mean:

> As spreading oilslicks
> burned the seas,
> the doctors confirmed
> metastasis.
>   (*AJ*, p. 40)

> *   *   *

> Black Gabriel, riding
> To the gallows tree,
> In this last hour
> What do you see?
>   (*Heart-Shape*, p. 23)

In general, Hayden's use of sound involves three types of effects – the rhythm or flow of line, which is effected by accentual stress, the interplay of one sound off another (alliteration, assonance, rhyme, etc) and the inherent tone certain words evoke (*r*'s and *s*'s may be soft and soothing; gutturals, harsh and grating). As with Hayden's poetic forms, his use of metrical effects are characterized by incredible variety. In 'Frederick Douglass' he uses long, formal lines in iambic and dactylic feet to achieve the high rhetoric appropriate to the oratorical tone of the piece:

When it is finally ours, this freedom, this liberty, this beautiful and terrible

thing needful to man as air,

usable as earth; when it belongs at last to all,

when it is truly instinct, brain matter, diastole, systole . . .

(AA, p. 131)

Another good example of his organic use of metrics is in the abundant stresses and onomatopoetic pace of the lines in 'Runagate Runagate'. Like the rhythm of the title, the meters in the poem suggest the frenetic pace of the running slaves and the steady, rumbling movement of a train, appropriate to the motif of the Underground Railroad:

> Runs falls rises stumbles on from darkness into darkness
>
> and the darkness thicketed with shapes of terror
>
> and the hunter pursuing and the hounds pursuing . . .

(AA, p. 128)

A number of Hayden's metrical effects are derived from or relate to various musical rhythms. At the end of 'Runagate Runagate' he alludes to a Negro spiritual: 'Mean mean mean to be free.' Similarly, in 'Mourning Poem for the Queen of Sunday' Hayden mixes a hymnal refrain ('Oh who and oh who will sing Jesus down') with a blues motif:

> Oh, Satan sweet-talked her,
> and four bullets hushed her.
> Lord's lost Him His diva,
> His fancy warbler's gone.
> Who would have thought,
> who would have thought she'd end that way?

(AA, p. 110)

The interesting juxtaposition of these two rhythms aptly hints at the focal irony of the poem – that this exquisite voice in the Sunday choir has been silenced in dubious circumstance.

Hayden also used blues rhythms in such poems as 'Soledad', 'Homage to the Empress of the Blues' and '"Summertime and the Living . . ."', and he used other musical modes as well, like the tonally complex *juba* in 'O Daedalus, Fly Away Home':

> Drifting night in the Georgia pines,
> coonskin drum and jubilee banjo.
> Pretty Malinda, dance with me.

> Night is juba, night is conjo.
> Pretty Malinda, dance with me.
>   (*AA*, p. 124)

The regular rhythm repeated throughout the poem conveys the sense of Congolese drums, chants and dance appropriate to the slave's longing for his homeland. Likewise the contrapuntal development reflects the interplay between sadness and gaiety. Hayden stated that while most of the lines are trochaic, he slowed it up 'in places, shifting the accent from the first syllable to the second' in order to emphasize the dance movement, and, in fact, the poem has been danced.[6]

In general Hayden's metrics do not utilize set patterns, but the pace of the lines always relates to the poetic situation. In '[American Journal]' he employs the telegraphic prose rhythm of a journal, as he does with the log entries in 'Middle Passage' or the diary in 'from *The Snow Lamp*'. In the associational thought which he presents in 'The Diver' and 'The Tattooed Man' Hayden uses brief lines in a continuous flow to capture the mood of the persona's emotion. In 'The Diver', which conveys the narcotic state of the persona, there are no metrical pauses at the ends of lines, because Hayden employs enjambment to capture the feeling of a liquid, continuous experience, not circumscribed thoughts, but a dreamlike, eerie flow from one image to another. The meters in 'The Tattooed Man' start and stop as his emotions change from the proud rehearsing of his devotion to his art, to his plaintive longing for affection, to his stoic resolve that his destiny is set:

> These that were my pride
> repel the union of
> your flesh with mine.
> I yearn I yearn.
> And if I dared
> the agonies
> of metamorphosis,
> would I not find
> you altered then?
> I do not want
> you other than you are.
> And I—I cannot
> (will not?) change.
>   (*AJ*, pp. 20–21)

It would require a considerable study of Hayden's metrics to assess adequately his artful control of his lines. It is sufficient to note here that Hayden was clearly aware of how metrics contributed to his poetic images, and that, well grounded as he was in both traditional poetic forms and music, he had the capacity to employ whatever metrical devices a given poem required. I would be remiss, however, if I did not mention a device which was clearly one of his favorite means of controlling pace and tone: it was his consistent use throughout his career of 'oh' and 'o' to form repetitions, to lengthen the metrics of a line, and to establish an imploring tone:

> Oh, not with statues' rhetoric . . .
> > from 'Frederick Douglass' (*AA*, p. 133)

> Oh who and oh who will sing Jesus down . . .
> from 'Mourning Poem for the Queen of Sunday (*AA*, p. 110)

> Oh, summer summer summertime —
> from '"Summertime and the Living . . ."' (*AA*, p. 111)

> oh surely this is the road she took
> > from 'A Road in Kentucky' (*AA*, p. 103)

> That gaiety oh
> that gaiety I love . . .
> > from '"Lear is Gay"' (*AA*, p. 70)

> Oh, hear the stuffed gold eagle sing.
> > from 'On Lookout Mountain' (*AA*, p. 46)

> Oh praised my honer, harshener . . .
> > from 'The Ballad of Nat Turner' (*AA*, p. 127)

> *But, oh, the living look at you* . . .
> > from 'Middle Passage' (*AA*, p. 122)

> oh, as I see them leap—
> > from 'The Lions' (*AA*, p. 64)

> oh dreadfully, our humanness must be achieved.
> > from 'Words in the Mourning Time' (*AA*, p. 59)

> And he swings
> oh swings: beyond complete immortal now.
> > from 'Soledad' (*AA*, p. 40)

> oh they took all the prizes one Hallowe'en.
> > from 'Beginnings' (*AA*, p. 4)

it is beginning oh
it begins now
from *'The Snow Lamp'* (*AJ*, p. 51)

He danced
through jeering streets
to death; oh sang . . .
from 'Dawnbreaker' (*AA*, p. 80)

What we yearned
but were powerless to do
for them, oh we
will dare, Michael, for you, . . .
from 'The Year of the Child' (*AJ*, p. 44)

And oh it was just as frightened
as we were.
from 'Ballad of the True Beast' (*NBC*, p. 14)

In the tradition of Gerard Manley Hopkins and Dylan Thomas, Hayden also loved the rich use of sounds playing off sounds – alliteration in particular, though often he relished the emotional quality that a single word might have. He fell in love with some particular words which he would use repeatedly because they had such a profound tonal quality. The word *plangent* or *plangency*, for example, he used in 'The Night-Blooming Cereus', 'October' and 'Veracruz' because the word itself seems to reverberate like the sound it describes, and yet it also seems to convey an emotion quite beyond sound alone. The word *chimera(s)* Hayden used in 'from *The Snow Lamp*', 'The Tattooed Man' and 'October', again because it has an inherently poetic sound, but also because it bridges the senses, connoting at once imaginative and various color, and, from the mythological monster it names, becoming a symbol of the seasonal nature of the year. Thus Hayden in 'October' describes 'chimera colors'; in 'from *The Snow Lamp*', the 'chimera's land', and in 'The Tattooed Man', the arms as 'prized chimeras'. The word *mica* Hayden used in 'Gulls' and 'A Plague of Starlings', the word *gelid* as 'gelid eyes' in 'Middle Passage' and a 'gelid mass' in 'Perseus'.

But it is in the context of his poems that we observe and appreciate Hayden's use of his favorite sound effect, alliteration. To convey the crazed horror of Arachne as she is transformed from woman into spider, Hayden constructs an intricate web of sounds:

Human face becoming locked insect face
mouth of agony shaping a cry it cannot utter
eyes bulging brimming with the horrors
of her becoming

Dazed crazed
by godly vivisection husking her
gutting her
cutting hubris its fat and bones away
(*AA*, p. 23)

The alliterating of *bulging, brimming, becoming,* the assonance of *dazed* and *crazed,* of *husking, gutting* and *cutting* all contribute to the intertwining of lines in a web-like whirl of confusion and fright.

In one stanza of 'The Night-Blooming Cereus' Hayden indicates the speaker's awe and perplexity at the mysterious incipience of the flower bud by combining a fused metaphor (with 'snake' and 'eyeless bird head' as vehicles) with intricate sound effects:

sometimes—snake,
eyeless bird head,
beak that would gape
with grotesque life-squawk.
(*AA*, p. 24)

The lines jerk and start in birdlike chatter as the sounds play off each other – *beak* with *snake* and *gape, snake* with *squawk* and *gape, bird* with *beak.*

In 'Snow' Hayden creates a soft, quiet, neutral tone by using few accents in the three rhymed couplets and an abundance of *r* and *s* sounds to recreate the soft texture of snow:

Snow

Smooths and burdens,
endangers, hardens.

Erases, revises.
Extemporizes

Vistas of lunar solitude.
Builds, embellishes a mood.
(*AA*, p. 84)

The incorporation of the title into the poem makes the poem itself a simple series of verbs denoting the various capacities of snow to enhance a subjective emotional state.

There are, to be sure, a multitude of poems which demonstrate Hayden's use of sound and the other subtleties of his craftsmanship. For example, much could be said about the way he manipulates tone through various types of irony, from the grating, agonizing tone of 'Night, Death, Mississippi', 'Middle Passage', 'Words in the Mourning Time' and ' "From the Corpse Woodpiles . . ." ', to the gentle twists in 'Electrical Storm', 'The Moose Wallow' and 'The

Performers'. But to acquire any substantial appreciation of what Hayden's finishing touch involves, to understand why and how the poet polishes the rough edges and shapes the poem for his special purposes, one must observe the process in motion though the drafts of the poet's work.

What one finds in examining Hayden's drafts is the evidence of two basic processes, both analogous to sculptural methods. For example, Hayden may begin with an image, a setting, a character, and as a sculptor extracts the form from stone, he will cut away the excess, the dross. In other instances he will piece together images, details, ideas, as a sculptor might flesh out an armature with clay. Obviously most poems involve both processes in an infinite variety of combinations. But the drafts of three Hayden poems I have chosen will demonstrate how he shaped his poetry for three different kinds of effect, in each case using slightly different methods.[7]

In the drafts of the short poem 'The Moose Wallow' Hayden revised towards a human perspective. He began with the sensually perceived details of the natural setting, which must have seemed at first the best way to relate the sense of mystery and expectation the place evoked for him:

I

> I think of the evergreen forest where
> daylight became a haunting dusk
> and the scent of pine and cedar and earth and mold

Throughout the next three drafts, Hayden toyed with the lines, trying to select the right combination of details and sensual imagery which would create the setting in the reader's mind:

2

> I think of the evergreen forest where
> daylight became a haunting dusk
> and pine and cedar and earth and mold

3

> I think of the evergreen forest where
> daylight became a haunting dusk
> and the scent of pine and cedar and earth
> and mold.

4

> I think of the evergreen forest where
> the daylight changed to haunting dusk
> redolent with odors of pine
> and cedar and earth and mold.

Suddenly with the fifth draft Hayden seems to have realized that it was not the forest itself which had conveyed to him the subtle blending of emotions; it was the possible presence of moose. Therefore, he focused on the moose and let the reader's imagination create the forest:

5

Friends warned of moose
found often at the wallow near
the forest path. I feared
Yet hoped to see
the tall ungainly creatures
in their battle crowns.

In the final revision Hayden broke the poem into three triplets, each containing a complete sentence and a separate thought. In the final triplet he added an implied speculation about his attraction to this sensation by tying the poem to his frequently used symbol, a mysterious presence in the dark:

6

Friends warned of moose that
often came to the wallow
near the path I took.

I feared, hoped to see
the tall ungainly creatures
in their battle crowns.

I felt their presence
in the dark (hidden watchers)
on either side.

(*AA*, p. 19)

Hayden's final drafts of 'Richard Hunt's "Arachne"' demonstrate the crafting of a poem for tonal effect. Among the five drafts I have selected the poem is essentially the same idea, the same fundamental image. But as the poem evolved, Hayden gradually fashioned layers of detail, enhancing the sensual perception of the image, and, perhaps more importantly, shaping the lines for meter and sound so that the lines reflect the terror they describe.

Even in the first draft Hayden had captured the essence of the literal portrait of the statue, but he had not satisfied himself that he had depicted the sense of total isolation which Arachne's transitional state represents:

I

Agony mouth screaming unable to scream
Woman face becoming insect face
eyes goggling at horror of her change

Dazed, crazed by the vivisection
opening her, she is husked, gutted,
the layers of her being cut away

her isolation

In the second draft Hayden determined to create the isolation rather than
discuss it, and tried to fashion an image which would convey the anguish of
the 'Deathbed childbed age', an existential state of being in the midst of
awesome change:

2

Agony mouth screaming unable to scream
Woman face becoming locked insect face
eyes goggling at the horror of her change

Dazed, crazed by the vivisection
opening her body, she is husked, gutted
the layers of her being cut away

Arachne becoming Arachnid
encysted, enwebbed in the moment of becoming

In the third draft Hayden fleshed out the last section even more substantially
by including as a source of Arachne's isolation not just her becoming, but her
dying to the previous identity. He was still shackled to the direct statement of
fact, the 'terrible mutation', because he had not yet discovered an effective
correlative for that emotion:

3

Agony mouth screaming unable to scream
woman face becoming locked insect face
eyes goggling at the horror of her change

Dazed, crazed by the vivisection
opening her flesh, husking her, gutting her,
cutting the layers of being away

Encysted, enwebbed in the moment of
terrible mutation, the terror not yet
fulfilled, Arachne dying changing becoming.

In the fourth draft Hayden changed the word *being* in the second stanza to *hubris*, implying almost a cleansing, positive transformation. He substituted 'fat and ganglia' for 'layers' to make the image more concrete. He further fleshed out the third stanza by naming the two identities rather than talking in abstractions about 'becoming', but he was still itching to include some major clue that would link this image to the Bahá'í perception of the world situation – that there is yet more terror to come before the transformation is complete:

4

> mouth of agony screaming unable to scream
> human face becoming locked insect face
> eyes bulging with the horror of her change
>
> Dazed crazed by godly vivisection
> opening her flesh, gutting her, husking her
> cutting hubris, its fat and ganglia, away
>
> In goggling terror fleeing unable to flee
> and fixed in chrysalis of the moment's
> mutation, Arachne not yet arachnid
>
> and no longer woman, the terror not yet
> fulfilled, the moment

In the final version Hayden gave up on making the Bahá'í allusion too obvious. He decided instead that the image of an agonizing metamorphosis was sufficient. He then replaced 'chrysalis' with 'centrifuge', thus de-emphasizing the literal properties of this change as related to an insect's creation and replacing the abstract term (for the tertiary stage in an insect's development) for a more visual image. Beyond these word changes Hayden also spent incalculable time literally shaping the lines to create the effect of a centrifuge of confusion and terror. The end result is possibly Hayden's most powerful correlative for the anxiety this historical period evokes, especially for those unaware of its ultimate benignity:

Richard Hunt's 'Arachne'

> Human face becoming locked insect face
>   mouth of agony shaping a cry it cannot utter
>   eyes bulging brimming with the horrors
>   of her becoming
>
>   Dazed crazed
>   by godly vivisection husking her
>   gutting her
>   cutting hubris its fat and bones away

In goggling terror fleeing powerless to flee
Arachne not yet arachnid and no longer woman
in the moment's centrifuge of dying
becoming.

(*AA*, p. 23)

Hayden's most complex poems required a more complex method of revision, a process of synthesizing a number of themes into a unified poetic image. In 'Middle Passage' he achieved this with the synthesis of different poetic forms and voices. In 'The Peacock Room' he fused a variety of themes into one poetic structure and a single voice in what is clearly one of his finest lyrics. From the myriad drafts of the poem it is clear that Hayden did not start out with synthesis in mind, but resorted to it only after lengthy experiments, many of which are entirely different poems:

Down one corridor I saw a sign, 'The Peacock Room'. I went in, walked around, then sat down imagining Betsy on her twelfth birthday having ice cream and cake there. For four years I made notes, very deliberately, and tried to write the poem. Betsy has been dead several years now, but it was only last summer [1972] that I was able to complete the poem. When I got it all together I saw that the motif of the poem, although not deliberate on my part, was: What is life? What is art?[8]

From Hayden's copious notes and drafts I have selected four versions of the poem which convey something of that process which tested the poet's skill as much as any poem he ever wrote.

The first draft is an early treatment in poeticized prose which speaks directly to two thoughts that the experience evoked: the room's Victorian environment is shelter from the macrocosmic chaos churning outside this time capsule, and the ornate beauty of the place contrasts ironically with the circumstance of its embittered creation:

I

The day roars past outside
and men who would rather die
than let their fellows live
are busy and everywhere like virus.
Violence and horror no longer appall,
are craved like sex, like heroin,
and a fix is daily provided.
The day wars pant outside
with stormy vibrations harsh enough
to have shattered the glass and china.
Heat gleamed in this room
in its pristine and more delicate state
to have shattered the room itself, one feels.

This Victorian aesthete's whimsey, this Pre-Raphaelite
Chamber that pleasured and disappointed
an English Lord and drove an architect
to gibbering despair
Whistler disdaining no doubt
the grossness of utility
trapped an artist in the spider web of shelves
and drove him to gibbering despair.
This room was not meant for quarrels
but note the flying feathers of those peacocks.

In another version Hayden concentrated exclusively on describing the room as connoting the embittered quarrel which brought about the work of art. Hayden's thematic concern here was with the irony that while the quarrel had ceased and the combatants had died, the room which had been Whistler's weapon of vengeance endured to eclipse the circumstance of its creation:

2

Quarrelsome Whistler is dead and his quarreling
peacocks luxuriate in a dead room preserved
like a delicate rare shell that has survived
the lives it sheltered and the jeweller's hand.

The Greek girl's tycoon father was displeased
with the portraits of his daughter Whistler made—
its languorous colors, impressionist echoes of
the Japanese—'The Porcelain Princess':

exotic fantasy offending what was proper and quotidian?
Ignoring art's responsibility to life?
The painting's hung at last as Whistler contended it
should be. On opposite peacock blue

satiric arabesque of golden peacocks in fury trampling
heaped gold: Thus art upbraids (according to the guidebook)
the stingy aristocrat and out of rancorous dissonance
creates, we may infer, perhaps, exacting harmony.

In still another version of the poem Hayden alluded briefly to the irony that art outlives the artist, and totally ignored the history of the room, concentrating instead on Betsy. He employed minimal description of the art work itself so that the poem became a straightforward elegy:

3

Ars longa vita brevis
And which is crueler, art or life?
Thoughts the Peacock Room,
elegant, harmonious, fin de siècle,
was not deigned to shelter.

Gold peacocks on walls of peacock blue
in mannered fury trampling
coins of gold: I saw them first
through her clear eyes, a gift
to the eye — blank now.

Her body, by her bequest,
is a med-school cadaver now.
I had a birthday party in
the Peacock Room when I was twelve,

She told me. Her essence brims
and implores my mind. The room
is like a shell flower floating on
the formaldehyde, her grave.

Following this version in Hayden's papers are a number of drafts in which the poet began to assemble the diverse poems into one poem. He experimented with combinations of thought and poetic forms, from unembellished free verse to triplets, to six-line stanzas. Some he focused on Betsy, some on Whistler, some on topical allusion, some on the enigmatic nature of art. Draft after draft he switched the order of images until he finally found a structure that worked. He assembled the diverse ingredients, divided the poem into six stanzas, each representing more-or-less a complete thought in the persona's pattern of mental associations. He then further synthesized the different thoughts by bracketing the whole experience with philosophical questions. At the beginning he ponders, 'Which is crueler, life or art?' At the end he asks the more fundamental question., 'What is art and what is life?' The answer to these questions, which the persona seems to discover as he notices the smile on a bronze Bodhisattva in the museum, is that art, like the events in our lives, symbolizes a benign spiritual process which we must struggle to understand before we can resolve life's enigmas:

The Peacock Room

(in memory of Betsy Graves Reyneau)

Ars Longa   Which is crueler
Vita Brevis   life or art?
       Thoughts in the Peacock Room,
where briefly I shelter. As in the glow
(remembered or imagined?)
       of the lamp shaped like a rose
my mother would light
for me some nights to keep
       Raw-Head-And-Bloody-Bones away.

Exotic, fin de siècle, unreal
and beautiful the Peacock Room
       Triste metaphor.
Hiroshima   Watts   My Lai.
Thus history scorns
       the vision chambered in gold
and Spanish leather, lyric space;
rebukes, yet cannot give the lie
       to what is havened here.

Environment as ornament.
Whistler with arrogant art designed
       it, mocking a connoisseur
with satiric arabesque of gold
peacocks on a wall peacock blue
       in fury trampling coins of gold.
Such vengeful harmonies drove
a rival mad. As in a dream
       I see the crazed young man.

He shudders in a corner, shields
his face in terror of
       the perfect malice of those claws.
She too is here—ghost
of the happy child she was that day.
       When I turned twelve,
they gave me for a birthday gift
a party in the Peacock Room.
       With shadow cries

the peacocks flutter down,
their spread tails concealing her,
        then folding, drooping to reveal
her eyeless, old—Med School
cadaver, flesh-object
        pickled in formaldehyde,
who was artist, compassionate,
clear-eyed. Who was belovéd friend.
        No more. No more.

The birds resume their splendored pose.
And Whistler's portrait of
        a tycoon's daughter gleams
like imagined flowers. What is art?
What is life?
        What the Peacock Room?
Rose-leaves and ashes drift
its portals, gently spinning toward
        a bronze Bodhisattva's ancient smile.
                                (*AA*, pp. 28–9)

Clearly this is one of Hayden's masterpieces, as superb an example of his craftsmanship as one could wish. In reading and rereading these finely tuned lines, we might never suspect the amount of effort that the poet invested to achieve the seemingly facile grace of each image, the easy flow from one thought to another. But dogged persistence, the willful pursuit of excellence, the relentless forging of artistic form from the common materials available to us all, these are the hallmarks of Hayden's workmanship. And whether or not critics understood or appreciated his themes or perspective, not one has ignored the sheer beauty of his style.

Robert Hayden did not produce vast quantities of poems, but virtually every poem he did write reflects this same caliber of careful craftsmanship, this amazing attention to detail, because from his first encounter with poetry as a youth until his untimely death, all he aspired to be was a poet. It was his delight, his profession, and he pursued it with a deathly seriousness.

In answer to Paul McClusky's question about why he wrote poetry, Hayden answered, 'If one could answer the question, "Why do you go on living?" then perhaps one could come up with a convincing answer to "Why do you write poetry?"'[9] To experience Hayden's poetry one must approach his art with a similar seriousness, realizing that however much effort we put into unleashing his art within us, he invested infinitely more care in ensuring that our efforts would never be wasted.

Afterword

For the poet is a light and winged and holy thing . . .[1]

Socrates in Plato's *Ion*

Emerson affirmed that 'the world seems always waiting for its poet'.[2] Eliot asserted that the great poet 'in writing himself writes his times'.[3] Roy Harvey Pearce observed that 'Poems, like men, have their life only *in* a world'.[4] But if the age is not aware of its own identity, it is hardly likely to recognize the great poet who occupies that world and writs that time. It is, in fact, most often the case that we can recognize and appreciate the great poets only after they have passed from the scene, along with the age they give voice to.

Critic after critic lamented through the years Hayden's belated recognition, bemoaned his meager reputation which, in spite of auspicious beginnings, awaited his parting years to garner a station befitting his talents. Many reasons could be cited for this tardiness in recognition. His poetry did not neatly fit any of the popular trends. He was Black, but his poetry was not. His poetry was 'modern', but his themes were not. My own opinion is that there are two main reasons. The first is that until recently few critics had taken the poet at his word that he was a symbolist, and consequently they had not approached Hayden's poems with sufficient daring and imagination to unleash the power of his work. The second is that critics did not believe him when he clearly and unmistakably professed that his themes were strongly influenced by his beliefs as a Bahá'í.

Some recent scholars have tried to elucidate Hayden's themes and symbols as they allude to the Bahá'í Faith.[5] Just as many have perceived his religious beliefs as detrimental to his art.[6] Not one has yet understood the scope of this relationship because none to date has had both a firm grounding in Bahá'í beliefs and an equally sound understanding of Hayden's poetic technique.

Not that Hayden was preaching with his poetry or asking his readers to accept the Bahá'í perspective as their own; certainly he was not writing for an exclusively Bahá'í audience. What George Williamson observed about T. S. Eliot's religious beliefs in relation to his poetry applies equally well to

Hayden's attitude: 'His poems are not sermons, or substitutes for them, but at most the experience of religious feeling in our time. In good poets religious feeling has intensified rather than narrowed the sensibility and has deepened their awareness of life.'[7]

Whether a Bahá'í or not, the reader of Hayden's poetry must be willing to exert himself in examining the 'religious feeling' of the persona and how that persona views 'our time'. Of course, if Hayden's beliefs are accurate, if indeed this is a time of crucial transition and transformation, a climactic point in man's spiritual journey, it could well be that in the future Hayden will be viewed as the poet of this special age. If he is so regarded, it will matter little that during his lifetime his efforts were largely unheralded. As James Cotter observed, 'Robert Hayden will survive in his poems long after current fashions of literature fade.'[8]

Appendix I

List of poems quoted in their entirety in the text

Title	From	Page in original	Page in this book
The Falcon	HSD	13	65
Speech	HSD	27	66
Sunflowers: Beaubien Street	HSD	12	98
What Is Precious Is Never To Forget	HSD	52	99–100
Sonnet To E.	HSD	31	103
Rosemary	HSD	37	103
Old Woman With Violets	HSD	54	103
Leaves In The Wind	HSD	55	104
The Prophet	FT	14	122–3
'Lear is Gay'	FT	19	125
Those winter Sundays	BR	29	131
Theme and variation	BR	40–41	133
The Diver	SP	11–12	145–7
Dawnbreaker	SP	16	150
Sphinx	WMT	11	164
Words in the Mourning Time, part X, And all the atoms cry aloud	WMT	50–51	173–4
Smelt fishing	NBC	12	188
'Dance the orange'	NBC	13	189
Traveling through fog	NBC	15	192
Akhenaten	AA	17	204
Crispus Attucks	AA	20	206
Elegies for Paradise Valley, part I	AJ (1978)	25	211
Snow	AA	84	287
The Moose Wallow	AA	19	289
Richard Hunt's 'Arachne'	AA	23	291–2
The Peacock Room	AA	28–9	295–6

Appendix II

The Tables of Contents of Hayden's volumes of poetry

Note: In his earlier publications, Hayden frequently used lower case for the titles of both books and poems, but in later volumes the same titles were usually printed with capital letters. For the sake of consistency, capitals have been adopted for this book. But the reader may find the original style in this appendix.

I. Heart-Shape in the Dust (1940)

Autumnal
'We Have Not Forgotten'
'He Is Foredoomed'
Sunflowers: Beaubien Street
The Falcon
To A Young Negro Poet
Dedication
Southern Moonlight
    Words This Spring
  I. Spring Offensive
 II. Primaveral
III. Words This Spring
Poem In Time Of War
Prophecy
The Wind, The Weathercock And The Warrior's Ghost
Gabriel
The Mountains
The Negro To America
Speech
Obituary
Essay On Beauty
Poem
Sonnet To E.
Allegory

Monody
This Grief
Three Leaves
Orison
Rosemary
An Old Song
    Religioso
 I. Brown Girl's Sacrament
II. Religioso
Poem For A Negro Dancer
Shine, Mister?
Diana
Bacchanale
Coleman
'We Are The Hunted'
    World's Fair
 I. Body Of Tomorrow
II. Time Capsule
Litany
The Departure
Ole Jim Crow
'What Is Precious Is Never To Forget'
Elegy
Old Woman With Violets
Leaves In The Wind
These Are My People

II. the lion and the archer (1948)

magnolias in snow
a ballad of remembrance
homage to the empress of the blues
eine kleine nachtmusik
invisible circus
the lion

III. Figure of time: Poems (1955)

'Summertime and the living . . .'
Locus
    from *The Coney Island Suite*
 i. 42nd Street Times Square and All
ii. Congress of Freaks
'The Burly Fading One'
'Incense of the lucky virgin'

Perseus
Figure
In light half nightmare and half vision
The Prophet
On the Maine Coast (i, ii and iii)
A road in Kentucky
'Lear is gay'

IV. A ballad of remembrance (1962)

one

A ballad of remembrance
Locus
Tour 5
On Lookout Mountain
A road in Kentucky
On the coast of Maine (i, ii and iii)
Homage to the Empress of the Blues
The burly fading one . . .
Incense of the Lucky Virgin
Witch doctor (i, ii, iii and iv)
Mourning poem for the Queen of Sunday

two

Summertime and the living
The whipping
Those winter Sundays
Weeds
The web
The anguish
The wheel
Eine kleine Nachtmusik (i, ii and iii)
Figure
Perseus
Lear is gay . . .
Theme and variation (i and ii)
In light half nightmare and half vision
The prophet

three: 'an inference of Mexico'

Day of the dead
Veracruz (i and ii)
Idol
El Cristo

Sub specie aeternitatis
Market
La corrida
  i. el toro
 ii. el matador
iii. sol y sombra

four

Middle Passage (i, ii and iii)
O Daedalus, fly away home
The ballad of Nat Turner
Frederick Douglass

V. Selected Poems (1966)

One

The Diver
Electrical Storm
Full Moon
Dawnbreaker
The Rabbi
Belsen, Day of Liberation
Approximations
Snow
The Ballad of Sue Ellen Westerfield
Night, Death, Mississippi

Two: 'An Inference of Mexico'

Day of the Dead
Mountains
Veracruz
Idol
Sub Specie Aeternitatis
Market
Kid
La Corrida

Three

A Ballad of Remembrance
Tour 5
Gulls
A Road in Kentucky
Homage to the Empress of the Blues

'The Burly Fading One'
'Incense of the Lucky Virgin'
Witch Doctor
Mourning Poem for the Queen of Sunday

Four

'Summertime and the Living . . .'
The Whipping
Those Winter Sundays
The Web
The Wheel
Perseus
Theme and Variation
'From the Corpse Woodpiles, From the Ashes'
Bahá'u'lláh in the Garden of Ridwan

Five

Middle Passage
O Daedalus, Fly Away Home
The Ballad of Nat Turner
Runagate Runagate
Frederick Douglass

VI. words in the mourning time (1970)

one

Sphinx
The Dream
'"Mystery Boy" Looks for Kin in Nashville'
The Broken Dark
The Mirages
Soledad
Aunt Jemima of the Ocean Waves

two

Locus
On Lookout Mountain
Kodachromes of the Island
Zeus over Redeye
Unidentified Flying Object

three: words in the mourning time

El-Hajj Malik El-Shabazz
Words in the Mourning Time

four

Monet's 'Waterlilies'
The Lions
October
The Return
'Lear is Gay'
A Plague of Starlings

VII. The night-blooming cereus (1973)

1. Richard Hunt's Arachne
2. The night-blooming cereus
3. The performers
4. The Peacock Room
5. Smelt fishing
6. 'Dance the orange'
7. Ballad of the true beast
8. Traveling through fog

VIII. Angle of Ascent (1975)

I *Angle of Ascent*

Beginnings
Free Fantasia: Tiger Flowers
For a Young Artist
Stars
Two Egyptian Portrait Masks
      I   Nefert-iti
      II. Akhenaten
Butterfly Piece
The Moose Wallow
Crispus Attucks

II *The Night-Blooming Cereus*

Richard Hunt's 'Arachne'
The Night-Blooming Cereus
The Performers
The Peacock Room
Smelt Fishing
'Dance the Orange'
Traveling through Fog

Homage to the Empress of the Blues
'The Burly Fading One'
'Incense of the Lucky Virgin'
Witch Doctor
Mourning Poem for the Queen of Sunday
'Summertime and the Living . . .'
The Whipping
Those Winter Sundays
Perseus
Theme and Variation
'From the Corpse Woodpiles, from the Ashes'
Bahá'u'lláh in the Garden of Ridwan
Middle Passage
O Daedalus, Fly Away Home
The Ballad of Nat Turner
Runagate Runagate
Frederick Douglass

IX. American Journal (1978)

A Letter from Phillis Wheatley
Paul Laurence Dunbar
Elegies for Paradise Valley
Names
The Rag Man
The Prisoners
The Point
Killing the Calves
Zinnias
The Islands
from The Snow Lamp
Astronauts
American Journal

X. American Journal (1982)

One

A Letter from Phillis Wheatley
John Brown
Theory of Evil

Two

Paul Laurence Dunbar
Homage to Paul Robeson

The Rag Man
The Prisoners
The Tattooed Man

Three

Elegies for Paradise Valley

Four

Names
Double Feature
The Dogwood Trees
Letter
Ice Storm
'As my blood was drawn'
Killing the Calves
The Year of the Child
The Point
Zinnias
The Islands

Five

from THE SNOW LAMP
Astronauts
[American Journal]

Bibliography

Only titles which are referred to more than once are included here. The
details of other titles will be found in the notes.

'ABDU'L-BAHÁ, *Selections from the Writings of 'Abdu'l-Bahá*, trans. by a Committee at the
Bahá'í World Centre and by Marzieh Gail (Haifa: Bahá'í World Centre, 1978).
——*Some Answered Questions*, trans. Laura Clifford Barney (Wilmette, Illinois: Bahá'í
Publishing Trust, rev. edn. 1981).

ABRAMS, M. H., *The Mirror and the Lamp: Romantic Theory and the Critical Tradition* (New
York: Oxford University Press, 1953).

American Writers: A Collection of Literary Biographies (New York: Charles Scribner's Sons,
1982).

Bahá'í Prayers (Wilmette, Illinois: Bahá'í Publishing Trust, 1982).

Bahá'í World Faith, Selected Writings of Bahá'u'lláh and 'Abdu'l-Bahá (Wilmette, Illinois:
Bahá'í Publishing Trust, 1976).

BAHÁ'U'LLÁH, *Gleanings from the Writings of Bahá'u'lláh*, trans. Shoghi Effendi (Wilmette, Illi-
nois: Bahá'í Publishing Trust, 2nd rev. edn. 1976).
——*Synopsis and Codification of the Laws and Ordinances of the Kitáb-i-Aqdas*, trans. Shoghi
Effendi (Haifa: Bahá'í World Centre, 1973).
——*The Hidden Words of Bahá'u'lláh*, trans. Shoghi Effendi (Wilmette, Illinois: Bahá'í
Publishing Trust, 1954).
——*The Kitáb-i-Íqán: The Book of Certitude* (Wilmette, Illinois: Bahá'í Publishing Trust,
1950).
——*The Seven Valleys and the Four Valleys* (Wilmette, Illinois: Bahá'í Publishing Trust, 1975).

BARKSDALE, RICHARD, AND KINNAMON, KENNETH, eds., *Black Writers of America: A Comprehensive Anthology* (New York: Macmillan Publishing Co., Inc., 1972).

BROOKS, CLEANTH, *The Well Wrought Urn: Studies in the Structure of Poetry* (New York:
Reynal and Hitchcock, 1947).

BROOKS, CLEANTH, AND WARREN, ROBERT PENN, eds., *Understanding Poetry* (New York: Holt,
Rinehart and Winston, 1976).

CARMICHAEL, STOKELY, *Black Power: The Politics of Liberation in America* (New York:
Random House, 1967).

Conversations with Writers (Detroit: Gale Research Co., 1977).

COOK, REGINALD, ed. *Selected Prose and Poetry* (New York: Holt, Rinehart and Winston, 1961).

DAVIS, ARTHUR P., *From the Dark Tower: Afro-American Writers 1900-1960* (Washington, DC:
Howard University Press, 1974).

ELIOT, T. S., *Selected Essays* (New York: Harcourt, Brace and Co., 1932).

ESSLEMONT, J. E., *Bahá'u'lláh and the New Era* (Wilmette, Illinois: Bahá'í Publishing Trust, 4th
rev. edn. 1975).

GAIL, MARZIEH, *Bahá'í Glossary* (Wilmette, Illinois: Bahá'í Publishing Trust, 1965).

GAYLE, ADDISON, JR., ed., *The Black Aesthetic* (Garden City, New York: Doubleday and Co.,
1971).

GENDRON, DENNIS JOSEPH, *'Robert Hayden: A View of his Life and Development as a Poet'*, Diss. University of North Carolina, 1975.

GIBSON, DONALD B., *Modern Black Poets* (Englewood Cliffs, NJ: Prentice-Hall, 1973).

GRAFF, GERALD, *Literature Against Itself: Literary Ideas in Modern Society* (Chicago: University of Chicago Press, 1979).

HARPER, MICHAEL S., AND STEPTO, ROBERT B., eds. *Chant of Saints: A Gathering of Afro-American Literature, Art, and Scholarship* (Chicago: University of Illinois Press, 1979).

HAYDEN PAPERS, National Bahá'í Archives.

HAYDEN, ROBERT, 'From the Life: Some Remembrances', unpublished autobiographical notes. The Hayden Papers, National Bahá'í Archives.

HAYDEN, ROBERT, ed. *Kaleidoscope: Poems by American Negro Poets* (New York: Harcourt, Brace and World, Inc., 1967).

HOLMAN, C. HUGH, *A Handbook to Literature* (Indianapolis, Indiana: Odyssey Press, 1975).

How I Write, 'Robert Hayden, The Poet and his Art: A Conversation' (New York: Harcourt, Brace, Jovanovich, 1972).

Interviews with Black Writers, ed. John O'Brien (New York: Liveright, 1973).

JEMIE, ONWUCHEKWA, *Langston Hughes: An Introduction to the Poetry* (New York: Columbia University Press, 1976).

JOHNSON, JAMES WELDON, ed., *The Book of American Negro Poetry* (New York: Harcourt, Brace and World, 1959).

KERLIN, ROBERT T., ed., *Negro Poets and their Poems* (Washington, DC: Associated Publishers, Inc., 4th edn. 1947).

KUBLER-ROSS, ELISABETH, *On Death and Dying* (New York: Macmillan Publishing Co., Inc., 1969).

LEROI JONES, *Home: Social Essays* (New York: William Morrow, 1966).

LEWIS, DAVID LEVERING, *When Harlem was in Vogue* (New York: Alfred A. Knopf, 1981).

LITTLEJOHN, DAVID, *Black on White: A Critical Survey of Writing by American Negroes* (New York: Grossman Publishers, 1966).

LOCKE, ALAIN, ed., *The New Negro* (New York: Johnson Reprint Corporation, 1968).

LOWELL, AMY, *Tendencies in Modern American Poetry* (New York: Octagon Books, 1971).

MACK, MAYNARD, ed., *Modern Poetry* (Englewood Cliffs, NJ: Prentice-Hall, Inc., 2nd edn. 1961).

PEARCE, ROY HARVEY, *The Continuity of American Poetry* (Princeton, NJ: Princeton University Press, 1961).

POOL, ROSEY E., ed., *Beyond the Blues: New Poems by American Negroes* (Lympne, Kent, England: The Hand and Flower Press, 1962).

RANDALL, DUDLEY, ed., *The Black Poets* (New York: Bantam Books, 1971).

RANSOM, JOHN CROWE, *The New Criticism* (Norfolk, Connecticut: New Directions, 1941).

ROBINSON, JAMES K., AND RIDEOUT, WALTER B., eds., *A College Book of Modern Verse* (New York: Harper and Row, 1958).

SHOGHI EFFENDI, *God Passes By* (Wilmette, Illinois: Bahá'í Publishing Trust, 1957).

——*The Advent of Divine Justice* (Wilmette, Illinois: Bahá'í Publishing Trust, 1939).

——*The Promised Day is Come* (Wilmette, Illinois: Bahá'í Publishing Trust, rev. edn. 1980).

——*The World Order of Bahá'u'lláh* (Wilmette, Illinois: Bahá'í Publishing Trust, 2nd rev. edn. 1974).

SIMPSON, LOUIS, *An Introduction to Poetry* (New York: St Martin's Press, 1967).

SMITH, JAMES H., AND PARKS, EDD W., *The Great Critics: An Anthology of Literary Criticism* (New York: W. W. Norton and Co., Inc., 3rd edn. 1951).

The Divine Art of Living: Selections from Writings of Bahá'u'lláh and 'Abdu'l-Bahá, compiled by Mabel Hyde Paine (Wilmette, Illinois: Bahá'í Publishing Trust, rev. edn. 1960).

The Individual and Teaching: Raising the Divine Call (Wilmette, Illinois: Bahá'í Publishing Trust, 1977).

TURNER, DARWIN T., ed., *Black American Literature* (Columbus, Ohio: Charles E. Merrill Publishing Co., 1970).

WILLIAMS, PONTHEOLLA T., 'A Critical Analysis of the Poetry of Robert Hayden through his Middle Years', Diss. Columbia University Teachers' College, 1978.

Notes

FOREWORD

1. W. H. Auden, 'In Memory of W. B. Yeats', *Modern Poetry*, ed. Maynard Mack (Englewood Cliffs, NJ: Prentice-Hall, Inc., 2nd edn. 1961), p. 208.
2. John Ciardi, 'Dialogue with the Audience', *Saturday Review*, November 22, 1958, p. 42.
3. Ibid.
4. Robert Hayden, 'Frederick Douglass', *Angle of Ascent* (New York: Liveright, 1975), p. 131.

PART I: FROM PARADISE VALLEY TO POET LAUREATE

1. Michael S. Harper quoted in John S. Wright, 'Homage to a Mystery Boy', rev. of *American Journal*, by Robert Hayden, *The Georgia Review*, winter (1982), 911.
2. William Meredith, *Proceedings of the American Academy and Institute of Arts and Letters*, Second Series, No. 31, 1981, p. 74.
3. Dennis Joseph Gendron, 'Robert Hayden: A View of his Life and Development as a Poet', Diss. University of North Carolina, 1975, p. 151.
4. Editorial, *World Order*, 16, No. 1(1981), 6.
5. Julius Lester, 'In Memoriam: In Gratitude for Robert Hayden', *World Order*, 16, No. 1 (1981), 55.
6. Robert M. Greenberg, 'Robert Hayden 1913–1980', *American Writers: A Collection of Literary Biographies* (New York: Charles Scribner's Sons, 1982), p. 364.

1. *Paradise Valley (1913–1930)*

1. Robert Hayden, '"Summertime and the Living . . ."', *Angle of Ascent* (New York: Liveright, 1975), p. 111.
2. Robert Hayden, 'From the Life: Some Remembrances', unpublished autobiographical notes. The Hayden Papers, National Bahá'í Archives, p. 3.
3. Pontheolla T. Williams, 'A Critical Analysis of the Poetry of Robert Hayden through his Middle Years', Diss. Columbia University Teachers' College, 1978, p. 10. Williams obtained her information about Hayden from personal interviews in 1972 and 1973. Hayden alludes to this event, albeit fictionally, in his poem 'The Ballad of Sue Ellen Westerfield', *Angle of Ascent*, p. 85.
4. Williams states in her study (p. 8) that Hayden was ten or twelve years old; in an interview with me May 22, 1981, Erma Hayden recalled his age as sixteen. I have arbitrarily chosen a middle age.
5. Robert Hayden, 'From the Life', p. 6.
6. Ibid., p. 2.
7. Ibid., p. 4.
8. Hollie I. West, 'Plaudits at Last for a Poet in Perfect Pitch', *Washington Post*, March 21, 1976, sec. L, p. 3, col. 3.

9. Hayden, *Angle of Ascent*, p. 86.

10. Ibid., p. 112.

11. Robert Hayden, unpublished notebook in National Bahá'í Archives in Wilmette, Illinois, where the Hayden Papers reside.

12. Quoted in *Conversations with Writers* (Detroit: Gale Research Co., 1977), pp. 157–8.

13. Quoted in 'Robert Hayden, The Poet and his Art: A Conversation', *How I Write.*/*1*/(New York: Harcourt, Brace, Jovanovich, 1972), p. 142. Of the several interviews with Hayden that have appeared in print, this is by far the most remarkable insight into his poetry.

14. Quoted in *Conversations*, p. 159.

15. Ibid., p. 160.

16. Quoted in *How I Write*, p. 136.

17. Gayle Morrison, *To Move the World: Louis G. Gregory and the Advancement of Racial Unity in America* (Wilmette, Illinois: Bahá'í Publishing Trust, 1982), p. 4n.

18. Pontheolla T. Williams, p. 22.

2. *The Apprenticeship (1930–1940)*

1. Robert Hayden, 'From the Life', p. 11.

2. Ibid., p. 10.

3. Ibid.

4. Quoted in *Interviews with Black Writers*, ed. John O'Brien (New York: Liveright, 1973), p. 113.

5. Ibid., pp. 113–14.

6. Letter from S. E. Walper, September 28, 1966, in Hayden Papers, National Bahá'í Archives.

7. Quoted in *How I Write*, p. 138.

8. Robert Hayden quoted in typescript of 'Oral History of Robert Hayden of the Michigan Federal Writers Project', interviewed by Paul Sporn of Wayne State University (Detroit, Michigan, August 30, 1978), p. 8.

9. Ibid., p. 9.

10. Ibid., p. 16.

11. Personal interview with Erma Hayden, May 22, 1981.

12. Quoted in *Conversations*, p. 162.

13. Quoted in *How I Write*, p. 141.

14. Williams, p. 40.

3. *The Poet Comes of Age (1941–1946)*

1. Quoted in *Conversations*, p. 165.

2. Arthur P. Davis, *From the Dark Tower: Afro-American Writers 1900–1960* (Washington, DC: Howard University Press, 1974), p. 177.

3. Ibid., p. 176.

4. In *Conversations*, p. 163.

5. Quoted in 'Plaudits at Last', *Washington Post*, March 21, 1976, p. 3, col. 2.

6. Quoted in *How I Write*, p. 140.

7. Quoted in *Interviews with Black Writers*, p. 114.

8. Ibid.

9. Quoted in *Conversations*, p. 165.

10. Robert Hayden quoted in a video tape interview at Bahá'í House of Worship, Wilmette, Illinois, 1976; the tape was never shown and is currently in the Archives.

11. Quoted in 'From the Life'., pp. 15–16.

12. Stephen Vincent Benét, *John Brown's Body* (New York: Rinehart and Co., Inc., 1968), p. 354, l. 933.

13. Quoted in *How I Write*, pp. 169–70.

4. *The Early Years at Fisk (1946–1960)*

1. 'In Memoriam', *World Order*, 16, No. 1 (1981), p. 51.

2. Quoted in *Conversations*, p. 170.

3. Quoted in 'Conversations with Americans', *World Order*, 10, No. 2 (1975–6), 46.

4. Quoted in *Conversations*, p. 168.

5. Julius Lester, rev. of *Words in the Mourning Time*, by Robert Hayden, *New York Times Book Review*, January 24, 1971, p. 4.

6. Hayden, subscription flier for Counterpoise series, April, 1948 (Nashville, Tennessee).

7. Selden Rodman, 'Negro Poets', *New York Times Book Review*, October 10, 1948, p. 27.

8. Quoted in *How I Write*, p. 198.

9. Ibid., p. 203.

10. Ibid., p. 204.

11. Gene Olson, *Sweet Agony* (Grants Pass, Oregon: Windyridge Press, 1972), p. 117.

12. Ibid.

13. Hayden notebook, National Bahá'í Archives.

14. Robert Hayden, 'Names', *American Journal* (New York: Liveright, 1982), p. 35.

15. Quoted in *How I Write*, p. 143.

16. Ibid.

17. 'Abdu'l-Bahá in *Bahá'u'lláh and the New Era*, by J. E. Esslemont (Wilmette, Illinois: Bahá'í Publishing Trust, 4th rev. edn. 1975), p. 94. He states: 'If a man has ten good qualities and one bad one . . . look at the ten and forget the one; and if a man has ten bad qualities and one good one . . . look at the one and forget the ten.'

18. Quoted in *How I Write*, pp. 142–3.

19. Bahá'u'lláh, *Gleanings from the Writings of Bahá'u'lláh*, trans. Shoghi Effendi (Wilmette, Illinois: Bahá'í Publishing Trust, 2nd rev. edn., 1976), p. 278.

20. Bahá'u'lláh, *The Hidden Words of Bahá'u'lláh*, trans. Shoghi Effendi (Wilmette, Illinois: Bahá'í Publishing Trust, 1954), (Persian) No. 39.

21. Shoghi Effendi in *The Individual and Teaching: Raising the Divine Call* (Wilmette, Illinois: Bahá'í Publishing Trust, 1977), p. 26.

22. Bahá'u'lláh in *Tablets of Bahá'u'lláh revealed after the Kitáb-i-Aqdas* (Haifa: Bahá'í World Centre, 1978), p. 26.

23. Ibid., p. 52.

24. 'Abdu'l-Bahá, *Selections from the Writings of 'Abdu'l-Bahá*, trans. by a Committee at the Bahá'í World Centre and by Marzieh Gail (Haifa: Bahá'í World Centre, 1978), p. 144.

25. I am acquainted with more than one Bahá'í artist who has been troubled from within and without by this apparent conflict. One Bahá'í friend gave up a promising career in ballet to teach the Bahá'í Faith in a remote Central American village. Several years later he had to return from this post and found himself without a vocation and too old to regain the crucial years he

had lost. No doubt a loving Deity is capable of accepting such sacrifice as it was intended, but I personally feel that such a gesture can result in an unnecessary waste of talent.

26. Quoted in House of Worship video tape.

27. Ibid.

28. Langston Hughes and Arna Bontemps, eds., *The Poetry of the Negro* (Garden City, New York: Doubleday and Co., Inc., 1949), pp. 288–96.

29. In *Conversations*, p. 170.

5. The Crucial Years (1960–1969)

1. Jo Thomas, 'Acclaim Comes to Robert Hayden', *Detroit Free Press*, September 12, 1976, Sunday Supplement, p. 33, col. 2.

2. Quoted in 'Anne Frank: "The Child and the Legend"', *World Order* (Spring, 1972), p. 52.

3. Ibid., p. 51.

4. Letter from Clyde Watkins, November 27, 1965, in Hayden Papers, National Bahá'í Archives.

5. In Hayden Papers, National Bahá'í Archives.

6. In House of Worship video tape.

7. Olson, p. 30.

8. In Hayden Papers, National Bahá'í Archives.

9. *Angle of Ascent*, p. 39.

10. Dr Rosey E. Pool, unpublished article. I am deeply indebted to Marion Hofman, to whom Rosey Pool gave these papers, for allowing me to utilize them in this study. In fact, it was at Marion's suggestion that Rosey first set the plan in motion to submit Hayden's book.

11. Ibid.

12. Ibid.

13. Unpublished letter to Rosey Pool, August 12, 1966; this letter is also among the papers from Mrs Hofman's collection.

14. David Llorens, 'Writers Converge at Fisk University', *Negro Digest*, 15 (June, 1966), 62.

15. Ibid.

16. Counterpoise flier.

17. Quoted in 'Conversations with Americans', *World Order*, 10, No. 2 (1975–6), p. 49.

18. Robert Hayden, ed., *Kaleidoscope: Poems by American Negro Poets* (New York: Harcourt, Brace and World, Inc., 1967), p. xxiii.

19. Ibid., pp. 208–9.

20. Personal interview with Hugh Semple, May 23, 1981, Ann Arbor, Michigan.

21. Hayden published Margaret Danner's book *To Flower* in 1963 as part of the Counterpoise series, and she has been anthologized in most collections of work by Black poets.

22. Letter from Margaret Danner, March 30, 1968, in Hayden Papers, National Bahá'í Archives.

23. Ibid.

24. Letter from William Bernhardt, October 6, 1967, in Hayden Papers, National Bahá'í Archives.

25. Quoted in *How I Write*, p. 142.

6. The Poet Laureate (1969–1980)

1. Quoted in 'Conversations with Americans', *World Order*, 10, No. 2 (1975–6), p. 52.

2. Robert Hayden, 'Words in the Mourning Time', *Words in the Mourning Time* (New York: October House, 1970), p. 41.

3. Ibid., p. 51.

4. Robert Hayden, 'Traveling through fog', *The Night-Blooming Cereus* (London: Paul Breman, 1973), p. 15.

5. Julius Lester, rev. of *Words in the Mourning Time*, p. 22.

6. Quoted in *Interviews with Black Writers*, p. 113.

7. Ross Beatty, Jr., 'Time to Wake up to Robert Hayden', letter to Editor, *Washington Star*, January 4, 1977.

8. Grace Cabalière, 'Poets and Small Presses', letter to Editor, *Washington Star*, January 15, 1977.

9. Michael S. Harper, rev. of *Angle of Ascent*, by Robert Hayden, *New York Times Book Review*, February 22, 1976, p. 34.

10. Michael S. Harper, quotation on cover of *Angle of Ascent* (New York: Liveright, 1975).

11. Harper, rev. of *Angle of Ascent*, p. 34.

12. Jo Thomas, 'Of Quietly Crafting Words', *Detroit Free Press*, Sunday Supplement, p. 32, col. 1.

13. Quoted in House of Worship video tape.

14. Robert Hayden, '[American Journal]', *American Journal*, p. 60.

15. Michael S. Harper, rev. of *American Journal* by Robert Hayden, *New York Times Book Review*, October 21, 1979, p. 20.

16. The volume published by Effendi Press was in limited edition (one hundred hard-bound, one thousand paperback); the edition with Liveright adds ten new poems and divides the poetry into five groups.

17. Niara Sudarkasa, quoted in 'Michigan Poet Dies at Age 66', by Rich Quackenbush, *Ann Arbor News*, February 26, 1980, sec. A, p. 1.

18. Harold P. Shapiro, quoted in 'Robert Hayden, Talented Poet', by Andrea Ford, *Detroit Free Press*, February 27, 1980, sec. B. p. 7, col. 1.

19. 'Milestones', *Time Magazine*, March 10, 1980, p. 46.

20. William Meredith, press release, February 26, 1980, in the Hayden Papers.

21. *Empyrea* 3 (1980), 1.

22. Laurence Goldstein, 'Robert Hayden: A Poet Who Sang to Humanity', *Detroit Free Press*, April 20, 1980, magazine section, p. 23.

PART II: THE MINOTAURS OF EDICT

1. 'Words in the Mourning Time', *Words in the Mourning Time*, p. 49.

7. The Problem of a 'Black Aesthetic'

1. James Weldon Johnson, ed., *The Book of American Negro Poetry* (New York: Harcourt, Brace and World, 1959), p. 41.

2. Quoted in *Beyond the Blues: New Poems by American Negroes*, ed. Rosey E. Pool (Lympne, Kent, England: The Hand and Flower Press, 1962), p. 25.

3. Ibid., p. 26.

4. W. E. B. Du Bois, *The Souls of Black Folk: Essays and Sketches* (Greenwich, Connecticut: Fawcett Publications, Inc., 1961), p. 182.

5. Langston Hughes, 'The Negro Artist and the Racial Mountain', *The Nation*, June 23, 1926, p. 692.

6. Ibid., p. 693.

7. Ibid.

8. Ibid., p. 694.

9. Ibid.

10. Ibid.

11. Langston Hughes, Letter, 'American Art or Negro Art?', *The Nation*, June 23, 1926, p. 151. George S. Schuyler's article 'The Negro-Art Hokum', appeared in *The Nation*, June 16, 1926, pp. 662–3.

12. Ibid.

13. Allan H. Spear in *The New Negro*, ed. Alain Locke (New York: Johnson Reprint Corporation, 1968), p. viii.

14. Ibid., p. ix.

15. Ibid., p. xiii.

16. Ibid., p. 3.

17. Ibid., p. 7.

18. Ibid., p. 11.

19. Ibid., p. 15.

20. Robert Hayden, *Kaleidoscope*, p. xxii.

21. Ibid.

22. James E. McCall, 'The New Negro', *Beyond the Blues*, p. 142.

23. David Levering Lewis, *When Harlem was in Vogue* (New York: Alfred A. Knopf, 1981), p. 71.

24. Ibid., p. 77.

25. Onwuchekwa Jemie, *Langston Hughes: An Introduction to the Poetry* (New York: Columbia University Press, 1976), p. 7.

26. Ibid., p. 12.

27. David L. Lewis, *When Harlem was in Vogue*, p. 305.

28. Onwuchekwa Jemie, *Langston Hughes*, p. 13.

29. Rosey E. Pool, *Beyond the Blues*, pp. 26–7.

30. Ibid., p. 27.

8. *The Birth of the Hayden Stand*

1. Arthur P. Davis, *From the Dark Tower: Afro-American Writers 1900–1960* (Washington, DC: Howard University Press, 1974), p. 177.

2. Sterling Brown, quoted in *Beyond the Blues*, p. 21.

3. David L. Lewis, *When Harlem was in Vogue*, p. 131.

4. Quoted in 'From the Life', p. 12.

5. Robert Hayden, *Heart-Shape in the Dust* (Detroit, Michigan: The Falcon Press, 1940), p. 13.

6. Robert Hayden, 'Speech', *Negro Poets and their Poems*, ed. Robert T. Kerlin (Washington, DC: Associated Publishers, Inc., 4th edn., 1947), p. 321.

7. Pontheolla T. Williams, 'A Critical Analysis', pp. 31–3.

8. Ibid., p. 34.

9. Ibid., p. 35.

10. Dudley Randall, 'The Black Aesthetic in the Thirties, Forties, and Fifties', *The Black*

Aesthetic, ed. Addison Gayle, Jr. (Garden City, New York: Doubleday and Co., 1971), p. 224.

11. Ibid.

12. Ibid.

13. Ibid., p. 231.

14. Pontheolla T. Williams, 'Robert Hayden: A Life Upon these Shores', *World Order,* 16, No. 1 (1981), p. 23.

15. Ibid., p. 24.

16. Ibid., p. 26.

17. Ibid. Dennis Gendron infers the same thing in his dissertation ('Robert Hayden', p. 54), but gives no reference to anything Hayden said in their interviews to substantiate such a contention, leaving the reader to assume that these conclusions are totally speculative.

18. Ibid.

19. Robert Hayden, 'From the Life', p. 12.

20. Quoted in 'Conversations with Americans', *World Order,* 10, No. 2 (1975–6), p. 49.

21. In Philadelphia in 1912, quoted in *The Promulgation of Universal Peace* (Wilmette, Illinois: Bahá'í Publishing Trust, rev. edn. 1982), p. 181.

22. Bahá'u'lláh, *Gleanings,* p. 277.

23. Ibid., p. 279.

24. Quoted in House of Worship video tape.

25. Shoghi Effendi, *The Advent of Divine Justice* (Wilmette, Illinois: Bahá'í Publishing Trust, 1939), p. 28.

26. See Part I, n. 3.

27. Quoted in 'The becoming of a poet . . . the becoming of poetry', *English High Lights 9–12* (Glenview, Illinois: Scott, Foresman and Company, 1972). Hayden said essentially the same thing in the McClusky interview *How I Write,* p. 162, and in the Layman interview in *Conversations with Writers,* p. 165, and on page 16 of this book.

28. Robert Hayden quoted by Saundra Ivey in 'Noted Black Poet Sees Race Relations Decline', *The Nashville Tennesseean* , September 15, 1978, p. 49.

29. Quoted in 'Plaudits at Last for a Poet in Perfect Pitch', sec. L, p. 3, col. 1.

30. C. L. Wrenn, *A Study of Old English Literature* (New York: W. W. Norton and Company, Inc., 1967), p. 103. This quote is often cited and may also be found in a number of other studies of the period.

31. 'Abdu'l-Bahá in *The Individual and Teaching: Raising the Divine Call* (Wilmette, Illinois: Bahá'í Publishing Trust, 1977), p. 7.

32. Personal interview with Hugh Semple, May 23, 1981.

33. Geoffrey Nash, 'Can There be a Bahá'í Poetry?', *Response to the Revelation, Bahá'í Studies,* Vol. 7 (1980), p. 1.

34. Ibid., p. 6.

35. Quoted in *How I Write,* p. 135.

36. Robert M. Greenberg, 'Robert Hayden 1913–1980', *American Writers . . .,* p. 371.

37. Quoted in *Interviews with Black Writers,* p. 115.

38. Robert Hayden, 'Words in the Mourning Time', *Words in the Mourning Time,* p. 49.

9. *The Controversy*

1. Wilburn Williams, Jr., 'Covenant of Timelessness and Time: Symbolism and History in Robert Hayden's *Angle of Ascent*', *Chant of Saints: A Gathering of Afro-American Literature,*

Art, and Scholarship, eds. Michael S. Harper and Robert B. Stepto (Chicago: University of Illinois Press, 1979), p. 84, n. 9.

2. Dudley Randall, ed., *The Black Poets* (New York: Bantam Books, 1971), p. xxiii.

3. Personal telephone interview with Dudley Randall, October 14, 1982.

4. Julius Lester, 'In Memoriam', *World Order*, 16, No. 1 (1981), p. 53.

5. Quoted by David Llorens, 'Writers Converge at Fisk University', *Negro Digest*, 15 (June, 1966), p. 54.

6. Stokely Carmichael, *Black Power: The Politics of Liberation in America* (New York: Random House, 1967), p. 41.

7. Ibid., pp. 34–5.

8. Ibid., p. 161.

9. LeRoi Jones, 'A Dark Bag', *Poetry*, 103 (March, 1964), p. 397.

10. LeRoi Jones (Amiri Baraka), *Home: Social Essays* (New York: William Morrow, 1966), p. 251.

11. Ron Karenga, 'Ron Karenga and Black Cultural Nationalism', *Negro Digest* (January, 1968), 5; reprinted in *The Black Aesthetic,* p. 32.

12. Julius Lester, 'In Memoriam', *World Order*, 16, No. 1 (1981), p. 53.

13. Quoted by David Llorens, 'Writers Converge at Fisk University', *Negro Digest* (June, 1966), p. 62.

14. Ibid., p. 63.

15. Ibid., p. 65.

16. Ibid.

17. Rosey E. Pool, 'Robert Hayden: Poet Laureate', *Negro Digest* (June, 1966), p. 41.

18. Robert Hayden, 'From the Life', p. 12.

19. Julius Lester, 'In Memoriam', *World Order,* 16, No. 1 (1981), p. 53.

20. Rosey E. Pool, 'Robert Hayden', *Negro Digest* (June, 1966), p. 43.

21. Ibid.

22. Ibid.

23. Dudley Randall, 'The Black Aesthetic', p. 226.

24. Julius Lester, 'In Memoriam', *World Order*, 16, No. 1 (1981), p. 53.

25. Ibid.

26. Quoted in 'Black Writers' Views on Literary Lions and Values', *Negro Digest* (January, 1968), p. 33.

27. Personal interview, October 13, 1982.

28. Robert Hayden, Letter, *Negro Digest* (April, 1968), p. 98.

29. David Littlejohn, *Black on White: A Critical Survey of Writing by American Negroes* (New York: Grossman Publishers, 1966), p. 82.

30. Ibid., p. 81.

31. Gwendolyn Brooks, rev. of *Selected Poems*, by Robert Hayden, *Negro Digest* (October, 1966), p. 51.

32. Ibid.

33. Rev. of *Selected Poems*, by Robert Hayden, *Choice*, 4 (May, 1967), p. 288.

34. Quoted in *How I Write*, p. 184.

35. Robert Hayden, *Kaleidoscope*, p. xix.

36. Ibid.

37. Ibid., p. xx.

38. Ibid.

39. Ibid., p. xxiii.

40. Ibid., p. xxiv.

41. Ibid., p. 95.

42. Ibid., p. 150.

43. Ibid., p. 208.

44. Ibid., p. 209.

45. Ibid., p. 108.

46. Julius Lester, 'In Memoriam', *World Order*, 16, No. 1 (1981), p. 53.

47. Rev. of *Kaleidoscope*, by Robert Hayden, *Saturday Review*, May 11, 1968, p. 85.

48. Don L. Lee, rev. of *Kaleidoscope*, by Robert Hayden, *Negro Digest* (January, 1968), p. 52.

49. Ibid.

50. Ibid., p. 90.

51. Ibid., pp. 93–4

52. 'Black Writers' Views', *Negro Digest* (January, 1968), p. 33.

53. Ibid.

54. Ibid.

55. Ibid., pp. 84–5.

56. Darwin T. Turner, ed., *Black American Literature* (Columbus, Ohio: Charles E. Merrill Publishing Co., 1970), p. 245.

57. Richard Barksdale and Keneth Kinnamon, eds., *Black Writers of America: A Comprehensive Anthology* (New York: Macmillan Publishing Co., Inc., 1972), p. 676.

58. Julius Lester, 'For a World Where a Man is a Man, a Poet a Poet', rev. of *Words in the Mourning Time*, by Robert Hayden, *New York Times Book Review*, January 24, 1971, p. 5.

59. Ibid., p. 22.

60. Ibid.

61. Jerome Cushman, rev. of *Words in the Mourning Time*, by Robert Hayden, *Library Journal* (March, 1971), p. 839.

62. Daniel Jaffe, rev. of *Words in the Mourning Time*, by Robert Hayden, *Saturday Review*, April 3, 1971, p. 33.

63. Carolyn Gerald, rev. of *Afro-American Literature: An Introduction*, ed. Robert Hayden, *Black World* (July, 1972), p. 51.

64. Arthur P. Davis, *From the Dark Tower*, p. 175.

65. Angela Jackson, rev. of *The Night-Blooming Cereus*, by Robert Hayden, *Black World* (September, 1975), p. 87.

66. Ibid.

67. Onwuchekwa Jemie, *Langston Hughes*, p. 166.

68. Ibid.

69. Ibid., p. 167.

70. Michael S. Harper, 'A Symbolist Poet Struggling with Historical Fact', rev. of *Angle of Ascent*, by Robert Hayden, *New York Times Book Review*, February 22, 1976, p. 34.

71. Quoted by James E. Harvey, 'Poet Feels, and Wants to be Judged, Part of Mainstream', *Flint Journal*, January 23, 1976, sec. C, p. 2, cols 1–2.

72. Quoted by Hollie I. West, 'Plaudits at Last for a Poet in Perfect Pitch', *Washington Post*, March 21, 1976, sec. L, p. 3, col. 1.

73. Jo Thomas, 'Of Quietly Crafting Words', *Detroit Free Press*, September 12, 1976, Sunday Supplement, p. 33, col. 1.

74. Quoted by Saundra Ivey, 'Noted Black Poet Sees Race Relations Decline', p. 49.

75. LeRoi Jones (Amiri Baraka), 'A Dark Bag', *Poetry*, 103 (March, 1964), p. 397.

76. Haki Madhubuti (Don Lee), 'In the Mourning Time: Robert Hayden', *Black Books Bulletin*, 7, No. 1 (1980), p. 3.

PART III: THE CONTINUITY OF HAYDEN'S POETRY. I

1. Robert Hayden, House of Worship video tape.

2. Robert M. Greenberg, p. 367.

3. Dennis Gendron, 'Robert Hayden: A View of His Life and Development as a Poet'; Gendron does an excellent job of surveying the major influences and developments in Hayden's career throughout his first three chapters, and in chapter four he begins to show Hayden's grouping of lyrics; in chapter five he discusses the thematic continuity in *Words in the Mourning Time* and, to a less extent, in *The Night-Blooming Cereus*. Pontheolla T. Williams discusses the works in chronological sequence up through *Selected Poems*, but her presentation is more of a casual, thumbnail sketch of each volume rather than an attempt to demonstrate any thematic design within or without Hayden's volumes.

4. As I will discuss later, among these are such studies as Charles T. Davis, 'Robert Hayden's Use of History', *Modern Black Poets*, ed. Donald B. Gibson (Englewood Cliffs, NJ: Prentice Hall, 1973), pp. 96–111; Constance Post, 'Image and Idea in the Poetry of Robert Hayden', *CLA Journal*, 20, No. 2 (1976), pp. 164–75; Howard Faulkner, '"Transformed by Steeps of Flight": The Poetry of Robert Hayden', *CLA Journal*, 21, No. 1 (1977), pp. 282–91; Wilburn Williams, Jr., 'Covenant of Timelessness and Time: Symbolism and History in Robert Hayden's *Angle of Ascent*', *Chant of Saints*, pp. 66–84.

10. *Heart-Shape in the Dust (1940)*

1. Robert Hayden, *Heart-Shape in the Dust* (Detroit, Michigan: the Falcon Press, 1940), p. 53; all subsequent references to poems from this volume will be indicated in the text; except for the publication of some of these poems in periodicals, this text is the only source for most of these poems.

2. Arthur P. Davis, *From the Dark Tower*, p. 176.

3. William Harrison, 'A New Negro Voice', rev. of *Heart-Shape in the Dust*, by Robert Hayden, *Opportunity*, 19, No. 3 (1941), p. 91.

4. James W. Ivy, 'Concerning a Poet and a Critic', rev. of *Heart-Shape in the Dust*, by Robert Hayden, *Crisis*, 48, No. 4 (1941), p. 128.

5. Quoted in 'Plaudits at Last', *Washington Post*, March 21, 1976, sec. L, p. 3, col. 1.

6. Quoted in 'Of Quietly Crafting Words', *Detroit Free Press*, September 12, 1976, Sunday Supplement, p. 33, col. 1.

7. See Gendron's first chapter 'Robert Earl Hayden: Poetry and Color', pp. 1–18.

8. Gendron, p. 31.

11. *The Lion and the Archer (1948)*

1. Robert Hayden, *The Lion and the Archer* (Nashville, Tennessee: Hemphill Press, 1948); the pages are not numbered but the poems are; 'The Lion' is no. 6. With those poems which later appear in the comprehensive collection of Hayden's poetry *Angle of Ascent* (1975), sometimes

in revised form, I will indicate in the text that reference as well. For 'The Lion' it is p. 64 ('The Lions').

2. Selden Rodman, 'Negro Poets', *New York Times Book Review*, p. 27.

3. Counterpoise flier; see Chapter 4, n. 6.

4. Quoted in *Conversations with Writers*, p. 171.

5. Quoted in *How I Write*, p. 161.

12. *Figure of Time (1955)*

1. Robert Hayden, *Figure of Time* (Nashville, Tennessee: Hemphill Press, 1955), p. 12. All references to poems in this volume are from this edition. Here too I indicate where appropriate the reference in *Angle of Ascent* (*AA*). 'Figure' is not included in this collection.

2. Quoted by Gendron, pp. 73–4, from his personal interview, March 16–19, 1974.

3. Hayden, quoted in 'From the Life', p. 2.

4. As Hayden explains in his own notes for the collection, the woman is burning incense, relying on 'High John the Conqueror' – a 'root said to have magical properties'.

5. As I discuss later, Gendron, Pontheolla T. Williams, Wilburn Williams, Jr., and Robert Greenberg, among others, often see Hayden's perspective as a poet in conflict with his perspective as a Bahá'í, his religious conviction as only a surface belief which belies his doubts and anguish, and his religious allusions as forced and injurious to his art. While Hayden freely admitted that spiritual growth was a struggle for him, a fuller understanding of his artistic purposes resolves these apparent conflicts and demonstrates that his themes and beliefs are quite in accord, and that his poetry is empowered by his Bahá'í perspective, not injured by it.

6. This event is a milestone in Bahá'í history and is commemorated annually as the Festival of Riḍván, a twelve-day period (April 21 through May 2) which celebrates the announcement by Bahá'u'lláh to His followers that He was 'Him Whom God will make manifest', the promised Manifestation whose coming the Báb had foretold. The event took place in the rented Najíbíyyih Garden outside Baghdad immediately prior to Bahá'u'lláh's further exile to Constantinople. This is the 'holiest and most significant of all Bahá'í festivals'. (*Bahá'í Glossary*, p. 42.) For further description see Shoghi Effendi, *God Passes By* (Wilmette, Illinois: Bahá'í Publishing Trust, 1957), pp. 151–5.

7. Shoghi Effendi, *God Passes By*, p. 153.

8. Bahá'u'lláh, *The Hidden Words*, (Arabic) no. 62.

9. Ibid., (Persian) no. 30.

10. Bahá'u'lláh, *The Seven Valleys and the Four Valleys* (Wilmette, Illinois: Bahá'í Publishing Trust, 1975), p. 12. The poet is Iṣfahání.

11. 'Abdu'l-Bahá, *Some Answered Questions*, trans. Laura Clifford Barney (Wilmette, Illinois: Bahá'í Publishing Trust, rev. edn. 1981), p. 74.

12. *ubi sunt* is a lyric formula deriving its name from the Latin phrase, *Ubi sunt qui ante nos ferunt*, a lyric refrain which translates, 'Where are those things that were before us?' It can be found in the lyric tradition of most periods and cultures as a catalogue of questions, as in the Anglo-Saxon poem 'The Wanderer': *'Hwaer cwom sybla gesetu? Hwaer sindon seledreamas?'* (Where have the feast seats gone? Where are the hall-joys?)

13. See 'The Ballad of Sue Ellen Westerfield', *Angle of Ascent*, p. 85, and Chapter 1, p. 7.

14. William Butler Yeats, 'Lapis Lazuli', *A College Book of Modern Verse*, eds. James K. Robinson and Walter B. Rideout (New York: Harper and Row, 1958), p. 80, l. 16.

15. Quoted in *Interviews with Black Writers*, pp. 117–18.

13. *A Ballad of Remembrance (1962)*

1. Robert Hayden, *A Ballad of Remembrance* (London: Paul Breman, 1962), p. 41. All references to poems are from this edition.

2. According to Erma Hayden in a personal interview May 22, 1981, Hayden had in mind Daddy Grace; Gendron quotes Hayden as stating it was based on Prophet Jones (p. 94). Most critics agree the figure is an indictment of all religious charlatanism, not the re-creation of a particular individual.

3. See further explanation of these symbols in Chapter 22; see also Bahá'u'lláh, *The Kitáb-i-Íqán: The Book of Certitude* (Wilmette, Illinois: Bahá'í Publishing Trust, 1950), pp. 33–44.

4. 'Concerning the Nature of Things', the great philosophical poem by Lucretius, the 1st-century BC Roman poet, in which, among other things, he adopts an atomic theory of matter. The title has come to designate a genre of poetic and philosophical discourse.

5. Constance Post, 'Image and Idea in the Poetry of Robert Hayden', p. 170.

6. Gendron, p. 113.

7. Wilburn Williams, Jr., *Chant of Saints*, p. 67.

8. 'Abdu'l-Bahá, *Some Answered Questions*, p. 233.

9. Bahá'u'lláh, *Gleanings*, p. 184.

10. Ibid., p. 250.

11. Gendron, p. 74.

12. 'Abdu'l-Bahá in *The Divine Art of Living: Selections from Writings of Bahá'u'lláh and 'Abdu'l-Bahá*, compiled by Mabel Hyde Paine (Wilmette, Illinois: Bahá'í Publishing Trust, rev. edn. 1960), p. 89.

13. Ibid., p. 90.

14. Quoted in *How I Write*, pp. 197–8.

15. Ibid., p. 169.

16. Bahá'u'lláh, *Synopsis and Codification of the Laws and Ordinances of the Kitáb-i-Aqdas*, trans. Shoghi Effendi (Haifa: World Centre, 1973), p. 62. The ring inscription reads: 'I came forth from God, and return unto Him, detached from all save Him, holding fast to His Name, the Merciful, the Compassionate.'

17. Gendron, p. 108; see also *How I Write*, pp. 181–5.

18. Quoted in *How I Write*, p. 183.

19. 'John Brown', *American Journal* (New York: Liveright Publishing Corporation, 1982), p. 5.

14. *Selected Poems (1966)*

1. Robert Hayden, *Selected Poems* (New York: October House, Inc., 1966), p. 11. All references to poems are from this edition.

2. Gwendolyn Brooks, rev. of *Selected Poems*, by Robert Hayden, *Negro Digest* (October, 1966), p. 51.

3. Ibid.

4. Ibid.

5. Ibid.

6. Robert D. Spector, 'The New Poetry of Protest', rev. of *Selected Poems*, by Robert Hayden, *Saturday Review*, February 11, 1967, p. 38.

7. David Galler, 'Three Recent Volumes', rev. of *Selected Poems*, by Robert Hayden, *Poetry*, 110 (1967), p. 268.

8. Ibid.

9. Rev. of *Selected Poems*, by Robert Hayden, *Choice*, 4 (May, 1967), p. 288.

10. Pontheolla T. Williams, 'A Critical Analysis', p. 160.

11. Gendron, p. 73.

12. Robert M. Greenberg, *American Writers*, p. 372.

13. Pontheolla T. Williams, 'A Critical Analysis', p. 176.

14. Maurice J. O'Sullivan, Jr., 'The Mask of Allusion in Robert Hayden's "The Diver"', *CLA Journal*, 17, No. 1 (1973), pp. 85–92; see p. 92 in particular.

15. Gendron, p. 75.

16. Quoted in *How I Write*, p. 166.

17. Gendron, p. 74.

18. Wilburn Williams, Jr., *Chant of Saints*, p. 67.

19. Ibid., p. 68.

20. *Selected Poems*, pp. 29–30.

21. See later discussion with regard to Hayden's most overtly Platonic poems in *The Night-Blooming Cereus*, and in the discussion in Chapter 22 of Hayden's symbolism.

22. Bahá'u'lláh, *The Hidden Words*, (Arabic) no. 7; this theme of striving for detachment is one of the preeminent motifs that permeate the Bahá'í Writings.

23. Bahá'u'lláh, *The Hidden Words*, (Persian) nos. 5, 69, 76; this ostensibly simple dictum underlies the entire Bahá'í analysis of spiritual development in this life as wrought through existential exercises, that words or knowledge by themselves are not indices to character.

24. Socrates in Plato's *Republic, The Dialogues of Plato*, trans. B. Jowett, Vol I (New York: Random House, 1937), Book VII, pp. 773 ff. I prefer alluding to the ideas of the Socratic dialogues as belonging to Socrates, inasmuch as I consider Socrates the genius and Plato the sublime literary artist. I base this distinction on the loftiness and clarity of the early Socratic dialogues versus the later non-Socratic ones.

25. The Socratic notion of the 'Forms' or 'Ideas' as the abstract reality which is given metaphorical or symbolical correspondence in the phenomenal world is discussed in numerous dialogues. In the *Republic* it is discussed most clearly in Book V. The *Symposium* is another of my favorite sources for this discussion.

26. 'the exile's path' here refers to an appellation of Bahá'u'lláh as the 'Blessed Exile', which Hayden uses in 'Words in the Mourning Time', *Words in the Mourning Time*, p. 59: 'through power of/ The Blessed Exile's/ transilluminating word.' In both cases Hayden is alluding to the fact that Bahá'u'lláh, a native of Ṭihrán, was exiled by the various governmental authorities (the Shah and the Sultan) to Baghdad, to Constantinople, to Adrianople, and finally to the prison city of 'Akká in what is now Israel. Bahá'ís believe that these travels fulfilled a number of prophecies from the Old and New Testaments and the Koranic traditions.

27. See Shoghi Effendi, *God Passes By*, pp. 77–8.

28. William Butler Yeats, 'The Second Coming', *A College Book of Modern Verse*, p. 65, l. 6.

29. 'Frederick Douglass', *Selected Poems*, p. 78; *Angle of Ascent*, p. 131.

PART IV: THE CONTINUITY OF HAYDEN'S POETRY. II

1. p. 176.

2. 'John Brown', *American Journal*, p. 5.

3. Pontheolla T. Williams, 'A Critical Analysis', p. 178.

4. Gendron, p. 114.

5. Though now in common parlance in discussion of poetry, the term was coined by T. S. Eliot to designate the use of tropes; see T. S. Eliot, *Selected Essays* (New York: Harcourt, Brace and Co., 1932), pp. 124–5; see also further discussion of this matter in Part V.

6. A critical term coined by Matthew Arnold, 'The Study of Poetry', *The Great Critics: An Anthology of Literary Criticism*, eds. James H. Smith and Edd W. Parks (New York: W. W. Norton and Co., Inc., 3rd edn. 1951), p. 637.

15. *Words in the Mourning Time (1970)*

1. Robert Hayden, *Words in the Mourning Time* (New York: October House, Inc., 1970), p. 51. All references to poems in this volume are from this edition.

2. Pontheolla T. Williams, 'A Critical Analysis', p. 178.

3. There are numerous Bahá'í books which deal with this theme. Bahá'u'lláh in *Kitáb-i-Íqán* treats the thesis of Progressive Revelation; 'Abdu'l-Bahá in *Some Answered Questions* responds to specific questions regarding the nature of the Bahá'í view of history as cyclical but ever-advancing.

4. Shoghi Effendi, *The Promised Day is Come* (Wilmette, Illinois: Bahá'í Publishing Trust, rev. edn. 1980). In this volume Shoghi Effendi describes the process by which world leaders rejected the guidance of Bahá'u'lláh, and the consequence of their actions in the prospect for future world peace.

5. Bahá'u'lláh quoted in *The World Order of Bahá'u'lláh*, by Shoghi Effendi (Wilmette, Illinois: Bahá'í Publishing Trust, 2nd rev. edn. 1974), p. 194.

6. Bahá'u'lláh, *Gleanings*, p. 11.

7. Shoghi Effendi, *The Promised Day is Come*, p. 3.

8. Quoted in *Interviews with Black Writers*, p. 119.

9. The occasion was the Bahá'í Centennial celebration held in Chicago, October, 1967.

10. Quoted in *Interviews with Black Writers*, p. 119.

11. Robert M. Greenberg, *American Writers*, p. 371.

12. Ibid.

13. William Wallis, rev. of *Words in the Mourning Time*, by Robert Hayden, *Prairie Schooner*, 45 (fall, 1971), p. 279.

14. Daniel Jaffe, rev. of *Words in the Mourning Time*, by Robert Hayden, *Saturday Review*, April 3, 1971, p. 33.

15. Jerome Cushman, rev. of *Words in the Mourning Time*, by Robert Hayden, *Library Journal*, March 1, 1971, p. 839.

16. Julius Lester, 'For a World Where a Man is a Man, A Poet a Poet', rev. of *Words in the Mourning Time*, by Robert Hayden, *New York Times Book Review*, January 24, 1971, p. 4.

17. Ibid., p. 5.

18. Dennis Gendron, p. 117.

19. There are other versions of the myth and the question in particular. For example, according to Robert Graves, *The Greek Myth* (Baltimore, Maryland: Penguin Books, 1955), Vol. 2, p. 10, the riddle asks, 'What being, with only one voice, has sometimes two feet, sometimes three, sometimes four, and is weakest when it has the most?'

20. Gendron, p. 117.

21. According to Marzieh Gail, *Bahá'í Glossary* (Wilmette, Illinois: Bahá'í Publishing Trust, 1965), p. 7, 'Alláh'u'Abhá' translates as 'God is All-Glorious', and is 'The Greatest Name',

adopted during the period of Bahá'u'lláh's exile in Adrianople as a greeting among Bahá'í's. It is also used as a brief prayer of thanksgiving and praise.

22. Bahá'u'lláh in *Bahá'í Prayers* (Wilmette, Illinois: Bahá'í Publishing Trust, 1982), p. 87.

23. 'Crystal' or crystal methadrene, a blue amphetamene popular in the 'drug culture' during the late 1960s and early 1970s, an 'upper' in drug parlance.

24. *Figure of Time*, p. 7.

25. p. 21; *AA*, p. 44; Hayden here effectively combines two sorts of irony; the one a humorous image of 'Aunt Jemima' on a sculpted baroque shell by Cellini is clearly a parody on the painting 'The Birth of Venus' by Botticelli (c. 1485); the overriding tone, however, is a serious and poignant irony reflecting the dire circumstance which gives birth to Aunt Jemima's sad life – the 'slave-ships on fantastic seas'. This simple stanza is thus a masterpiece of understatement.

26. William Butler Yeats in 'The Circus Animals' Desertion', *Modern Poetry*, ed. Maynard Mack, 2nd edn. (Englewood Cliffs, NJ: Prentice-Hall, Inc., 1961), p. 98, states 'I sought a theme and sought for it in vain', and asks 'What can I but enumerate old themes?' He concludes, 'Now that my ladder's gone,/ I must lie down where all the ladders start,/ In the foul rag-and-bone shop of the heart.' Yeats' title calls to mind Hayden's poem 'The Invisible Circus' and, perhaps more directly, 'The Lion', since it is clear that Hayden's symbol of the lion refers to his inner fears and emotions encountered in the 'rag-and-bone shop of the heart', what Hayden calls the 'gilt and vermilion cage' (*The Lion and the Archer*, poem 6).

27. According to the Bahá'í Writings, world peace is inevitable, a natural consequence of a divinely ordered history and God's plan for man's spiritual evolution. The 'Most Great Peace', the complete fulfillment of that promise, has been delayed, according to Bahá'u'lláh, because of the neglect or rejection by kings and rulers of His letters urging the establishment of a world federation of governments. Consequently, Bahá'u'lláh stated that before the 'Most Great Peace' would be attained mankind would first achieve an intermediary stage, the 'Lesser Peace', a cessation of active warfare, a condition which, according to 'Abdu'l-Bahá, will obtain around the end of this century. Bahá'u'lláh stated: 'Now that ye have refused the Most Great Peace, hold ye fast unto this, the Lesser Peace, that haply ye may in some degree better your own condition and that of your dependents' (*Gleanings*, p. 254). It is crucial to understand all the ingredients of this perspective in order to grasp the subtle mixture of hope and fear, of expectation and dread which is such a vital part of the tone in many of Hayden's poems.

28. The 'Short Obligatory Prayer' is prayed each day by Bahá'ís at noon. It states: 'I bear witness, O my God, that Thou hast created me to know Thee and to worship Thee. I testify, at this moment, to my powerlessness and to Thy might, to my poverty and to Thy wealth. There is none other God but Thee, the Help in Peril, the Self-Subsisting' (*Bahá'í Prayers*, p. 4).

29. Socrates in Plato's *Phaedo*, *The Dialogues of Plato*, Vol. I, p. 448.

30. Ibid., p. 450.

31. *The Hidden Words*, (Arabic) no. 32.

32. *Gleanings*, p. 345.

16. *The Night-Blooming Cereus (1973)*

1. Robert Hayden, *The Night-Blooming Cereus* (London: Paul Breman, 1973), p. 4. All references to poems in this volume are from this edition.

2. Quoted in *Interviews with Black Writers*, p. 113.

3. See Charles T. Davis, 'Robert Hayden's Use of History', *Modern black Poets*, ed. Donald B. Gibson (Englewood Cliffs, NJ: Prentice-Hall, 1973), pp. 96–111; Fred M. Fetrow, 'Robert

Hayden's "Frederick Douglass": Form and Meaning in a Modern Sonnet', *CLA Journal*, 17, No. 1 (1973), pp. 79–84; and Maurice J. O'Sullivan, Jr., 'The Mask of Allusion in Robert Hayden's "The Diver"', *CLA Journal*, 17, No. 1 (1973), pp. 85–92. After 1973 many other studies began to appear.

4. Angela Jackson, rev. of *The Night-Blooming Cereus*, by Robert Hayden, *Black World*, September 1975, pp. 87–8.

5. Ibid., p. 87.

6. Ibid., p. 88.

7. See Chapter 13, n. 16.

8. John Keats, 'Ode on a Grecian Urn', *English Romantic Poetry and Prose*, ed. Russell Noyes (New York: Oxford University Press, 1956), pp. 1193–4. Observing the pastoral setting on the ancient vessel, the speaker concludes:

> When old age shall this generation waste,
> Thou shalt remain, in midst of other woe
> Than ours, a friend to man, to whom thou say'st,
> 'Beauty is truth, truth beauty,—that is all
> Ye know on earth, and all ye need to know.'

9. See Part IV, Introduction, n. 5.

10. As a topical allusion this passage reflects an observation made to me by Erma Hayden (May 22, 1981) that 'Poets are in mortal combat with life', and it also recalls Hayden's own statement that he had 'a lover's quarrel with life' (House of Worship video tape). In any case, the reactions imply two distinct personalities – the optimistic woman awaits the bloom; the poet-worrier imagines something ominous.

11. Bahá'u'lláh in *The Hidden Words*, (Persian) no. 13, states, 'I fear lest, bereft of the melody of the dove of heaven, ye will sink back to the shades of utter loss, and, never having gazed upon the beauty of the rose, return to water and clay.'

12. In effect, awaiting the flower's bloom may symbolize the couple's search, and the flower's bloom may symbolize the fulfillment of that search in discovering the Bahá'í Faith.

13. In the traditional Italian or Petrarchan sonnet the fourteen lines are divided into two parts, the octave and the sestet; the octave states the problem, and the sestet resolves it.

14. See 'English High Lights', *Interviews with Black Writers*, pp. 120–22; and Dennis Gendron, pp. 137–41.

15. See Chapter 23.

16. As I explain in Chapter 22, 'raw-head-and-bloody bones' is a childhood symbol (which he uses in 'Night, Death, Mississippi') that represents a visual image of nighttime terror too dreadful to name or describe. It becomes for Hayden a symbol of dehumanized evil.

17. Bahá'u'lláh, *Gleanings*, p. 215; 'All men have been created to carry forward an ever-advancing civilization.'

18. See Chapter 23 for further discussion of this poem.

19. The haiku is commonly distinguished as a three-line poem of five, seven, and five syllables respectively. My personal opinion is that the heart of this poetic form is in the imagistic equation it establishes. Take, for example, Pound's own rendering of a haiku in 'In a Station of the Metro', *Understanding Poetry*, eds. Cleanth Brooks and Robert Penn Warren (New York: Holt, Rinehart and Winston, 1976), 4th edn., p. 71:

The apparition of these faces in the crowd;
Petals on a wet, black bough.

In short, I feel the metrics of an English haiku are largely irrelevant.

20. See Gendron, p. 141.

21. See Matthew Arnold's 'Dover Beach' and T. S. Eliot's 'Wasteland'.

22. William Butler Yeats, 'Sailing to Byzantium', *A College Book of Modern Verse*, eds. James K. Robinson and Walter B. Rideout (New York: Harper and Row, 1958), p. 69.

23. *The Hidden Words*, (Persian) no. 20.

24. Rainer Maria Rilke, *Sonnets to Orpheus*, trans. Karl H. Siegler (Vancouver, Canada: Talonbooks, 1977), sec. I, sonnet 1.

25. Ibid., sec. I, sonnet 15.

26. Wallace Stevens, 'Peter Quince at the Clavier', *A College Book of Modern Verse*, pp. 259–60.

27. 'Abdu'l-Bahá, *Some Answered Questions*, p. 264.

17. *Angle of Ascent (1975)*

1. Robert Hayden, *Angle of Ascent* (New York: Liveright, 1975), p. 10. All references to poems in this volume are from this edition.

2. See Chapter 16, n. 3.

3. Quoted in Gendron, p. 234.

4. Michael S. Harper, 'A Symbolist Poet Struggling with Historical Fact', rev. of *Angle of Ascent*, by Robert Hayden, *New York Times Book Review*, February 22, 1976, p. 34.

5. Ibid., p. 35.

6. William Logan, rev. of *Angle of Ascent*, by Robert Hayden, *Poetry* (July, 1977), p. 228.

7. Ibid., p. 227.

8. Richmond Lattimore, rev. of *Angle of Ascent*, by Robert Hayden, *The Hudson Review*, 29, No. 1 (1976), p. 125.

9. Ibid., p. 127.

10. James Cotter, rev. of *Angle of Ascent*, by Robert Hayden, *America*, 134 (February 7, 1976), p. 103.

11. Ibid., p. 104.

12. Rev. of *Angle of Ascent*, by Robert Hayden, *Choice*, 13 (April, 1976), p. 223.

13. Lewis Turco, '*Angle of Ascent*: The Poetry of Robert Hayden', *Michigan Quarterly Review*, (Spring, 1977), pp. 199–219.

14. Wilburn Williams, Jr., 'Covenant of Timelessness and Time . . .', *Chant of Saints* (see Chapter 9, n. 1, above).

15. Howard Faulkner, op. cit.

16. John S. Wright, 'Homage to a Mystery Boy', rev. of *American Journal*, by Robert Hayden, *Georgia Review*, 36 (Winter, 1982), p. 909.

17. Robert Hayden, 'Smelt Fishing', p. 30.

18. Howard Faulkner, p. 285.

19. Samuel Taylor Coleridge, 'Kubla Khan: Or, A Vision in a Dream', *English Romantic Poetry and Prose*, p. 392.

20. Constance Post; 'Image and Idea in the Poetry of Robert Hayden', p. 167.

21. Bahá'u'lláh, *The Kitáb-i-Íqán*, p. 36.

22. John 8: 31–2, *The Holy Bible*, rev. standard version (New York: Thomas Nelson and Sons, 1953).

23. Constance Post, 'Image and Idea in the Poetry of Robert Hayden', p. 166. As Post notes, ample explanation of the significance of the number *nine* in Bahá'í symbology is given by the Hand of the Cause A. Q. Faizi, 'Explanation of the Emblem of the Greatest Name', *Bahá'í News*, No. 451 (October, 1968), pp. 8–12.

24. Interestingly, some authorities attribute Akhenaten's religious belief to the influence of Tiy, his commoner mother.

25. See 'Akhenaton', *The New Encyclopaedia Britannica*, Macropaedia, Vol. 1, 1974, p. 403.

26. p. 76.

27. 'The Broken Dark', p. 39.

28. 'Abdu'l-Bahá in *Bahá'í World Faith*, p. 382.

18. *American Journal (1978)*

1. Robert Hayden, *American Journal* (Taunton, Massachusetts: Effendi Press, 1978). Because the poems in this volume are unnumbered and because all poems in this edition appear in the 1982 Liveright edition, I have included in the text the page numbers for the Liveright edition, but the description of the poems and their arrangement refers to the Effendi Press edition. (Opening quotation, p. 57.)

2. Michael S. Harper, 'Three Poets', rev. of *American Journal*, by Robert Hayden, *New York Times Book Review*, October 21, 1979, p. 18.

3. Ibid., p. 20.

4. Ibid.

5. Robert G. O'Meally, 'Poems and the Nation', rev. of *American Journal*, by Robert Hayden, *Book World*, June 25, 1978, G6.

6. Ibid.

7. Reginald Gibbons, 'Hayden, Peck, and Atwood', rev. of *American Journal*, by Robert Hayden, *Ontario Review*, 10 (1979), p. 87.

8. Ibid., p. 88.

9. See Fred M. Fetrow, 'American Poet', rev. of *American Journal*, by Robert Hayden (Liveright version), *Poet Lore*, 77, No. 1 (Spring, 1982), p. 36. Fetrow states, 'Hayden called "A letter from Phillis Wheatley" a "psychogram".' However, in his review of the Effendi Press *American Journal* Harper himself coins the phrase 'epistolary psychograph' to describe the poem (p. 18).

10. *Heart-Shape in the Dust*, p. 10.

11. Reginald Gibbons, *Ontario Review*, 10 (1979), p. 87.

12. Personal interview with Erma Hayden, May 22, 1981.

13. Ibid.

14. As far back as the early 1960s Hayden had contemplated an epical treatment of Matthew Henson. Cf. Chapter 5, n. 5.

15. Prefatory notes to *Americal Journal*.

16. 'Veracruz', *Angle of Ascent*, p. 92.

17. *Angle of Ascent*, p. 39.

18. Robert Stepto, 'After Modernism, After Hibernation: Michael Harper, Robert Hayden, and Jay Wright', *Chant of Saints*, pp. 470–86.

19. Ibid., p. 480.

20. Counterpoise flier.

21. Ibid.

22. 'For a Young Artist', *Angle of Ascent*, p. 9.

19. *American Journal (1982)*

1. Robert Hayden, *American Journal* (New York: Liveright, 1982), p. 21. All references to poems in this volume are from this edition.

2. Fred M. Fetrow, 'American Poet', *Poet Lore*, 77, No. 1, p. 39.

3. Ibid., p. 40.

4. John S. Wright, 'Homage to a Mystery Boy', *Georgia Review*, 36 (Winter, 1982), p. 905.

5. Fred M. Fetrow, *Poet Lore*, 77, No. 1, p. 36.

6. Ibid., p. 41.

7. Quoted in *How I Write*, p. 135.

8. John S. Wright, *Georgia Review*, 36 (Winter, 1982), p. 906.

9. Fred M. Fetrow, *Poet Lore*, 77, No. 1, p. 39.

10. Ibid.

11. Elisabeth Kubler-Ross, *On Death and Dying* (New York: Macmillan Publishing Co., Inc., 1969).

12. Mentioned under 'Acknowledgments, Notes' in *American Journal.*

13. Quoted in *How I Write*, p. 163.

14. Robeson is still a controversial figure, and there are currently efforts being made to redeem his reputation.

15. 'The Lion', *The Lion and the Archer.*

16. John S. Wright, *Georgia Review*, 36 (Winter, 1982), p. 905.

17. *Heart-Shape in the Dust*, p. 31.

18. Reference to the martyrdom of Bahá'ís, but preceding the ongoing slaughter of Bahá'ís in Iran.

19. *Gleanings*, p. 80.

20. Ibid., pp. 39–40.

21. Ibid., p. 213.

22. 1979.

23. 'The Good' as the essentially unknowable, animating and creative force in the universe is mentioned by Socrates in virtually every Socratic dialogue. See the Jowett Index, p. 863, for particular references.

PART V: THE POET OF PERFECT PITCH

1. Roy Harvey Pearce, *The Continuity of American Poetry* (Princeton, NJ: Princeton University Press, 1961), p. 13.

2. In the pre-literate tribal stage of virtually every culture there exists a position of equivalent function and status; it is only in the last several decades that research has revealed to us a complete understanding of how these poets composed according to the oral-formulaic tradition.

3. William Faulkner, 'The Stockholm Address', *Masterworks of World Literature*, Vol. II, eds. Edwin Everett, Calvin S. Brown and John D. Wade (New York: Holt, Rinehart and Winston, 1955), p. 957.

4. Ibid.

5. Quoted in 'Plaudits at Last . . .', sec. L, p. 1, col. 2.

6. Ibid., sec. L, p. 3, col. 2.

7. Quoted in *How I Write*, p. 165.

8. Ralph Waldo Emerson, 'The Poet', *Selected Prose and Poetry*, ed. Reginald Cook (New York: Holt, Rinehart and Winston, 1961), p. 320.

20. *The Poet and the Poetic Process*

1. Quoted in *Interviews with Black Writers*, p. 112.

2. Quoted in Jo Thomas, 'Of Quietly Crafting Words', *Detroit Free Press*, p. 35, col. 2.

3. C. Hugh Holman, *A Handbook to Literature* (Indianapolis, Indiana: Odyssey Press, 1975), 3rd edn., p. 298.

4. Ibid., p. 299.

5. Quoted in *How I Write*, p. 153.

6. Ibid.

7. Quoted in 'English High Lights'.

8. Quoted in *How I Write*, p. 154.

9. Samuel Taylor Coleridge, *Biographia Literaria*, *English Romantic Poetry and Prose*, ed. Russell Noyes (New York: Oxford University Press, 1956), p. 427.

10. Quoted in *Interviews with Black Writers*, pp. 111–12.

11. Samuel Taylor Coleridge, 'The Eolian Harp', *English Romantic Poetry and Prose*, p. 382, ll. 39–40.

12. Percy Bysshe Shelley, 'A Defence of Poetry', *English Romantic Poetry and Prose*, p. 1097.

13. See F. O. Matthiessen, *The American Renaissance: Art and Expression in the Age of Emerson and Whitman* (Oxford: Oxford University Press, 1941), p. 54.

14. I take the term 'outer mystery' as coined by my former professor and noted Shakespearean authority R. H. West in his study *Shakespeare and the Outer Mystery* (Lexington: University of Kentucky Press, 1968). He uses this term, as I do here, to designate a sense of a divinely ordered spiritual reality which gives ultimate order and meaning to the phenomenal realm.

15. See Emerson's essays 'The Oversoul' and 'The Poet' for an ample discussion of this process.

16. Charles Baudelaire, 'Correspondances', *Charles Baudelaire: Selected Poems* (London: Falcon Press Ltd., 1946), p. 27. The translation is my own.

17. According to Jowett, the 'forms' or 'ideas' are 'unchangeable and invisible, and therefore akin to the divine elements in us, that is, the soul'. He states further that the 'ideas' 'may be reached by the "gracious aid" of a dialectic, which uses the objects of sense as steps by which we are able to mount to the sphere of the absolute'. *The Dialogues of Plato*, Vol. II, p. 874.

18. Quoted in *How I Write*, p. 154.

19. M. H. Abrams, *The Mirror and the Lamp: Romantic Theory and the Critical Tradition* (New York: Oxford University Press, 1953), p. 59.

20. Emerson, 'The Poet', *Selected Prose and Poetry*, p. 327.

21. See the dialogue 'Phaedrus', l. 244, p. 248, in the Jowett edition, in which Socrates explains how words once bore an intimate, organic, poetic relationship with the things they name.

22. Robert Hayden, 'From the Life', p. 11.

23. *Gleanings*, p. 184.

24. In the Sura 'The Cow', God dumbfounds the angels by placing Adam on earth as His emissary and by giving him the authority and knowledge to name creation: 'And he taught Adam the names of all things, and then set them before the angels, and said, "Tell me the names of these, if ye are endured with wisdom." . . . He said, "O Adam, inform them of their names." And when he had informed them of their names, He said, "Did I not say to you that I know the hidden things of the Heavens and of the Earth, and that I know what ye bring to light, and what

ye hide?"' *The Koran*, II: 29–31, trans. J. M. Rodwell (London: J. M. Dent and Sons Ltd., 1953), p. 341.

25. Louis Simpson, *An Introduction to Poetry* (New York: St Martin's Press, 1967), p. 6.

26. Quoted in *How I Write*, p. 135.

27. Quoted in House of Worship video tape.

28. Quoted in *How I Write*, p. 154.

29. The *Kitáb-i-Íqán*, p. 255.

30. Matthew 13: 14–15, *The Holy Bible*, rev. standard version.

31. In *Tablets of Bahá'u'lláh revealed after The Kitáb-i-Aqdas*, p. 57.

32. Shelley, 'A Defence of Poetry', *English Romantic Poetry and Prose*, p. 1101.

33. 'To A Young Negro Poet', *Heart-Shape in the Dust*, p. 14.

34. Quoted in *How I Write*, p. 169.

35. Emerson, 'The Poet', *Selected Prose and Poetry*, p. 320.

36. T. S. Eliot, 'Shakespeare and the Stoicism of Seneca', *Selected Essays* (New York: Harcourt, Brace and Company, 1932), p. 117.

37. Ibid.

38. Quoted in *Interviews with Black Writers*, p. 114.

39. Shelley, 'A Defence of Poetry', *English Romantic Poetry and Prose*, p. 1109.

40. William Wordsworth, 'Preface to *Lyrical Ballads*', *English Romantic Poetry and Prose*, p. 358.

41. Quoted in *Interviews with Black Writers*, p. 112.

42. Quoted in Jo Thomas, 'Of Quietly Crafting Words', *Detroit Free Press*, Sunday Supplement, p. 35, col. 1.

43. 'Abdu'l-Bahá, 'The Quickening Spirit', *Foundations of World Unity* (Wilmette, Illinois: Bahá'í Publishing Trust, 1945), p. 101.

44. 'Abdu'l-Bahá in *Bahá'í World Faith*, p. 383.

45. See *Synopsis and Codification of the Laws and Ordinances of the Kitáb-i-Aqdas*, p. 11; see also *Gleanings*, p. 70, and *The Hidden Words*, (Persian) no. 76.

46. Emerson stated about the poem 'Days': 'I have written within a twelvemonth verses which I do not remember the composition or correction of, and could not write the like today, and have only, for proof of their being mine, various external evidences as the manuscript in which I find them.' *The Heart of Emerson's Journals*, ed. Bliss Perry (New York: Dover Publishers, Inc., 1958), p. 258.

47. See *English Romantic Poetry and Prose*. p. 391, for a detailed account of that experience.

48. Coleridge, 'Biographia Literaria', *English Romantic Poetry and Prose*, p. 427.

49. Ibid.

50. Wordsworth, 'Preface', *English Romantic Poetry and Prose*, p. 359.

51. Ibid.

52. Quoted in *How I Write*, p. 146.

53 .T. S. Eliot, 'Tradition and the Individual Talent', *Selected Essays*, p. 10.

54. Ibid., p. 11.

55. See Amy Lowell, *Tendencies in Modern American Poetry* (New York: Octagon Books, 1971), pp. 239–46. In this work, which originally appeared in 1917, Lowell explains these 'simple rules' which had appeared in the preface to the 1915 anthology *Some Imagist Poets*.

56. William Empson, *Seven Types of Ambiguity* (London: Chatto and Windus, 1930).

57. I. A. Richards, *The Meaning of Meaning* (London: Routledge and Kegan Paul Ltd., 1956).

58. Cleanth Brooks and Robert Penn Warren, *Understanding Poetry* (New York: Holt, Rine-

hart and Winston, 1976). See also Cleanth Brooks, *The Well Wrought Urn: Studies in the Structure of Poetry* (New York: Reynal and Hitchcock, 1947).

59. T. S. Eliot, *Selected Essays*, pp. 124–5.

60. Cleanth Brooks and Robert Penn Warren, *Understanding Poetry*, p. 69.

61. George Williamson, *A Reader's Guide to T. S. Eliot* (New York: Noonday Press, 1953), p. 29.

62. Louis Simpson, *Introduction to Poetry*, p. 11.

63. George Williamson, *A Reader's Guide to T. S. Eliot*, p. 30.

64. John Keats in 'Selections from Keats' Letters', *English Romantic Poetry and Prose*, p. 1211.

65. George Williamson, *A Reader's Guide to T. S. Eliot*, p. 30.

66. Quoted in *How I Write*, p. 144.

67. Quoted in *Interviews with Black Writers*, p. 116.

68. Quoted in 'English High Lights'. Scott, Foresman's News Periodical for 9th thru 12th Grade English Teachers (Winter, 1972).

69. Quoted in House of Worship video tape.

70. Gendron, p. 14.

71. James Weldon Johnson, ed. *The Book of American Negro Poetry* (New York: Harcourt, Brace and World, 1959), pp. 41–2. See Chapter 7, n. 1.

72. Wilburn Williams, Jr., 'Covenant of Timelessness', *Chant of Saints*, p. 67.

73. Dudley Randall, 'The Black Aesthetic', pp. 224 ff.

74. T. S. Eliot, 'Hamlet', *Selected Essays*, pp. 124–5.

75. Lewis Turco, '*Angle of Ascent*: The Poetry of Robert Hayden', *Michigan Quarterly Review* (Spring, 1977), p. 216.

76. Coleridge, 'Kubla Khan', *English Romantic Poetry and Prose*, p. 392.

77. Ezra Pound, *The Spirit of Romance* (London: Peter Owen Ltd., 1960), p. 14.

78. George Williamson, *A Reader's Guide to T. S. Eliot*, pp. 20–21.

79. Matthew Arnold, 'Dover Beach', *Victorian Poetry*, ed. E. K. Brown (New York: Ronald Press, 1942), p. 458.

80. Gerald Graff, *Literature Against Itself: Literary Ideas in Modern Society* (Chicago: University of Chicago Press, 1979), p. 45.

81. Ibid., p. 46.

82. Quoted in 'Conversations with Americans', *World Order*, 10, No. 2 (1975–6), p. 45.

83. Quoted in 'Recent American Poetry – Portfolio I', *World Order*, 5, No. 3 (Spring, 1971), p. 33.

21. *Shaping the Poem*

1. Emerson, 'The Poet', *Selected Prose and Poetry*, p. 320.

2. Pearce, *Continuity of American Poetry*, p. 13.

3. Quoted in *Interviews with Black Writers*, p. 112.

4. *Physiologus* is an Anglo-Saxon poem belonging to the Cynewulf school which derives from the Latin Bestiaries. Found in the *Exeter Book*, the Anglo-Saxon version consists of two complete beast-fables, 'The Panther', and 'The Whale', the first of which is a symbol of Christ, the second of which symbolizes the devil.

5. Wilburn Williams, Jr., *Chant of Saints*, p. 81.

6. Quoted in *How I Write*, p. 147.

7. Fred M. Fetrow, 'American Poet', *Poet Lore*, 77, No. 1 (Spring, 1982), p. 36.

8. Jackson Blyden and Louis Rubin, Jr., *Black Poetry in America*, p. 80.

9. Quoted in *How I Write*, p. 177.

10. Ibid., p. 153.

11. Quoted in Cleanth Brooks and Robert Penn Warren, *Understanding Poetry*, p. 13.

12. Ibid.

13. Quoted in *How I Write*, p. 198.

14. See Chapter 16, n. 19.

15. See Fred M. Fetrow, '"Middle Passage": Robert Hayden's Anti-Epic', *CLA Journal*, 22, No. 4 (1979), 304–18.

16. See Chapter 20, n. 55.

17. *American Writers*, p. 367.

18. George Herbert (1593–1633) was one of the so-called Metaphysical poets, of whom John Donne was, no doubt, the most noteworthy. Herbert's 'The Collar' is among the most anthologized poems from this school.

19. 'The Collar', *The Norton Anthology of Poetry*, rev. (New York: W. W. Norton and Co., Inc., 1975), p. 294.

20. Ibid., p. 295.

21. See Chapter 15. n. 28.

22. Image and Symbol

1. Emerson, 'The Poet', *Selected Prose and Poetry*, pp. 326–7.

2. As C. Hugh Holman acknowledges in *A Handbook to Literature*, p. 264, the term *image* 'has a great variety of meanings'. In the ensuing discussion I attempt to inform the reader of my special uses.

3. I. A. Richards, *The Philosophy of Rhetoric* (Oxford: Oxford University Press, 1936), p. 94.

4. I. A. Richards, *The Meaning of Meaning*, p. 11.

5. Ibid.

6. 'Abdu'l-Bahá, *Some Answered Questions*, pp. 84–5.

7. See *Gleanings*, p. 321, p. 327 and p. 193, for example.

8. See *Bahá'í World Faith*, p. 262; *Gleanings*, p. 34 and p. 139, to cite but a few.

9. *Kitáb-i-Íqán*, p. 33.

10. Ibid., p. 36.

11. Ibid., p. 37.

12. Ibid., p. 38.

13. See Wilburn Williams, Jr., 'Covenant of Timelessness', *Chant of Saints*, p. 81.

14. Bahá'u'lláh wrote *The Seven Valleys and the Four Valleys* as a response to inquiries by Súfí mystics. Using the form of the mystical treatise, which traditionally delineates the graduated intensity of the mystic's experience, Bahá'u'lláh explains that spiritual ascent takes place only by means of divine intervention by the Manifestations, that by ourselves we are helpless. Interestingly, while some critics sense a mystical tenor to Hayden's work, his two overt portraits of mystics depict misguided and ultimately unfortunate figures.

15. *Kaleidoscope*, p. xx.

16. See his chapter 'No Relieving Shade', pp. 112–49.

17. See Charles T. Davis, 'Robert Hayden's Use of History', and pp. 77–81 in *Black Poetry in America* (1974).

18. Constance Post, 'Image and Idea in the Poetry of Robert Hayden', *CLA Journal*, 20, No. 2 (1976), pp. 164–75.

19. Howard Faulkner, '"Transformed by Steeps of Flight": The Poetry of Robert Hayden', *CLA Journal*, 21, No. 1 (1977), pp. 282–91.

20. Wilburn Williams, Jr., 'Covenant of Timelessness', *Chant of Saints*, p. 67.

21. Dennis Gendron, p. 210; Constance Post, 'Image and Idea in the Poetry of Robert Hayden', p. 165. Gendron refers to Stauffer's theory of 'obsessive' imagery on page 210 of his study, and Post alludes to Stauffer's thesis of 'coherent patterns' of imagery on page 165 of her article. Stauffer himself enumerates 'the characteristics of these imaginative poetic symbols' and shows how these patterns work in Yeats' poetry. *The Golden Nightingale* (New York, Hafner Publishing Co., 1971), pp. 28–9.

22. William Butler Yeats, 'The Second Coming', *A College Book of Modern Verse*, p. 65.

23. Quoted in Cal Samra, 'Poet Wants Freedom to Respond', *Ann Arbor News*, February 15, 1971, p. 7.

24. Unofficially the nine-pointed star symbolizes the Bahá'í Faith because it represents the nine extant world religions (Sabean, Hindu, Jewish, Zoroastrian, Buddhist, Christian, Islamic, Bábí, and Bahá'í). Thus, the star is a symbol of Progressive Revelation. The more weighty significance of the number is explained by the Hand of the Cause, A. Q. Faizi, in his article 'Explanation of the Emblem of the Greatest Name'), *Bahá'í News*, No. 451 (October, 1968), pp. 8–12. See Chapter 17, n. 23.

25. *Black Poetry in America*, p. 78.

26. The title of Bahá'u'lláh's work derives from the Hidden Book of Fáṭimih, 'which was believed to have been revealed by the Angel Gabriel through the Imám 'Alí for the consolation of Muhammad's grief-stricken daughter after the Prophet's death, but which has remained hidden from the world's knowledge till now made known'. (*The Hidden Words*, 1939 edn., Introduction, p. i.) I feel the title also connotes the poetic qualities of these teachings which are often metaphorical and thus hidden or concealed.

27. *The Republic of Plato*, trans. Francis MacDonald Cornford (New York: Oxford University Press, 1958), pp. 230–31. I prefer Cornford's translation of this passage to that of Jowett.

28. See 'Symposium', *The Dialogues of Plato*, Vol. I (New York: Random House, 1937), pp. 334–5.

29. See Bahá'u'lláh, *The Seven Valleys and the Four Valleys*, trans. Marzieh Gail (Wilmette, Illinois: Bahá'í Publishing Trust, 1975).

30. See C. Hugh Holman, *A Handbook to Literature*, p. 233.

23. *The Finishing Touch*

1. John O'Brien, *Interviews with Black Writers*, p. 110.

2. John Crowe Ransom, *The New Criticism* (Norfolk, Connecticut: New Directions, 1941), p. 22.

3. 'Frederick Douglass', *Angle of Ascent*, p. 131.

4. Gerard Manley Hopkins, 'The Windhover', *A College Book of Modern Verse*, p. 34. I interpret this line as meaning that the sheer drudgery of ploughing a field one furrow at a time ultimately makes the whole field shine, in the same way that Christ's daily work among men ultimately made God's power and majesty meaningful.

5. Quoted in *How I Write*, p. 149.

6. Ibid., p. 181.

7. Drafts of Hayden's poetry are from the Hayden Papers, National Bahá'í Archives.

8. 'English High Lights'. Scott, Foresman's *News Periodical . . .* (Winter, 1972).

9. Quoted in *How I Write*, p. 136.

AFTERWORD

1. *The Dialogues of Plato*, Vol. I. p. 289.

2. Emerson, 'The Poet', *Selected Prose and Poetry*, p. 320.

3. T. S. Eliot, 'Shakespeare and the Stoicism of Seneca', *Selected Essays*, p. 117.

4. Roy Harvey Pearce, *The Continuity of American Poetry*, p. 12.

5. Dennis Gendron and Constance Post in particular.

6. Wilburn Williams, Jr., and Robert M. Greenberg in particular.

7. George Williamson, *A Reader's Guide to T. S. Eliot*, p. 20. He is actually paraphrasing what Eliot himself said in a 1945 lecture 'The Social Function of Poetry', *Critiques and Essays in Criticism*, ed. Stallman (New York: Ronald Press, 1949), pp. 105–16.

8. James Cotter, rev. of *Angle of Ascent*, by Robert Hayden, *America*, 134 (February 7, 1976), p. 103.

Index of Poems

Poems are indexed according to the last published spelling of the titles.

Index of Names